Study of the Land in the Old Testament

Biblical Hermeneutics Rediscovered

The Series as the name suggests will focus on Biblical Hermeneutics, i.e., literary works concerned with methods of interpreting the Old and New Testaments of Bible via different stream of topics like Literature & Poetry, Indigenous Philosophizing, Ethical response towards Ecology, Health & Healing, Science & Technology, Feminist Theology, Sociological approach towards Human Rights, Law & Politics, Arts, History of Ideas, Ancient Civilizations, Cultural Contiguity, Religious Cosmologies & Mysticism, Appraisal of various Theologians, World Peace & Harmony, Global Capitalism, Network Marketing, Cybertheology, Population & Demographics, Epigraphic Studies, Contextualized Education, and many others. We welcome a Mss. on any topic/s mentioned, whether they are original works, scholarly monographs, collections of conference papers, revised dissertations, or translations of historical documents. Through the Series we, the Publishers, are striving to put forward published works that may help Institutions, Academic Bodies, Researchers, Scholars and the World at large in furthering their respective knowledge and understanding on the concerned subject. We welcome your comments on our efforts and further suggestions on how we can enshrine new ray of analysing & explaining the written Texts through our upcoming books.

Biblical Hermeneutics Rediscovered - 6

Study of the Land in the Old Testament

Theological Traditions & Socio-Historical Events

Kiyeho Sema

CWI

Christian World Imprints™

First Published in 2017 by

Christian World Imprints(TM)
Christian Publishing & Books from India
H-12 Bali Nagar, **New Delhi-110015**
info@christianworldimprints.com
www.ChristianWorldImprints.com
Phone: +91 11 25465925

ISBN: 978-93-5148-194-2 (HB) ISBN: 978-93-5148-195-9 (PB)

Cataloging in Publication Data--DK
Courtesy: D.K. Agencies (P) Ltd. <docinfo@dkagencies.com>

Sema, Kiyeho, 1976- **author.**
Study of the land in the Old Testament : theological traditions & socio-historical events / Kiyeho Sema.
pages cm. -- (Biblical hermeneutics rediscovered ; 6)
Includes bibliographical references.
ISBN 9789351481942 (HB)
ISBN 9789351481959 (PB)

1. Bible. Old Testament--Criticism, interpretation, etc. 2. Bible. Old Testament--Theology. 3. Land tenure--Religious aspects--Christianity. 4. Land tenure--Biblical teaching. 5. Tradition (Theology) I. Title. II. Series: Biblical hermeneutics rediscovered ; 6.

BS1199.L28S46 2017 DDC 221.830632 23

Printed in India.

Foreword

Land is an inseparable part of human life. Our existence on this earth is an evidence to that fact. Various dimensions of land as living space, agricultural field, political kingdom, source of water and air are studied in the academic departments of biology, economics, political science, sociology and geology in the Universities and Colleges. Many kinds of researches are going on the issues of land for so many years. Land ownership and tenure systems during the early monarchical period, colonial period and post-independent period are studied even today. Land reforms related to the problems of Zamindari system, Ryotwari system and Mahalwari system during the colonial and post-independent period became an interesting topic for those who specialize on revenue system of land. Vinobhave effort of promoting Bhoodhan movement to donate land to the landless following the ideals of Gandhi was successful for a short period but could not continue due to the lack of support from the government and landlords. Today, many have become landless and a few have become land owners of large estate in our country.

Churches and seminaries have neglected this important aspect of land for a long period and failed to produce a suitable land theology for India. But thank God, a few doctoral students in seminaries are focusing their attention on studying what the Bible says about land and relating the teachings of the Bible to develop contextual theology and challenge the trend of rich becoming richer and poor becoming poorer. One such effort is taken by Dr. Kiyeho Sema who did his doctoral research on the relationship between God, land and Israel in the Old Testament. He explored the historical events and theological traditions about the tripartite relationship in the OT to formulate a strong basis to know how the 8th century prophets Hosea, Amos, Micah and Isaiah (chs. 1-39) used these historical events in proclaiming God's justice. During his research in SAIACS, Bangalore he examined the key texts in these prophets and brought out the way they presented the tripartite relationship between God, land and Israel and based their prophecy of judgment or salvation. He spent a few months in UK to collect material on his topic and had opportunity to meet and discuss with scholars there. He defended his thesis first in front of the Doctoral committee of SAIACS and then answered the external examiner earning the Ph.D.

We do not have many books on land theology. His effort in revising and bringing it out as a book will be a valuable contribution to the study of land in the Bible. I wish, he would continue his research on relating the study of land to the context of North East India in the coming years.

Revd. Dr. Jesudason Baskar Jeyaraj
Director, Jubilee Institute, Madurai.
Former Professor and HOD, Old Testament, SAIACS, Bangalore
12th October, 2016.

Acknowledgment

"Thanks to God for my Redeemer, Thanks for all Thou dost provide! Thanks for times now but a memory, Thanks for Jesus by my side!" (August Ludvig Storm).

Several people have contributed in the successful completion of my Research. Thanks to Dr. J.B. Jeyaraj for his invaluable help in leading me from a basic idea to a concise, clear and well-argued research. Thanks to Dr. Havilah Dharamraj, the Head of the Department, Old Testament and Dr. Iain Payne, the Principal, SAIACS for encouragement and also for support in raising partial scholarship for my studies in 2008-2009 and for arranging my overseas study component in April-June, 2010 to Trinity College, Bristol, UK.

I wish to express my gratitude to Rev. Canon George I. Koover, the Principal, Trinity College, Bristol, England for offering me a three month World Church Fellow scholarship. My gratitude also goes to Dr. John Currie, Dean of post Graduate Studies, Trinity College, UK, for giving me the opportunity to present the findings of my research at the Centre for World Christianity. I receive helpful comments and constructive criticisms from many scholars during the seminar particularly from Professor Gordon Wenham who has helped me see the relationship between the book of Hosea and Deuteronomy. I received valuable help from my friend and professor Dr. Paul Barker, Australia, who sincerely did the editing and proofreading work of my research. Besides, there are several friends and churches who have helped me financially and encouragement me in times of my crisis. Thank you!

Thanks to the staff and Librarians of United Theological College (UTC, Bangalore), South Asia Institute of Advanced Christian Studies (SAIACS, Bangalore) and Trinity College, Bristol, United Kingdoms, for giving me access to their library resources. I also express my gratitude to all my professors and especially to Dr. Mayer Gruber, Israel, and Dr. Lindsay Wilson, Australia, who taught me various Old Testament subjects and enabled me to complete this research work. I would not have come this far in my theological studies without the support of my parents who taught me since my early days to know God and to fear and serve him faithfully. God bless you!

Kiyeho Sema

Abbreviation

AB	:	Anchor Bible
ABD	:	Anchor Bible Dictionary
AJSL	:	*American Journal of Semitic Languages and Literatures*
AJTR	:	*Arasaradi Journal of Theological Reflection*
ANE	:	Ancient Near East
BA	:	*Biblical Archeology*
BASOR	:	*Bulletin of American Society for Oriental Research*
BCE	:	Before Common Era
BHS	:	Biblia Hebraica Stuttgartensia
BST	:	Bible Speaks Today
CBC	:	Cambridge Bible Commentary
CBQ	:	*Catholic Bible Quarterly*
CTJ	:	*Calvin Theological Journal*
CTR	:	*Criswell Theological Review*
CV	:	*Communio Viatorum*
FCC	:	Form Critical Comments
FOTL	:	Form of the Old Testament Literature
HBT	:	*Horizons in Biblical Theology*
HTR	:	*Harvard Theological Review*
HUCA	:	*Hebrew Union College Annual*
IBD	:	The Interpreter's Bible Dictionary
ICC	:	International Critical Commentary
IDB	:	The Interpreter's Bible Dictionary
ISPCK	:	Indian Society for the Promotion of Christian Knowledge
JAOS	:	*Journal of the American Oriental Studies*
JAOS	:	*Journal of the American Oriental Society*
JBL	:	*Journal of Biblical Literature*

JBQ	:	*Jewish Bible Quarterly*
JBTh	:	*Jahrbuch fur Biblische Theologie*
JETS	:	*Journal of Evangelical Theological Studies*
JNES	:	*Journal of Near Eastern Studies*
JNSL	:	*Journal of Northwest Semitic Languages*
JSOT	:	*Journal for the Study of Old Testament*
JSOTSS	:	*Journal for the Study of Old Testament Supplementary Series*
JSS	:	*Journal of Semitic Studies*
JTS	:	*Journal of Theological Studies*
LXX	:	Septuagint
Mss	:	Manuscript
MT	:	Massoretic Text
NAC	:	New American Commentary
NIB	:	New Interpreter's Bible
NICOT	:	New International Commentary on the Old Testament
NIDOTTE	:	New International Dictionary of Old Testament Theology and Exegesis
NT	:	New Testament
OT	:	Old Testament
OTL	:	Old Testament Library
PEQ	:	*Palestine Exploration Quarterly*
PTR	:	*Pacific Theological Review*
SBL	:	*Society of Biblical Literature*
SBT	:	*Studies in Biblical Theology*
SJOT	:	*Scandinavian Journal of the Old Testament*
SJT	:	*Southwestern Journal of Theology*
SPCK	:	Society for the Promotion of Christian Knowledge
TCC	:	Text Critical Comments
TDOT	:	Theological Dictionary of the Old Testament
TLOT	:	Theological Lexicon of the Old Testament
TOTC	:	Tyndale Old Testament Commentaries
TWOT	:	Theological Word Book of the Old Testament
VT	:	*Vetus Testamentum*
VTS	:	*Vetus Testamentum, Supplements*
ZAW	:	*Zeitschrift fur de altestamentiche*

Contents

Chapter 1

Introduction

In the Old Testament (OT), the ownership of land is protected by Yahweh in the Tenth Commandment, "You shall not covet your Neighbor's house (בית)."[1] Protection of an individual's right and access to land is one of the theological fundamentals and sociological dynamics of the early Israelite society. During the settlement period every Israelite had equal access to land and each tribe settled within the allocated portion of land (Jud. 2:6).[2] The perpetuation of such practice is envisaged by the Law of Moses, *"The land shall not be sold in perpetuity, for the land is mine,"* (Lev. 25:23). This apodictic law with an emphatic negation לא *(you shall not...)*, prohibits the permanent sale of land (ארץ).[3] There is an undergirding theological sanction in the prohibition, that is, the "land" belongs to Yahweh and therefore the Israelites cannot sell the land from the ultimate owner,

[1] Exodus 20:17. According to Marvin Chaney בית in the Ten Commandments originally refers to the neighbor's plot of arable land held in redistributional domain by an Israelite extended family. M. L. Chaney, "You Shall Not Covet Your Neighbor's House", *Pacific Theological Review* 15 (1982) 6. Cited in D. N. Premnath, "Latifundialization and Isaiah 5:8-10", *JSOT* 40 (1988), 55. Similarly, after extensive study of the Accadian *bitu* in Ugaritic documents from the second millennium, which deals with the transfer of immovable property, W. Moran concludes that property in these texts is referred to as house *(bitu)*, field *(eqlu)*. W. Moran, "The Conclusion of the Decalogue (Ex. 20:17= Dt 5:21)", *CBQ* 29 (1967)549-52.

[2] The book of Joshua gives a picture of how the land was divided according to tribes and ancestral families as גורל, usually translated as "lot" or "allotted land" (Jos. 15:1; 16:1; 17:1; 18:11; 19:1; etc), and as "נחלה", which can mean "inheritance or entitlement" (Jos. 14:2). Cf. Norman C. Habel, *The Land is Mine: Six Biblical Land Ideologies* (Minneapolis: Fortress Press, 1995), 54-74.

[3] This legislation is given in the context of property redemption, which allows the Israelites to buy and sell the land albeit within the right to reclaim it. The legislation reminds the buyer that the ownership of the land does not extend beyond the Jubilee year. Jacob Milgrom, *Leviticus 23-27*, AB, 3B (New York: Doubleday, 2000), 2138.

Yahweh.[4] This law ensures the inalienability of land and secures the right to the access of land and its resources.

With the emergence of the monarchy, however, slowly there was a shift in land tenure system. The kings who acquired the power to rule started appropriating the land and its resources within the dominion of their empire.[5] Such monarchical authorities that change the ownership of ancestral land are found in the incidents of David and Mephibosheth[6] and Ahab and Naboth.[7] Both the instances show the authority of the kings to transfer the land from the owners. In such context, Walter Brueggemann rightly comments that the kings, who are entrusted to manage and care for the land, became the "instrument" of mismanagement of land during the monarchy.[8]

The problem of land ownership, dispossession and landlessness, which begins with the emergence of monarchy, was further heightened during the eighth century BCE.[9] We see the echo of fraudulent appropriation and deceitful accumulation of land in the prophetic oracles of the eighth century prophets. In Amos 2:6, the prophet brings an indictment for selling the needy 'אביון' for a pair of sandals 'נעלים'. Since in ancient Israelite society, the sandal transfer was practiced as a symbol of land transaction, the terms here indicate the issue of land alienation and latifundialization.[10] Similar language is found in Isaiah "*Woe to*

---

[4] Another important term in connection with לא is לִצְמִתֻת which is interpreted as a sale "in derogation of the seller's right of redemption." J.E. Hogg cited in Christopher J.H. Wright, *God's People in God's Land: Family, Land and Property in the Old Testament* (England/Grand Rapids, Michigan: Paternoster/Eerdmans, 1990), 59. לִצְמִתֻת basically means 'completion, finality.' Cf. R. Larid Harris, Gleason L. Archer and Bruce K. Waltke (eds), *Theological Wordbook of the Old Testament*, vol. 1 (Chicago: Moody, 1980). In other words, לִצְמִתֻת along with לא states an apodictic prohibition, which denies complete and final claim of the land by the buyer.

[5] D. N. Premnath traces the beginning of latifundialization during the period of the monarchy. With Israel's expansion of its territory to the Canaanites plains, there aroused a need of administrative reforms, which resulted in a far reaching impact upon the land tenure system. Premnath asserts that the royal payments to the officials were carried out through a system a land grant in patrimonial and prebendal domains. Such situation created a new system of Israelite landed aristocracy. D. N. Premnath, "Latifundialization and Isaiah 5:8-10", 53.

[6] In the case of David, he handed over the ancestral land of Saul's family to divide between Mephibosheth and his servant, Ziba (2 Sam. 19:29-30 cf. 16:1-4; 9:9-10).

[7] In the incident of Naboth, the king Ahab took away Naboth's plot of land, despite Naboth's unwillingness to part from נחלה "the ancestral land" (1 Kgs 21:3).

[8] Walter Brueggemann, *The Land: Place as Gift, Promise, and Challenge in Biblical Faith* (London: SPCK, 1978), 104.

[9] The eighth century prophets include, Amos, Hosea, Micah and Isaiah (chs 1-39). Unlike the arrangement in the English bible, we have placed Amos first followed by Hosea, Micah and Isaiah (1-39). Such arrangement in the present research is based on the general scholarly consensus of their period of ministry. For the discussion on the period of their ministry, see the historical backgrounds of chs three to six.

[10] The expression 'garments taken as pledge' (Am. 2:8); who 'oppress the poor and the needy' (Am. 4:1) etc, speaks of oppressive social policy and exploitative economic offence that are closely

those who add house to house and join field to field." (Is. 5:8); Micah accuses that "*They covet fields, and seize them; and houses, and take them away; they oppress a man and his house, a man and his inheritance.*" (Mic. 2:2). Hosea, likewise, indicts the princes of Judah for removing "*the landmark*" (Hos. 5:10). Against such practices, Yahweh intervenes in judgment and announces that the land will fail to produce its yield, land as political nation will be destroyed and the inhabitants will be alienated from their homeland and exiled to a foreign nation.[11] These prophetic oracles against the land acquisitions raise a few questions: What makes the prophet pronounce judgment against the "land" when the perpetuators of injustice are Israelites themselves? What were the factors that contributed to the rise of latifundialization?

The eighth century was an important period of transition in the history of Israel and Judah. On the one hand, it was an era of peace and expansion for Israel and Judah while on the other hand it was also a beginning period of decline for both the kingdoms. During this period, Israel and Judah pursued their national agenda of territorial expansions and brought most international trade centers under their control.[12] Under Jeroboam II (786-746 BCE, Northern Kingdom),[13] and Uzziah (783-742 BCE, Southern Kingdom),[14] Israel and Judah consolidated themselves with great political and economic success.[15]

---

associated with the land appropriation.

[11] Am. 2:5, 13-16; 3:11, 15; 5:16-17, 27; 6:7; 7:17; Hos. 8:13; Mic. 2:5; 3:12; Isa 1:7; 5:8-10.

[12] Stanley E. Peter states that after the fall of Assyrian capital, Damascus, the Aramean kingdom slowly declined ca. 801 B.C.E., which gave opportunity for Jeroboam II to annex Gilead and the Transjordan area. Gilead and the Transjordanian cities of Lo-debar and Karnaim (6:13–14) were the King's Highway, which controlled the major trade route from the Tigris-Euphrates to the Gulf of Aqaba and Egypt. Israel thus controlled the major trade route in the region, which in turn brought great economic prosperity. Stanley E. Peter, 'The Book of Amos,' in David Noel Freedman and others, *ABD,* vol. 1 (New York: Doubleday, 1992), 205.

[13] International business and commerce flourished with huge revenue (Amos: 3:9; 8:15). Building activities increased with both summer and winter houses (Amos 3:10, 12, 15; 5:11; 6:4, 8). Viticulture and cattle raising became good business with great demands (Amos 5:11; 6:4). Moreover, the confiscation of wealth from the military campaigns added to the prosperity of their economic growth. Cf., Joseph Blenkinsopp, *A History of Prophecy in Israel: From Settlement in the Land to the Hellenistic Period* (Philadelphia: Westminster John Knox Press, 1983), 95.

[14] In the south, under Uzziah's reign Judah saw her increasing economic growth (Is 2:7). The luxurious fortifications of towers as symbol of its economic growth and national pride increased. Cf. Is. 2:15; 30:25. Jacob Milgrom, "Did Isaiah Prophecy During the Reign of Uzziah?", *VT* 14 (1964) 164-167. Viticulture, orchard, livestock rearing, and farming of various products increased. Moreover, extraction of huge tributes from the annexed kingdoms such as, Ammonite added more wealth to their national exchequer. Cf., B. Obed, "The Historical Background of Syro-Ephairmite War Reconsidered", *CBQ* 34 (1972) 157.

[15] The archeological findings also confirm the prosperity of the time. Peter notes that over 500 ivory fragments belonging to the 9th and 8th century BCE were found at Samaria (cf Am 3:15), also two palaces stood in each others' direction were excavated from Zinjirli, which possible explains

However, the economic prosperity resulted in creating a new situation in which the Yahwistic egalitarian social ideal began to fade away with the emergence of a new form of capitalistic market-oriented society.[16] The rich became richer while the poor became poorer.[17] Since the agrarian and pastoral nations like Israel and Judah generated their wealth mostly from the land, injustice, corruption, exploitation and other socioeconomic offences were closely linked to the issue of the land appropriation.[18] In other words, the growth of agro-economy trade in the eighth century and the persistent intention of the rich people to add more land and accumulate wealth and labor with secondary regard to the Yahwistic social imperatives led to the alienation of land. In such a context, the eighth century prophets emerged with a theological message of transformative social norms, which is closely associated with the issues of land. Therefore, it is important to understand how the eighth century prophets understand land and how they respond to the issues of land during the period of the eighth century.

OT scholarship has largely neglected the eighth century prophets' understanding of land for three main reasons. First, the land studies in the OT have focused mostly on the Pentateuchal and Historical books due to the interest of the scholars in the promise-fulfillment scheme of land.[19] Second, land studies have also been concentrated mostly on Joshua and Judges due to scholars' preoccupation on the issue of whether Israel's settlement in the land is through conquest or

---

the description of summer and winter houses in Amos 3:15. "Houses of hewn stone, or ashlar masonry (Amos 5:11), are found at Samaria." These archeological findings confirm the prosperity mentioned in the corpus of the eighth century prophets. Peter, *The Book of Amos*, 205.

[16] Hans Walter Wolff, *Joel and Amos* (Philadelphia: Fortress Press, 1977), 89-90.

[17] The excavations at Tizzah (Tell el- Farah) show that houses in the 10th century BCE were of uniform small size while in the 8th century there were both large expensive houses and small huddled houses. This shows the contrast of luxury of the rich and the misery of the poor people in the 8th Century. James Luther Mays, *Amos: A Commentary*, OTL (Philadelphia: Westminster, 1969), 2-3.

[18] The poor were exploited, dispossessed, and sold to slavery (Amos 2:6; 8:6). Falsifying weights and measures and dishonest gain became the order of business (Amos 8:5-6). In court, the poor were denied justice because bribery became the means for judicial decision. Also heavy taxation was levied on the poor people and sexual satisfaction was demanded from them. Wolff, *Joel and Amos*, 103.

[19] Gerhard von Rad, "The Promised Land and Yahweh's Land", in *The Problem in the Hexateuch and Other Essays*, trans. by Trueman Dicken (Philadelphia/London: Fortress/SCM, 1984); Brueggemann, *The Land*; Elie Assis, "How Long Are you Slack to go to Posses the Land" (Jos. 28:3): Ideal and Reality in the Distribution Descriptions in Joshua 13-24", *VT* 53 (2003) 2-25; Dorothy Jones, "Surveying the Promised Land: Elizabeth Jolley's Milk and Honey", *Semeia* 88 (2001) 97-111; Bernhard Lang, "The Social Organization of Peasant Poverty in Biblical Israel" *JSOT* 24 (1982) 47-63; Patrick D. Miller, "The Gift of God: The Deuteronomic Theology of the Land", *Interpretation* 23/4 (1969) 451-465; Horst Seebass, "Holy' Land in the Old Testament: Numbers and Joshua", *VT* 56/1 (2006) 92-104; Bruce S. Marshal, "Israel's Stake in the Land", *Theology Today* 35/4 (1979) 413-420; Jeffrey L. Townsend, "Fulfillment of the Land Promise in the Old Testament", *Bibliotheca Sacra* (1985) 320-337.

infiltration or internal peasants' revolution.[20] Third, in the corpus of the classical prophets' literature, mostly the references to land occur in accusation prophecy, particularly in socioeconomic offences. As such, the scholarship of the eighth century prophets has mostly concentrated on the wider context of socioeconomic criticism. Despite several contributions of scholars on the land research in the OT,[21] as mentioned, attempts have been made mostly on the Pentateuchal and Historical books. Only some representative scholars whose work is pertinent to the present research are dealt with in the following section.

Gerhard von Rad mostly understood "land" as referring to the whole land of Israel that came under Israel's occupation and was apportioned to the tribes of Israel. He attempted to understand "land" by categorizing a "cultic" and "historical" conception of land. The promise of land to the patriarchs is conceived as the original form of patriarchal religion and the fulfillment of that promise during Joshua's time, is understood as the historical conception of land, while the affirmation that "the land belongs to Yahweh" is regarded as the cultic conception of land. Though von Rad's historical and cultic conceptions of land is

[20] Alan J. Hauser, "Israel's Conquest of Palestine: A Peasant's Rebellion?", *JSOT* 7 (1978) 2-19; Walter C. Kaiser, "The Promised Land: A Biblical-Historical View", *Bibliotheca Sacra* (1981) 302-312; Keith W. Whitelam, "Israel's Traditions of Origin: reclaiming the Land", *JSOT* 44 (1989) 19-42; Timothy G. Crawford, "Taking the Promised Land, Leaving the Promised Land: Luke's Use of Joshua for a Christian Foundation Story", *Review and Expositor* 95 (1998) 251-261; Etan Levine, "The Land of Milk and Honey", *JSOT* 87 (2000) 43-57; Paul. W. Lapp, "The Conquest of Palestine in the Light of Archaeology", Concordia Theological Monthly; John J. Bimson, *Redating the Exodus and Conquest* (Sheffield: Almond, 1981); Richard S. Hess, "Early Israel in Canaan: A survey of Recent Evidence and Interpretation", *Palestine Exploration Quarterly* 12 (1930) 125; Norman. K. Gottwald, *The Hebrew Bible: A Socio-Literary Introduction* (Philadelphia: Fortress Press, 1985), 138 ff; Richard S. Hess, "Early Israel in Canaan: A Survey of Recent Evidence and Interpretation", *PEQ* 125 (1993) 127ff; W.F. Albright, "The Israelite Conquest in the Light of Archaeology", *BASOR*, 74 (1939) 12; G.E. Mendenhall, "The Hebrew Conquest of the Palestine", *BA* 25/3 (1962); Bimson, "Merenpath's Israel and Recent Theories", *JSOT* 49 (1991) 18.

[21] Apart from the above mentioned works of scholars in the footnotes no. 18 and 19, other scholars have also contributed much in land studies of the OT, such as, John Andrew Dearman, *Property Rights in Eighth Century Israel*, SBL Dissertation Series 106 (Atlanta: Scholars, 1988); Christopher J.H. Wright, *God's People in God's Land: Family, Land and Property in the Old Testament* (Grand Rapids, Michigan: William B. Eerdmans Publishing Company, 1990); Jeffrey A. Fager, *Land Tenure and Biblical Jubilee: Uncovering Hebrew Ethics through the Sociology of Knowledge*, JSOTSup. 155 (Sheffield: JSOT, 1993); Elmer A. Martens, *God's Design: A Focus on Old Testament Theology*, 2nd edn. (Grand Rapids, Michigan: Baker Books, 1994); Norman C. Habel, *The Land is Mine: Six Biblical Land Ideologies,* Overtures to Biblical Theology, (Minneapolis: Fortress Press, 1995); D. N. Premnath, "Latifundialization and Isaiah 5:8-10", *JSOT* 40 (1988) 49-60; Michael L. Barré, "*'rṣ (h)hyym-* 'The Land of the Living'?", *JSOT* 41 (1988) 37-59; Abraham Berkowitz, "The Law and the Land: Why Biblical Israel has Artificial Territorial Boundaries?", *Tradition* 28/2 (1994) 34-43; Zipporah G. Glass, "Land, Slave Labor and Law: Engaging Ancient Israel's Economy", *JSOT 91* (2000) 27-39; Thomas W. Mann, "Israel and the Land: A Note From a Christian Perspective", *Theology Today* 35/4 (1979) 421-426; Walter Brueggemann, "To Whom Does the Land Belong? 2 Sam. 3:13", *Journal for Preachers* 30/3 (2007) 28-35.

a ground-breaking work in land studies, Christopher Wright states that von Rad's understanding on "cultic" and "historical" conception of land divides the wedge too far, which in fact, should be seen as complementary to each other.[22]

Walter Brueggemann attempts to explain "land" at two levels. First, he states that "land" refers to "actual earthly turf where people can be safe and secure, where meaning and well being are enjoyed without pressure or coercion."[23] Second, he states that "land" symbolically expresses "the wholeness of joy and well-being characterized by social coherence and personal ease in prosperity, security, and freedom."[24] He traces the biblical history of land under three categories of Israel's history:[25] the history of the promise of land to the patriarchs; the history of land management from Joshua's time to the exile and the history of the loss of the land (exile) and culminates in kingdom. Brueggemann's approach on land studies rests on the hermeneutical presupposition that land is one of the central themes of the Old Testament. Due to the lack of exegetical approach, the richness of various terms used for land in the Old Testament could not be adequately explained.

Walter Zimmerli's article on "land" offers two observations on Amos' understanding on land. First, in Amos' understanding, Israel is not indigenous to the land as Israel was brought into Canaan by Yahweh (Am. 2:9). Second, Israel was sent out or removed from her land as a consequence of her iniquities[26] for oppressing the poor (Am. 2:8). This reflects the older stipulation of the covenant code (Ex. 22:25-27),[27] which, according to Zimmerli indicates that Amos' judgment against the people and land is based on the tradition of the ancient legal demands of God who brought Israel into the land.

For Zimmerli, Isaiah's understanding of land is shaped by the Zion tradition, which conceives land as the site of God's presence.[28] Yahweh thus demands the practice of righteousness and justice in the land and that the portrayal of devastated Jerusalem (29:1-8) is linked with the issue of justice and righteousness. On the other hand, Micah confronts land encroachers (2:1-2) since he understood that such practice destroys "the beneficial divine distribution of the land...". The punishment for unjust dealings in land distribution brings destruction (Is. 5:9-10) and the land fails to yield adequate produce. Also the people themselves were alienated from the land by sending them off to exile. Significantly, Zimmerli sees that Hosea's understanding of land is shaped by the traditions of Exodus,

[22] Wright, *God's People in God's Land*, 12. See Appendix A for further discussion.

[23] Brueggemann, *The Land*, 2.

[24] Brueggemann, *The Land*, 2.

[25] Brueggemann, *The Land*, xv.

[26] Walter Zimmerli, "The 'Land' in the Pre-exilic and the Early Post-Exilic Prophets", in James T. Butler, Edgar W. Conard and Ben C. Ollenburger (eds), *Understanding the Word: Essays in Honour of Bernhard W. Anderson*, JSOTSS 37 (Sheffield: JSOT, 1985), 247-248.

[27] Zimmerli, "The 'Land' in the Pre-exilic and the Early Post-Exilic Prophets", 248.

[28] Zimmerli, "The 'Land' in the Pre-exilic and the Early Post-Exilic Prophets", 249.

Wilderness and the Conquest. This, Zimmerli thinks, is the reason of Hosea's emphasis that the land is a gift of God.

Zimmerli's work briefly offers a synoptic view of the eighth century prophets' understanding of land. It needs to be noted that, however, the understanding of land is not only shaped by the ancient legal or Zion or Exodus traditions. Traditions like creation, theophany, Torah and remnant also influenced the understanding of land, which will be explained later in the exegetical sections.

D.N. Premnath's work explains the growing process of latifundialization in the eighth century Israel. By employing sociological categories, he explains how a few wealthy elites accumulated land by depriving the poor peasants.[29] He traces this process to the period of David's territorial expansion during which he gave land grants to his palace officials and military commanders especially in the occupied territory. This, he argues, resulted in a new landed aristocracy in Israel.[30] Premnath further argues that the landed aristocrats utilized the large estate for commercial crops like vine and olive to meet the demand in the international market. This process had a far-reaching impact on the land tenure system in Israel. Since various means of production such as, water, seed, and work animals were procured at high rate, the poor peasants had no option but to borrow from the wealthy elites with a high cost of interest. Unable to repay the borrowed money, the poor peasants had to foreclose their land, which resulted in a large scale of latifundialization. Premnath argues that these dynamics were operative in the time of Uzziah in the south and Jeroboam II in the north during the eighth century, the period of which is considered as the worst form of latifundialization.[31]

Premnath employs Is. 5:8-10 as a case in point in which the phrase בָּתִּים רַבִּים is understood as referring to a "large landholdings"[32] while מקום as small landholding (cf. Gen. 23:20; Judg. 9:55; 19:28; 1 Sam. 2:20; 27:5; 29:4; 2 Sam.19:40). He also defines יושב as referring to the proprietors or lords of the upper political structure.[33] As such, he concludes that "it is these members of the ruling class who owned large estates, and in Isa. 5.8, 9 the verbal and nominal forms ישב should be seen in the context of the process of land accumulation."[34] Premnath's analysis helps us see the factors leading to the problem of land acquisition and how it brought far reaching consequences on the land tenure system. However, since his primary concern is focused on Isa. 5:8-10, he could not deal with other key texts of the eighth century prophets that deals with the issue related to land.

John Andrew Dearman's work addresses the issues of the land grants in the eighth century Israel/Judah. He argues that the prophets' indictment against the

---

[29] D. N. Premnath, "Latifundialization and Isaiah 5:8-10", *JSOT* 40 (1988) 49.

[30] Premnath, "Latifundialization" 53.

[31] Premnath, "Latifundialization" 54.

[32] Premnath, "Latifundialization" 55.

[33] Premnath, "Latifundialization" 55-56.

[34] Premnath, "Latifundialization" 56.

unjust land acquisition was directed against the clan and military leaders who used their influence to accumulate their landed property.[35] He argues that no strict prohibition against land alienation is found in the OT but only some measures are promulgated to protect the right of inheritance and family property.[36] This he considered as the customary law for land right protection that had its basis on Yahwistic traditions.[37] Contrary to Dearman's viewpoint, Christopher Wright argues that the inalienability of land is rooted in the covenant tradition, which he thinks is the foundation of the OT understanding of land. Further, he argues that from Israel's viewpoint, "land" is the land of promise and gift and from Yahweh's viewpoint, "land" ultimately belongs to him and that Israel must acknowledge the prior divine ownership in its legal and cultic institutions.[38] Thus, he argues, although Israel owns the land, it is Yahweh who remained the ultimate owner of the land.

Wright provides insightful information on the tripartite relationship of God, people and land. He asserts that the breaking of the relationship between God and Israel leads to the judgment and expulsion from the land. In order to return to the land, Israel must first return to God and then only Israel can be restored back to the land. Wright argues that such relationship stems from "the existence of covenant relationship between Yahweh and Israel which imposed obligations and conditions, sanctioned by threats of judgment."[39] In other words, "Israel's land gift traditions must be understood and interpreted in the light of the belief in the covenant relationship established at Sinai."[40] Thus, he concludes that Israel and its land are bound together as an "umbilical"[41] relationship, "determined by the nature of Israel's own relationship to God."[42]

Another significant contribution on land tenure system and the purpose of Jubilee law of land comes from Jeffrey A. Fager. He locates the historical setting of the Jubilee law of land to the Babylonian exile. He argues that after the Jews were deported to Babylon, the landless peasants occupied the deserted land and became the landholders in Judah.[43] With the return of the exilic Jews, the Palestinian Jews claimed that the deportees had been expelled from the cultic community, thus forfeiting the right to claim the land.[44] Fager argues that during

---

[35] Dearman, *Property Rights*, 103.

[36] Dearman, *Property Rights*, 69.

[37] Dearman, *Property Rights*, 76-77.

[38] Wright, *God's People in God's Land*, 10.

[39] Wright, *God's People in God's Land*, 13.

[40] Wright, *God's People in God's Land*, 15.

[41] He borrowed the term from Davies to describe the relationship between Israel and its land. Wright, *God's People in God's Land*, 9.

[42] Wright, *God's People in God's Land*, 9.

[43] Fager, *Land Tenure and Biblical Jubilee*, 45-46.

[44] Cf. Ezek. 11:14-17. Fager, *Land Tenure and Biblical Jubilee*, 47-48.

this period the priestly group sought to organize a new society based on the system of redistribution of land[45] and therefore, reformulated the traditions of the jubilee law of land and sanctioned a theological legitimacy to it by linking the jubilee law of land to Sinai covenant.[46] Fager argues that the "land", which the jubilee law deals with, is a "cultivable land" that provides the "basis of survival",[47] and that the enacted law serves to offer a periodic land distribution (every 50 years) "that would restore every family to the land to which it had an absolute right."[48] Fager's work shows how different schools of thought (Priestly group and Ezekielian's group) came into conflict with different alternatives to land reform after the exile.

A brief overview on the OT understanding of land is presented by Elmer Martens. He states that "land" and "people" belong to each other and that both belong to Yahweh. This is indicated by the land promise that is "interlaced" with the promise of descendents (Gen. 13:14-16; 26:4; 27:3; 35:9-12)[49] and such an interlaced promise operates with an affirmation that God would be their God (Gen. 17:4-8; 28:13-15). This, according to Martens, is based on the covenantal relationship. "Land" is understood as "gift"[50] as such, Israel's merit of acquiring land is precluded;[51] she possessed the land as gift and inheritance from Yahweh (Num. 14:39-45) as such, no one can be alienated from the land.[52] Martens also argues that the promise and gift dimensions emphasize Israel's responsibility in the land: *"when you possess it [land] … you shall be careful to do all the statutes…"* (Deut. 11:31-32).[53] The law that should govern the lifestyle of Israel includes the moral and cultic responsibilities, rules about the use of land and other cultic

---

[45] Fager argues that the purpose of Jubilee land law is threefold: "(1) to preserve the ancient traditions now endangered by the Babylonian conquest, (2) to explain the conquest in terms of divine punishment, and (3) to provide a foundation for proper living in the future." Fager, *Land Tenure and Biblical Jubilee*, 54.

[46] He argues that the Jubilee tradition and the Sinai tradition were originally independent of each other; however, the priestly group links the jubilee tradition with Sinai for theological reasons. Sinai is more remote than the Davidic dynasty and the temple, Sinai is a literal mountain but its exact location remains mystery. Sinai is thus semi-mythic historically and semi-mythic geographically. Therefore, no force can destroy Sinai. In other words, Sinai legislations remain inviolable. Fager, *Land Tenure and Biblical Jubilee*, 54-57.

[47] Fager contends that the terms אחזה and שׂדה refers to the cultivable land. Thus, he concludes that "the jubilee legislation is strictly agrarian legislation whose sole land is to effect the distribution of land that produces food, that is, land that forms the basis of survival." Fager, *Land Tenure and Biblical Jubilee*, 89.

[48] Fager, *Land Tenure and Biblical Jubilee*, 97.

[49] Martens, *God's Design*, 105.

[50] For instances, Deut. 5: 31; 9:6; 11:17; 12:1; 15:7, 20; 26:9.

[51] Deut. 6:10; 8:17; 9:6.

[52] Martens, *God's Design*, 110-112.

[53] Cf. 4:5, 14; 5:31; 6:1.

festivals with agricultural orientations. Failure to observe the commands not only pollutes the land; it also will result in the expulsion of Israel from the land.[54]

Against the law that forbids the accumulation of land and its resources (Deut. 17:15-20), the kings started to amass wealth and resources of the land and even evicted or alienated commoners from the land (Naboth's vineyard, cf 2 Kgs 17:23). Martens states that such violation of laws urges the prophets to intervene with the judgment about the imminent loss of the land and concludes that "continual occupancy of the land... was contingent on their compliance with God's commandment."[55]

Martens rightly sees that "land" is the fulcrum upon which the relationship between Yahweh and Israel hinged. He observes correctly that the mismanagement of land during the monarchy ultimately led to the loss of land. In affirming that the land is "a gift from Yahweh, and Israel, through preoccupation with it, has her attention continually called to Yahweh,"[56] Martens shows how the relationship between Yahweh, Israel and land are inseparably linked with each other. He demonstrates how the motif of land enjoined with responsibilities, such as, proper ethical behavior, regulation for land use in sabbatical and jubilee year, laws of festivals associated with the production of land linked land with Yahweh and points to Israel's responsibilities to live in the land before Yahweh. The tripartite relationship of God, humans and land is thus discussed; however, the basis and traditions of such tripartite relationship could not be dealt with by Martens in his work.

Habel demonstrates how concepts, images and beliefs used in the biblical texts show various land ideologies in the OT.[57] He categorizes six major land ideologies[58] and argues that each ideology is associated with a particular social group, who seeks to acquire, gain, or maintain control of the land. Habel's contribution to the land study of the OT has shown that that "there is no monolithic concept of land in the Hebrew Scriptures. There is, rather, a spectrum of land ideologies, with diverse images and doctrines of land."[59] It is surprising, however, to note that despite his attempt to articulate the prophetic ideology, the eighth century prophets' view on land is neglected in his treatment on the prophetic ideology. In fact, this has been the case in most major studies on land

---

[54] Lev. 26:32-33, 43; 2 Chro. 36:21.

[55] Martens, *God's Design*, 192.

[56] Martens, *God's Design*, 119.

[57] Habel defines an ideology as "a pattern of beliefs [which] functions to promote the social and political cause of a particular group in society, to justify its vision, and to promote its interpretation of reality as truth". Habel, *The Land is Mine,* 12.

[58] Royal Ideology (1 Kings 3-10, royal psalms), Theocratic Ideology (Deuteronomy), Ancestral Household ideology (Joshua), Prophetic Ideology (Jeremiah), Agrarian Ideology (Leviticus 25-27), Immigrant Ideology (the Abraham narratives).

[59] Habel, *The Land is Mine*, 148.

in the OT. As stated above, much attention on land study has been focused in the Pentateuch and Historical books, due to the primary interest of the scholars in the Promise-Fulfillment tradition of the land.

What we have discussed so far concerning various scholars' contributions has shown us the following: First, land study in the OT scholarship has been mostly concentrated on the Pentateuchal and historical books partly because of the scholars' preoccupation with the promise-fulfillment tradition of the land.

Second, some scholars have contributed to the prophets' understanding of land; however, the focus has been mostly on the exilic prophets like Jeremiah and Ezekiel due to the scholarly interest in the exile and return to the land scheme. Thus, the eighth century prophets' books are largely neglected in the land studies. Studies on land in the individual prophets of the eighth century appear in the work of some scholars mentioned above. However, the four prophets, Amos, Hosea, Micah and Isaiah have not been treated together to provide a synoptic view of the understanding of land and the issues involved in it during the eighth century Israel and Judah.

Third, the study on land has also been mostly a theological enterprise thereby the exegetical approach has largely been neglected. Due to the lack of exegetical approach, various usages of the terms like, ארץ[60], אדמה[61], תבל[62], נחלה[63], שׂדה[64], and

---

[60] The term ארץ has a wide range of meanings in the Old Testament. Basically, the term ארץ refers to the dry earth in cosmological sense in contrast to heavens and waters; the physical turf of ground upon which one stands; the geographical regions of land and finally the political realm of governed area of a particular nation. Cf. H.H. Schmid "ארץ", in Ernst Jenni and Claus Westermann (eds), *Theological Lexicon of the Old Testament,* vol. 1. Trans. by Mark E. Biddle (Massachusetts: Hendrickson, 1997), 173; Ottoson, "ארץ" in G. Johannes Botterweck and Helmer Ringgren (eds), *Theological Dictionary of the Old Testament*, vol. 1. Trans. by John T. Wallis (Grand Rapids, Michigan: William B. Eerdmans Publishing Company, 1974), 394; Christopher J. H. Wright, "ארץ" in Willem A. VanGemeren (ed), *New International Dictionary of the Old Testament Theology and Exegesis,* vol. 1 (Carlislie, Cumbria: Paternoster, 1996), 519.

[61] In most instances, the word אדמה is closely connected to cultivable land. In Genesis 2:5, אדמה is used in connection with the tilling of the land "לעבד את־האדמה" (Gen 3:23; 4:2, 12; 9:20; 47:23; 2 Sam. 9:10; Zech. 13:5; 1 Chro. 27:26.). J. G. Ploger, "אדמה", *TDOT* 1: 88.

[62] The term תבל is generally understood as "world" in cosmic sense, the whole world as a single entity. In Job 37:12 and Proverbs 8:31, תבל appears in conjunction with ארץ conveying the idea of the entire earth and the inhabited earth. Wright, "תבל" *NIDOTTE* 4:272.Cf. van Meeteren, "תבל" *TDOT* 15:558.

[63] "נחלה" is an inherited portion of land received as grant according to the lineage of one's household, clan or tribe. Cf. Christopher J. H. Wright, "נחלה" *NIDOTE* 3: 77; G. Wanke, "נחלה" in Ernst Jenni and Claus Westermann (eds), *Theological Lexicon of the Old Testament*, vol. 2. trans. by Mark. E Biddle (Peabody, Massachusetts: Hendrickson, 1997), 731.

[64] שׂדה in (Gen. 2:5; 4:8-10; Jer. 32:43) refer to the fields that are situated around and outside humans' inhabited location in contrast to the city or village. שׂדה refers to a productive and cultivable land that can yield agricultural products for the sustenance (Ex. 23:16; Lev. 19:19; 25:3-4; Ps. 107: 37).

אחוזה[65] are interpreted generally as "land." Such generic interpretation makes it hard to treat the subject of land in depth.

Finally, a tripartite understanding of God, humanity and land has not been adequately dealt with except by a few scholars like Wright and Martens. However, even in Wright and Martens' work, due to their preoccupation in the ethical dimensions of land, the traditions behind the tripartite relationships are not clearly explained. In other words, exegetical studies on land have not given adequate attention to the particular tradition that has shaped the meaning and theology of land in the eighth century prophets.

The generic interpretation of various Hebrew terms, ארץ, אדמה, חבל, נחלה, שׂדה, and אחוזה, as "land" fails to adequately convey the understanding of land since these terms refer to land as "living/residential space", "agricultural plot", "uncultivable space", and "territory for political nation." The eighth century prophets' understanding of land was shaped and influenced by various traditions that inseparably link "land" with "God" and "Humans" in which humans' relationship with God is seen as determinant factor for the existence in the land. However, the traditions are mostly neglected in the land studies of the eighth century prophets, which fail to sufficiently provide a helpful understanding of the eighth century prophets' theology of land.

As mentioned above, the eighth century prophets used various Hebrew terms, which are translated generally as "land." Such generic rendering of "land" does not convey the precise meaning of the words in particular texts. These terms could mean either as agricultural land or dry land without cultivation or living territory or a garden for plantations or a political nation. In other words, the various usages of the terms with divergent meanings show the shallowness of translating these terms as "land." This raises certain issues, such as, what does "land" refer to in particular texts? What is the understanding of "land" in the eighth century prophets' sense? What are the ranges of the meaning of the term in different contexts? How do different usages of the term contribute to the understanding of the land concept in the eighth century? These problems can be addressed by finding and exegeting the relevant texts to determine the meaning of these words in particular texts, which will help understand and establish a deeper meaning of the land theology in the eighth century prophets' literature.

"Land" in the eighth century prophets' oracles convey a tripartite relationship: "God, humanity and land." Israel's disobedience to God not only strains the relationship between God and Israel, but also between Israel and

---

[65] Mostly the term אחוזה occurs "in reference to land that belonged to or was promised to the patriarchs or the children of Israel as their place in which to live." Cf. William T. Koopmans, "אחוזה" in Willem A. VanGemeren (ed.), *New International Dictionary of Old Testament Theology and Exegesis*, vol. 1 (Carlisle, Cumbria: Paternoster, 1997), 358.

land.[66] The eighth century prophets reinforce such tripartite relationship between God, humanity and land in their prophetic speeches. Thus, when Israel/Judah sinned against Yahweh either by worshipping other gods and/or by oppressing their fellow humans, Yahweh announced judgment to withhold the productivity of the land (Am. 4:7-9; Hos. 2:3,9), to destroy houses and cities in the land (Am. 3:9-11; 7:7-9; Mic. 2:3-5; 3:12) and to alienate the inhabitants of the land by exiling them to foreign land (Is. 5:13). Such tripartite relationship raises some crucial issues. What is the basis of this kind of tripartite relationship? Is it based on the tradition of land promise and fulfillment or is it based on the tradition of election and covenant or some other traditions? The eighth century prophets seem to emphasize one or more of these theological traditions in their oracles. It is, therefore, important to find out what theological traditions each of these eighth century prophets emphasize when they speak of tripartite relationship. Proper understanding of such traditions will help determine other issues, such as, how Israel and Judah's sins affect their relationship with land? What are the consequences of strained relationship between the people and land and Yahweh? What are the reasons and consequences affecting the relationship mentioned in the texts? How is Israel and Judah's relationship with God and land explained by alienating the people from the land?

In short, the above discussions point to three crucial problems that are closely interrelated to each other, which will be addressed in the following chapters:

i. to establish the exact meaning of the terms for "land" in the oracles of the eighth century prophets,
ii. to study the tradition of the tripartite relationship between God, humanity and land, the basis of such relationship and the reason and consequences of breaking the tripartite relationship,
iii. to derive, out of exegetical study, the theology of land in the understanding of the eighth century prophets.

The above mentioned issues are investigated in the following chapters based on the presupposition that the tripartite relationship between God, Israel/Judah and land in the eighth century prophets' literature is based on the traditions of Creation, Exodus, Election, Covenant, Promise-fulfillment of land, Remnant,

---

[66] Some instances of humans' sin in other texts of the Old Testament, which strains the relationship between God and humanity and its consequence extending to the land are as follows: Adam and Eve sinned and they were banished from Eden to till the land אדמה (Gen. 3:23-24); Cain shed innocent blood and he became a restless wanderer upon the earth ארץ (Gen. 4:6-12); Corruption and violence increased during Noah's time and the Lord destroyed the earth ארץ (Gen. 6: 13ff); the people rebelled at Bablel and the Lord scattered them over all the earth ארץ (Gen. 11:8-9). During the period of judges, the cycle of sin, oppression and deliverance pictures how Israelites did evil in the sight of God and how it brought consequences upon living in the land (Judg. 2:11-14; 3:7-8, 12-14; 6:1-5; 10:6-10; 13:1). In all these instances, the consequences of sin extents to the land and the entire community had to bear the consequences of judgment.

Zion and other traditions. Such presupposition on the traditions behind the eighth century prophets' land theology of tripartite relationship will be assessed by examining the relevant texts.

The main aim of the present work is twofold: first, to explore the understanding of "land" in the writings of the eighth century prophets. In it, the researcher argues that the meaning of the Hebrew terms used for "land" have four dimensions, they are, "land" refers to the entire earth, particular living or residential space, as agricultural and cultivable space and as territory for political governance. Second, it is argued that in the understanding of the eighth century prophets "land" is viewed in terms of tripartite relationship, *God, people and land.* This relationship is based on the earlier traditions of election and covenant and/or promise and fulfillment of land. The basic premise of the above position rests on the eighth century prophets' assertion that sin not only estranges people from God but sin also alienates people from the land. Such alienation includes the rejection as God's people, withdrawal of the fertility of land, displacement from the houses and cities and deportation to a foreign land. This means all the four dimensions of land as entire earth, as living space, as agricultural and cultivable space and as political nation will be affected.

Issues such as, what constitute the meaning of the term "land" in a particular context and on what basis "land" is inseparably understood in term of tripartite relationship have not been clearly defined in the work of most scholars. Scholarships in the classical prophets have been engaged mostly on the wider issue of socioeconomic justice and thereby the questions pertaining to the alienation of land have not been answered satisfactorily. To find explanation to the above issues, the present writer has dealt with some relevant texts in Amos, Hosea, Proto-Isaiah and Micah. Based on the exegesis of the texts, the meaning of land in a particular context is defined and explained how the tripartite relationship of God, people, and land is articulated in the corpus of the classical prophets.

Methodology of the Book

Since the main task of this study is to understand the motif of "land" in the eighth century prophets' literature, primarily, an exegetical method is employed here. The reason of selecting Amos, Hosea, proto-Isaiah and Micah is that these prophets had both direct observation of their society concerning the issues of land and present their understanding about it, while at the same time they explicate in their message how the land was misused against the Law of Yahweh and how its inhabitants' survival were threatened. In other words, to understand the issue of land in the eighth century, it is helpful to incorporate all the four prophets to gain a synoptic view for the proper explication of the texts and fuller understanding of the message of the eighth century prophets.

For exegesis,[67] the present writer has mainly employed the Form Critical and Traditio-Historical approaches.[68] Unlike the narratives, the prophetic oracles spoken on different occasions are imbedded together in the texts giving an impression that different messages are spoken in the same context. Such disjointed materials can be separated by using the Form Critical analysis, thereby enabling the exegetes to understand the setting of a particular text. By employing the Form Criticism, we seek to analyze the texts, particularly the forms,[69] structures[70] and settings[71] (*genre* and *Sitz im Leben*); thereby the message of the texts is thrust to the reconstructed social contexts. On the other hand, the Traditio-Historical Criticism[72] seeks to establish the traditions[73] (i.e., the use of prior materials) and the situations, which produced the texts thereby the theological meaning and intention of the texts, are investigated. In other words, by employing the Traditio-Historical Criticism we assume that behind the present layers of the literary materials, there was a tradition known to the biblical writers, which the authors adapted, reinterpreted and gave a new meaning so as to address their new situation. By inquiring into the tradition, the Traditio-Historical approach can help us interpret the setting of the life and beliefs that produced and contributed

---

[67] The term 'exegesis' refers to a method of interpreting and establishing the intended meaning of the author/s as embedded in the text. Cf. Peter Cotterell and Max Turner, *Linguistics and Biblical Interpretation* (Downers Grove, Illinois: IVP, 1989), 72.

[68] The Form Critical and Traditio-Historical methods share a common or complementary assumption that the statement of the Old Testament texts were formed "under influences and shaping devices which provided the author the prerequisites of possible linguistic utterances." Odil Hannes Steck, *Old Testament Exegesis: A Guide to the Methodology*, trans. by James D. Nogalski (Atlants, Georgia: Scholars, 1998), 121.

[69] The analysis of the literary types/forms of a passage includes the identification of whether the type of a passage is a myth, legend, poem, saga, genealogy, promise, blessing, curse, legal saying, and speeches/oracles or other.

[70] The identification of structures, which in a brief and independent manner comprises a unity of thought determine the beginning and ending of literary unit.

[71] Certain assumptions underlie in determining the setting of the texts, such as, literary type arises out of a specific life situation and the variety of types point to the varied social setting and that the settings in life are often closely related, if not identical, with institutions.

[72] Ambiguity exists among the traditio-historical scholars. The German scholars mostly focus on the study of the oral transmission of a unit prior to its written formulation. However, since in the prophetic books evidence of earlier stage of oral transmission is lacking, the European scholars have "broadened the tradition-historical approach to include *traditionsgeschichtlich*, which investigates not the oral transmission of the text but the conceptions and notions that lie behind the text, and the 'stream of tradition' in which a text is rooted". Ben C. Ollenburger, *Zion, the City of the Great King: A Theological Symbol of the Jerusalem Cult*, JSOTSS 41(Sheffield: JSOT, 1987), 14. Our investigation will follow this approach of tradition-historical method.

[73] "...the word tradition can even refer to the process of transmission (the *tradition*) as well as to the materials themselves that are being handed down (the *traditum*). Douglas A. Knight, "Tradition and Theology", in Douglas A. Knight (ed), *Tradition and Theology in the Old Testament* (Philadelphia: Fortress Press, 1977), 2.

to the production of the present texts, thereby the intended meaning of the texts can be established.[74] The prophets employ many forms and traditions in their prophetic oracles in different social settings. Thus, the use of Form Critical and Traditio-Historical methods provide certain advantages in exegesis, such as, the knowledge and insights into the nature of the prophets' audience, socio-cultural context, form and traditions and establish the intended meaning of the texts of the prophets.

However, the book is also not too exclusive in using the above mentioned approaches. Certain helpful insights from exegetical tools such as, textual criticisms, social criticism, historical criticism and other methods are also employed as and when these methods appear to provide useful information for the present work.

To narrow down the limit of the present work, it is inevitable to be selective in the present approach. Land theology pervades through the entire OT, however, this book restricts itself to the eighth century prophets: Amos, Hosea, Micah and Proto Isaiah. Within the corpus of the eight century prophets, not all the land related text are exegeted. Only the land relevant texts where tradition(s) are apparent are dealt with for exegesis. Thus the selections of the text do not include every reference to land but representative texts of land that show the tripartite relationship imbedded with major traditions are chosen. The selected texts are chosen in unit and not just an individual verse in order to avoid the danger of isolating the text from the particular theology of a literary unit. The exegetical passages are restricted within the literature of the eighth century prophets. Occasional references to other sections of the Old Testament are made only by way of illustration and/or evidence and not necessarily to exegete for the arguments of land theology in the eighth century prophets.

[74] Walter Harrelson, "Faith, Life, and the Emergence of Tradition", in Knight (ed.), *Tradition and Theology*, 19.

Chapter 2

Historical Events[1] Leading to the Tripartite Relationship A Brief Survey

2.1. Definition of "Tripartite Relationship"[2]

The use of the term "tripartite" needs some explanations and justifications. Since in the eighth century prophets' literature, the term "land" often appears in connection with Yahweh and Israel indicating a symbiotic relationship, the term "tripartite" can be a helpful theological term to refer to the relationship between Yahweh, Israel and land. Christopher Wright uses the term 'triangle' and describes the relationship between God, People of Israel and Land from ethical, social and economic angles.[3] E.A. Martens, on the other hand, uses the term 'triad' to describe the similar relationship between Yahweh, Israel and land.[4] The words such as 'triangle', 'triad' used by scholars and 'tripartite" do not appear in the Bible. However, the word, 'tripartite' is used here as a theological concept to refer to the corresponding relation between Yahweh, Israel and land, while the term "relationship" is used to refer to a bond, link and connection between Yahweh,

---

[1] By "Historical Events" we refer to those events that are considered and accepted as happened in the history of Israel. Scholars have debated about the historicity of various events mentioned in the Bible, which are not discussed here since such discussion would merit another thesis.

[2] Though the exact expression "tripartite relationship" does not appear in any known research work of the Old Testament theology of land, the idea of "tripartite relationship" is not entirely new as Elmer Martens and Christopher Wright have used similar expression. Both the scholars convey the idea diagrammatically by employing the triangle to explain the relationship between Yahweh, Israel and land. See, Christopher J.H. Wright, *Old Testament Ethics for the People of God* (Secunderabad: Authentic, 2004), 19; idem, *God's People in God's Land*, 105; Martens, *God's Design*, 118.

[3] Wright, *God's People in God's Land*, 19-62.

[4] Elmer Martens, *Plot and Purpose in the Old Testament* (Leicester: InterVarsity, 1981), 113.

Israel and land. The tripartite relationship thus refers simply to the way in which Yahweh, Israel and land relate to, correspond with and explain each other. Beginning from the creation narrative, we see the emphasis of the relationship between God and humanity (and later Israel) in the light of the land. Walter Brueggemann thus understood land as a "prism" through which the faith and history of Israel is explicated and construed.[5] By employing "tripartite relationship", we assume that Israel's existence and identity as a nation is understood and explained in relation to Yahweh and land.

For a better understanding on how this corresponding relationship between Yahweh, Israel and land is explicated, we have briefly surveyed some major historical events of the OT. These events became Israel/Judah's cherished traditions and remembered by the future generations. Encountering Yahweh through revelations and historical events established Israel's relationship with Yahweh and shaped Israel's understanding of land in connection with her relationship with Yahweh. The historical experiences and revelations of Yahweh concerning the nation and land instilled a strong faith in those who experienced it. As their faith or memories of their belief were passed on to the generations, they became religious and historical traditions. Such traditions were cherished, remembered, perpetuated and restated by the prophets to shape their community's life in times of their crisis. The eighth century prophets utilized these historical and religious traditions as a source of their theology to address some theological issues related to land. The process can be shown in a simple way as follows:

Divine revelation
&
Israelite's Experience] → Belief → Tradition → becomes a basis of Theology

A few of the important questions discussed here include, how is land explained to highlight the relationship between God and Israel? How is Israel's life understood in the light of her relationship with Yahweh and land? How does Israel recount her past history in the light of the relationship with God and Promised Land? These issues are briefly discussed as follows.

2.2. The Creation Event and Primeval History Account (Gen. 1-11)

The Genesis account of creation affirms that God created the entire universe and everything in it. God is portrayed as the creator God who is the ultimate owner of and the sovereign ruler over the entire universe. He created humanity (האדם), according to the P's (priestly) account, in his image (בצלם) and likeness (צדמות) and gave them the authority to rule (רדה) the creatures while the earth

[5] Brueggemann, *The Land*, xii.

was to yield its fruits for the sustenance of humanity.[6] J (Yahwist), on the other hand, states that humanity (האדם) is formed out of the ground/land (האדמה)[7] and humanity is placed upon Eden to till (לעבדה) and to keep (ולשמרה) the land. The land is stated to be an arena upon which Yahweh walks and visits humanity.[8] Humanity, as Walter Zimmerli states, is thus bound with the land in two ways, "he [humanity] is incorporated into it [world], and he is to rule over it."[9] Viewing the P and J accounts of creation synoptically, we find other aspects of relationship between God, humanity and land at least in three important ways: first, God is portrayed as the creator and therefore the owner and ruler of the entire earth; humanity is described as the bearer of God's image to rule the earth on God's behalf while the earth/land is portrayed as an agent of God's providence for the sustenance of humanity.[10] Second, the creation account inseparably connects the life and vocation of humanity with the land by stating that the land is the very material out of which humanity is fashioned and that the land is the very object of humanity's labor.[11] Third, the creation accounts also portray an existent harmonious relationship between God, humanity and land by showing the land as an arena upon which God has fellowship with humanity.

The harmonious relationship between God and humanity was strained after the fall, which had far reaching consequences on the land. Humanity was expelled from the fertile and productive Garden of Eden. Instead of its fecundity and fertility, land became cursed with thorns and thistles upon it. The productivity of the land became subjected only to humans' toil and sweat (Gen. 3:17-19). Later, with Cain's sin against his fellow brother (Abel), the arable land (אדמה) he cultivated (4:2) refused to produce its yield anymore and even worse, Cain was expelled from the arable land (האדמה) and become a fugitive and wanderer upon the earth (בארץ, cf. 4:12). In other words, humans' sin against God and against fellow humanity affected the tripartite relationship in following ways. First, sin expels humanity from the presence of God, עדן) to arable land (אדמה) to become a toiling laborer. Second, sin alienates humanity from arable land (האדמה) to the earth (הארץ) to become a fugitive and wanderer upon the land (Gen. 4:12). Thus, in Gen. 2-4 account of tripartite relationship, sin alienates humanity from

---

[6] Gen. 1:26, 30.

[7] Gen. 2:7.

[8] Cf. Gen. 2:15.

[9] Walter Zimmerli, *The Old Testament and the World*, trans. by. John J. Scullion (Atlanta: Westminister John Knox Press, 1971), 24.

[10] Land as an agent of God's blessing to yield fruits for the sustenance of humanity (Gen. 2:9) is not considered as a "self-contained" organism with its own internal law of nature, rather Yahweh is portrayed as the God who causes the fertility upon the earth to yield its fruit. Yahweh is also portrayed as the God who comes, visits and communicates personally to humanity (Gen. 3:8). Zimmerli, *The Old Testament and the World*, 27.

[11] Theodore Heibert, *The Yahwist's Landscape: Nature and Religion in Early Israel* (New York/ Oxford: Oxford, 1996), 34-35.

God and the alienation from God virtually estranges humanity from אדמה עדן to הארץ.

During Noah's time the pervasiveness of humans' wickedness further aggravated the relationship between God, humanity and land. Yahweh decrees not only to destroy humanity but also the earth, "I will destroy…[humanity] along with the earth (הארץ)."[12] The earth (הארץ) thus suffers the judgment of destruction as a result of failed relationship between humanity and God. Sin among humanity evidenced itself again at Babel as humanity attempted to build a tower as high as heaven to make a name for themselves (Gen. 11:4). Yahweh intervened in judgment and scattered humanity upon the face of all the earth (כל־הארץ). Thus, humanity did not only alienate itself from God and from the land but humans were also estranged from one another upon the face of the earth.

In sum, the creation event and primeval history show the existence of a harmonious tripartite relationship and the reason of breaking such relationship. With the entry of sin the rapport between God, humanity and land was broken resulting in expulsion from עדן to אדמה; alienation from אדמה to הארץ; destruction of both humanity and land (at Flood) and separation of humanity upon the earth (הארץ). With every committed sin, humans were alienated both from God and from land. Thus, the creation and primeval history present the history of tripartite relationship in terms of communion and fellowship to expulsion, alienation and separation of humanity from God and from land.[13]

2.3. Divine Revelation and Promises to the Ancestors

The explicit reference which redefines the tripartite relationship in the patriarchal narrative is stated in the Abrahamic promise.[14] Against the background of the above-mentioned humans' disobedience and the consequent expulsion, alienation and separation of humanity from God and land (Gen. 1-11), God promised to restore his relationship and his blessing of land to humanity through Abraham's descendents. Land is thus seen as a focal point for the outworking of the divine plan to reverse the state of alienation in the Abrahamic narrative (Gen. 12:1-7; 15: 7-21; 17: 8). In contrast to earlier humans' disobedience, Abraham obeyed God's call (Gen. 12:1-4) and his obedience to God's command is followed by a promise to give the land (הארץ Gen. 12:7) as possession (לרשתה cf. Gen. 15:7-21; 17:1-8).[15] In other words, the land that was earlier a "threat agent" to "destroy humanity" became an "object of promise"[16] to "possess". Land is thus no longer

---

[12] Gen.6:13.

[13] Brueggemann, *The Land*, 15.

[14] See Brueggemann, *The Land*, 19.

[15] Jeffrey L. Townsend, "Fulfillment of the Land Promise in the Old Testament", *Bibliotheca Sacra* (1985) 321.

[16] Cf. Brueggemann, *The Land*, 19.

an arena of human's expulsion and alienation but an object of promise, a place to possess and in which to dwell (Gen.12:7, 15:7).

The promise of land was repeatedly confirmed to Abraham (13:14-16; 15:18-21; 17:8), Isaac (26:3-4, 24) Jacob and his descendents ((28:3f.; 13-15; 35:9-12) as a place to possess, to dwell in and to populate their descendents as stars of the heavens. The basis of Yahweh's promise of land to Abraham and his descendents is clearly stated as the covenant (ברית), which Yahweh cut (כרת) with Abraham (Gen. 15:7-21; 17:1-8).[17] That covenant is firmly established as indicated by the ratification of covenant (ברית) in which God passed between the pieces of slain animal (Gen. 15:9-17). Based on the ANE practice of covenant ritual, scholars have found the significance of walking between the pieces of slain animals as a form of self-maledictory oath signifying that "may the fate of the animals be the fate of the promise maker if he fails to keep the covenant."[18] Commenting on Abrahamic covenant in Gen. 15, Ludwig Schmidt states that in passing between the slain animal, Yahweh binds himself with a promise to guarantee the gift of the land to Abraham's descendants (15:9-17).[19] The covenant relationship between Yahweh and Israel in relation to land is mentioned again in Gen.17: 1-9 in which God established (√קים) his covenant (ברית) with Abraham and his descendents. In this covenant, the content is spelled out clearly by stating that the deity would "be God for you [Abraham] and for your descendents after you" (v.7), which is accompanied by the promise of the gift of the land (v.8).[20] In short, in the patriarchal narratives of divine revelation and event of making promise, covenant is seen as a determining factor to the relationship between Yahweh, Abraham (and his descendents) and land. The tripartite relationship is thus seen in terms of the promise in which Yahweh is portrayed as the God who covenanted to give Abraham and his descendents the land, Abraham and his descendents as receiver of the promise of land as gift of God to possess.

2.4. The Exodus Event

Towards the fulfillment of the above mentioned promise of God to bless Israel and the land, Israel found herself under Egyptian slavery. The Egyptians introduced corvee and child infanticide to contain the growth of the Israelites' population (Ex. 1:1-16). Such oppressive policy against Israel is linked with their status as landless sojourners in Egypt but who did not belong to it nor could they take root in it.[21] The Israelites' identity in Exodus is thus seen as landless slaves and their status as landless slaves is associated with oppression and exploitation. Amidst their

---

[17] Townsend, "Fulfillment of the Land Promise", 232.

[18] Martens, *God's Design*, 104; Townsend, "Fulfillment of the Land Promise", 232.

[19] Ludwig Schmidt, "Genesis 15", *VT* 42/2 (2006) 260.

[20] Rolf Rendtroff, *The Covenant Formula: An Exegetical and Theological Investigation*, trans. by Margaret Kohl (Edinburgh: T & T Clark, 1998), 15.

[21] Brueggemann, *The Land*, 22.

persecution, God heard (שמע) their groaning and promised to deliver them and to lead them to a "good land" (3:8). The basis of this promise of exodus and land is stated to be the "covenant" (ברית), which Yahweh established with the ancestors ("I establish my covenant with them", Ex. 6:4).[22] Two important observations on the tripartite relationship can be made: first, it is the covenant that moves Yahweh to act for the liberation of Israel and to lead Israel to the Promised Land. In Yahweh's redemptive plan for Israel, land becomes an inseparable element. Second, the Exodus event presents Yahweh as "deliverer", land as "God's gift" and Israel as beneficiary of God's deliverance and gift. Liberation and land is thus seen in close relation as mere deliverance is not enough since without land Israel could become slaves again to another nation. So, liberation with the gift of land for living with freedom and self-governance became necessary.

The tripartite relationship is further expressed in Ex. 6:7-8 in which Yahweh assures to take Israel as his "people" and to be their "God" (v.7) with a promise that he will give Israel the land as he swore to give as possession (v.8). "I will take you for my people and I will be your God" is a formula of covenant,[23] which expresses an intimate loyalty and mutual solidarity.[24] In other words, the tripartite relationship within the covenantal framework sees "Israel" as the "people of God", "Yahweh" as the "God of Israel" and "the land" as the "gift of God" for Israel to enjoy God's blessing. In this tripartite relationship, Israel's relation with Yahweh as their God and Israel's anticipation to possess the land as God's gift is seen only in relation with the covenant. Thus, the Exodus narrative expresses the relationship between Yahweh, Israel and land on the basis of the covenant and on the basis of this covenant Yahweh promised to lead Israel to the sworn land. The tripartite relationship is thus established, perpetuated and sustained on the basis of the covenant.

2.5. The Sinai Event and Covenant Making

After the deliverance from Egyptian bondage, Israel camped at Sinai from where they entered into the covenant with Yahweh. Before the formalization of the covenant at Sinai, Yahweh reiterates what he has done for Israel: "you have seen what I did to the Egyptians and how I … brought you to myself" (Ex. 19:4). Yahweh then offers a proposal of covenant, "If you obey" (Ex. 19:5) with a promise of special relationship, "you will be my treasured possession" and a special position, "priestly kingdom and a holy nation" (vv. 5-6).[25] Israel accepted the proposal

[22] Modayil Mani Chacko, *Liberation and Service of God: A Theological Evaluation of Exodus 1:1-15:21* (Delhi: ISPCK, 2002), 176.

[23] Martens, *God's Design*, 72.

[24] Walter Brueggemann, *The Covenanted Self: Explorations in Law and Covenant* (Minneapolis: Fortress Press, 1999), 32.

[25] Thomas B. Dozeman, *God on the Mountain: A Study on Redaction, Theology and Canon in Exodus 19-24* SBL 37 (Atlanta, Georgia: Scholars, 1989), 41. For the discussion on the descriptions

with an affirmation, "everything that Yahweh has spoken we will do" (Ex.19:8).[26] However, for Israel to exist as Yahweh's treasured possession, both the land and laws were required to exist as nation and to govern her covenantal relationship with Yahweh. This leads to the promulgation of the Decalogue (Ex. 19:1-17) that sets the norms for Israel to live as God's treasured possession (Ex. 19:22-24:7) and also obligates Israel to follow those obligations as a condition to live in the land. The covenant was ratified with sacrifice at Sinai (Ex. 23:3-8) by spilling the blood upon the altar to seal the covenant. Since blood is the life (Gen. 9:4; Lev. 17:11; Deut. 12:23), the blood that pours out upon the altar signifies "life pours out" in a sacrificial act symbolizing "the life of God poured out for Israel with that of Israel poured out for God."[27] It is a symbol of union between Yahweh and Israel.[28] The covenant thus brought Yahweh and Israel into a close relationship and demands Israel's exclusive "focus of loyalty" to Yahweh.[29] In other words, the Sinai covenant formulates the laws to regulate Israel's relationship with Yahweh and sets condition to govern lifestyle in the land.

Following his covenant faithfulness, Yahweh not only provided Israel's needs, but also appeared (Ex. 19:17) and spoke to Israel (Ex. 20:22) in a very intimate way.[30] However, Israel's idolatry, "These are your gods, O Israel who brought you out of the land of Egypt" (Ex. 32:4), infuriated Yahweh and he threatened to withdraw from Israel, "I will not go up with Israel in the land" (Ex. 33:3). Thus, Israel's covenant disloyalty not only strained her relationship with Yahweh but it also jeopardized the land promise as Yahweh threatened to "consume" Israel before she enters the Promised Land (Ex. 32:11). However, Moses pleaded with Yahweh by appealing to the patriarchal "covenant" that promises the progeny and land (Ex. 32:13), which saved Israel from the certain destruction of Yahweh. Covenant faithfulness is thus seen to be a central factor to determine Israel's relationship with Yahweh and her existence upon the land.

In short, Israel as a community at Sinai entered into a special relationship with Yahweh through the covenant. The covenant consists of laws and commandments

---

"special possession", "kingdom of priests", and "holy nations", see, Joseph Blenkinsopp, *Treasures Old and New: Essays in the Theology of Pentateuch* (Grand Rapids, Michigan/Cambridge, UK: William B. Eerdmans Publishing Company, 2004), 163-165.

[26] Dale Patrick, *The Rhetoric of Revelation in the Hebrew Bible* (Minneapolis, Fortress Press, 1999), 35.

[27] George A.F. Knight, *Theology as Narration: A Commentary on the Book of Exodus* (Grand Rapids, Michigan: 1976), 157.

[28] Dennis J. McCarthy, *Treaty and Covenant: A Study in Form in the Ancient Oriental Documents and in the Old Testament*, Analecta Biblica 21a (Rome: Biblical Institute, 1978), 268.

[29] Patrick, *The Rhetoric of Revelation*, 71.

[30] David J. A. Clines, *The Theme of the Pentateuch,* JSOTSS 10 (England; Sheffield, 1978), 49.

to govern Israel's relationship with Yahweh and to shape Israel's life in the land.[31] The perpetuity of the tripartite relationship remains conditional on Israel's covenantal loyalty. Israel's relationship with Yahweh and her anticipation to inherit the land is thus bound by her obedience to the covenant law.

2.6. The Giving of Law at Sinai and Conditions for Living in the Land

In view of the impending fulfillment of the promise of land, God gave the Israelites the law, which became norms for living in the land.[32] The formula, "these are the statutes… follow when you enter the land"[33] expresses that the land is not only the gift to enjoy Yahweh's blessing, but the land "is also the sphere in which Israel does what Yahweh requires (4:5, 14; 5:31; 6:1; 12:1)."[34] Israel must diligently follow the laws "in the land", which was given by "Yahweh", the "God of your fathers."[35] Two important observations can be made concerning the tripartite relationship. First, the relationship between Yahweh and Israel is connected by the epitaph, "God of your fathers"- a relational expression, which shows how Israel is related to Yahweh as the children of his promise.[36] Yahweh is thus seen as the "giver" of the land while the Israelites are its [land] legitimate occupants as the descendents of God's promise. Second, the tripartite relationship is further connected by the law, which Israelites were to "diligently follow" in the land (Deut. 12:1). Obedience to the Yahweh's covenant is connected to Israel's secured and continual existence in the land, while disobedience would bring defilement, guilt (Deut. 21:23; 24:4), war, catastrophe, death and the loss of land (4:25-26). In other words, the covenant law appears as a connecting factor between the relationship of Yahweh and Israel and Israel's existence upon the land.

Most covenant law in the legal corpus deals with the land and the norms for Israel's existence in the land, such as, the law of sharing resources (Deut. 15:1-7); law of Sabbath for the land (Ex. 23:10-11; Lev. 25: Deut. 15:1-3); law of redemption of the land (Lev. 25); law of landmark (Deut. 19:14).[37] These laws were given on the basis of theological understanding that land belongs to Yahweh, (the land is mine) and that the Israelites are גרים 'sojourners' and חשבים 'strangers' in the land (Lev. 23:25). Israel's relationship with Yahweh and land is thus explained in terms

[31] Murray Lee Newman, *The People of the Covenant: A Study of Israel from Moses to Monarchy* (London: Carey Kingsgate, 1962), 49.

[32] Martens, *God's Design*, 104.

[33] Deut. 11:31-32; 4:4, 14; 5:31; 6:1; 12:1.

[34] Patrick D. Miller, "The Gift of God: The Deuteronomic Theology of the Land", in *Interpretation* 23 (1969) *459*-459.

[35] Deut. 12:1.

[36] Cf. Augustine Pagolu, *The Religion of the Patriarch*, JSOTSS 277 (England: Sheffield, 1998), 114.

[37] Miller, "The Gift of God", 459-460.

of resident aliens who live as Yahweh's tenants in the land.[38] Apart from this cultic law of the land, other civil laws[39] are also promulgated as a prescribed form of tenants' conduct appropriate for life in the land (Lev. 23; 25:2, 8; 26:36). Failure to live by these stipulations would amount to the violation of the tenancy law, which would result in expulsion from the land (Lev. 26:33, 38-41) or the land itself would vomit out Israel (Lev. 18:25, 28; 20:22; 26:33, 38-42). Israel's relationship with Yahweh and with the land is thus seen in terms of tenancy status and that Israel's settlement in the land remains conditional upon her faithfulness to the covenant obligation. Israel's response to the law is therefore understood to have a direct bearing on land. In other words, the laws outline Yahweh's requirements for the maintenance of the Yahweh-Israel relationship. Thus, for Israel to dwell in the land there is an integral responsibility to fulfill the law's demand.

2.7. Wilderness Event

On various occasions in the wilderness, the tripartite relationship was put in a precarious situation. Despite Yahweh's kind act of deliverance, Israel rebelled against Yahweh by expressing their yearnings to return to Egypt (Num. 11:5; 14:1-4; 21:15). Despite the covenant with Yahweh and the assurance of covenantal blessings, Israel doubted Yahweh's ability to provide her needs and her safe passage to the Promised Land. Such mistrusts and rebellions of Israel threatened the relationship between Yahweh and Israel and jeopardized Israel's hope to enter the Promise Land.

At Taberah Israel complained before Yahweh and the punishment of fire came to devour the Israelites (Num. 11:1-3). Israel complained about the food (Num. 11:4-6) as an act of rejecting Yahweh himself (Num. 11:20) and Yahweh struck Israel with plague (Num. 11:33). As an act of disobedience to Yahweh's command (Num. 14:11) Israel rejected Yahweh's order to conquer the land from the south (Num. 13:31-33), which lead to the death of all the Exodus generation (except Caleb and Joshua) without entering the Promised Land (Num. 14:10-38). The grumbling of Korah and his followers ignited God's anger to destroy the entire Israelites' assembly, which finally resulted in the death of fourteen thousand seven hundred Israelites (Num. 16:49). Israel's complaint about the lack of water angered Moses and prompted him to act beyond God's command. The result was unfortunate as Moses and Aaron were forbidden to enter the Promised Land (Num. 20:12). The Israelites spoke against God and Moses (Num. 21:5) and in

[38] Jesudasan B. Jeyaraj, "Ownership, Tenancy and Care of Land in Leviticus 25-27", *AJTR* 4/2 (1991) 18-31.

[39] Such as, the year of release (Deut. 15:1 ff.); judicial procedure (Deut. 16:18-20); law of kingship (Deut. 17:14 f f.); law against abominable practices (Deut. 18:9 ff.); cities of refuge (Deut. 19:1 ff.); not removing a landmark (Deut. 19:14); expiation for an unknown murder (Deut. 21:1 ff.); law against leaving a hanged man's body on a tree (Deut. 21:22 f.); just weights and measures (Deut. 25:13-16); divorce law (Deut. 24:1-4). Cf. Miller, "The Gift of God", 459-450.

his anger Yahweh sent venomous snakes, which resulted in the death of "many Israelites" (Num. 21:6).[40]

The above incidents of rejection, rebellion, disobedience, and complaints contradicted Israel's affirmed loyalty to the covenant, "everything that Yahweh has spoken we will do (Ex.19:8)". In other words, these incidents amounted to Israel's covenant infidelity with Yahweh. Such acts of disloyalty not only jeopardized the relationship between Yahweh and Israel but they also put Yahweh's promise of land into a precarious situation. Two important observations with regard to the tripartite relationship need to be noted. First, disloyalty brings destruction and annihilation and thereby the possibility to enter the Promised Land was debarred from the rebellious people. Second, disloyalty not only prolonged the misery of wilderness life but it also prevented Israel's timely entry into the Promised Land. Israel's anticipation to enter the land is thus constantly referred to in the light of her relationship with Yahweh expressed through covenantal loyalty. The wilderness experience points to us that it is the covenant that regulated the relationship between Yahweh and Israel and it sustains Israel's hope to enter the land promised by Yahweh.

2.8. Settlement

The key term that describes the relationship between Yahweh, Israel and land during the settlement period is inheritance (נחלה).[41] Israel as Yahweh's inheritance (Deut. 4:20) now possess the land of Canaan as her inheritance (Josh. 18:7; 19:1, 9). In other words, Israel is Yahweh's inheritance and the land is Israel's inheritance, which is to say that both Israel and land are Yahweh's נחלה and that both belong to him.[42] Such understanding of land as inheritance shows Israel's relationship with Yahweh in terms of sonship. Wright states that, "it is because Israel is Yahweh's firstborn son that the land is given as an inheritance."[43] The tripartite relationship is thus expressed in a unique bond that exists between Yahweh and Israel in the light of the settlement in the land as inheritance. But how did Israel settle in or occupy the land? Whether or not Israel's settlement is

---

[40] T. Desmond Alexander, *From Paradise to the Promised Land: An Introduction to the Main Themes of the Pentateuch* (Grand Rapids, Michigan: Baker, 1995), 150-153.

[41] Wright, *God's People in God's Land*, 18-19.

[42] John Goldingay, *Old Testament Theology: Israel's Gospel*, Vol. 1 (Downers Grove, Illinois: IVP, 2003), 517.

[43] Wright, *God's People in God's Land*, 20.

through conquest[44] or peaceful infiltration[45] or through peasants' revolts[46] is less important here. The significant issue in our discussion is how Israel remembered their settlement in Canaan. According to Joshua 21:43-45 and 23:14, it is because Yahweh promised and gave to Israel all the land, Israel possessed, settled and rested in the land. The settlement in Canaan is therefore seen as a possession of inheritance, a period of promise-fulfillment and an era of rest (Josh. 11:23). Israel's possession of and relationship with the land is thus explained in reference to Yahweh and his faithful execution of his promise.

Another dimension that explains Israel's connection with the land is seen in terms of Yahweh's righteous judgment. Yahweh categorically states that Israel's dispossession of the Canaanites is not because of Israel's righteousness but because of the iniquity of the Canaanites, "it is because of the wickedness of these nations that Yahweh is dispossessing them (Deut. 9:4)". The same yardstick applies to Israel that just as Yahweh gave the land to Israel because of the wickedness of other peoples, Yahweh would also take the land from Israel because of their iniquity,[47] "if you transgress the covenant of Yahweh...you shall quickly perish from the good land" (Josh. 23:16). If Israel disobeys, especially in idolatry, they would be regarded in God's eyes as pagans and thus they would be disqualified from the land. So, that as pagans are to be conquered and exterminated from the land, the same applies to Israel if she ends in idolatry (Deut. 26:16ff). Israel's exclusive devotion to Yahweh is linked with her survival in the land.

The settlement era was a period of "adaptation and adjustment"[48] for Israel during which Israel was influenced by the Canaanite culture and religion.[49] Such influence had a bearing on Israel's understanding of land, which needs a brief mention here. Macintosh points out that it was a historical reality among the nations that surround Israel to understand the tradition of the conquered land

---

[44] The Conquest Hypothesis (the 13th Century, also known as the theory of the Baltimore school) Israel entered into Canaan from outside through conquest. Adherents of this theory include W.F. Albright, G.Ernest Wright, John Bright. John Bright, *A History of Israel*, 4th edn. (Louisville, Kentucky: Westminster John Knox Press), 129-143; Cf. R.K. Harrison, *The Archaeology of the Old Testament* (New York: Harper and Row, 1963) 48. John Bimson, "The Origins of Israel in Canaan: an examination of recent theories", *Themelios* 15/1 (1989), 4-15.

[45] Peaceful infiltration theory proposed by Albrecht Alt believes that without any form of violence Israel peacefully occupied the uninhabited or sparsely inhabited areas and into the gaps between the Canaanite cities.

[46] Peasant Revolt Theory developed by G.E. Mendenhall (1962) affirms that there was no mass destruction, no total displacement of population but the serfs overthrew only ruling classes. G.E. Mendenhall, The Hebrew Conquest of the Palestine,' *BA* 25/3 (1962).

[47] Bruce S. Warshal, "Israel's Stake in the Land" *Tradition Today* 35/4 (1979) 414.

[48] Bright, *A History of Israel*, 177.

[49] For the discussion on the influence of Canaanite culture and religion, see Mark S. Smith, *The Early History of God: Yahweh and the Other Deities in the Ancient Israel*, 2nd edn. (Grand Rapids, Michigan: William B. Eerdmans Publishing Company, 2002), 19-31.

and worship its gods in order to live secured life in the land (cf. 2 Kgs 17:26).[50] As Israel sought to understand the Canaanite concept of land and agriculture, she was tempted to know the lore of the land, which introduced her to Baal religion. In the Canaanite Baal religion, nature and its forces like rain, earthquake and sea are personified as deity that are either destructive or beneficial to the land and people against which humanity remain helpless.[51] The fertility of the land is seen to be dependent on Baal's fight against chaotic forces that threatens humans' life. Baal's subduing of chaos help the land regains its vitality and assures humanity of the future.[52] However, for Israel nature and its forces are but God's creation and he controls the cycle of nature to moisturize the land and offers the bounty of crops as his gifts for his people. Thus, unlike Canaanite concept of land, for Israel land is Yahweh's blessing and gift and a place of rest.[53] (For further discussion on Canaanite religion, see the following discussion on Religious Context at 4.2.3).

In sum, the settlement tradition sees the land as Israel's inheritance granted by Yahweh's to his firstborn son. Just as Israel possessed the land as her inheritance, Yahweh possesses Israel as his inheritance affirming that belongingness governs the tripartite relationship. Israel's could possess the land because Yahweh fulfilled his promise and just as Yahweh fulfilled his promise, he demands Israel to fulfill her covenantal agreement by living a righteous life in the land. Israel thus remembered that her ethics of and settlement in the land is provisional upon loyalty to Yahweh, "so that you may live and that it… you may live long in the land" (Deut. 5:33).

2.9. Monarchy and Enlarging of Borders

The Davidic-Solomonic era see a greater fulfillment of land promise (Gen 15:18-21 cf. 1 Kgs 4:21). What could not be taken or occupied during the settlement era was, according to Eberhard Ruprecht, finally brought under the control of Israel during the united monarchy.[54] The extent of David's territorial expansion is seen in his census mentioned in 2 Sam 24; 1 Chro. 21:1-27. Joab and his men undertook the census starting from Aroer in Transjordan to the point near Dan at the foot of Mount Hermon in the north to then eastward from Galilee to the cities of Sidon and Tyre. These men also covered the Negev of Judah to Beersheba and the entire western side of Jordan as far as Edom and Moab.[55] Further clarity on the limits of the Israelite kingdom is mentioned in the account of Solomon's

---

[50] A.A. Macintosh, *Hosea*, ICC (Edinburgh: T&T Clark, 1977), 49.

[51] Alfred J. Horeth and others (eds), *Peoples of the Old Testament World* (Grand Rapids, Mich./ Cambridge: Baker/Lutterworth, 1994), 169.

[52] Horeth, *Peoples of the Old Testament World*, 172-173.

[53] Martens, *God's Design*, 112-114.

[54] Eberhard Ruprecht, "Vorgegebene Tradition Und Theologische Gestaltung in Genesis 12:1-3", *VT* 29/2 (1963) 185.

[55] Walter C. Kaiser, *A History of Israel: From Bronze Age Through the Jewish Wars* (Nashville, Tennessee: Broadman & Holman, 1998), 255.

summons to bring the ark of covenant (1 Kgs 8). Verse 65 reads that "Solomon held the festival at that time, and all Israel with him-a great assembly, people from Lebo-hamath to the Wadi of Egypt" (1Kings 8:65). Lebo-hamath and the wadi of Egypt are prominent border points of the north and south respectively in the descriptions of the land (cf. Num. 13:21ff).[56] Other passages that provide information on the territories of Solomon's rule include, 1 Kgs 4:21 (cf. 2 Chron. 9:26) which states that "Solomon was sovereign over all the kingdoms from the Euphrates to the land of the Philistines, even to the border of Egypt" adding that "they brought tribute and served Solomon all the days of his life". What is significant here is not whether these nations were brought under the direct rule of Israel; rather the significance is the extent of Israel's control of the entire boundaries of the Promised Land through tributary imposition.

Israel's domination over these nations began to decline by the end of Solomon's reign. One main reason provided for such decline and subsequent division of the kingdom is "apostasy". Yahweh was angry with Solomon because "his heart had turned away from Yahweh... he did not observe what Yahweh commanded.... Therefore Yahweh said to Solomon... I will surely tear the kingdom from you" (1 Kgs. 11:9). Covenantal disloyalty against Yahweh is understood to be the reason of the decline of Israel's political hegemony and subsequent division of the kingdom between Israel and Judah. Disloyalty and violation of the covenantal law became a common practice among the successive kings of both Israel and Judah, which resulted first in the loss of their own territory controlled by Israel after Solomon and finally the loss of their own land in the future (Israel was deported to Assyria followed by Judah to Babylon). For Israel and Judah, existence or destruction in the land is all determined by faithful or unfaithful relationship with Yahweh. In short, Israel's departure from Yahweh and from his covenantal laws first declines Israel's dominations and later disintegrates her nations. Subsequent departure from Yahweh finally alienates her from her homeland land to exile.

2.10. The Exile and the Loss of Political Governance

According to 2 Kgs 17:1-6, Hoshea the last king of Israel defaulted the tribute payment to Assyria and entered into negotiation with Egypt to throw off Assyria's yoke. The Assyrian king, Shalmeneser V, thereupon captured Samaria and deported its population and reduced the whole of Israel's territory to a province of Assyrians (722 BCE). This brought the political history of the northern kingdom to an end.[57] The deported people of Israel were settled at Halah in Gozan (2 Kgs 17:6), while people from Babylon, Cutah, Avva, Hammath and Sepharvaim (2 Kgs 17:24) and later another foreign group of people were re-settled in Samaria during the reigns

[56] Townsend, "Fulfillment of the Land Promise", 330.

[57] Rolf Rendtorff, *The Old Testament: An Introduction* (Philadelphia, Fortress Press, 1986), 47.

of Esarhaddon (680-669 BCE) and Ashurbanipal (668-627).[58] Israel's loss of and alienation from the land is explained in terms of Israel's disloyalty to Yahweh despite knowing that covenantal disloyalty will lead to the forfeiture of the gift of land (2 Kgs 17:7-18).[59]

More than a century after the fall of Samaria, the Babylonian troops ravaged Jerusalem (587 BCE) along with the temple, royal palace and houses by fire. The temple treasury, priests, royal officials, military commanders, provincial leaders were all carried away and many of them were executed by Nebuchadnezzar (2 Kgs 25:8-17; Jer 52:12-23). The "pleasant land" of Judah was ravaged (Zech. 7:14) and their existence as political nation was put to an end.

Both Israel and Judah lost their land and became landless survivors in strange lands. Two observations are noteworthy. First, by alienating the population from their land and deporting to Assyria and Babylon, the possibility of the nations building in the future were bunged. Second, by enforcing the deportees as manpower or labor force of the Assyrian and Babylonian's empires, Israel and Judah were reduced to their former status as slaves in Egypt. Such historical fate is not understood to be the result of Yahweh's inability to save Judah; rather, the loss of land is understood in terms of the divine punishment.

The eighth century prophets understood the existence in and the desolation of the land in terms of fidelity and infidelity to Yahweh. Such theological perspective on the loss of land is based on the past tradition, the covenant. Violation of the covenant is expressed in terms of injustice, oppression and denial of human rights (Am. 2:6-8; 5:10-12; 6:4), which are stated to be the reason of bringing the nation to an end. Jeremiah reiterates the Leviticus tradition and states that the loss of the land is because of polluting the land (Jer. 2:7; 3:1-10. Cf. Lev. 25).[60] In the exilic setting of tripartite relationship, covenant punishment is seen to have enforced in which Israel and Judah's unfaithfulness to Yahweh is stated as reason for devastation of the land. The prophetic oracles explain the reasons for losing the land, which is dealt with in the following exegesis. Israel and Judah's ethical behavior is seen to be directly affecting the land and the consequences on land affect the living condition of Israel and Judah.

2.11. Post Exile and the Return to the Land

Amidst desolation of and alienation from the land, the exilic people continued to live in hope to return back to their land (Jer. 24:1-10; 29:10-14; Ezek. 36:8-15;

[58] J. Maxwell Miller and John Hayes, *A History of Ancient Israel and Judah* (Philadelphia: Westminster, 1980), 338-339.

[59] Kaiser, *A History of Israel*, 356.

[60] Jeremiah laments over the helplessness state of exile in the following terms, Israel has 'none to comfort' (Lam. 1:2, 9, 17, 21); 'none to help' (Lam. 1:7; cf. 1:3; 5:5, 8).

Isa. 10:1).[61] When Yahweh restores the exilic people in the future, he will also restore the land back to his people. Land becomes the central point of emphasis in Yahweh's restoration of Israel. Israel will be resurrected as a nation and will be united under one king (Ezek. 37:22) and one God (Ezek. 37:23). Like in Joshua's time, there will have a redistribution of land. Land for the temple (Ezek. 45:1-5), for the city (Ezek. 45:6), for the princes (Ezek. 45:7-8), and different land will be assigned to several tribes (Ezek. 47:13-48:29).[62] Yahweh's promise to restore both the land and people back to the harmonious relationship with him is based on the new covenant. The new covenant assures the exilic community of returning to the land and rebuilding the cities (Jer. 31; 33:38; Ezek. 37:26).

After king Cyrus of Persia issued an edict (538 BCE) allowing the Jews to return back to their homeland, the people of Judah once again experienced a new exodus. Despite various opposition, the returned people reconstructed the temple, rebuilt the ruined walls and under the leadership of Ezra, the people of Judah sought to regulate their lives in conformity with God's written law as the divinely appointed way of life in the land. In the post exilic setting, land remained a central theme in the relationship between Yahweh and Israel. As a result of renewed covenant between Yahweh and Israel, the alienated people were also brought back to their homeland. A return to the covenant relationship is thus seen as the basis for restored tripartite relationship in the exile.

Conclusion

The above discussion shows a close connection between Yahweh, Israel and land. The symbiotic relationship between Israel and land is determined by the harmonious relationship Israel keep with Yahweh. For Israel, to depart from Yahweh is to virtually depart from the land and to remain loyal to Yahweh is to remain located in the land. The components of the tripartite relationship are thus inseparably connected with one another. In the following exegesis, we seek to establish that the eighth century prophets utilized the above mentioned historical and religious experiences as their traditions to emphasize their theological understanding of the tripartite relationship and the consequences and results that are stated in the event of breaking or restoring the tripartite relationship.

---

[61] R.E. Clements, *Old Testament Theology: A Fresh Approach* (London: Marshall, Morgan & Scott, 1978), 147.

[62] Bruce C. Brich and others (eds), *A Theological Introduction to the Old Testament* (Nashville: Abingdon Press, 1999), 361.

Chapter 3

The Understanding of Land in the Book of Amos

3.1. Amos, the Prophet

According to the superscription (Am. 1:1), Amos comes from Tekoa, a village in Judea located about ten miles south of Jerusalem, but he carried out his prophetic ministry in the North (7:15). His particular place of ministry is not mentioned but the narratives and speeches of Amos locate him in places, such as, the royal palace (3:9-4:3; 6:1-11), the sanctuary at Bethel (7:10-17; cf. 5:4ff),[1] a market place (8:4-8) and also at a place of community gathering for cultic festivals (2:8; 3:14; 4:4; 5:5ff; 5:21-27).[2] A brief mention about the prophet in 7:14-15 tells us that Amos did not come from a prophetic lineage or from a royal family. He comes from a rural setting and engaged in the profession of a breeding sheep (בוקר) and dressing of sycamore trees (בולס). Since בוקר is understood as an owner in charge of other shepherds, Amos would have been a respected man among his community.[3] His profession as sheep breeder and dresser of sycamore trees probably engaged him in business that demanded him to travel widely in his country and contact with other travelling traders from nearby nations. His interactions with different people during such travels probably gave him an opportunity to gather the vast information concerning the social conditions and various religious traditions of Israel and the historical information of other nations (cf. 1:3-8, 13-2:3; 9:7).

---

[1] Jorg Jeremias, *The Book of Amos: A Commentary* (Louisville, Kentucky: Westminister John Knox Press, 1995), 1.

[2] James Luther Mays, *Amos: A Commentary* (Philadelphia: Westminister John Knox Press, 1969), 4.

[3] Mays, *Amos*, 4.

3.2. Historical Context of Amos' Period

Since the superscription (Am. 1:1) places Amos' ministry during the reign of Jeroboam II (786-746 BCE)[4] and Uzziah (783-742 BCE),[5] most scholars consider that Amos delivered his oracles between 760 and 750 BCE.[6] No scholarly consensus exists concerning the precise date of Amos' ministry,[7] however, the absence of any reference to political reversal in the aftermath of Jeroboam II's death (ca.746 BCE) and the nonappearance of Tiglath-Pileser III's ascendency in Assyria and his policy of territorial expansion in the southwest within the text suggest that Amos' began his ministry in a relatively peaceful era.[8] The reference, "two years before the earthquake" in 1:1 offers some clues on Amos' prophetic ministry. According to Wolff, "Stratum VI of Hazor shows evidence of destruction caused by a great earthquake, traces of which have also been uncovered in archeological work as Samaria. Independently of exegetical considerations... the excavators have dated this earthquake *circa* 760."[9] This suggests that Amos most likely began his prophetic ministry ca. 760-762 BCE. This was a period of successful military campaigns, economic growth, religious syncretism, and deteriorating social conditions in Israel. The following section briefly highlights some aspects of Amos' historical setting.

---

[4] Mays, *Amos,* 1.

[5] Mays, *Amos,* 1.

[6] James L. Mays, "Words about the Words of Amos", *Interpretation,* 13 (1959) 263; John Bright, *A History of Israel* (Philadelphia: The Westminster Press, 1969), 244; J. D. Smart, "Amos", *IDB,* I (Nashville: Abingdon Press, 1962), 118; Jeremias, *The Book of Amos,* 2; John H. Hayes, *Amos, Eighth Century Prophet: His Times and His Preaching* (Nashsville: Abingdon Press, 1988), 16-27, 45-47; Larry J. Rector, "Israel's Rejected Worship: An Exegesis of Amos 5", *Restoration Quarterly* 21/3 (1978) 161; Moltz, "A Literary Interpretation of the Book of Amos", 61.

[7] Due to the internal discrepancies of the monarchical chronology presented in 1 & 2 Kings and 1 & 2 Chro., scholars usually find it difficult to precisely date the time of the kings. Instead only approximate dates are offered. Some proposals of Jeroboam II's date are as follows: Cogan and Tadmor date Jeroboam II's at around 789-748 BCE; Menahem Haran, 789-787 BCE; Albright, John Bright, MacLean, Philip J. King, 786-746; Miller and Hayes, 785-745; Cohen, 784-744; Edwin, R. Thiele, 793-753. Cf. Edwin, R. Thiele, *The Mysterious Numbers of the Hebrew Kings: A Reconstruction of the Chronology of the Kingdoms of Israel and Judah* (Grand Rapids, Michigan: 1965); Hayes and Hooker, 788-748. Cf. John H. Hayes and Paul K. Hooker, *A New Chronology for the Kings of Israel and Judah and its Implication for Biblical History and Literature* (Atlanta: Westminister John Knox Press, Barnes, 784-744. Cf. William Hamilton Barnes, *Studies in the Chronology of the Davidic Monarchy of Israel* (Atlanta: Scholars, 1991). Cited in P.P. Thomas, *Jeroboam II the King and Amos the Prophet: A Social-Scientific Study on the Israelite Society During the 8th Century BCE* (Delhi: ISPCK, 2003), 139. no. 1.

[8] Shalom M. Paul, *Amos* (Minneapolis: Fortress Press, 1991), 1.

[9] Wolff, *Joel and Amos,* 124.

3.2.1. Political Context

Prior to the period of Jeroboam II, Israel suffered severe onslaughts of the Arameans during the last quarter of the ninth century. However, the Arameans' domination was reduced considerably after the rise of Adad-nirari III of Assyria (806-783BCE).[10] Around 796 BCE, Adad-nirari III marched southwest for the fourth time,[11] captured the capital Damascus and forced the Aramean kingdom to pay tribute to the Assyrian king.[12] This reduced the Arameans' political and military strength greatly, while Assyria's domination in the region reached the helm. However, soon after Adad-nirari III's death, Urartu kingdom under Sardur III (810-743) started its territorial expansions and engaged into war with the Assyria, while at the same time Assyria faced internal problem of revolts and successions for almost forty years.[13] Thus, Assyria also started to decline by the end of the ninth century, which paved way for the resurgent Israel under Joash and Jeroboam II to rise at the international arenas.[14] The political scenario was thus marred by warfare and onslaughts between the nations to expand the political territories. Descriptions of brutalities, atrocities, forceful deportations, and slave trade mentioned 1:3-2:16 are all mentioned in the backdrop of such crimes for territorial expansions. Amos indicts those foreign nations who were responsible for such crimes and pronounces Yahweh's judgment against them either in the form of exile and alienation from the land or the defeats and fall of their political nation (1:4, 7, 10, 12, 14, 2:3, 5, 13-16).

After the decline of Assyria, Jeroboam II defeated Damascus and restored the northern Davidic boarder as far as Syria (2 Kgs. 14:25).[15] Cities, such as, Lo-debar and Karnaim as the King's Highway were brought under Israel's control, which served as the major trade route from the Tigris-Euphrates to the Gulf of Aqaba and Egypt.[16] Israel's monopolization of all the major trade routes between Egypt and Mesopotamia that connected the Mediterranean seaports[17] gave her the opportunity to take control of the strategic commercial centers. This ushered in a period of prosperity in Israel.

3.2.2. Socioeconomic Context

Jeroboam's II successful policy of territorial expansion brought far reaching consequences in Israel. The annexed kingdoms brought huge tributes to Israel

---

[10] Wolff, *Joel and Amos*, 89.

[11] 805, 804, 802, 796 BCE. Thomas, *Jeroboam II the King and Amos the Prophet*, 163.

[12] Cf. Thomas, *Jeroboam II the King and Amos the Prophet*, 163.

[13] Thomas, *Jeroboam II the King and Amos the Prophet*, 164.

[14] Stuart A. Irvine, "The Southern Boarder of Syria Reconsidered", *CBQ* 56 (1994) 24.

[15] Rector, "Israel's Rejected Worship", 161. For the discussion on the territorial expansion of Jeroboam II, see Thomas, *Jeroboam II the King and Amos the Prophet*, 144-162.

[16] Peter, 'The Book of Amos,' 205.

[17] Thomas, *Jeroboam II the King and Amos the Prophet*, 180.

while the control of commercial centers generated huge profits in the form of taxations and aggressive business practices (8:5b). Such profits were invested in building activities, money lending and acquiring of lands and large estates. The luxury of the Israelites during this period is indicated by the construction of both the summer and winter houses (Am. 3:10, 12, 15; 5:11; 6:4, 8)[18] and indulgent lifestyle (4:1ff; 6:4-6). Such phenomenal growth of economy in the eighth century Israel is confirmed by some archeological findings. The excavations at Tirzah (Tell el- Farah) show that houses in the tenth century BCE were of uniform small size while in the eighth century there were both large expensive houses and small huddled houses. This shows the contrast of luxury of the rich and the misery of the poor people in the eighth Century.[19]

Since the control of commercial centers under Jeroboam II's reign, the elite class began to involved in a large scale business of viticulture and cattle rising that were of great demand in the international market (5:11b; 6:4b). The outcome of such result was a shift from a subsistence economy to a market-oriented economy. In order to maximize the profits, viticulture was intensely cultivated, which required a huge area of land to grow and to produce. The rich people thus resorted to various form of injustices to acquire land from the peasants. The victims of such corrupted practices are identified as the "weak", "poor", "afflicted" and "righteous" (2:6-8; 4:1; 5:11; 8:4-6). The *modus operandi* of the rich to encroach into the peasants' land was in the form of money lending. During the time of agricultural failures due to natural calamities (4:7-9), the poor peasants had to mortgage their land in order to borrow from the money lenders. However, when the money could not be repaid due to the exorbitant interest rate, the mortgaged lands were forcibly taken away albeit for just a paltry amount (Am 2:6). Thus, the system of *latifundialization* slowly crept into the Israelite society, which made the rich richer while impoverishing the poor to the extreme form of poverty. However, when the cases of injustice were brought to the court, the judges instead of restoring back the land to the poor, they perverted justice by accepting the bribes from the rich and settled the case in favor of the rich (Am. 2:6; 5:7, 10). Such practice was a clear departure from the traditional norm of the inalienability of the land.

3.2.3. Religious Context

The dominant religious practice of eighth century Israel was a syncretistic blend of Yahweh worship with fertility cult of Syro-Palestinian religion.[20] The Baal

[18] According to Peter, two palaces stood in each direction were excavated from Zinjirli, which possibly explains the description of summer and winter houses in Amos 3:15. "Houses of hewn stone, or ashlar masonry (Amos 5:11), are found at Samaria." These archeological findings confirm the prosperity mentioned in the book of Amos. Peter, *The Book of Amos*, 205.

[19] Mayes, *Amos*, 2-3; Lloyd J. Ogilvie, *Hosea, Joel, Amos, Jonah*, The Communicator's Commentary, 20 (Dallas, Texas: Waco, 1990), 261-262.

[20] Blenkinsopp, *A History of Prophecy in Israel*, 104.

worshippers believed that through their devotion and rituals, Baal could be influenced to send rain for the fertility of the crops and the success of animals and human reproduction. Baal worship was also associated with the practice of sacred prostitution. Since it was believed that the sexual intercourse among the gods and goddesses caused fertility on the land, the worshippers of Baal engage in the sexual act at the shrines in order to influence the gods to do likewise so that the fertility of the land would be ensured.[21] The motivation behind this syncretistic worship was to ensure successful harvest.

Frequent and elaborate sacrifices were conducted with expensive sacrifices. However, such sacrifices offered to God were drawn from the corruption in the court and from the oppression of the poor. The poor were exploited, dispossessed, and sold to slavery for excessive fines and travail debts (Amos 2:6; 8:6). Falsifying weights and measures and dishonest gain became the order of trade and commerce (Amos 8:5, 6). In court, the poor were denied justice because bribery became the means for judicial decision. Also, heavy taxation was levied on the poor people and sexual satisfaction was demanded from them. The poor class fell prey to poverty, oppression and slavery on account of the elite class's unjust demands.[22] Social cataclysm was thus manifested in different forms despite their outward religiosity. Injustice and piety, oppression and worship, immoral conduct and sacrificial offerings prospered together during the eighth century Israel.[23] Justice and ethical ideals became totally void in religious activities.

Amidst such context, Amos announces Yahweh's judgment in the form of agricultural failures, military defeats, the loss of land and exile to other nations. Such pronouncement of judgment shows a close link between Yahweh, Israel and land by affirming that Israel's departure from Yahweh would finally alienate her from the land. In the following exegesis, we attempt to investigate the issue of land in the light of the tripartite relationship by inquiring into the traditions upon which Amos based his prophetic oracle concerning the land issues.

3.3. Exegetical Studies on the Tripartite Relationship in Amos

The following exegeses seek to bring out Amos' understanding of land in the light of various traditions that are imbedded in the texts. The selection of the following texts for exegeses is based on the relationship between Yahweh and Israel that is stated in connection with the land. Not all the texts in the following exegeses employ land terminologies, such as, the oracles against Tyre (צר), Edom (אדום) and

---

[21] Ogilvie, *Hosea, Joel, Amos, Obadiah, Jonah*, The Communicator's Commentary, vol. 20 (Dallas, Texas: Word Books, 1990), 263. The archaeological discovery from Kuntillet of eighth century BCE excavated in 1975-76 show the invocation of blessings in the name of Baal, Yahweh and Asherah.

[22] Wolff, *Joel and Amos*, p. 103.

[23] Stephen WinWard, *A Guide to the Prophet* (London: Hodder and Stoughton, 1968), p. 79.

Judah (יהודה 1:9-10; 11-12; 2:4-5). However, the terms צר, אדום and יהודה speak of land in the sense of political nations.

In what follows, we have consistently pursued the following exegetical steps.

i. First, we provide working translations of the texts with some text critical comments on grammatical and syntactical problems to establish the meaning of the texts.
ii. This is followed by form critical comments that seek to establish the form, setting and unit of a passage to see how they shape the message of the text.
iii. The findings of the textual meaning and the shape of the message from the critical comments are elucidated in the light of the traditions embedded in the texts. These are the exegetical steps followed to establish the meaning of land and tripartite relationship in the light of the traditions.

In short, the above exegetical steps on translation, text critical comments, form critical comments and tradition and theological comments do not stand aloof but they are integrated together, which establish the meaning of the texts and theology of the land in the eighth century prophets.

3.4. Tradition of Brotherhood Covenant (Amos 1:9-10)

The oracle against Tyre is based on the tradition of the brotherhood covenant (v.9). Tyre failed to honor the covenant of brotherhood and delivered up her captives (Israel) to Edom (v.9). This refers to a forceful alienation of Israel from her land, which is also stated as the reason of Yahweh's destructive judgment against Tyre as a political nation. The tripartite relationship is thus explained by employing the tradition of brotherhood covenant in 1:9-10.

3.4.1. Translation of Amos 1:9-10

9 Thus, says Yahweh, [a]"For three violations[b] of Tyre, and for four,[a] I will not turn it back; because they delivered up a whole captivity to Edom,[c] and did not remember the covenant of brotherhood[d].

10 Therefore I will send a fire[a] upon the wall of Tyre, and it shall devour her strongholds."

3.4.2. Text Critical Comments (TCC)[24] on Amos 1:9-10

V.9a-a: The phrase, "for three transgression and for four" appears eight times in the oracles against the nations (1:3, 6, 9, 11, 13; 2:1, 4, 6).[25] Citing the biblical

[24] Hereafter the Text Critical Comments are abbreviated as TCC.

[25] Cf. John H. Hayes, "Amos's Oracles Against the Nations (1:2-2:16)", *Review & Expositor* 92 (1995) 167.

and extra-biblical examples of numerical sayings,[26] Wolff contends that such sayings appear mostly in listing the wicked behavior, the pattern of which Amos uses here to list the crimes of the indicted nations. He argues that the numerical saying itemizes wrong actions until the final one singularly mentions a climactic point to convey the irrevocability of the divine punishment.[27] Wolff's argument on the graduated numerical saying as "climactic" appears plausible since the final crime is explicitly stated as the basis of divine punishment. Concerning שלשה (three) and ארבעה (four), Meir Weiss argues that the "three" and "four" together forms a number seven, which he thinks is a symbolic expression of completeness or fullness of sin.[28]

V.9b. פשע appears at least ten times in Amos,[29] and refers mostly to the infractions of property and personal rights.[30] פשע also describes the violation of covenant or treaty agreement by the vassal against the suzerain. In 2 Kings 1:1; 3:5, 7; 8:20 פשע. is associated with the Moabites' act of rebellion against Israel. Andersen and Freedman argue that פשע in the present context refers to the violation of morality "expressed in inhumane treatment of one nation by another."[31] Such explanation appears plausible since 1:3, 11 and 13 mentions the setting of committed atrocities and violation of human rights in the war. The following clause "and did not remember the covenant of brotherhood" conveys the idea of violating the covenantal obligations (see the following section on the tradition and theological comments). Thus, פשע in v.9 can mean violation and infractions of property rights, violation of human rights and covenantal obligations.

V.9c. לאדום "to Edom" refers to the destination of the Tyrian slave trade. BHS suggests לאדום "to Edom" could be rendered as לארם "to Aram." The suggestion emerged from the assumptions that since geographically and economically Tyre shares close proximity with Aram rather than Edom and also on the supposition that the Hebrew consonant ר (לארם) is mistranslated as ד (לאדום) as the two consonants ר and ד appears similar.[32] Hayes objects such emendation since there is no textual evidence to support the alternative reading "to Aram"[33] In any case,

---

[26] The biblical examples Wolff cites are: Prov. 30:15-16; Sir. 50:25-26; Ps 62:12-13[11-12]; Job 5:19-27; 33:14-15. The extra-biblical examples include: the saying of Ahiqar (6.92-92), which mentions three modes of conduct that delight Shamash. Cf. *ANET* 3: 428. "A Ugaritic saying names kinds of misdemeanor (at the sacrificial meal) which Baal hates. Wolff, *Joel and Amos*, 137.

[27] Wolff, *Joel and Amos*, 137-138.

[28] Meir Weiss, "The Pattern of Numerical Sequence in Amos 1-2: A Re-examination", *JBL* 86 (1967) 420-412.

[29] 1:3, 6, 9, 11, 13; 2:1, 4, 6; 3:14; 5:12.

[30] Wolff, *Joel and Amos*, trans, 152.

[31] Francis I Andersen and David Noel Freedman, *Amos: A New Translation with Introduction and Commentary*, AB 24A (New York: Doubleday, 1989), 231.

[32] Marven A. Sweeney, *The Twelve Prophets*, vol. 1, Berit Olam (Collegeville, Minnesota: Liturgical, 2000), 209.

[33] Hayes, "Amos's Oracles Against the Nations", 159.

the significance of the judgment oracle against Tyre lies on the specification of their crime rather than on the destination of their trade. We retain לאדום as it is rendered in the MT text.

V.9d: In the ANE, the term "brotherhood" is used in the context of covenant making. Based on several ANE texts, Gerstenberger convincingly illustrates that the nations who had no blood relationship and were in the past hostile to each other could by virtue of the treaty effected between them be brought into a relationship of "brotherhood."[34] Marvin A. Sweeney states that certain technical terms of ANE treaty are used to describe the relationship between Tyre and Israel during the time of Hiram, David and Solomon (1 Kgs 5:1).[35] One such term is אהב (love), which describes Hiram's love for David, "Hiram always "loved" (√אֹהֵב) David". The term אֹהֵב, according to Sweeney, is "the standard technical term to convey faithfulness and loyalty in treaty relationship."[36] Further he argues that Hiram's address to Solomon as my "brother" (אחי) is a technical term in the ANE "parity treaties" between two parties.[37] The use of ANE technical term of covenant (אהב) in 1 Kgs 5:1ff suggests that the historic relationship between Tyre and Israel is of the "parity treaty" that mutually and equally bind and obligate both the parties. Sweeney's argument appears plausible in the context of 1 Kings 5:12 [MT 5:26], where the term covenant "ברית" is used to describe the treaty concluded between Solomon and Hiram of Tyre. Since the literary context of 1 Kings 5 traces back the relationship between the two kingdoms to the time of David, it appears likely that the parity treaty between Tyre and Israel existed since the time of David in the tenth century. Apart from the above mentioned "covenant" in 1 Kings 5:12 [MT 5:26], there is no known established treaty between Tyre and Israel either in the Bible and the ANE documents, thus most likely the covenant of brotherhood here refers to the historic cooperation between the Phoenician king Hiram and the Israelite kings, David and Solomon (cf. 2 Sam 5:1; 1 Kgs 5:1, 11).[38] Such treaty is understood in terms of "covenant of brotherhood" not because of any

---

[34] E. Gerstenberger, "Covenant and Commandment", *JBL* 84 (1965) 40-42; John Barton, *Amos's Oracles Against the Nations*, The Society for Old Testament Studies Monograph Series, 6 (Cambridge: Cambridge University, 1980), 20.

[35] Sweeney, *The Twelve Prophets*, 208.

[36] Sweeney, *The Twelve Prophets*, 208.

[37] Sweeney, *The Twelve Prophets*, 208.

[38] Mays, *Amos: A Commentary*, 34; William Rainey Harper, *Amos and Hosea*, ICC (Edinburgh: T&T Clark, 1979), 29; C.F. Keil, *Minor Prophets*, vol. 10 (Grand Rapids, Michigan: William B. Eerdmans Publishing Company, 1982), 247; Thomas Edward McComiskey, "Amos", in Frank E. Gæbelein and others (eds), *Daniel and the Minor Prophets,* The Expositor's Bible Commentary, vol. 7 (Grand Rapids, Michigan: Zondervan, 1985), 287; Andersen and Freedman, *Amos*, 261; Ogilvie, *Hosea, Joel, Amos, Obadiah, Jonah*, 278; Billy K. Smith and Frank S. Page, *Amos, Obadiah, Jonah*, NAC, 19b (Nashville, Tennessee: Broadman & Holman, 1995), 53; Donald E. Gowan, *The Book of Amos: Introduction, Commentary and Reflection*, NIB, 7 (Nashville: Abingdon Press, 1996), 361; Sweeney, *The Twelve Prophets*, vol. 1, 208.

blood relations but because of the treaty initiated between the two parties that bind them equally and mutually to each other.

V.10a: "I will send a fire… and it shall devour…" specifies the nature of impending judgment. The term "fire", which consumes the enemies, belongs to the vocabulary of the Holy War tradition that appears in the descriptions of Yahweh's destruction of military catastrophe.[39] Amos uses the traditional formulaic expression to convey the impending catastrophe that will destroy the military and political establishments of the indicted nations.

3.4.3. Form Critical Comments (FCC)[40] Amos 1:9-10

The oracles against the foreign nations and the messenger-speech formula[41] appear for the first time in Amos.[42] The messenger formula "Thus says Yahweh" is rooted in the ambassadorial style of international diplomacy. In the ANE, the king's emissary acts as spokesperson to convey the message in diplomatic terms. For example, when Sennacherib's messenger spoke in the name of the king, he said, "… Thus the great king has said" (2 Kgs 18:19). When Hezekiah sends his messengers to the prophet Isaiah, the emissaries said, "Thus Hezekiah has said" (2 Kgs 19:3). In these occurrences, the emissaries spoke on king's behalf wherein the formula of "thus says…" appears as a protocol of diplomacy. Amos employs the form of diplomatic communication style to represents himself as messenger of Yahweh to announce judgment against the nations.[43]

The Tyre oracle in 1:9-10 is a complete unit that carefully follows a structured pattern of judgment oracle:

Messenger formula:	Thus, says Yahweh
General accusation:	"For three violations of Tyre and for four…
Specific indictment:	because they delivered up a whole captivity to Edom, and did not remember the covenant of brotherhood.
Sentence:	so I will send a fire upon the wall of Tyre and it shall devour her strongholds."

According to Wolff, Amos probably delivered the oracle during "the occasion of the festival assembly" in Israel.[44] He argues that such an assumption is possible since Amos' presence at Bethel is mentioned in 7:10-17, where Amos

---

[39] P.D. Miller, "Fire in the Mythology of Canaan and Israel", *CBQ* 27 (1965) 256.

[40] Hereafter the Form Critical Comments is abbreviated as FCC.

[41] The messenger formula appears fourteen times in Amos (1:3, 6, 9, 11, 13; 2: 1, 4, 6; 3:11, 12; 5:3, 4, 16; 7:17).

[42] Gerhard F. Hasel, *Understanding the Book of Amos: Basic Issues in Current Interpretations* (Grand Rapids, Michigan: Baker, 1991), 17; Wolff, *Joel and Amos*, 135.

[43] Partlow, "Amos's Use of Rhetorical Entrapment", 23.

[44] Wolff, *Joel and Amos*, 149.

probably came to attend a festival that was celebrated at the end of harvest (cf. 1 Kgs 12:23).[45] It is difficult to determine the crimes mentioned in 1:9 with some known historical event. Sweeney seems to suggest that the crime refers to the Arameans' occupation of Gilead and Bashan in the aftermath of Ahab's death. He states that the violation of the treaty mentioned here refers to the withdrawal of the Ph'enicians' cooperation with Israel during the Arameans' invasion. After the overthrow of the Omride dynasty, Jehu assassinated Joram, king of Israel, Ahaziah, king of Judah, and Jezebel, Ahab's wife (2 Kgs 9:14-27), who were either the children or grandchildren of the Phoenician king. Such a turn of assassination by Jehu forced the Phoenicians to withdraw their support to Israel at the time when Hazael occupied Israel's territory of Gilead and Bashan.[46] Sweeney states that the entire Israelite population, which comes under Aram's occupation, was exiled. Jehu's dynasty viewed Tyre's failure to come to Israel's aid during this time as an act of violation of the treaty.[47] If this explanation is viable, then Tyre's crime refers only to her failure to cooperate and that the accusation of delivering up the people to Edom would in fact, refer to Aram. Such explanation is possible if אדם (Edom) is amended to ארם (Aram). However, as mentioned above in the TCC on v.9c, such emendation is not necessary in the present context. Stuart states that the attempts to show contemporary international development of brutal events in Amos' time to "a narrow time limit" are "ill-founded" as there are not enough data to prove the case.[48] Stuart thus suggests a broad time line that the mentioned atrocities seems to refer to the border wars, which probably occurred during the late years of Solomon's reign ca 940 BCE. till Amos' time in the mid-eighth century.[49]

3.4.4. Traditions and Theological Comments in the Light of Tripartite Relationship

Amos' oracle against Tyre is based on the tradition of the brotherhood covenant. Amos indicts Tyre for she did "not remember" (לא זכר) the "covenant of brotherhood" (ברית אחים).[50] As stated above in the TCC on v.9d, the "covenant of brotherhood" refers to the historic cooperation between Tyre and Israel. Such cooperation includes Tyre's supply of timber, mason and building experts to Israel for palace and temple constructions (economic cooperation, cf. 2 Sam. 5:11ff; 1 Kgs 5). Later, the ties between the two nations were further strengthened by

---

[45] Wolff, *Joel and Amos*, 149.

[46] Sweeney, *The Twelve Prophets*, 209.

[47] Sweeney, *The Twelve Prophets*, 209.

[48] Stuart, *Hosea-Jonah*, 309.

[49] Stuart, *Hosea-Jonah*, 309.

[50] Priest has demonstrated convincingly the accuracy of "covenant of brotherhood" in Am. 1:9 as referring to the treaty between Tyre and Israel. See, Priest, "The Covenant of Brothers", 400-406.

Ahab's marriage to Jezebel, daughter of Ethbaal (political cooperation, cf. 1 Kgs 16: 31ff). The centuries-long ties between Tyre (Phoenicia) and Israel over the period of time had become a shared tradition of cooperation between the two nations. Such tradition involves economic cooperation (for instance, supplying of timber, mason and the experts or skilled men) and political solidarity (for instance, Hiram's "love" for David and Hiram's address to Solomon as "my brother", the wise king). However, the past heritage which shaped the spirit of solidarity and cooperation has not been honored. Instead Tyre handed over her victims as captives to another political nation, Edom. This, according to Amos, is a violation of the covenant of brotherhood, which serves as the basis of judgment against Tyre.

Yahweh's specific indictment against Tyre is based on the charge that Tyre "delivered up" a whole captivity to Edom. In the Old Greek Translation "שלמה" (whole) is transliterated as "of Solomon" to show that the captives were the Israelites. Though the identity of Tyre's victims is not specified, scholars do not doubt that Israel/Judah is indicated here.[51] Whether or not the delivering up of whole people to captivity refers to slave trade is debatable.[52] In any case, three observations can be noted with regard to the issue of land. First, when the entire inhabitants are deported to another nation, the victims' land becomes free, open, unoccupied and devastated land. Second, in delivering up the whole population to Edom, the victims were forcibly alienated from their land. Third, the victims delivered to Edom possibly became landless slaves and lost their dignity. If the above three observations can be sustained, then the issues here include the devastation of the victims' land, forceful alienation of victims from their land and making the victims the landless slaves. Such act of the Tyrians, according to Amos, amounts to violation (פשע). In this case, פשע refers to an act of infringement into others' political territory and violation of the victims' liberty to dwell in the land. This is considered as a violation of the tradition of brotherhood covenant between Tyre and Israel/Judah. Tyre's failure to honor this covenant is used as the basis of indictment and punishment against her land.

As mentioned in the above FCC, Amos' use of the messenger formula has shown that Yahweh is the sovereign ruler over the nations and that the nations are accountable before Yahweh. As the ultimate ruler, Yahweh enters into judgment against Tyre for violating the brotherhood covenant. Yahweh's speech, "I will"[53] emphasizes God's active participation in bringing destruction upon Tyre. The object of Yahweh's judgment is stated as "fire" that would devour Tyre's wall and stronghold. The impenetrable fortress, massive walls and the king's elite army will

---

[51] Gary V. Smith, *Amos: A Commentary* (Grand Rapids, Michigan: Zondervan, 1989), 38.

[52] Most scholars seem to understand that delivering up the whole population to Edom refers to Edom's involvement in slave trade. Cf. Harper, *Amos*, 25; Smith, *Hosea, Amos, Micah*, 241; Ogilvie, *Hosea, Joel, Amos, Obadiah, Jonah*, 277; Stuart, *Hosea-Jonah*, 312-313; Sweeney, *The Twelve Prophets*, 207; Gowan, "The Book of Amos", 361; Andersen and Freedman, *Amos*, 261.

[53] "I will" appears repeatedly in the oracles against the nations. cf. 1:4, 7, 10, 12, 14; 2:2, 5.

not be able to protect the strongholds of the nation from Yahweh's judgment. "Stronghold" as a symbol of national pride and political and military centre will be destroyed and turned to ruins by fire. Setting the conquered cities to fire was a military tactic in the ANE to cripple the political and military infrastructure of the defeated nations.[54]

The breakdown of this tradition affects the relationship between Yahweh, Israel/Tyre and land. The tripartite relationship is seen in terms of Yahweh's ultimate sovereignty. As sovereign ruler, Yahweh judges the national affairs of Tyre and as found guilty Tyre, as political nation, is sentenced to destruction of fire. Tyre's crime includes alienation of Israel from her land. Tyre's crime not only affected her relationship with Israel and Yahweh, but it even affected her relationship with the land, that is, her political land would be devastated. Yahweh's relationship with Israel is also expressed in terms of his judgment on behalf of the Israelite victims. As victims of oppression, Israel's relationship with her land is also affected in that she is alienated from her land and became a captive in foreign land. In sum, Yahweh is portrayed as the ultimate observer and arbitrator of the affairs between the nations. Yahweh is also portrayed as the God who protects the weak, judges the powerful and establishes his justice on the earth.

3.5. Kinship Tradition (Amos 1:11-12)

The Edom-Israel/Judah relationship is stated by the term "brother" (v.11), which refers to the patriarchal tradition of kinship between Esau and Jacob as uterine brothers. Edom's failure to honor the kinship tradition not only results in warfare and destruction of the land of Israel/Judah but it also calls for Yahweh's intervention to bring destruction upon Edom. Destruction upon the land is stated as Yahweh's act occasioned by Edom's failure to honor the kinship tradition. The tripartite relationship is thus explained by employing the kinship tradition in 1:11-12.

3.5.1. Translation on Amos 1:11-12

11 Thus, says Yahweh: "For three violations of Edom, and for four, I will not turn it back; because he pursued[a] his brother[b] with the sword, and he destroyed[c] without compassion,[d] and his anger tore[e] perpetually,[f] and he kept his wrath for ever.

12 So, I will send a fire upon Teman, and it shall devour the strongholds of Bozrah."

[54] cf. Josh. 6:24; 11:11; Judg. 9:52; 1 Sam. 30:14; 1 Kgs 16:18; 2 Kgs 25:9; Isa. 1:7; Jer. 37:10; 39:8.

3.5.2. Text Critical Comments on Amos 1:11-12

V.11a. √רדף "to pursue" refers to "hot pursuit after battle" (cf. Gen. 14:15).[55] The following term √שחת "to destroy" states the goal of their hot pursuit, that is, to eliminate Israel completely.[56] The two terms "pursue" and "overtake" are a well-established sequence that appears frequently in the context of combat.[57]

V.11b. Sweeney thinks that "his brother" (אחיו) indicates more of political relationship, which Edom had violated rather than the allusion of ethnic bond between the two nations.[58] Since "his brother" (אחיו) refers to the victim of Edom's crime and since the patriarchal tradition recounts Esau and Jacob as brothers, Edom's persuasion of "his brother (אחיו)" with sword could refer to Israel in a comprehensive sense of the term.[59] We consider "brother" as referring to the kinship relationship (cf. Gen 25:19ff; 27:40-41; Num. 20:14; Deut. 2:4; Obad. 10, 12).

V.11c. The word שחת can mean to "murder" a person (2 Sam. 1:14), or "destroy" a nation (Hos. 11:9), cf. Gen. 6:17; 9:15; 2 Sam. 14:11; Ezek 5:16; 20:17.[60] The perfect שחת with ואו consecutive follows the infinitive (רדפו), which expresses the idea of frequent actions.[61]

V.11d. The LXX reads רחמיו as ארתֵהמ, which by metonymy is translated as "mother". Based on the ANE treaty terminology, Fishbane proposes רחמיו and אחיו as a synonymous pair, which are understood as "ally."[62] Likewise Andersen and Freedman state that רחם refers to "a person or a group in a covenant relationship with another person or group."[63] Thus they argue that רחמיו can be interpreted within the framework of covenant as "ally."[64] Considering the two terms אחיו (his brother) and רחמיו (his ally) to be together, Andersen and Freedman conclude that the Edomites are, thus, the brother and ally of Israel/Judah, which reflects both kinship and covenant obligation.[65] The idea of covenant is present in the term "brother;" however, to render רחם as "ally" in the present context may not be tenable. רחם in the tradition of Edom-Jacob is associated with the idea of compassion as uterine brothers. As such, Yahweh warned Israel neither to hate

---

[55] Andersen and Freedman, *Amos*, 266.

[56] Andersen and Freedman, *Amos*, 266.

[57] Michael L. Barre, "Amos 1:11 Reconsidered", *CBQ* 47 (1985), 426.

[58] Sweeney, *The Twelve Prophets*, 209.

[59] Andersen and Freedman, *Amos*, 266.

[60] Sweeney, *The Twelve Prophets*, 209.

[61] Harper, *Amos and Hosea*, 34.

[62] For detail discussion, see Fishbane, "The Treaty Background of Amos 1:11", 313-318; idem, "Critical Note: Additional Remarks on RHMYW (Amos 1:11)", *JBL* 91 (1972) 391.

[63] Andersen and Freedman, *Amos*, 266.

[64] Andersen and Freedman, *Amos*, 266.

[65] Andersen and Freedman, *Amos*, 266.

Edom nor to annex Edom's territory (Deut. 23:7-8; 2:5). In this case, רחם can be understood as compassion, which was expected to be a determining factor in Edom-Israel relationship, which Edom failed to reciprocate since the beginning of their history.

V.11e. The MT version of ויטרף "and he tear apart" is rendered in the Samaritan Pentateuch and Vulgate as ויטר from the root נטר probably to express parallelism with √שמר "to keep". Following these renderings, Drivers, Coote, Fishbane and Held think that the verbs in the last clause of v.11e are נטר ("to keep or maintain" and שמר "to keep" instead of טרף (to tear/rend) and שמר (to keep) of MT.[66] However, emending the MT version of טרף (to tear/rend) to נטר ("to keep or maintain" for the sake of mere parallelism would lose the intensity of Amos' accentuation of the crimes of Edom. We retain MT version of √טרף (to tear/rend) in our exegesis.

V.11f. For לעד, the LXX reads "for a witness."[67] It is appropriate to retain MT's reading לעד meaning "perpetually" in the context of the Edomite-Israelite continued conflicts during the course of their history. The centuries-long hostilities of the Edomites against Israel and Judah are mentioned in the following section on the tradition and theological comments.

3.5.3. Form Critical Comments on Amos 1:11-12

The oracle against Edom (1:11-12) employs the same form and formulaic pattern as in the above oracle against the Tyre (see the FCC on vv.9-10). The judgment oracle against Edom can be outlined as follows:

Messenger formula:	Thus, says Yahweh
General accusation:	"For three violations of Edom and for four, I will not turn it back;
Specific indictment:	because he pursued his brother with the sword … destroyed without compassion… his anger tore perpetually, and he kept his wrath for ever
Announcement of judgment:	So, I will send a fire upon Teman and it shall devour her strongholds".

Edom-Israel relationship was strained since the time of David on the issue to control the Gulf of *'el-Aqabah*, which continued till the time of Uzziah and Amos (2 Kgs 14:22). According to Wolff, the Judean kings aggressively campaigned

[66] G.R. Driver, "Studies in the Vocabulary of the Old Testament III", *JTS* 32 (1931), 361-63; R.B. Coote, "Amos 1:11", 208 no. 13; Fishbane, "The Treaty Background of Amos 1:11", 317 no. 21; M. Held, "Studies in Biblical Homonyms in the Light of Akkadian", *JANESCU* 3 (1970-71) 47-51.

[67] Stuart, *Hosea-Jonah*, 313.

throughout the Edomite territory "to the east and west of the *Wedi 'el-Arabah* between the Dead Sea and the Gulf of 'el-Aqabah", which fuelled Edom's anger against Judah.[68] Wolff argues farther that Edom took advantage of Jerusalem's fall in the aftermath of Babylonian's conquest in 587 BCE, and avenges the centuries long anger against the defenseless Judah. Wolff thus considers that the indictment of pursuing "his brother with sword" refers to the post 587 BCE events.[69] Wolff's argument on alluding Edom's crime to the exilic setting is difficult to sustain since Edom's attack on Israel is mentioned even before the Babylonian attack. Contrary to Wolff, Stuart argues that Edom's crime of pursuing his brother refers to the pre-conquest event of the Edomites who refused Israel a safe passage and instead pursued Israel with the sword (בחרב; Num. 20:14-21; esp. vv. 18, 20). Edomite-Israelite hostility continued thereafter.[70] Perhaps Amos had in mind the long history of hostility between Edom and Israel since the time of the Exodus.[71]

Edom remained under Israel's control since the period of the united monarchy.[72] Shortly before the time of Amos, the Omride dynasty was overthrown by Jehu and subsequently Judah lost its control on Transjordan region. This event was followed by Edom's "revolt" against Judah, after the death of Ahab, during Jehoram ben Jehoshaphat's period (2 Kgs 8:20-22). Since "revolt" in 2 Kgs 8:20 presupposes bloodshed, the reference to Edom "pursued his brother with sword" (1:11) perhaps presupposes the atrocities committed during such revolts. The biblical records provide ample instances of the long standing animosity of Edom against Israel/Judah. Amos would have been aware of Edom's revolts and attacks that had happened before this period. All these events show Edom's bitter relations with Israel both in the early and later period of Edom's history.

3.5.4. Tradition and Theological Comments in the Light of Tripartite Relationship

Amos' judgment in 1:11-12 is based on the tradition of kinship between Edom and Israel. The kinship tradition of Edom and Israel dates back to the patriarchal age of Esau and Jacob, the eponymous ancestors of Edom and Israel (Gen. 25:24ff). As uterine brothers, the biblical accounts encourage promoting the kinship tradition for harmonious existence between the two nations. Such tradition promotes forbearance and tolerance with one another and forbids hatred and bigotry, "you shall not abhor an Edomite; for he is thy brother ... their third generation... may enter the assembly of the LORD" (Deut. 23:7-8). It was also a tradition of territorial protection, which is rooted in a theological conviction that both Edom and Israel received the land as gift from Yahweh. Thus, Israel is warned not

[68] Wolff, *Joel and Amos*, 160.

[69] Wolff, *Joel and Amos*, 160.

[70] Stuart, *Hosea-Jonah*, 313.

[71] Barton, *Amos's Oracles Against the Nations*, 32.

[72] 2 Sam. 8:13-14; 1 Kgs 14:7, 22; 1 Kgs 11:15-17.

to appropriate even a foot of Edomite land, "... I will not give you any of their land... because I have given Mount Seir to Esau as a possession" (Deut. 2:5). In other words, the relationship between Edom and Israel is supposed to be governed by the practice of kindness, acceptance, and respect for territorial protection as the recipients of land as God's gift. However, aggression, hostility and brutality became the trade mark of Israel-Edom relationship, which is stated to be the reason of judgment against Edom.

Edom is accused for pursuing his brother with the sword. As noted above in the TCC on v.11b, "his brother" refers to both Edom-Israel/Judah as uterine bothers that is supposed to be characterized by kinship obligations. However, instead of perpetuating such kinship responsibility, Edom engaged in military combat and pursues "רדף" his brother with sword. Edom is also accused of destroying his brother without compassion. √שחת "to destroy" refers to damaging or ruining the objects such as, corps, buildings, and cities with total destruction and extermination and the degree of such large scale destruction is permitted to God, not to humans.[73] שחת thus specifies Edom's action to totally annihilate and destroy his brother's cities and population. Such an act of total destruction is carried out without compassion "רחם". The image used here to picture Edom's action is that of a lion that attacks and guards its prey. The clause ויטרף אעד אפו literally "and tore forever his anger" employs the verb טרף, which means "he tore (meat like a lion)" i.e., "his anger tore perpetually."[74] Moreover, the phrase "and he kept/watched his wrath forever", indicate the image of a lion watching its dead prey. The usage of these verbs indicates Edom's crimes in war against Israel/Judah. Since in Amos the term פשע also refers to an act of infringement into others' political territory and violation of the liberty of victims' land, Edom's crimes here involve not only an attempt to annihilate and destroy her brother's population but also to infringe into the territory of his brother. Such act is contrary to the tradition of brotherhood, which envisages the respect for territorial protection. Amos sees this to be the reason for Yahweh's judgment against Edom.

Based on the above crime of Edom, Yahweh sentences his judgment of fire upon Teman and Borzah. Teman was Edom's southernmost city while Borzah was the northernmost city and both lay in the ancient king's highways stretching from Damascus to the Gulf of Aqaba.[75] Teman and Borzah thus figuratively represent the entire territory of Edom,[76] which indicates that the destruction would be large scale devastation. Such magnitude of national disaster is stated as Yahweh's judgment against Edom for her betrayal of kinship tradition.

The kinship tradition explains the tripartite relationship in that both Edom and Israel/Judah are not only understood as uterine brothers but both the brothers

[73] Andersen and Freedman, *Amos*, 264.

[74] Sweeney, *The Twelve Prophets*, 210.

[75] Stuart, *Hoseah-Jonah*, 313.

[76] Gowan, "The Book of Amos", 362.

are remembered as recipients of land as gifts from God. The kinship tradition thus encourages the respect for territorial integrity between the sister nations. However, Edom's constant engagement in war against Israel/Judah is seen as a violation of kinship tradition and an affront to the divine land gift tradition, which forbids the encroachments into each other's territory. In acting against Israel, Edom angered Yahweh who gave her the land (Mount Seir) as a possession. Yahweh's anger affects Edom's relation with the land in that the fire from Yahweh devours Edom's entire political territory. As in the case of Tyre, the tripartite relationship here is also seen in terms of Yahweh's ultimate sovereignty. As sovereign ruler, Yahweh judges the entire affairs of Edom and as he finds Edom guilty, as a political nation, Edom is sentenced to destruction by fire.

3.6. The Torah Tradition (Amos 2:4-5)

The terms "Torah of Yahweh" (תורת יהוה), "to keep" (שמר), "to follow" (הלך) in v.4 indicate that the Judah oracle (2:4-5) is rooted in the Torah tradition. Judah's rejection of Yahweh's Torah is stated to be the reason of judgment of fire upon the land. The effect of the tripartite relationship is thus explained by employing the Torah tradition in 2:4-5.

3.6.1. Translation on Amos 2:4-5

4 Thus, says Yahweh: "For three violations of Judah, and for four, I will not turn it back; because they have rejected[a] the Torah of Yahweh, and have not kept his statutes, but their idols[b] have led them astray, after which their fathers walked.

5 So, I will send a fire upon Judah, and it shall devour the strongholds of Jerusalem."

3.6.2. Text Critical Comments on Amos 2:4-5

v.4a: מאס is probably derived from the Akkadian equivalent *mêšu*, meaning to despise, to have contempt for, and to disregard the gods and their rites.[77] מאס frequently appears in Amos, Hosea, Isaiah, Jeremiah and Ezekiel to convey the idea of outright rejection of the Lord and his word.[78]

v.4b: כזבהם literally means "their lies", a cacophemistic expression to describe idolatry in the Bible.[79] Since Judah is indicted for "walking" (%lh) "after them" (אחריהם),[80] probably the idols are in view here, as such, כזבהם can be interpreted as

---

[77] Shalom. M. Paul, *Amos*, Hermeneia (Minneapolis: Fortress Press, 1991), 75.

[78] Andersen and Freedman, *Amos*, 296.

[79] Paul, *Amos*, 75.

[80] The expression "to walk after" false gods appears prominently in Deuteronomy and the Deuteronomistic history (Deut. 8:19; 11:28; 28:14; Judg. 2:12, 19; 1 Kgs 11:10; 18:18; 21:26. Cf. Finley, *Joel, Amos and Obadiah*, 159), which led scholars to assume the hand of some later editorial work. Cf. Thomas J. Finley, *Joel, Amos and Obadiah*, The Wycliffe Exegetical Commentary

"their idols." Paul states that the Akkadian equivalent expression "*arki...alāku*" ("to follow after") is a diplomatic language of the ANE, which expresses the concept of political loyalty while another expression "*rē' û māt Aššur ālik arkiki*" ("The shepherd of Assyria who follows you [Ishtar]") appears in the religious context.[81] Paul thus concludes that the phrase "to follow after" expresses the idea of loyalty to (God or gods).[82] Niehaus studies the eighteenth century BCE letter addressed to Hammurabi, the king of Mari, which reads, "Ten to fifteen kings walk after Hammurabi...". Based on such examples, Niehaus concludes that "In the ancient Near East the concept of walking after someone indicated a subordinate or, in some cases, a suzerain-vassal relationship."[83] "To walk after" probably refers to Judah's loyalty and allegiance to other gods instead of subordinating herself to Yahweh.

3.6.3. Form Critical Comments on Amos 2:4-5

Except for the charge of violation, the oracle of Judah follows the same formula as in the above oracles of Tyre and Edom (see the above FCC on 1:9-10). Scholars doubt the authenticity of the Judah oracle due to some characteristic Deuteronomistic terminology, such as, the Torah of Yahweh (תורת יהוה), to keep (שמר), to follow (הלך).[84] However, Paul argues that the phrase תורת יהוה appears in the earlier pre-exilic source (Is. 5:24), which is neither considered as secondary nor of Deuteronomic influence, while the term "שמר" also appears in other passages that are not related to the Deuteronomic literature.[85] Further the phrase הלך אחרי "to walk after" appears in pre-Deuteronomic literature (cf. Hos. 2:7, 15; 5:11; 11:10). Thus, Paul contends that the style of language that became a marked characteristic of the Deuteronomistic tradition had precedents, as such, these phrases cannot be taken as valid ground to consider that Judah oracle is the work of a later editor(s).[86] Since the publications of the works of Paul and Andersen and Freedman, the supposed linguistic relationship with the Deuteronomistic historians is no longer considered to be strong grounds to invalidate the authenticity of

(Chicago: Moody, 1990), 159. See also, Jorg Jeremias, *The Book of Amos: A Commentary*, OTL (Louisville, Kentucky: Westminster John Knox Press, 1995), 44; Mays, *Amos*, 41. However, such conclusion appears to be conjectural since the phrase "to walk after" is not exclusively a Deuteronomic phraseology as we find its occurrence in the pre-Deuteronomic literature (Hos. 2:13 [MT 2:15]). Finley, *Joel, Amos and Obadiah*, 159.

[81] Paul, *Amos*, 75-76.

[82] Paul, *Amos*, 75.

[83] Jeffery Niehaus, "Amos", in Thomas Edward McComisky (ed), *The Minor Prophets*, vol. 1 (Grand Rapids, Michigan: Baker, 1992), 361.

[84] Harry Mowvley, *The Book of Amos and Hosea* (London: Epworth, 1991), 27-28; Hayes, "Amos' Oracles Against the Nations", 162.

[85] Paul, *Amos*, 21-22.

[86] Paul, *Amos*, 21.

Judah oracle.[87] We consider 2:4-5 as authentic and a self contained unit of Amos' oracle that deals with the nation of Judah. The Judah oracle uses a short form like the oracles against the Tyre and Edom, yet the oracle of Judah is significantly different from all the six preceding oracles in that it does not mention any specific war crimes as the basis of judgment. Instead, "a sweeping theological accusation is made,"[88] that is, the rejection (מאס) of the Torah and not keeping Yahweh's statutes since their fathers' time. This indicates a long history of infidelity to Yahweh. Amos announced that Judah will be destroyed by the divine fire.[89] The unit of Judah oracle is outlined as follows:

Messenger formula:	Thus, says Yahweh (v.4)
General Accusation:	"For three violations of Judah and for four, I will not turn it back (v.4)
Specific indictment:	because they have rejected the Torah of Yahweh, and have not kept his statutes, but their idols have led them astray, after which their fathers walked (v.4)
Announcement of Judgment:	So, I will send a fire upon Judah and it shall devour the strongholds of Jerusalem (v.5)

3.6.4. Tradition and Theological Comments in the Light of Tripartite Relationship

As stated above, the reference to Judah's rejection of Yahweh's Torah and his statues (v.4) indicates that the oracle against Judah is rooted in the Torah tradition. In the Torah tradition, the tripartite relationship is closely associated with the Sinai covenant in which Yahweh became "Israel's God", Israel became Yahweh's "treasured possession", while Israel's loyalty to Yahweh became the condition for her survival in the land.[90] To sustain, perpetuate and govern the tripartite

---

[87] Shalom, *Amos*, 20-24; Andersen and Freedman, *Amos*, 302-306. See also Gray, *Amos*, 80.

[88] Mays, *Amos*, 42.

[89] The prophecy was fulfilled during the Babylonian siege of Jerusalem (cf. 2 Kgs. 25:9).

[90] Earlier scholars rejected the idea of covenant in the book of Amos. However, recent studies have shown that covenant is one of the bases of the prophet's indictment in Amos. John D. Watts and Arvind S. Kapelrud adopt the covenant as the basis Amos' indictment against Israel. John D. Watts, *Vision and Prophecy in Amos* (Leiden: Brill, 1958); Arvind S. Kapelrud, *Central Ideas in Amos* (Oslo: University Press, 1961). H. Graf Reventlow interprets Am. 4: 6-11 after the pattern of covenantal curse list of Lev. 26 (and even Deut. 28). Similarly, Delbert R. Hillers and F. Charles Fensham opine that the knowledge of the covenant provides "the plausible premise for the parallels between Near Eastern treaty curses and the dooming oracle sentences of Israelite prophetic literature". Delbert R. Hillers, *Treaty Curses and the Old Testament Prophets* ("Anteclecta Biblica," vol. xvi; Rome: Pontifical Biblical Institute, 1964); F. Charles Fensham, "Common Trends in Curses of the Near Eastern Treaties and *Kudurru*-Inscriptions Compared with Maledictions of Amos and Isaiah", *ZAW* 75 (1963) 155-175. Synder argues that Amos uses covenant to measure the nation of Israel as a whole. George Synder, "The Law and Covenant in Amos", *Restoration Quarterly* 158.

relationship, Yahweh gave the law to Israel, which became the tradition of Torah, the embodiment of Yahweh's will concerning Israel/Judah. Failure to follow the law of Torah and its statutes and following idols are stated as the basis of indictment against Judah. Since the tradition of Torah obligates Judah to live by the teachings of the Torah, Judah is now judged by the standard of the Torah, which they have rejected. The Torah tradition warns that disobedience will bring catastrophe and expulsion from the land (Lev. 26:33, 38-41; Cf. Deut. 4:25-26). As Judah failed to live by the law of Torah, Yahweh decrees the judgment that fire will devour the strongholds of Jerusalem, which refers to the destruction of her land as a political nation. The breaking of the tripartite relationship is thus explained by employing the Torah tradition in 2:4-5.

As stated in the above FCC, the specific indictment of Judah includes, the rejection (מאס) of the Torah and not keeping (לא שמר) Yahweh's statutes (חקיו) since the time of their fathers (אבותם). This means Judah's infidelity to Yahweh's Torah dates long back to the history of their forefathers. The indictment is described by the term "to reject"(√מאס) which as mentioned in the TCC in v.4a, refers to Judah's utter contempt and disregard to follow and live according to the statutes of Yahweh's Torah. The content of Torah which Judah has rejected is not specifically mentioned but in the light of Amos' call to seek good so as to live before Yahweh (5:14) and to practice justice (5:15) and also in the light of Amos' condemnation of injustice (2:7-8), Judah's rejection of Yahweh's Torah and statutes could be referring to the absence of justice and righteousness in interpersonal relationships as envisaged by Yahweh for Israel in the Sinai covenant.

Based on the above indictment in v.4, Yahweh pronounces the sentence of destruction on Judah in v.5. Yahweh's agent of destruction, as in the preceding oracles, is fire (אשׁ), which is associated with the divine wrath (Gen. 19:24; Ex. 24:17; Num. 11:1-3).[91] In the tradition of Holy War, חרם, the accursed things are destroyed by fire (Deut. 7:25-26; 12:3; Num 31:10; Judg. 1:8). How the fire judgment is related to the Holy War tradition is already discussed in the above TCC on v.10b. To highlight briefly, the fire imagery portrays Yahweh as military leader, who would devour Judah's stronghold (ארמנות), a fortification of royal palace and a defense wall to withstand the enemies' attack. Judah's stronghold here indicates the land of Judah as political nation. Using the Holy War imagery, Amos presents that Yahweh will intervene to set ablaze the stronghold of Judah to cripple her military and administrative centre. In other words, Judah's rejection of living according to the Torah tradition affected the tripartite relationship in the following way: Judah's rejection of Yahweh's Torah leads to the destruction of her political land (strongholds). This means, for Amos, disloyalty to Yahweh's instruction (Torah) and occupation of the land are mutually exclusive to each

Brueggemann likewise argues that Am. 4: 4-13 depends ultimately on the covenant tradition. Walter Brueggemann, "Amos 4:4-16 and Israel's Covenant Worship", *VT* 15 (1965) 1-15.

[91] Stuart, *Hosea-Jonah*, 311.

other. Judah's existence in the land and her perpetual disobedience to Yahweh cannot go together. Judah's occupation in the land is sustained by her continual obedience to Yahweh.

3.7. The Exodus, Wilderness and Conquest Traditions (Amos 2:6-16)

"I destroyed the Amorites", "I led you forty years in the wilderness" and "I brought you out of the land of Egypt" speak of the Exodus, Wilderness and Conquest traditions (vv. 9-11). The divine intervention, such as, Yahweh's deliverance of Israel from Egypt (Exodus tradition), Yahweh's guidance of Israel for forty years (Wilderness tradition) and Yahweh's destruction of the Amorites (Conquest tradition) are all linked with Israel's possession of the land as Yahweh promised. But because of her domestic violence, Yahweh will bring Israel into judgment of defeat, death and exile (vv.13-16). Such expressions explain how the relationship between Yahweh, Israel and the land is established and broken by employing the intertwining traditions of Exodus, Wilderness and Conquest traditions in 2:6-16.

3.7.1. Translations on Amos 2:6-16

6 Thus, says Yahweh, for three transgressions of Israel, and for four, I will not turn it back; because they sell[a] the righteous[b] for silver, and the needy[b] for a pair of shoes

7 they that trample the head of the poor into the dust of the earth and turn aside the way of the afflicted[a]; a man and his father go in to the same maiden[b], so as to profane my holy name;

8 they lay themselves down beside every altar upon garments taken in pledge[a]; and in the house of their God they drink the wine of those who have been fined[b].

9 "But I, I destroyed the Amorite before them[a], whose height was like the height of the cedars, and who was as strong as the oaks; I destroyed his fruit above, and his roots beneath[b].

10 And I, I brought you up out of the land of Egypt[a], and I led you forty years in the wilderness[b], to possess the land of the Amorite.

11 And I, I raised up some of your sons for prophets, and some of your young men for Nazirites[a]. Is it not indeed so, O people of Israel?" declares Yahweh.

12 But you made the Nazirites drink wine, and commanded the prophets, saying, "You shall not prophesy".

13 Behold, I will press you down in your place, as a cart full of sheaves presses down.

14 Flight shall perish from the swift, and the strong shall not retain his strength, nor shall the mighty save his life;

15 he who handles the bow shall not stand, and he who is swift of foot shall not save himself, nor shall he who rides the horse save his life;

16 and he who is stout of heart among the mighty shall flee away naked in that day, says Yahweh.

3.7.2. Text Critical Comments on Amos 2:6-16

V.6a. √מכר "to sell" is generally understood as referring to the bribery of the judges who, for the sake of money, denied the just cause of the poor.[92] Paul, Finley and Jeremias, however, reject such interpretation by arguing that מכר occurs nowhere in the Bible to refer to bribery.[93] It is mostly understood as referring to the sale of the poor into debt slavery[94] as found in the patriarchal narratives where מכר is used in the context of selling of human beings as slaves (Gen. 37:27, 28, 36; 45:5, 6) and even in the Mosaic law מכר refers to the debt slavery but never to bribery (Ex. 21:7-8; Lev. 25:39; Deut. 15:12).[95] Also, in the ANE, the war captives and especially the indebted poor were forced into slavery in lieu of the debts.[96] In the agrarian context of ancient Israel, the jubilee law permits the impoverished farmer to sell himself as a way to get out from his economic impoverishment (Lev. 25:39, 47ff; Deut. 15:12).[97] Amos' usage of the term מכר probably refers to the grotesque abuse of such traditional institution of slavery by the creditors "even in the case of the most trifling debt,"[98] and sealed off the fate of the poor man's independent existence.

V.6b: צדיק "righteous" in a legal sense refers to a guiltless and innocent person before the law.[99] אבון refers to "defenseless" or "the needy" victims "who have no means whatsoever at their disposal to protect themselves from being sold into debt slavery."[100] According to Dearman, "poor" (v.6) and "needy" (v.7) are the terms used in the context of "disenfranchisement and the loss of possession". He argues that the poor and needy are the people who lose their land and right

---

[92] H.W. Robinson, *Amos: Hebrew Text* (London: SPCK, 1923); E. Hammershaimb, *The Book of Amos: A Commentary*, trans. by J. Sturdy (Oxford: Basil Blackwell, 1970), 46. Cited in Paul, *Amos*, 77; Cripps, *A Critical and Exegetical Commentary on the Book of Amos*, 140.

[93] Paul, *Amos*, 77; Finley, "Amos", 163; Jeremias, *The Book of Amos*, 35.

[94] Ex. 21:7-8; Lev. 25:39; Deut. 15:12; Isa. 50:1; Neh. 5:8. Cf. Wolff, *Amos*, 165; cf. Jeremias, *The Book of Amos*, 35; J. Alberto Soggin, *The Prophet Amos: A Translation and Commentary* (England: SCM, 1987), 47; Mays, *Amos*, 45. Andersen and Freedman argue that "selling… for a pair of sandal" is "a reference to and description of debt slavery" in which the righteous poor are sold off as slaves for a petty debt that is just a value of a pair of sandal. Andersen and Freedman, *Amos*, 313.

[95] Jeremias, *The Book of Amos*, 35.

[96] Mays, *Amos*, 45.

[97] Jeremias, *The Book of Amos*, 35.

[98] Jeremias, *The Book of Amos*, 35.

[99] Wolff, *Amos*, 165; Mays, *Amos*, 46; Paul, *Amos*, 77; Finley, "Amos", 162-163; Jeremias, *The Book of Amos*, 35; Soggin, *The Prophet Amos*, 47; Cripps, *A Critical and Exegetical Commentary on the Book of Amos*, 140.

[100] Thomas, *Jeroboam II the King and Amos the Prophet*, 186.

of possession and not those who lacked them.[101] If Dearman's contention can be sustained, then the poor refer to the former property owners, who probably would have borrowed cash from the money-lenders because of crops failure by pledging their agricultural returns and mortgaging the land. If unfortunately the harvest fails due to natural calamities or some other reasons and if the indebted peasants fail to repay the borrowed amount, the lenders would take away the mortgaged land in lieu of the borrowed כסף.[102] Thus, the cultivable land of the peasants (land owners) was transferred to the hand of the money lenders through unscrupulous means. This is another indication of the violation of the covenant law that demands a kind treatment to the vulnerable people (Ex. 22:21-24) for the Israelites themselves know how they live a vulnerable life in Egypt (Ex. 23:9).[103] In short, "righteous" and "needy" refer to innocent victims of the socioeconomic conditions of Amos' day.

V.7a: Wolff thinks that ודרךְ ענוים יטו "and turn aside the way of the afflicted" refers to the perversion of justice at the judicial proceedings in the city gate. He argues that to "pervert the way" (נטה דרך hip'il) is equivalent to "to pervert the course of justice (הטות ארחות משפט Pro. 17:23)."[104] Paul argues that the suggestion of דרך as synonymous to משפט is possible "only when the context and vocabulary are explicitly within the legal sphere (for example, Jer. 5:4,5)."[105] Since this is not the case in Amos 2:7c, Paul states that the accusation does not refer to the perversion of judicial procedures, rather he thinks it to be a figurative expression to convey that the "underprivileged classes are bullied and oppressed by the wealthy, who deprive and block them from obtaining the privileges and prerogatives to which they are naturally entitled."[106] Though such figurative meaning of oppression cannot be ruled out, it needs to be noted that the נטה used in v.7c appears in a legal context in 5:12 and in Ex. 23:6. As such, we can consider that the phrase refers to the perversion of justice against the poor in the legal setting.

V.7b: Generally נערה refers to a young and minor girl. However, if "to go unto" is understood in a sense of "to copulate with", as Wolff suggests, then נערה denotes a girl of marriageable age.[107] נערה is neither defined as wife nor as sister or as daughter in law or "female servant", it is also different from קדשה, the cultic

---

[101] Dearman, *Property Rights*, 53.

[102] According to Mayes, the definite article before כסף "money" shows that a particular amount as debt is indicated. Mayes, *Amos*, 45.

[103] Herbert Wolf, *An Introduction to the Old Testament Prophets* (Chicago: Moody, 1991), 153.

[104] Wolff, *Joel and Amos*, 166.

[105] Paul, *Amos*, 81.

[106] Paul, *Amos*, 81.

[107] Wolff, *Amos*, 166.

prostitute. It is thus difficult to precisely suggest what status נערה actually suggests.[108] Paul suggests that נערה belongs to the same category of דלים and ענוים, who were defenseless and became the object of exploitation. However, as mentioned in the TCC on v.6a that since מכר refers to a sale of person to debt-slavery for which Amos indicts Israel, we can assume that in v.7 נערה refers to those women who were forced to slavery because of their unpaid debt. In any case, relations with the same woman by both the father and son are considered as taboo in the Israelite society, which is strictly forbidden in the covenant code (Ex. 22:16-19).

V.8a: Following the LXX, Wolff removes the preposition על and interprets the phrase as "garments taken in pledge they spread out."[109] Paul contends that it is unnecessary to delete על since the preposition makes clear that it is not the garments that are being spread out but that "they are stretching themselves "upon" (על) these very garments.[110] בגדים חבלים is generally understood as referring to a legal instrument in which the debtor left the garment with the lender as a surety when a loan is granted.[111] Paul's extensive study on the term חבל both in the Bible[112] and in the ANE[113] has shown that both in a juridical context[114] and in wisdom literature,[115] "the verb חבל applies to distraints- persons as well as property- that take place only when the loan falls due and the debt is defaulted."[116] The legal tradition in Ex. 22:25-26 prohibits keeping the clothes of a poor man overnight as a pledge. Here Amos indicts the people for disregarding the legal tradition meant to protect the economically vulnerable and socially destitute people.

V.8b: Rudolph sees the grammatical form ענושים "wine" to be an abstract substantive similar to מגורים (sojourning: Gen. 17:8; 28:4; 47:9) and נעורים (youth: Gen. 8:21; Isa. 54:6; Pss 127:4).[117] Paul, however, argues that ענושים should be interpreted in parallel to חבלים "pledge" passive participle as in v.8a. He further argues that since the root of ענושים is ענש, which refers to "monetary fines and

---

[108] For detail discussion on the term "נערה" see, Hans M. Barstad, *The Religious Polemics of Amos: Studies in the Preaching of Am: 7b-8; 4:1-13; 5:1-27; 6:4-7; 8:14* (Leiden: Brill, 1984), 17-36.

[109] Wolff, *Amos*, 134.

[110] Paul, *Amos*, 86.

[111] Mays, *Amos*, 47.

[112] Paul states that the verb חבל in Job 24:9; 2 Kgs 4:1; Is. 50:1; Prov. 13:13 express the seizure by the creditors only when the loan is defaulted.

[113] The Aramaic Paryri from Elephentine refer to "the issue that the debtor can take no legal steps against the seizure of pledges"; the Mesopotamian sources on Nuzi and middle Assyrian mortgage texts show that in Hammurabi's law the seizure of pledges took place only after default. Paul, *Amos*, 84-85.

[114] Ex. 22:25; Deut. 24:6, 17.

[115] Prov. 13:13; 20:16; 27:13; Job 24:9.

[116] Paul, *Amos*, 83.

[117] W. Rudolph, *Jeremiah HAT* 1/12 (Tubingen: Mohr, 1958), 139. Cited in Paul, *Amos*, 86.

indemnity,"[118] he considers LXX's interpretation "to extort by false information", and Targum's אונסה "compulsion, force" as unlikely. He thus concludes that ענושים refers to "wine bought with money received from extracting fines from the poor".[119]

V.9a: ואנכי השמדתי "but I destroyed" introduces a transitional sentence in an emphatic term. The phrase contrasts Israel's oppressive treatment of the poor with the historical acts of Yahweh on behalf of the helpless Israel in the past. The verb used to state the extermination of invincible Amorites at the time of conquest is in Hip'il form (השמדתי), which shows the holy war context of total annihilation of the enemies.[120] The Amorites האמרי can refer to a particular tribe (Gen. 10:16; Ex. 3:8), but in the present context, the reference is to the whole population of the Canaanites (cf. Gen. 15:16; Josh. 24:15).[121] See the Tradition and Theological comments below for further discussion.

V.9b: The repetition of verb "שמד" (to destroy) emphasizes the forcefulness of total annihilation, which once again recounts the conquest tradition to stress that Israel's occupation of the land is only on Yahweh's action.

V.10a: The expression, העליתי "I brought up", which recalls Israel's Exodus event has generated much scholarly debate. Wolff thinks that עלה is employed here by a later Deuteronomic redactor[122] while J. Wijngaards thinks that it is added by Amos' disciple.[123] Paul rejects both the views by arguing that עלה appears in pre-Deuteronomic literature (cf. Mic. 6:4) and it is "an old conventional formula for the Exodus."[124] Also the phrase "ואנכי העליתי אתכם מארץ מצרים" (And I brought you up from the land of Egypt) is debated. Harper and Cripps think that the phrase should be transposed at the beginning of v.9 since the Exodus and Wilderness traditions are historically antecedent to the Conquest tradition.[125] Such transposition may not be necessary since the present MT order is in the form of inclusio, that is, "the prophet both begins (v.9) and concludes (v.10) with the theme of the Amorites."[126] In any case, whether v.10 is moved before v.9 or not, the meaning and intention of Amos' statement in vv.9-10 remains unchanged since the Exodus, Wilderness and Conquest traditions are encapsulated within Yahweh's action of total annihilation of the Amorites to make Israel's occupation in the land

---

[118] Paul, *Amos*, 86.

[119] Paul, *Amos*, 86.

[120] Wolff, *Amos*, 168.

[121] Finley, "Amos", 170.

[122] Wolff, *Amos*, 112-113, 169-170.

[123] J. Wijngaards, "הוציא and העלה: A Twofold Approaches to the Exodus", *VT* 15 (1965) 91-102.

[124] Paul, *Amos*, 87.

[125] Cripps, *A Critical and Exegetical Commentary on the Book of Amos*, 144; Harper, *Amos*, 53-54.

[126] Paul, *Amos*, 90.

possible. This also indicates, according to Zimmerli, that Israel is not indigenous to her land, but she was brought into the land by her God, Yahweh.[127]

V.10b: The phrase ואולך אתכם במדבר ארבעים שׁנה "and I led you forty years in the wilderness" reiterates the wilderness tradition. Wolff argues that this phrase is a later addition since he thinks that the motif of forty years wilderness journey does not appear before the Deuteronomistic literature.[128] Against such secondary characterization of v.10, Paul contends that the forty years wilderness motif appears in the early tradition and sources, such as, Num. 33-34; 32:13; Josh. 5:6; Ps. 95:10. Thus the wilderness theme, as Paul argues, is a "common property of the tradition", and it is "therefore totally unwarranted to interpret it as being dependent upon Deuteronomy and thus to deny its authenticity in Amos."[129] Wolff further argues that "to possess the land of the Amorite" is a characteristic mark of Deuteronomistic writings,[130] and therefore he suspects the authenticity of Amos' oracle in v.10.[131] However, Wolff's position needs critical evaluation since the expression, "to possess the land of the Amorite", is not exclusive to Deuteronomistic literature, as the same motif ויירשׁ את־המרי appears in the early tradition, such as, in Num. 21:32; 32:39.[132] Therefore, לרשׁת את־ארץ האמרי "to posses the land of the Amorite" in v.10 does not in any way indicate any editorial work; rather, it belongs to Amos' original oracle.

v.11a: The MT version of "נזרתם" (Nazirites) is rendered as "מלפין" (teachers) in Targum.[133] However, the MT rendering can be retained to juxtapose the Nazarites' abstention from wine with the charge of excessive wine drinking in v.8.[134]

3.7.3. Form Critical Comments on Amos 2:6-16

The Israel oracle serves as a movement towards the climactic point of Amos' judgment speech. The oracle follows the same formulaic pattern as in the preceding oracles. However, there are some marked differences in the oracle against Israel. First, the description of the crimes (vv. 6-8, 12) and the announcement of the judgment (vv.13-16) take an expanded form. Second, Israel's indictment is no longer on the basis of her international crimes (cf. 1:3-2:3) but on the basis of her domestic exploitation (2:6-8). Third, unlike the preceding oracles, the Israel oracle refers to specific acts of Yahweh in Israel's history (vv.9-10). Fourth, "second-person, direct address to the audience becomes interspersed with third-person,

---

[127] Zimmerli, "'Land' in the Exilic and the early Post-Exilic Prophets'", 247-248.

[128] Wolff, *Amos*, 170.

[129] Paul, *Amos*, 91.

[130] Deut. 2:31; 9:4-5; 11:31; Josh. 1:11; 18:3; Judg. 2:3.

[131] Wolff, *Amos*, 170.

[132] See, Paul, *Amos*, 91.

[133] See, Finley, "Amos", 171.

[134] See, Paul, *Amos*, 92-93.

indirect address. Fifth, the formulaic announcement of judgment, "I will send fire…" is dropped in the Israel oracle.[135]

The participial form in v.7 is different from all the other oracles and the historical recital in v.9 shows a break after v.8, which makes it difficult to understand where the oracle ends. However, since the oracle begins with the messenger formula, "Thus says Yahweh" in. v.6a and ends with a concluding formula, "declares Yahweh" in v.16, we will consider 2:6-16 to be a self contained unit. V.6a introduces the oracle with the messenger formula; vv. 6b-8 speaks of injustices and oppression in Israel; vv. 9-11 recounts Yahweh's act and intervention for Israel; v.12 further charges Israel of wrong doings and vv.13-16 announces judgment based on the Yahweh's charge. 2:6-11 can be outlined as follows:

Messenger formula:	Thus, says Yahweh (v.6)
General Accusation:	"For three violations of Israel and for four, I will not turn it back (v.6).
Specific indictment:	they trample the head of the poor… turn aside the way of the afflicted; a man and his father go in to the same maiden … they lay themselves down … upon garments taken in pledge; and in the house of their God they drink the wine of those who have been fined (vv.7-8).
Historical Recital:	".. I destroyed the Amorite … brought you up out of the land of Egypt… led you forty years…to possess the land of the Amorite… (vv.9-11).
Further Indictment:	but you made the Nazirites drink wine… commanded… "You shall not prophesy" (v.12).
Announcement of Sentence:	Behold, I will press you down in your place… Flight shall perish…the strong shall not retain his strength… the mighty save his life; he who handles the bow shall not stand, and he who is swift of foot shall not save himself, … the mighty shall flee away naked in that day, says Yahweh (vv.13-16).

The historical and geographical setting is not mentioned precisely in the oracle. However, the text indicates some possible locations or settings, which include the market place where people are sold, the city gate where fines (wine) are levied (agrarian exploitation) and where sandals are transferred (land acquisition)

[135] Hayes, "Amos's Oracles Against the Nations", 163.

and the religious shrine where the garments are laid behind the altars (v 6b-8).[136] In such setting, presumably the culprits include the rich traders, elders/judges in the society and the cultic priests in the shrines.

3.7.4. Tradition and Theological Comments in the Light of Tripartite Relationship

According to Zimmerli, Amos' indictment in 2:6-16 is based on the tradition of the ancient legal stipulation of the covenant code in Ex. 22:25-27. He rightly sees that Amos re-uses the legal tradition of the covenant code to assert that the practice of justice and righteousness are the legal demands of God who brought Israel into her land.[137] The covenant tradition is linked with the Exodus tradition, which is indicated by the verb עלה "to bring up" (v.10) that appears in connection with מארץ מצרים (from the land of Egypt), which shows how the landless slaves of Israel were delivered from Egypt by Yahweh to give the land of the Amorites. The expression "I led you forty years in the wilderness" (v. 10) speaks of Yahweh's guidance and sustenance of Israel on their way to enter the promised land while ואנכי השמדתי את האמרי "and I destroyed the Amorite" (v.9) refers to how Yahweh destroyed the invincible Amorites to make Israel's settlement in the land of Canaan possible. The Exodus, Wilderness and Conquest traditions are all linked with Yahweh's intervention on Israel's behalf, which makes possible for Israel to exist in the land. Instead of emulating Yahweh's kind act as a model to help the landless and sustain the vulnerable members of the society, Israel began to exploit the helpless for which reason Yahweh sentences Israel to defeat and escape from their land as exiles. By employing the Exodus, Wilderness and Conquest traditions, Amos explains how the tripartite relationship was strengthened in the past and by bringing the charge against Israel Amos also shows how the tripartite relationship is now affected.

Amos delivers Yahweh's charge against Israel as follows: (see also the FCC above). As Limburg notes, the indictments listed against Israel include (vv.6-8):[138]

selling the righteous;
selling the needy for a pair of sandal;
trampling the poor;
denying justice to the oppressed;
sexually exploiting the same maiden by both the father and son;
keeping garments taken pledge;
drinking wine taken in fines payment.

---

[136] Cf. Andersen and Freedman, *Amos*, 322.

[137] Zimmerli, "Land' in the Pre-Exilic and the early Post-Exilic Prophets", 248.

[138] James Limburg, "Sevenfold Structures in the Book of Amos", *JBL* 106 (1987) 219. See also, Partlow, "Amos's Uses of Rhetorical Entrapment", 28; Hayes, "Amos's Oracles Against the Nations", 163.

As mentioned above in the TCC about the wrongdoings of Israel, we now focus only on how the above indictments convey the issues related to the land. In the above list, the victims are identified as "poor" and "needy" who are also characterized as "righteous". As argued above in the TCC on vv.6c and 7c, the term "poor" does not refer to those who lack property but the "poor and needy" are those people who were formerly the property owners but had lost their land to the money-lenders and corrupt officials for not repaying the borrowed money on time. The oppression and injustice, which Amos indicts in vv.6-8, are thus related to the land and peasants problem.

The land issue became even more serious during the eighth century, which was partly contributed to by the growing agro-economic prosperity (see the discussion on "Socioeconomic Context" in the Historical Background of Amos). The archeological evidences have shown that during the eighth century, viniculture was intensively cultivated as wine and oil demands were increasingly high in the market both for domestic consumption and for international export.[139] Such intensification of viniculture required more land to cultivate, which lead to rampant acquisition of land by the powerful elites. As mentioned above, the devious method of acquiring the land was to foreclose the land by rich people in lieu of a trivial amount of borrowed money. In this process many peasants started to lose their cultivable land yet their rights were "trampled" and "turned aside" (v.7) since the judges for the sake of "silver" sold away the legal rights of the victims (v.7). In this case, "silver", as Bernhard Lang argues, refers to "money."[140]

The unjust form of land acquisition is expressed by the phrase "a pair of sandals" (v.6). Scholars debate whether "a pair of sandals" conveys a hyperbolic expression of a meager amount lent by the creditor[141] or whether "a pair of sandals" conveys a proverbial bribe to express a small sum for which the poor are sold.[142] Though the hyperbolic and proverbial meanings cannot be denied, what appears important is the significance of land transfer expressed by the phrase "a pair of sandals". Based on the findings of the social practice at Nuzi and also in ancient Israel (cf. Ruth 4:7), Speiser and Lang argue that the significance of "sandals" lies in the symbolic expression of formalizing the transaction.[143] Likewise, most

---

[139] Chaney states that the archaeological surveys suggest a proliferation of and innovation in rock-cut olive and grape processing installations in the eighth century B.C.E. For the discussion on the intensification of wine and oil production during the eighth century, see Chaney, "Whose Sour Grapes," 108.

[140] Bernhard Lang compares the Hebrew "כסף" with the Akkadian equivalent "kaspu" and the Ugarit "kaspi", which refers with both "silver" and "money" and argues that the Hebrew "כסף" can take a special nuance of "money". Cf. Bernhard Lang, "Sklaven und Unfreie im Buch Amos (2:6, 8:6)", *VT* 31/4 (1981) 482.

[141] Stuart, *Amos*, 316.

[142] Andersen and Freedman, *Amos*, 312.

[143] E.A. Speiser, "Of Shoes and Shekels", *BASOR* 77 (1990) 18; Lang, "Sklaven und Unfreie im Buch Amos", 483.

scholars agree that "a pair of sandals" refers to a legal process involving property of land.[144] Since in ancient Israelite society, the sandal transfer was practiced as a symbol of land transaction (cf. Ruth 4), we can interpret that the cliché "a pair of sandals" indicates the acquisitions of the victim's land and a transfer of the ownership of land.

The above indictment on unjust land acquisition (vv. 6-8) appears in total contradiction to Israel's recitals of salvation history. The Exodus tradition, "I brought you out from the land of Egypt" recounts Israel and her existence in the land in connection with Yahweh's salvific act. In the Exodus tradition, Yahweh is understood as Israel's deliverer, Israel as "Yahweh's people" (Ex. 5:1) while the land is understood as Yahweh's object of promise to Israel and Israel's object of possession for inheritance. The Exodus tradition is central in the memory of Israel as it evokes how the enslaved, exploited and landless Israel lived in Egypt (Ex. 3:8). Amos perpetuates here the Exodus tradition so that the memory of their past experience would delegitimize any form of exploitation in the society.[145] However, the Israelites started to exploit, enslave and rendered their fellow Israelites landless (vv.6-8), which is a total contradiction to Yahweh's saving act.

Yahweh also affirms that he led Israel "for forty years in the wilderness" (v.10). Two observations can be noted about Israel's wilderness experience in relation to land. First, Israel learned Yahweh's faithful providence, protection, and sustenance until she possessed the promised land. Second, Israel also learned that her disloyalty imperils her relationship with Yahweh and jeopardized her hope to possess the land. Israel thus learned that despite Yahweh's commitment to honor the land promise, if Israel remains disloyal to Yahweh, Israel will be debarred to possess the land. Despite these wilderness lessons, Israel continued to be unfaithful to Yahweh by committing the social crimes listed in vv. 6-8.

Another significant historical recital is the conquest tradition, "I destroyed the Amorites… to possess the land of the Amorites" (vv.9-10). In the conquest tradition, Yahweh acts on Israel's behalf for Israel is seen as "Yahweh's inheritance" and land is seen as "Israel's inheritance" (Josh. 18:7) and both Israel and land are seen as belonging to Yahweh. The conquest tradition affirms that Israel possessed the land of Canaan not because of her righteousness but because of the wickedness of its inhabitants for which Yahweh dispossesses them (Deut. 9:4-6). Likewise Yahweh threatens to take away the land from Israel for their iniquity (Josh. 23:16).[146] The conquest tradition also considers that the land of Canaan is the gift of God to Israel. As such, Israel not only owes her allegiance to Yahweh for his kind act but Israel's land ethics should also be governed by the same

---

[144] Cf. Ruth 4:7-8; cf. Deut 25:9-10. See, Gowan, "The Book of Amos", 365; Mayes, *Amos*, 45; Dearman, *Property Rights*, 21.

[145] Cf. Walter Brueggemann, *The Prophetic Imagination*, 2nd edn. (Minneapolis: Fortress Press, 2001), 9.

[146] Bruce S. Warshal, "Israel's Stake in the Land" *Tradition Today* 35/4 (1979) 414.

principle of kindness just as Yahweh did to her. Instead Israel, the recipients of Yahweh's gift, started exploiting their fellow citizens and started dispossessing the poor peasant (vv.6a-8). This, according to Amos, is the act of פשע "transgression", which deserves Yahweh's punishment. The indictment on Israel's social crimes (vv.6-8) and theological offence (v.12) is served as the basis of sentence that Israel will now result in exile "… flee away naked in that day" (v. 16).

In the above historical recitals in v. 10, the term "ארץ" appears twice and in both the cases it is defined by the genitive, "of Egypt/Amorite", which puts the land in relationship to the people living in it (the land).[147] The first occurrence "מצרים מֵארץ" (from the land of Egypt) refers to the land of Egypt in a sense of political nation ruled by king. Another occurrence, "ארץ האמרי" (the land of Amorite) also refers to the land of the Amorite in a political sense, but it assumes theological significance in the light of the verb לרשת "to possess."[148] √ירשׁ "to possess" in v.10 is associated with Israel's occupation of the land, which is designated here as the "land of Amorite". The verb "to possess" presupposes the priority of "giving" or stated differently, "to give off" precedes "to possess". This means Israel possessed the land of Canaan, her political territory, as a gift of Yahweh.

Two observations concerning the meaning of land can be stated here. First, the term ארץ, "land" refers to a political nation in the sense of territory ruled by kings in which Yahweh is seen as the God who controls/directs the destiny of each political nation. Second, land is understood in the sense of cultivable land which is seen as an object to engage in economic activity and an object of temptation to possess and to acquire as indicated by the transfer of sandals. In both the political and agrarian understanding of the land, Amos' emphasis is that Israel's existence in the land is solely a result of Yahweh's kind act. Therefore, Israel is likewise expected to act in kindness as benefactors of the helpless people. Instead the helpless ones became the target of exploitation in the hand of the greedy elites. Yahweh considers such mistreatment, oppression and exploitation as an act of violation פשע. Such an act of פשע affected the tripartite relationship in the following ways: Yahweh who brought Israel into the land will now send Israel out of the land to exile ("will not save their lives… flee in naked…" vv.14-16), while the land that was Israel's inheritance will now be an alienated land for Israel will be separated from her land. Just as Yahweh chased out the former inhabitants of Canaan for their iniquities during the exodus, wilderness and conquest period, likewise Yahweh will now send Israel out from the land for their act of פשע. For Amos, to be a recipient of Yahweh's gift of land, and to be the social exploitator are mutually excusive to each other. These cannot co-exist. Israel's dwelling in

---

[147] Ottosson, "ארץ" in G. Johannes Botterweck and Helmer Ringgren (eds), *The Theological Dictionary of the Old Testament*, vol. 1. trans. by John T. Wallis (Grand Rapids, Michigan: William B. Eerdmans Publishing Company, 1974), 400.

[148] לרשת qal infinitive construct from the root ירשׁ "to possess."

the land depends equally both on her theological obligation toward Yahweh and social obligation toward fellow people in the society.

3.8. Covenant Tradition (Amos 4:6-13)

The judgment described in the form of famine, drought, agricultural failures, and death in the battles (vv.6-9) are all rooted in the covenant curse judgment. These catastrophes came upon the land and the people because Israel did not return to Yahweh. The affect of the tripartite relationship is thus explained by employing the covenant tradition in 4:6-13.

3.8.1. Translation on Amos 4:6-13

6 I gave[a] you cleanness of teeth[b] in all your cities, and lack of bread in all your settlements, yet you did not return[c] to me, says Yahweh.

7 And I also withheld the rain from you when there were still three months to the harvest; I would send rain on one city, and send no rain on another city; one arable land[a] would be rained upon, and the arable land on which it did not rain withered;

8 so two or three towns wandered to one town to drink water, and were not satisfied; yet you did not return to me, says the Yahweh.

9 I struck you with blight and mildew[a]; I laid waste your gardens and your vineyards; the locust devoured your fig trees and your olive trees; yet you did not return to me, says Yahweh.

10 I sent among you a pestilence after the manner[a] of Egypt; I killed your young men with the sword[b]; I carried away your horses; and I made the stench of your camp go up into your nostrils; yet you did not return to me, says Yahweh.

11 I overthrew some of you, as when God overthrew Sodom and Gomorrah, and you were like a brand snatched from the fire; yet you did not return to me, says Yahweh.

12 Therefore[a] thus I have done to you, O Israel; because I have done this to you, prepare to meet[b] your God, O Israel!

13 For behold[a], the one who forms the mountains, creates the wind, reveals his thoughts to mortals, makes the morning darkness, and treads on the heights of the earth-Yahweh, the God of hosts is his name!

3.8.2. Text Critical Comments on Amos 4:6-13

v. 6a: וגם is an adversative, which introduces an antithesis to that which preceded. גם contrasts what the people have brought to God in the cult (vv. 4-5) to that which God has brought to Israel for their covenant infidelity (vv.6-11).[149] The גם formula appears again in v. 7.

[149] See, Paul, *Amos*, 142.

v.6b: נקיון שנים literally, "cleanness of teeth", refers to a scarcity of food. This explanation is further supported by the parallel mention of חסר לחם "lack of bread" in the cities, which shows that famine is meant.

v.6c: ולא־שבתם עדי: the preposition עד with a verb שוב is a rare term. שוב is a verb of conversion, which expresses the idea of turning from idolatry and polytheism to orthodox faithfulness to Yahweh.[150]

v.7a: חלקה "field" appears two times in v.7, which refers to an allotted portion of arable land.

v.9a: The words "שדפון and וירקון" (blight and mildew) always appear together (cf. Deut. 28:22; 1 Kgs 8:37; Hag. 2:17) indicating that the covenant curse is the common background of "blight and mildew" in these texts.

v.10a: דרך in v. 10 is usually translated as "way", but translated here as "manner" as the syntax indicates that דרך is used in the context of the plagues in Egypt.

v.10b: חרב "sword" and the mention of "camp" indicates that the military disaster with innumerable causalities and death. Though the exact historical event cannot be ascertained, there is a record of Hazael reducing Israel's horses to mere handful in 2 Kgs 13:7. It is possible that Amos could be referring to this event.[151]

v.12a: לכן "therefore" marks the transition from accusation to punishment, which indicates that though the punishment will continue as in the past, it will be in a larger scale in v. 12.[152]

v.12b: Brueggemann states that the verb כון "prepare" appears in three different contexts. First, it appears in the Sinai narratives (Ex. 19:11; 15; 34:2), in which Yahweh demands Israel to prepare themselves to meet him in an act of covenant-making or renewal.[153] Second, it is used in the context of war preparation, which includes "alertness in ambush, preparation of armaments and readiness of weapons."[154] Third, the verb is also used in the cultic context of the preparation for worship, such as, preparation of sacrificial animals (Num. 23:29), a place for the ark (1 Kgs. 6:19; 1 Chro. 15:1, 3,4; 2 Chro. 1:4); sacrifices (Zeph. 1:7), a place for the showbread (1 Chro. 9:32) and a variety of objects and personnel for temple use (1 Chro. 22:3, 5; 28:2, 2 Chro. 2:8-9; 29:35, 31:11, 33:16, 35:4, 10, 14-16, 20).[155] Arguing along the shared terminology of כון in the above mentioned contexts, Brueggemann contends that כון in 4:12 has a double meaning: a) reference to an act of war preparation in which the destroyer God comes against Israel and b) reference

[150] W. L. Holladay, *The Root SUBH in the Old Testament* (Leiden: E. J. Brill, 1958), 116-21.

[151] Andersen and Freedman, *Amos*, 443.

[152] Sweeney, *The Twelve Prophets*, 230.

[153] W. Brueggemann, "Amos iv 4-13 and Israel's Covenant Worship", *VT* 15 (1965) 3.

[154] Cf. Jer 51: 12; Ezek. 7:14; 38: 7; Ps. 7:13ff; Pro. 21: 31. See, Brueggemann, "Amos iv 4-13", 3.

[155] Brueggemann, "Amos iv 4-13", 4.

to an act of repentance which leads to renewal of covenant as in Ex. 19 and 34."[156] He thus concludes that כון in 4:12 has its roots both in "holy war language and more immediately in the covenant-making terminology of the Sinai tradition."[157]

Brueggemann makes again three observations on the term לקראת "to meet". First, לקראת appears mostly in holy war contexts referring to the encounters initiated by Yahweh and also of meeting the enemies in the battle field.[158] Second, the term is used in the context of paying tribute and allegiance to a king. In this case, לקראת concerns a meeting between persons or parties to effect a relationship. Third, Brueggemann argues that כון and לקראת appear together in Ex. 19:15ff. "in which Israel purified herself through cultic acts so that she could meet this sovereign in negotiation and enter into covenant."[159] Although Brueggemann rightly points out that כון and לקראת in the texts of Sinai traditions are used in the context of covenant making, it is doubtful if the same applies in v.12, since כון and לקראת in Amos 4:12 are used in the context of the divine punishment and not in a covenant renewal context. In any case, these terms indicates that the punishment in 4:6-13 has its basis in the covenant tradition (See the FCC and tradition and theological comments below).

v.13a: The phrase כי הנה "for behold" appears to be an abrupt beginning. However, in the present context, it shows a turn in the total unit, as Brueggemann opines, כי הנה is introduced here to affirm about the God whom Israel is to encounter, that is, he is the creator God. כי הנה thus "introduces a doxology on creation to motivate repentance and covenant renewal".[160] This explanation appears plausible since the pedagogical intention of the text is clear in the repeated refrain in (vv. 6, 8, 9, 10, 11).

3.8.3. Form Critical Comments on Amos 4:6-13

Most scholars delineate vv.6-11 from vv.12-13 due to the alleged inconsistency of joining the accusation (vv. 6-11) with a veiled reference in v. 12 and the hymn in v. 13.[161] Mostly v.12 is considered as gloss (Marti, Mowack, Hoelscher and

---

[156] Brueggemann, "Amos iv: 6-13", 3-4.

[157] Brueggemann, "Amos iv:6-13", 4.

[158] Num. 21: 23; Josh. 8: 14; 9: 20; Jud. 7: 24; 20: 31; 1 Sam. 4: 1, 2; 27: 2, 21, 48, 55; 23: 28; 2 Sam. 9: 9, 10, 17; 28: 6, Ps. 35: 3; Job 39: 21.

[159] Brueggemann, "Amos iv: 6-13", 5.

[160] Brueggemann, "Amos iv: 6-13", 11.

[161] Wolff, *Amos*, 217. Reventlow, who observed that vv.6-11 is a unit that was patterned after the covenant tradition and forms, excluded vv. 12-13. Reventlow, *Das Amt des Propheten bei Amos*, Frlant 80, 1962, 77, no. 1. Cited in Brueggemann, "Amos iv 4-13", 1.

Sellin)[162] or as transition to the doxology in v. 13 (Reventlow).[163] Brueggemann, however, argues that the phrase "prepare to meet your God" in v. 12 should be understood in terms of the covenant tradition as כון and לקראת in v. 12 have striking parallels in the Sinai covenant passages of Ex. 19 and 34.[164] He therefore argues that 4:12 has its root in covenant tradition and thus it is closely related to the entire unit.[165] As the covenant tradition in vv. 6-11 is not doubted and since v. 12 echoes the pattern of covenant traditions as Brueggemann argues, vv.6-11 and v.12 can thus be taken as a unit bound together by the covenant theme. The doxological conclusion in v. 13, which concerns the creation also seems to lack connection with the covenant curse accusation in 4:6-11, thus Mayes considers v.13 to be a fragment which is out of its present context.[166] Against such fragmentization of the unit, Brueggemann demonstrates the relation of v. 13 by arguing that the occurrences of כי in both Ps. 95 and Am 4:13 ascribe praise to Yahweh's creative work in which the covenant becomes more compelling because of Yahweh's creative work. Such creation deeds of Yahweh evoke both awe and terror among the Israelites in the Sinai narratives. Brueggemann thus contends that כי הנה introduces a doxology on creation to motivate repentance and covenant renewal. Whether כי הנה in v. 13 can be used to argue for covenantal renewal or not is debatable. However, it is much more plausible to consider v. 13 to be an integral part of the unit as 4:6-13 shares both terminological and phraseological similarities with the covenantal passages of Ex. 19, 34 and Ps. 95 as mentioned above.

Since the entire passage shows internal literary coherence, such as, the oracle is addressed to Israel and Yahweh remains the main speaker throughout and moreover the formula "says Yahweh" (נאם יהוה) consistently concludes each successive section (vv. 6, 8, 9, 10, 11, 13),[167] we can consider 4:6-13 to be a unit, which can be outlined as follows:

---

[162] Brueggemann, "Amos iv 4-13", 1, no. 4.

[163] Reventlow. Cited in Brueggemann, "Amos iv 4-13", 1.

[164] Brueggemann argues further from Reventlow's position and states that even vv. 4-5, which deals with the false or broken covenant, is connected to vv. 6-11 that deals with the judgment of breaking the covenant and concludes with vv. 12-13, which calls and praises for the renewal of the covenant. He thus considers that the unit consists of 4:4-13, the form of which he considers to be a liturgy of covenant renewal derived from the earlier covenant tradition. Brueggemann, "Amos iv 4-13", 13. Arguing further from Brueggemann's analysis, Boyle states that the unit begins from 3:1 and ends with 4:13. Boyle argues that 3:1-4:13 employ a prophetic *rib* speech, which is structured as follows: 3:1-4:3 as summon to hear and witness; 4:4-5 as introductory statement of the case; 4:6-11 as plaintiff's benevolent acts and indictment; 4:12 as sentence and warning and 4:13 as recognition. Boyle, "The Covenant Lawsuit", 340-342.

[165] For detailed discussion see, Brueggemann, "Amos iv 4-13", 5-6.

[166] Mayes, *Amos*, 82-84.

[167] Stuart, *Hosea-Jonah*, 336.

i. Covenant curse judgment that causes poverty and devastation on the land (vv.6-9)
Famine: Cleanness of teeth in all your cities and lack of bread in all your places v.6
Drought: I withheld the rain vv. 7-8

Agricultural Failures: Garden and Vineyards laying waste with blight and mildews; Fig tree and olives devoured by locusts v.9

ii. Covenant curse judgment that creates difficult life upon the land (vv.10-11)
Plague: pestilence sent after the manner of Egypt; killing of young men and loss of horses v. 10

Devastation of Habitation: overthrow like Sodom and Gomorrah v. 11.

iii. Further warning v.12
Warning: I will do thus to you, prepare to meet your God.

iv. Doxological affirmation v. 13.
Hymn: [He is the God] who forms the mountains
creates the wind
reveals his thoughts to mortals
makes the morning darkness
and treads on the heights of the earth, Yahweh, the God of hosts, is his name! v. 13.

The above outline shows a combination of genres, which includes prophetic judgment speech, historical reviews and the liturgical hymn of praise. The form of "prophetic judgment speech" sets the stage for judgment and states Yahweh's intention to punish Israel for disobedience, while the "liturgical hymn" praises Yahweh for his role as creator. In Ps 106, the liturgical hymn of praise consists of historical recital in which Yahweh's act of deliverance becomes the basis to praise Yahweh.[168] In Ps 78, the liturgical hymn cites historical review and catalogues Israel's transgressions to justify Yahweh's change of action in rejecting the site of Joseph and choosing Judah as the place for the palace and temple. Amos employs here the historical review to justify Yahweh's action, such as, withholding the bread and rain, causing the mildew, blight, locusts, plagues, invaders and destruction. Amos imbedded these forms together to show Israel the need to return to Yahweh, who is affirmed as the creator (v.13). Though we do not know for certain about the time and place of the events reviewed in vv.6-11, we can assume that Amos have selected the instances that may have happened anytime and anywhere.[169]

---

[168] Sweeney, *The Minor Prophets*, 228.

[169] Andersen and Freedman, *Amos*, 436.

3.8.4. Tradition and Theological Comments in the Light of Tripartite Relationship

Though "covenant" is not mentioned explicitly, as argued above in the TCC on v.12b and the FCC, the present passage is rooted in the covenant tradition. H. Graf Reventlow was the first to propose that Am. 4:6-11 is patterned after the covenant curse list of Lev. 26.[170] Despite minor differences on the form and structures, scholars have mostly followed Reventlow's proposal.[171] Since some vocabularies, such as, גשם "rain," המטיר "cause to rain," (v.7); כון "prepare"; לקראת "to meet" (v.12) and כי הנה "for behold" (v.13) show some striking similarities with the covenant sanction passages (Lev. 26:19; Deut. 28:22-24), the covenant tradition cannot be ruled out in Am. 4:6-13.[172] We have noted that in the covenant tradition of tripartite relationship, Yahweh became "Israel's God"; Israel became Yahweh's "people" while Israel's loyalty to Yahweh became the condition for Israel to survive in the land. The covenant tradition of tripartite relationship warns that disloyalty to Yahweh would bring disaster to Israel and her land. In vv.6-11 Israel is portrayed as a stubborn unrepentant nation for which reason Yahweh invokes covenant curse judgment that affects Israel's life and land. By embedding the covenant tradition, Amos shows that Israel's unfaithfulness has affected her agricultural land and habitation in vv. 6-11. As the covenant tradition understood punishments not necessarily as retributive, but as warning-invitation to force Israel's return to Yahweh,[173] Amos likewise uses the same pattern to show that Yahweh inflicts the calamities with an intention to cause Israel's return to Yahweh.

Vv.6-9 describes the covenant curse judgment that causes poverty and devastation on the land. The famine in the land is figuratively described in v.6 as "cleanness of teeth" (נקיון שנים).[174] Since one's teeth remain clean when there is nothing to eat, the expression here conveys an extreme food-scarcity. This is further explained by the lack of bread (חסר לחם) in the second colon. Unlike the selective-raining in v. 7, the famine in v. 6 covers the entire land as indicated by

---

[170] H. Graf Reventlow, *Das Amt des Propheten bei Amos* (FRLANT, 80 Göttingen: Vandenhoeck and Ruprecht, 1962).

[171] Scholars who consider the form of "covenant curse" pattern are as follows. W. Brueggemann, "Amos iv 4-13 and Israel's Covenant Worship", *VT* 15 (1965) 6-8; James. L. Mays, *Amos: A Commentary*, OTL (Philadelphia: Westminster John Knox Press, 1969), 77; Allen R. Guenther, *Hosea Amos,* Believers Church Bible Commentary (Ontario: Herad, 1997), 285; Douglas Stuart, *Hosea-Jonah*, WBC, *31:* (Dallas, Texas: Word Books, 1998), 337; H. Graf Reventlow, *Das Amt des Propheten bei Amos,* 75. Paul, *Amos*, 142. While other scholars who think that the present pericope takes the form of "covenant lawsuit" are Herbert B. Huffmon, "The Covenant Lawsuit in the Prophets" *JBL* 78 (1959) 290ff; Boyle, "The Covenant Lawsuit", 341-343.

[172] Stuart, *Hosea-Jonah*, 338; see also, Wolff, *Joel and Amos*, 213.

[173] Cf. Deut. 4:29–31; 30:1–10; cf. Hos 2:4–17; 14:2; Isa 10:20–27; Jer 32:30–42, etc.

[174] Paul, *Amos*, 144.

the phrase "in all your cities" (בכל־עריכם) and "in all your habitations" (מקומתיכם בכל). Though the famine mentioned here is historically difficult to ascertain, the nation-wide instances of famine are recorded as having taken place during the period of Ahab (1 Kgs. 17:12), and Jehoram (2 Kgs. 4:38; 8:1). In any case, the text asserts that the purpose of the famine is primarily pedagogical, that is, to teach Israel to return to Yahweh. However, Israel remained obstinate ("yet you did not return to me, says Yahweh" vv. 6, 8, 9, 10, 11).

Vv. 7-8 mention the drought that affects the cultivable land. The understanding of deity withholding rain to fulfill a curse was common in the ANE.[175] Amos uses a similar thought to express that the drought was of divine origin. "I withheld rain" (v.7) speaks of drought, which is erratically localized (rain on one city … and no rain on another city) and long-enduring ("three months") that finally leads to the deterioration of crops (תיבשׁ "withered", v.7). Since barley and wheat harvest begin during the months of May and June[176] and since v.7 mentions that the rains were withheld three months before the harvest, the reference could be of latter-rain (March and April), which affected the cultivation. The point is, not only the people (Israel) faced hardship; even the arable land (חלקה) was affected due to drought. The emphatic refrain וגם אנכי "and I also" that is repeated in vv.6, 7 emphasizes the divine origin of drought that affects both the people and the land. The significance with regard to the tripartite relationship is that, Yahweh withheld the rain and Israel suffered for the lack of bread and water, while the land suffered for drought and the crops of the land withered. Yahweh's role as creator and controller of nature is brought into focus by emphasizing that it is he who decides where to send and where to withhold rain.

Vv.11-13 describe how the covenant curse judgment creates difficult life upon the land. The mention of שׁדפון (blight) and וירקון (mildew)[177] in v. 9 stand as synecdoche for crop diseases in general. וירקון comes from the root word "ירק", which means yellow or pale.[178] Thus, !wqryw can be understood as withering of the crops. In the covenant tradition of Deut. 28:15 cf. 22; 1 Kgs 8:35 cf. 37, וירקון, and שׁדפון are mentioned as divine curses for Israel's disloyalty to her covenanted God. גזם (locusts) could refer to pests in general (Deut 28:38–42), which devoured the garden, vineyard, fig and olive (v.9). These are the produce of the land upon which survival for Israel depends. During the eighth century in Israel, the viniculture, orchards, livestock rearing, and various farm products were in great demand with increasing profits in the international market. All these revenue-generated cultivations are land resources, which form an important part

[175] Paul, *Amos,* 145.

[176] Wolff, *Joel and Amos,* 220-221.

[177] שׁדפון (blight) is caused by hot east wind, which scorches the grain and dries it up prematurely, so that the grain turns brown. Whereas, וירקון (mildew) refers to the turning of the tips of the green grain due to the build up of parasitic worms. Wolff, *Joel and Amos,* 221.

[178] Sweeney, *The Minor Prophets,* 227.

of the economy of the Israelites. However, the lack of rain and the increasing pests have progressively deteriorated the productivity of the cultivable land that affects the Israelites' vital economic resources.

Despite all these failures, Israel remained unrepentant, which finally affected the Israelite population by alienating them from the land. The idea of alienation from the land is expressed by the term שבי (v.10), which is used to describe the act of taking captive (cf. Num. 31:26; Deut. 21:10; 28:41; Lam. 1:5; Jer. 48:46; Ps. 78:61). Israel was finally overthrown (הפכתי.v.11) in which many people were slaughtered in battle and the unburied carcasses of those dead bodies caused stench in the nostrils (v.10). Whether the overthrowing (הפכתי) of the cities refers to the earthquake as mentioned in 1:1[179] or the Assyrian attack[180] is difficult to determine. In any event the "overthrow" would be devastating, as indicated by the phrase, "as God overthrow Sodom and Gomorrah" (v.11).

Yet Israel did not again return to God. Thus, further warning (v.12) is proclaimed against Israel to "prepare" and "meet" her God. Israel who did not return to God will now be met by Yahweh, not for covenant-making but for judgment.[181] The covenanted God, whom Israel is warned to meet is identified as the God who creates the mountains and winds. As such, he is responsible for natural disaster (famine, drought, blights, and mildews). He is the God who makes the morning into darkness as such; he reverses Israel's history by defeating and alienating Israel from the land they once conquered. He is Yahweh of Hosts, the God with whom Israel entered into covenant.

In the above exegesis, the terms such as, חלקה "field" (v.7), כרם "vineyard" and גן "garden" (v.9) refer to land in a sense of arable plots upon which agricultural activities for survival are carried out while עיר "city" speaks of land in a sense of a place of habitation where the people have their settlement "מקום" (v.6). Land as a place of habitation and cultivation remains affected as a result of Yahweh's withdrawal of blessings, which was propelled by Israel's unrepentance. In this tripartite relationship, the covenanted God, Yahweh is portrayed as the creator who controls and holds authority over nature and withholds all the gifts of nature causing the land to wither as a result of Israel's failure to turn to God. Israel is thus portrayed as the distressed community who suffers because of their unfaithfulness to Yahweh. Israel fails to fulfill the covenantal obligations and Yahweh chastises Israel by causing drought, crops failure and finally Yahweh destroyed his people and alienated Israel from the land. The effect on the tripartite relationship is thus explained by employing the covenant tradition.

---

[179] Soggin, *The Prophet Amos*, 75.

[180] Wolff, *Joel and Amos*, 222.

[181] Mays, *Amos*, 82. Finley states that "part of that historical fulfillment came in the Assyrian invasion; when the Israelites encountered the Assyrian, they were actually meeting God- in judgment (cf. Is. 10:5)". Finley, "Amos", 216.

3.9. Covenant and Wilderness Traditions (Amos 5:21-27)

References to Yahweh's leading of Israel for forty years in the wilderness (v.25) and the indictment against Israel's idolatry (v.26) indicate that vv.21-27 is rooted in the covenant and wilderness traditions. Despite Yahweh's faithful leading of Israel for forty years, Israel continued to violate the covenant, which is stated as the reason of Yahweh's rejection of Israel's worship and the loss of land and exile to other nations. The tripartite relationship is thus explained in 5:21-27 by employing the covenant and wilderness traditions.

3.9.1. Translation on Amos 5:21-27

21 [a]I hate, I reject[a] your festivals, and I take no delight[b] in your festive assemblies.
22 When you offer me your burnt offerings and grain offerings[a], I will not accept them[b]; and the peace offerings[c] of your fatted animals I will not look upon.
23 Take away from me the noise of your songs; I will not listen to the melody of your harps.
24 But[a] let justice[b] roll down like waters, and righteousness[c] like an ever-flowing stream.
25 Did[a] you bring to me sacrifices and offerings the forty years in the wilderness, O house of Israel?
26 But you bring to[a] the shrine of your Molech and to the abode of your images[b] the host of your gods which you have made for yourselves;
27 therefore I will take you into exile beyond Damascus, says Yahweh, whose name is the God of hosts[a].

3.9.2. Text Critical Comments on Amos 5:21-27

V.21a-a: שׂנא "to hate" appears three times in ch. 5. Israel "hates" justice (5:10), is unwilling to "hate" evil and in v.25 Yahweh himself "hates" Israel's cultic activities through which Israel sought to please God. מאס "to reject" in 1 Sam. 15:23 and Hos. 4:6 suggest that the divine rejection is the reaction of Yahweh to having been rejected by humans.[182] A similar idea of Yahweh's reaction against Israel's infidelity is attached here. The object of God's hatred and rejection is חגיכם "your festivals", which probably refers to the three annual pilgrimage festivals (feast of unleavened bread; festival of harvest and the feast of ingathering cf. Ex. 23:14-16; 34: 22, 25).[183]

V.21b: ולא אריח literally "I will not smell" refers to the unfavorable acceptance of sacrifices (cf. Gen 8:21; Ex. 30:38; Lev. 26:31; 1 Sam. 26:19),[184] which can be extended to mean "I take no delight". The object of Yahweh's disfavor is בצרתיכם

---

[182] Wolff, *Joel and Amos*, 262.

[183] Paul, *Amos*, 189.

[184] Paul, *Amos*, 189.

עצרתיכם, "your festive assemblies", which refers to the assembled place for prayer and sacrifice during the festivals and/or troubled times.[185]

V. 22a: מנחתיכם (a plural form of מנחה), translated here as "grain offering", is the term originally used for gift and presents to express: i. Reverence or respect (1 Sam. 10:27; 2 Kgs 8:8) ii. Gratitude (2 Chro.17:5); iii. Homage or allegiance (Gen. 32:14); and iv. Political alliances and tributes 1 Kgs 5:1; 2 Kgs 20:12; 17:3). Cripps, however, thinks that by the time of Amos, the term has come to signify a "meal offering" usually of grain or of its products that accompanied the animal sacrifice. This is primarily a gift offered to the Deity as such, it is either burned on the altar or assigned to the priests and the offerer ate no share.[186]

V.22b: לא ארצה "I will not accept", which in Hebrew and Aramaic means "to have pleasure in". The term is used in the cultic context to convey God's approval towards sacrifice or the offerers of sacrifice (2 Sam. 24:23; Hos 8:13; Mic. 4:7).[187]

V.22c: שלם "peace offering", in singular form appears only in Am. 5:22, although the plural form appears in the early cult (Ex. 20:21; 24:5; 1 Sam. 10:8; 11:15; 2 Sam. 6:17-18; 24:25). Since שלם appears alongside the two major sacrifices (עולה and מנחה), Paul thinks that "it [שלם] played a predominant role specifically in the cult of northern Israel."[188] In any event, these offerings are considered as "pleasant aromas" to Yahweh (cf. Lev. 1:13; 2:9; 3:16), as such, the Israelites commonly understood of them as pleasing to Yahweh. Amos, however, states that Yahweh refused to accept these offerings.

V.24a: H. Cazelles and J.P. Hyatt interpret ו as waw consecutive, but such rendering does not give the force of contrast. ו in ויגל can be interpreted as "adversative" that contrasts what God requires from that which Yahweh has rejected in vv. 21-23.

V. 24b: Kiel, A. Weiser, E. Sellin and others interpret משפט "justice" in terms of the judgment of God that will roll down on Israel like a river,[189] which is unlikely, since such rendering does not stress the contrast that juxtaposes "sacrifices and prayers" in vv. 22-23 with "justice and righteousness" in v. 24.[190] Instead of judgment, משפט is used as an admonition demanding of Israel what Yahweh requires, namely, justice, rather than the human effort of religiosity, such as, festivals, sacrifices and songs. משפט, in Amos' usage, mostly refers to the just and fair judicial trails carried out at the city gate, which includes "reparation for

---

[185] Paul, *Amos*, 190.

[186] Cripps, *A Critical and Exegetical Commentary on the Book of Amos*, 196.

[187] Cripps, *A Critical and Exegetical Commentary on the Book of Amos*, 196.

[188] Paul, *Amos*, 191.

[189] C.E. Kiel, *The Twelve Minor Prophets 1* (Grand Rapids, Michigan: William B. Eerdmans Publishing Company, 1954), 298; A. Weiser, *ATD* 24 (1964), E. Wurthwein and E. Sellin, *KAT* 12/1 (1929). Cited in Mays, *Amos*, 108; see also, Soggin, *The Prophet Amos*, 97.

[190] Wolff, *Joel and Amos*, 264.

the defrauded, fairness for the less fortunate, and dignity and compassion for the needy."[191]

V.24c: The term צדקה "righteousness", according to Cripps, in its original form probably belongs to a clan virtue, corresponding to "what is due" or it may also be a forensic term derived from the court of justice to determine the innocent party.[192] In Amos 8:5,6, the term is used to express the acts and deeds that are just and fair in social dealings. צדקה is thus a relational term that expresses a quality of life lived according to the accepted norms both in relationship with God and with fellow humans in the society.[193] Mays argues that "The two most important spheres for righteousness were the relationship between Yahweh and Israel defined in the covenant and expressed in the cult, and the relationship in the social order of the flock."[194]

V.25a: the ה of הזבחים is followed by dagesh in the following letter, which makes it appear like the definite article. The dagesh after the ה is applied to retain the short vowel with ה. Instead of reading it as the definite article, it is interpreted here as interrogative "did you?"

V.26a: Following Gevirtz's suggestion that the particle את on its own can function "exactly as does the preposition,"[195] we consider that את points to the following term סכות and interprets it as preposition "to".

V.26b: Whether the terms סכות[196] and כיון provide any evidence of astral worship[197] or indicate the impending judgment that Israel would be forced to worship astral gods by the conquering nation[198] or refer to Yahweh's indictment against Israel's idolatry have generated intense debate. Most modern scholars who interpret סכות and כיון as *sakkut* and *Kaywan*, the foreign astral deity named after the Saturn planet, based their argument on the celestial term כוכב "star."[199] However,

[191] Finley, "Amos", 251.

[192] Cripps, *A Critical and Exegetical Commentary to the Book of Amos*, 183-184.

[193] Mays, *Amos*, 92.

[194] Mays, *Amos*, 93.

[195] S. Gevirtz, "A New Look at an Old Crux: Amos 5:26", JBL 87 (1968) 275.

[196] LXX reads the MT version of Sakkoth as *την σκηνην του Μολχ* "the tent of Molech."

[197] Scholars who consider סכות and כיון as referring to astral worship mostly interpret these terms as *sakkut* and *Kaywan*, after the deity of Saturn planet. C. Torrey, "On the Text of Amos v. 26; vi. 1, 2 ; vii. 2," *JBL*, 13 (1894), 61 f. ; S. R. Driver, *The Books of Joel and Amos* Cambridge: Cambridge Bible, 1897, 189, no. 2; Eric Burrows, "Cuneiform and Old Testament: Three Notes," *JThS*, 28 (1927), 184 f.; E. A. Speiser, "Note on Amos 5:26," *BASOR*, 108 (1947), 5; R. S. Cripps, *A Critical and Exegetical Commentary on the Book of Amos*, 199 f. and 300-02; Jeremias, *The Book of Amos*, 105. Since, Sakkoth is believed to have been introduced into Israel after the Assyrian conquest (2 Kgs 17:30), Wellhausen, Schmidt and Rudolff consider it to be a later addition or interpolation. Cited in Paul, *Amos*, 194.

[198] Mays, *Amos*, 112.

[199] Scholars who support this view are mentioned in Barstad, *The Religious Polemics of Amos*, 119. no. 212.

Gevirtz suggests another possibility by using the example of *qittûl* and *mqtl* noun formations from other biblical occurrences.[200] He establishes an equation between כיון and מכון as "place or abode", and interprets the phrase כיון צלמיכם as "the abode of your images,"[201] while סכות is equated with the Phoenician מסכת (shrine) and since סכות is in construct relationship with מלככם, which is understood by Targum, Jonathan, LXX, Aquila, Syriac and Vulgate as referring to foreign gods, Gevirtz interprets the phrase סכות מלככם as the "shrine of your gods."[202] The meaning of these terms remains contentious. However, what appears clear is that these terms on the one hand appear in the context of Yahweh's rejection of Israel's cultic activities and on the other hand they appear in the context of Yahweh's indictment on Israel's deviation to other gods. As such we have interpreted these problematic terms as "the shrine of your Molech" and "the abode of your images".

V.27a: The title "Yahweh of hosts" could possibly refer to the earthly armies, or host of spiritual beings and heavenly messengers or even the heavenly bodies themselves, regarded as divine in some ANE cults. In any case, in Hebrew understanding, all these are subjected to Yahweh. The title thus signifies a "great, mysterious and irresistible power" of Yahweh.[203]

3.9.3. Form Critical Comments on Amos 5:21-27

Am.5:21-27 employs different styles within the prophetic speech of judgment oracle. First, vv. 21-23 employ a cultic form. Various terms such as, "I hate", "I despise" "I take no delight", "I will not accept" express negative cultic decisions. The form of cultic declaration is employed here to announce Yahweh's decision of whether the offerings of the worshippers are acceptable to Yahweh or not.[204] Second, v.24 takes the form of sapiential admonition,[205] which expresses Yahweh's injunctions that justice and righteousness must be practiced instead of cultic sacrifices. Third, v. 25 takes the rhetorical form, "Did you bring to me sacrifices… in the wilderness?, the obvious answer to which is "no". Such rhetorical form in v. 25 seeks to offer theological validity to Yahweh's demand for justice instead of sacrifices. Despite Yahweh's rejection of cults in vv. 21-23 and his demand for justice and righteousness in v. 24, Israel failed to heed Yahweh's instruction. Thus, vv. 26-27 pronounced the imminent judgment that Israel will go to exile.

---

[200] Some examples Gevirtz cites are: שקוי in Prov. 3:8 (drink)=משקה in Lev. 11:34; Isa. 32:6; סיפור ("narration, story")=מספר in Judg. 7:15. For detail examples of *qittûl* and *mqtl* noun formations, see Gevirtz, "A New Look at an Old Crux", 271-274.

[201] Gevirtz, "A New Look at an Old Crux", 272.

[202] Gevirtz, "A New Look at an Old Crux", 274.

[203] David Stacey, *Isaiah 1-39* (London: Epworth, 1993), xxvii.

[204] Wolff, *Joel and Amos*, 261; Mays, *Amos*, 106.

[205] Wolff, *Joel and Amos*, 261.

Though scholars agree that 5:21-27 is a unit, the authenticity of vv. 25-26 is often doubted.[206] Wolff argues that stylistically vv.25-26 are prose; grammatically, the singular form of מנחה (offering cf. v.25) does not go along with the plural form מנחתיכם (your offerings cf. v.22.); moreover, the subject of vv. 25-26 is no more Yahweh but Israel, which is addressed in second person plural.[207] As such, Wolff doubted that vv. 25-26 originally belonged to Amos. The reference of astral gods "Sokkuth, Kawain, and stars" in v.26, which are believed to have intruded into Israelites' worship after the Assyrian invasion is also cited as reason to consider vv. 25-26 to be a later addition or gloss.[208] However, as mentioned in the TCC on v.26b, Sokkuth and Kaiwan as gods were known to Israel long before the Assyrian invasion.[209] Thus, to suspect the authenticity of v. 26 on the ground that these astral gods would not have been known to Israel prior to the Assyrian period cannot be sustained. 5:21-27 could be considered as unit as the entire verses takes the first-person divine speech. Vv. 21-23 deal with Yahweh's denunciation of cultic activities; v. 24 deals with Yahweh's demand for just social order; v.25 poses a rhetorical question to justify Yahweh's demand for justice and righteousness over the cultic activities. V. 26 indicts Israel for her perpetual practice of idolatry and finally, v.27 talks about the coming punishment of exile. As such, there appears a thematic and logical connection from vv. 21-27. Thus, we consider that the present pericope is a self contained unit.

The historical setting surrounding 5:21-27 cannot be determined with certainty. According to Stuart, the time and setting of this oracle could be somewhere around 745 and 740 BCE, the time when Israel sought Yahweh's deliverance from the Assyrian territorial expansion.[210] Such presumed setting remains speculative in the absence of any textual evidence. On the other hand, Wolff thinks that the setting of this oracle could be the cultic place at Bethel where the prophet interrupted the speech of the official cultic spokesperson.[211] Judging by the textual tradition, Wolff's argument appears plausible as we see the elements of cultic decision, such as, "I hate", "I despise", "I take no delight", "I will not accept" and so on, which are all cultic/priestly declaratory vocabularies. This probably suggests that Amos proclaimed this oracle during the cultic festivals at Bethel, the official religious place for the northern Israel.

---

[206] Torrey, "On the Text of Amos v. 26", 61 f. ; Driver, *The Books of Joel and Amos,* 189, no. 2; Burrows, "Cuneiform and Old Testament", 184 f.; Snaith, *The Book of Amos,* 98-108; Hammershaimb, *Amos,* 90 f.; Speiser, "Note on Amos 5:26", 5; Cripps, *A Critical and Exegetical Commentary on the Book of Amos,* 199 f. and 300-02; Fosbroke, "The Book of Amos," 821 f.

[207] Wolff, *Joel and Amos*, 259-261.

[208] Larry J. Rector, "Israel's Rejected Worship: An Exegesis of Amos 5", *Restoration Quarterly* 21/3 (1978) 175.

[209] For the reference, see the footnote no 197.

[210] Stuart, *Hosea-Jonah*, 353.

[211] Wolff, *Joel and Amos*, 262.

3.9.4. Tradition and Theological Comments in the Light of Tripartite Relationship

Though the term covenant is not explicitly mentioned, Amos' oracle in 5:21-27 seems to have its root in the covenant tradition. (For the discussion on the tripartite relationship in the covenant tradition, see the Tradition and Theological Comments in Am. 2:4-5 and 4:6-13). The indictment against Israel's idolatry (v.26) reflects the Decalogue of Sinai covenant, "You shall have no other gods" (Ex. 20:3). The covenant tradition warns that Israel would lose the land and would be alienated from the Promised Land if she fails to live by the covenantal terms. The judgment of exile and consequent alienation of Israel from the land in v. 27 reflects such covenant tradition. Moreover, the covenant tradition affirms that covenantal loyalty is an essential requirement for Yahweh to accept Israel's offering otherwise their cultic activities would be unacceptable (cf. Lev. 26:31). Since the practice of justice and righteousness is an essential element of the covenantal stipulations, the absence of these qualities apparently serves as reason for Yahweh's rejection of Israel's cult in vv. 21-23. Amos considers the tradition of covenant as central in considering the relation between Israel and her survival in the land in 5:21-27.

Israel survived her historical predicament and landlessness in the wilderness period because of the covenantal relationship. (For the discussion on the tripartite relationship in the wilderness tradition, see the Am. 2:6-11). The wilderness sojourn was a period of the absence of lavish animal sacrifices yet it was also a period of the absence of social injustice and exploitation. Amos looked back to this historical precedent to drive his point that Israel's existence in the land is not based on the extravagant cultic practices but on the covenantal faithfulness that is marked with justice and righteousness. The covenant and wilderness traditions are thus intertwined in 5:21-27 to show how the tripartite relationship is affected. Israel's failure to live by the covenantal norms affects her relationship with God and her fellow humans. Significantly it also affects Israel's relationship with her land as she is alienated from her land and destined to exile.

In vv. 21-23, Yahweh rejects Israel's cult with seven verbs of negation (שׂנאתי "I hate", מאסתי "I reject", לא אריח "no delight" in v. 21; לא ארצה "not accept", לא אביט "not look" in v.22; הסר "take away", and אשמע לא "not listen" in v. 23), which represents a complete and comprehensive repudiation.[212] By employing these negative verbs, Amos makes clear that cultic offerings unaccompanied by the covenant virtues of justice and righteousness are not acceptable to Yahweh. Such understanding is made clear in the covenant tradition in Lev. 26, which warns that if the Israelites do not obey (לא תשמעו) or do not observe Yahweh's command (לא תעשׂו, cf. Lev. 26:14) or break the covenant (להפרכם את־בריח, cf. Lev. 26:15), then Yahweh will not accept their cultic offerings (לא אריח בריח ניחהכם

[212] Paul, *Amos*, 192.

cf. Lev. 26:31). The covenant tradition thus affirms that the cultic activities and covenantal loyalty are inseparable in worshipping Yahweh. The Israelite temple is not exclusively intended for cultic ceremonies, it was also a place for instruction about Yahweh's expectations of justice in the society.[213] However, Amos sees that despite the Israelites' regular temple attendance and maximized cultic ceremonies, there was no practice of justice and righteousness. This, according to Amos, makes their cult practices null and void before Yahweh.

After rejecting the cultic festivals, offerings and music in vv. 21-23, Yahweh asserts what he expects from Israel, namely, משפט "justice" and צדקה "righteousness". These terms appear three times as a word-pair in Amos (5:7, 24; 6:12). In 5:7 and 6:12, "justice" and "righteousness" appear in the context of the prophet's indictment for perverting the social norms and orders, whereas, in 5:24, the pair appears in the context of Amos' critique of the cult.[214] However, even in 5:24, the word-pair is closely connected with proper ethical behaviors in social relations. In Amos' term, the setting of משפט is the city gates (cf. 5:10, 12; 6:1), where legal disputes are investigated to establish what/who is right. This kind of legal practice helped maintain the social order by acquitting the just party and by ascertaining the wrong and correcting it. While the term צדקה "righteousness", according to Mays, refers to those who fulfill the responsibilities, which are expected of them in their relationship with others.[215] As mentioned in the TCC on v.24c, such relationship, on the one hand, involves Yahweh who outlines the contents of his will for Israel, and on the other hand, it includes the Israelites who are demanded by Yahweh to execute His will in the horizontal sphere of the society.[216] Yahweh demands that the adjudication of such justice, which protects the marginalized and vulnerable people from exploitation,[217] should roll down like water. Righteousness that fulfills the obligations of both the vertical and horizontal relationships must flow like the ever flowing streams. The metaphor of ever flowing water, which Amos draws from his familiarity of the agrarian setting, juxtaposes those streams (wadis) that overflow only during the rainy seasons and those rivers that continually flow despite the summer drought.[218] Just as the perpetual flow of rivers brings prosperity and life to the land, the perpetuation of justice and righteousness, which Israelites have set aside and turned into wormwood and poison (5:7; 6:12), can bring life to every member of the Israelite society. Yahweh's demand for "justice" calls the Israelites to ensure "right" and "protection" of the poor and weak in the court,

---

[213] Sweeney, *The Twelve Prophets*, 239.

[214] Mays, *Amos*, 92.

[215] Mays, *Amos*, 108.

[216] Cf. Mays, *Amos*, 108.

[217] The officials oppressed and ignored the poor of their needs (Amos 2:6-7; 8:4-6). They perverted justice, bribed judges and cheated the poor in the market place (5:10-12). Jannie du Preez, "'Let Justice Roll on Like…' Some Exploratory Notes on Amos 5:24", *JTSA* 109 (2001), 95.

[218] Soggin, *The Prophet Amos*, 97.

while "righteousness" demands fulfillment to the covenantal stipulations, which involves a daily obligation to Yahweh as well as fellow humanity. In other words, a call to justice and righteousness will not only promote social order for peaceful coexistence, they will effect blessing and prosperity amongst the people just as streams and rivers of the land bring gifts of fertility and life (Amos 5:24).

V.26 links the absence of justice and righteousness with idolatrous practice. The accusation that Israel brings "Molech", "images" and "the host of gods" indicates the prevalent idolatry. The verb עשׂה "to make" in v. 26 is used in the context of making the idols[219] indicating that Israel was after other gods, which is against the Decalogue of the Sinai covenant. This is a case of utter disloyalty to covenant stipulations that forbids any form of idolatry. As a result of Israel's covenant unfaithfulness, Yahweh pronounces the judgment of exile that Israel will be deported from her land (v.27). The phrase "beyond Damascus" refers to a distant geographical location where Israel will be exiled.[220] Whether or not "beyond Damascus" alludes to Assyria, the fate that overtakes Israel within the next few decades (2 Kgs 17:6) is difficult to determine. In any case, v.27 emphasizes the judgment of exile, which Yahweh himself will execute. hlG (exile) implies a "horror" which outruns the ruin and pain of defeat and capture by an enemy[221] and forceful alienation from the homeland. Mays states that "For Israel it meant being removed from the land promised to the fathers, displacement from geographical locus of the unfolding history of election, and so was in effect a kind of excommunication."[222] Israel's dislocation from the land is thus not a result of the natural order of disaster, but because of Yahweh's judgment.

By employing the covenant tradition, Amos presents that in the tripartite relationship no amount of animal sacrifices can sustain Israel's relationship with Yahweh and her existence in the land if exclusive devotion to Yahweh and the ethos of justice and righteousness remains absent. Israel's relationship with Yahweh and her survival in the land remains possible only in her faithfulness to Yahweh and in her ethical life patterned after the covenantal norms as in her wilderness period. Injustice, unrighteousness and idolatry are against the covenantal ethos. The prevalence of such practices indicates Israel's disloyalty to the covenant. Such disloyalty breaks up the tripartite relationship between Yahweh, Israel and the land in that Israel could no longer dwell in the land as she fails to live according to the qualities of life envisaged by Yahweh in his covenant. Yahweh considers Israel's idolatry as rejection of him as Israel's only God and the absence of justice and righteousness as a rejection of his covenant. Israel's rejections of Yahweh as her only God and his laws propel Yahweh to give up Israel. Israel is thus exiled beyond

---

219 Cf. cf. Ex. 20:4; 1 Kgs 14:9; 2 Kgs 17:29-31; Hos. 8:4, 6; 13:2. Paul, *Amos*, 197.

220 The theme of exile appears frequently in Amos' oracle of judgment (1:5, 15; 5:5; 6:7, 7: 11, 17).

221 Mays, *Amos*, 113.

222 Mays, *Amos*, 113.

Damascus and alienated from her land. In other words, Israel's relationship with Yahweh and land either stands or falls based on her commitment to the covenant stipulations.

3.10. Theophany, Creation and Exodus Traditions (Amos 9:5-8)

Yahweh touches the earth and it quivers (v.5); he builds the upper chamber and founded the vault upon the earth (v.6); and he brought Israel out from the land of Egypt" (v.7). These expressions speak of the theophany, creation and exodus traditions respectively. As the creator (creation tradition), Yahweh intervenes upon the earth (theophany tradition) to deliver and destine each political nation as a separate territory (exodus tradition). By embedding these traditions, Amos explains the tripartite relationship in 9:5-8.

3.10.1. Translation on Amos 9:5-8

5 Now the Lord, Yahweh of hosts[a], he who touches the earth[b] and it quavers[c], and all who live in it mourn[d], and all of it rises like the Nile, and sinks again, like the Nile of Egypt;

6 who builds his upper chambers[a] in the heavens, and founded his vault upon the earth; [b]who calls for the waters of the sea, and pours them out upon the surface of the earth-Yahweh is his name.[b]

7 Are you not[a] like the Cushites[b] to me, O people of Israel? says Yahweh. Did I not bring Israel up from the land of Egypt, and the [c]Philistines from Caphtor and the Arameans from Kir?[c]

8 Behold the eyes of God, Yahweh, are upon the sinful kingdom[a], and I will destroy it from the face of the earth-except that I will not utterly destroy the house of Jacob[b], says Yahweh.

3.10.2. Text Critical Comments on Amos 9:5-8

V.5a: צבאות "hosts" is commonly applied to a company of an army or angels (1 Kgs 22:19; Pss 103: 20-21; 148:2). Cripps argues that its first occurrence appears in the period of war with the Philistines (1 Sam. 5:10) in connection to the sacred ark.[223] Later it is also used in connection with Yahweh as the God of the armies of Israel (1 Sam. 27:45). Amos regularly uses the title "Yahweh, God of hosts" (cf. Am. 3:13; 4:13; 5:16, 27; 6:8, 14). Since there is a slight variation in the present title, "Lord, Yahweh of Host", scholars suspect the hand of redactor.[224] However, the use of divine title "אדני" does not necessarily indicate the editorial work since Amos does address God as אדני as in the case of his vision reports.

V.5b: ארץ "earth" in vv.5-6 is used to refer to the entire earth. Just as the crimes and injustices which Amos indicts occurred in the international arena

[223] Cripps, *A Critical and Exegetical Commentary on the Book of Amos*, 330.

[224] Mays, *Amos*, 155.

(cf. the oracles against the nations in Am. 1:3-2:16), Yahweh also demonstrates his manifestation upon the entire earth.

V.5c: The MT reads מוג (melts), which is rendered in the LXX as *και σαλευων αυτην* (and he who makes it shake) emphasizing the act of Yahweh. The same root word appears in v.13 but in Hithpolel form to indicate the dissolving of the hills. מוג connotes "deterioration from vertical to horizontal,"[225] thus it is possible to translate it as "melt". However, the context indicates the reeling of the earth as a consequence of Yahweh's action in which case it appears appropriate to render it as "quaver".

V.5d: √אבל "to mourn" appears in 1:2, where it is commonly translated as "wither". In 9:5 the subject of אבל is humans. It is thus appropriate to render אבל as "mourn". The mourning of the people who inhabit the land is expressed as a result of Yahweh's act of touching the earth.

V.6a: The LXX renders *αναβασιν αυτου* in singular form. The normal Hebrew term for upper chamber is עלייתו (cf. 2 Kgs 1:2; Neh 3:31, 32). Wolff thus argues that MT version of מעלותיו arose due to dittography as indicated by מ, while ו is the result of misreading the.י[226] Though such textual errors are common, Finley argues that it is possible to interpret "upper chamber" with the form of מ. MT's rendering מעלותיו is retained here as "his upper chambers".

V.6b-b: Wolff states that the bicolon in v.6b-b is originally a part of 5:8.[227] Whether this bicolon belongs to the second part of 5:8 or not is difficult to determine. In any case, v.6b-b is identical with the second part of 5:8. B.Z. Luria interprets this bicolon as referring to the tidal waves that accompany an earthquake.[228]

V.7a: The interrogation הלוא functions here as a negative question "are you not?" Scholars recognize the rhetorical force of the question, which introduces a disputation saying to counter the Israelites' misdirected belief that her Exodus event places her in a privileged position.[229]

V.7b: The title בני כשיים (children of Cushites or Ethopians) corresponds with the following בני ישראל (children of Israel). The Ethiopians, who live in Nubia, are not singled out disdainfully[230] because of their color[231] or slave status.[232] "They are

---

[225] Stuart, *Hosea-Jonah*, 389.

[226] Wolff, *Joel and Amos*, 336-337.

[227] Wolff, *Joel and Amos*, 336-337.

[228] B.Z. Luria, "'Who Calls the Water of the Sea and Spills Them on the Face of the Earth' [Amos 5:8; 9:6]", *BM* 101 (1984-1985) 259-262. Cited in Paul, *Amos*, 280.

[229] Paul, *Amos*, 282.

[230] Num. 12:1.

[231] Jer. 13:23.

[232] 2 Sam. 18:21; Jer. 38:7.

mentioned simply as representative of foreign and remote peoples who live on the outermost periphery of the known world".[233]

V.7c-c: The second rhetorical question places Israel squarely among the nations. Israel alone did not experience exodus. Yahweh also brought the Philistines out of Caphtor and the Arameans from Kir. The LXX renders the MT version of כפתור as אכִדאפפאכ (Cappadocia). Following the LXX, G.A. Wainwright, F. Cornelius and J.J. Prignaud identify Capthor with Cappadocia,[234] while Cripps and Soggin suggest Crete.[235] The exact reference of Capthor remains obscure. In any case, Yahweh emphasizes here that just as Israel is brought out from Egypt, he also brought up the Philistines from Capthor. Likewise, the Arameans too have a history of exodus from Kir but as a result of Yahweh's act. This means Israel's historical deliverance from Exodus accords her no unique position. Yahweh is sovereign over nations, as such he moves people from one land to another land.

V.8a: Wolff contends that בממלכה in Amos' usage refers to "kingship" in the sense of "royal house" and not kingdom.[236] To render בממלכה as kingship appears untenable since בממלכה appears in the context of referring to other political kingdoms (v.7), such as, Egypt, Philistia, Aram and others. It is thus fitting to interpret בממלכה as "kingdom". However, whether בממלכה is a generic term referring to any kingdom or whether it refers only to the North or inclusive of both North and South need further analysis. Harper asserts that "kingdom" refers to Israel alone.[237] Paul, on the other hand argues that since the first bicolon of v.8 is a continuation of v.7, בממלכה refers not only to Israel but it emphasizes "the total control of the Lord over all the nations."[238] Perhaps the usage of the definite article "the" in בממלכה indicates that the prophet has the Northern kingdom in mind. This interpretation corresponds to the reference of בני ישׂראל "children of Israel" in v.7.

V.8b: Though the phrase "house of Jacob" refers to the entire people of Israel (Israel/Judah) in a later time, in Amos' usage בית יעקב refers to the kingdom of Jeroboam (cf. 3:13; "Jacob" in 6:8; 7:2, 5; 8:7).[239]

---

233 Wolff, *Joel and Amos*, 347.

234 G.A. Wainwright, "Capthor-Cappodicia", *VT* 6 (1956) 199-210; *idem*, "The Septuagint's *Καππαδοκια* for Capthor", *JJS* 7 (1956) 91-92; *idem*, "Some Early Philistine History", *VT* 9 (1959) 73-84); F. Cornelius, "Genesis 14", *ZAW* 72 (1960) 5. no. 16; J.J. Prignaud, "Caftorim et Keretim", *RB* 71 (1964) 215-219. Cited in Paul, *Amos*, 238. no. 13.

235 Cripps, *A Critical and Exegetical Commentary on the Book of Amos*, 263; Soggin, *The Prophet Amos*, 142.

236 Wolff, *Joel and Amos*, 348.

237 Harper, *Amos and Hosea*, 193.

238 Paul, *Amos*, 284.

239 Mays, *Amos*, 160.

3.10.3. Form Critical Comments on Amos 9:5-8

Scholars recognize some characteristic hymn-forms in the hymnic doxologies of 9:5-6; 4:13 and 5:8f,[240] such as, the use of the predicative participles, the ascription of Yahweh's majestic works of creation and the concluding refrain "Yahweh (God of host) is his name.[241] The doxological hymn in vv.5-6 consists of theophany and creation traditions. The theophany tradition describes "the effect upon earth when Yahweh descends from heaven to touch its surface,"[242] while the creation tradition affirms the universe as the handiwork of Yahweh. Both the theophany and creation traditions employ the poetic form, and the prose section of vv.7-8 expands and comments on the poetry of vv.5-6.[243] The prose unit of vv.7-8 uses both a rhetorical question and announcement of judgment. The rhetorical form employs interrogation to counter Israel's attitude on their presumed privileged position due to the historical event of Exodus. Mays, thus, aptly considers v.7 as a disputation saying.[244] The disputation saying is then followed by the announcement of judgment in v.8 asserting that Yahweh sees the sinful kingdom and proclaims his judgment to destroy the kingdom (political nation) from the face of the earth.

The proclamation of the identity of God by the title "Yahweh of Hosts" (v.5) seems to break the style of the preceding unit and introduces a new section on hymnic doxology (vv.5-6).[245] Thus, scholars doubt the authenticity of 9:5-6[246] and only v. 7 and the first bicolon of v. 8 are considered to be genuinely Amos. The last part of v. 8 is considered to be a later addition. Cripps considers vv.5-8 to be a "composite passage,"[247] while Mays thinks that vv.5-6 and 7-8 are two different units.[248] A close analysis shows some compelling reasons to consider vv.5-8 as unit. The reference to Cushite/Ethiopian and Egyptian in v.7, as Stuart observes, corresponds to the hymn's reference to Egypt in v.5,[249] and so v.5 can hardly be an editorial insertion as Cripps has argued.[250] Moreover, vv.7-8 elaborates on the judgment language of the hymnic doxology of vv.5-6,[251] indicating that the prose

[240] Harper, *Amos and Hosea*, 190; Wolff, *Joel and Amos*, 341; Mays, *Amos*, 82; John Joseph Owens, "Exegetical Studies in the Book of Amos", *Review & Expositor* 63/4 (1966) 440.

[241] Mays, *Amos*, 155.

[242] Mays, *Amos*, 155.

[243] Stuart, *Hosea-Jonah*, 391.

[244] Mays, *Amos*, 156. For the instances of disputation sayings in Amos cf. 3:3-8; 5:18-20; 6:2.

[245] Mays, *Amos*, 155.

[246] Cripps, *A Critical and Exegetical Commentary on the Book of Amos*, 260. no. 3.

[247] Cripps, *A Critical and Exegetical Commentary on the Book of Amos*, 260.

[248] Mays, *Amos*, 155-157.

[249] Stuart, *Hosea-Jonah*, 390.

[250] Cripps, *A Critical and Exegetical Commentary on the Book of Amos*, 260. no. 3.

[251] Stuart, *Hosea-Jonah*, 390.

section of vv.7-8 expounds on the hymnic doxology of vv.5-6. Thus, we consider vv.5-8 to be a separate unit, which can be outlined as follows:

Yahweh's coming upon the earth, v.5
Yahweh, the creator and controller of nature, v.6
Yahweh questions Israel's understanding as unique people, v.7
Yahweh's judgment upon Israel, v.8

3.10.4. Tradition and Theological Comments in the Light of Tripartite Relationship

The oracle in Am. 9:5-8 is rooted in the traditions of Creation, Theophany, and Exodus. Amos wove these traditions together and explains the relationship between Yahweh, Israel (and other nations) and land. As mentioned in the above FCC, land belongs to God by virtue of his creation and that Israel and other nations exist as recipients of God's gift of land in each of their demarcated political territories. By portraying Yahweh as the creator, Amos also shows Yahweh as the ultimate and sovereign ruler over the earth; he demonstrates his authority by manifesting himself upon the earth (Theophany) and by delivering each nation and placing them in their designated territory (Exodus). In such context land appears as an arena of Yahweh's manifestation and a sphere of human's existence. Yahweh is portrayed as the God who controls the affairs of humanity and the God who destines the territories of each political nation.

Since Yahweh is said to "touch" the earth (v.5), scholars think that theophany is in view here.[252] In the tradition of theophany, Yahweh's manifestation is always accompanied by the quaking of the earth, raising of the water tides, and arousing awe and fear of the people (cf. Ps. 29; 46:6; 104:32; 144:5; Mi. 1:3 f). In using this tradition, Amos demonstrates the appearance of Yahweh and the consequent result that follows, such as, melting of the earth, rising and sinking of the River Nile and mourning of the people (v.5). The location of Yahweh's appearance is stated to be בארץ "in the earth" and the consequent result of the earth is described by the term מוג, which, as stated in the TCC on v.5c, "depicts the cosmic upheaval instigated by Yahweh himself."[253] The verb מוג here indicates a poetic hyperbole of an earthquake. In this theophany the place where Yahweh appears is ארץ, which refers to the entire earth as an arena of Yahweh's manifestation. The emphasis here is that Yahweh is in complete control of the earth.

Amos uses some creation terms, בונה (builder) and יסד (founder),[254] to portray Yahweh as the creator, which shows his dependence on the creation tradition. In the creation tradition of the tripartite relationship, Yahweh is portrayed as the creator God, who created humanity and everything upon the earth. Thus,

[252] Finley, "Amos", 317; Jeremias, *The Book of Amos*, 159; Paul, *Amos*, 280.

[253] Wolff, *Joel and Amos*, 342.

[254] Cf. Pro. 3:19; 8:27, 28; Isa. 51:16.

both humanity and land remain under the sovereign control of God. In v. 6 the subject of בונה and יסד is Yahweh, which serves as a basis to praise Yahweh as the creator. The vault and the upper chambers in heavens are all ascribed as Yahweh's handiwork, while the sea waters move in the course of Yahweh's direction. All these descriptions reflect Amos' reuse of the creation tradition to ascribe to Yahweh as both the creator and controller of nature. It is within this context ארץ appears two times in v.6. First, ארץ appears while extolling Yahweh as the one who founded "יסד" his vault upon the earth, as such, ארץ is understood as the handiwork or creation of Yahweh. Second, ארץ appears while affirming Yahweh as the one who directs the course of water upon the earth, as such, ארץ remains under the direction and control of Yahweh. In other words, ארץ, the cosmic arena where Yahweh appears in majesty (v.5) is also the creation of Yahweh and it is sustained and controlled by Yahweh himself (v.6). Such hymnic description not only praises Yahweh's power over the cosmos but also conveys the inescapability from the coming judgment of Yahweh. Amos identifies this God as Yahweh, the covenant God of Israel.[255]

Amos now turns to the Exodus tradition to counter Israel's false belief (v.7). Here the history of Exodus is stated from the viewpoint of Land Giving traditions to each ethnic group by Yahweh as his gift to live (cf. Deut. 32:8-9). Presumably the setting of rhetorical questions (v.7) was occasioned by the disputes that arose due to Israel's belief that her election is a guarantee that swords, destructions, exiles mentioned in 9:1-4 would not overtake Israel (cf. 9:10).[256] Amos unmasks such false theological positions by turning back to the exodus tradition and other historical traditions of their region.[257] The question, "Are you not like the Cushites/Ethiopians to me, O people of Israel?" delegitimizes Israel's false belief that Yahweh's past intervention "conferred some kind of unique or favorite position for them."[258] The Cushites/Ethiopians lived in a remote distance in the then known world. By comparing Israel with Ethiopia, "Yahweh asserts that Israel is just as distant and strange to YHWH as Ethiopia is to Israel."[259] Moreover, just as Yahweh delivered Israel from Egypt so too Yahweh brings out the Philistines from Capthor (Crete) and Arameans (Syrians) from Kir. These two arch enemies of Israel also experienced exodus events stirred by Yahweh himself. The exodus from Egypt thus accords Israel no special status,[260] unless she remains faithfully in the covenant with Yahweh. Though Yahweh caused the Philistines' exodus from Capthor, it did not stop him from threatening to destroy the Philistines (1:6-8)

---

[255] John Joseph Owens, "Exegetical Studies in the Book of Amos," 440.

[256] Soggin, *The Prophet Amos*, 143.

[257] Mays, *Amos*, 157.

[258] Christopher J.H. Wright, *The Mission of God: Unlocking the Bible's Grand Narrative* (Downers Groove, Illinois: IVP, 2006), 97.

[259] Sweeney, *The Twelve Prophets*, 271.

[260] Paul, *Amos*, 283.

and though Yahweh delivered the Arameans from Kir, it did not prevent him from threatening to destroy the Damascus (1:3-5). Likewise, Yahweh's deliverance of Israel from Egypt would not avert or preclude his punishments against the Israelites (cf. 2:6-8).[261]

In v.5, ארץ refers to the entire earth. ארץ appears as an arena upon which Yahweh demonstrates his power. V. 6 mentions that the entire earth (ארץ) is the creation of Yahweh, who controls and sustains it. V.7 states that the cosmic earth (ארץ) is also the place upon which Yahweh placed Israel, just as he placed other nations like, the Ethiopians, Philistines, and Arameans. V.7 further states that the Exodus is not the reason for Israel's secured existence; instead Israel's survival in the land is determined by חטא. Yahweh watches upon any kingdom that is החטאה (sinful) and he sees Israel to be a sinful kingdom (בממלכה החטאה). Yahweh thus pronounces his verdict to destroy the kingdom of Israel. √שמד "to destroy" describes a "violent and complete destruction" that will annihilate Israel from the face of the earth (פני האדמה). The word earth takes a different term in v.8. Instead of ארץ as in vv.5-7, v.8 employs האדמה, which is closely connected with ממלכה (kingdom). Thus, האדמה refers to the land in a sense of political territory or nation. In other words, Israel as a political entity will be destroyed; however, the children of Israel shall not be totally eradicated.[262] This is expressed by the negative לא before the infinitive absolute השמיד "exterminate/destroy," which emphasizes "the negation of the intensification, not of the action itself."[263] Though the act of destruction will be there, the intensity of extermination will be subsided, which will make possible for some remnant of Israel to survive. In Amos' understanding, the relationship between Yahweh, Israel and land stands not exclusively on the past history of salvation (the exodus) as to their present faithfulness. Israel cannot claim a special relationship with Yahweh and continue to indulge in sinful acts. Israel's sins make herself equally on par with other nations and therefore she will be judged like any other nation (cf. Am. 3:2). In other words, in Amos' understanding, the breaking of the tripartite relationship is חטא "sin."[264] Because of Israel's sin, Yahweh intervened in judgment and destined their political land to destruction (v.8).

3.11. Land Promise & Giving Tradition (Amos 9:11-15)

The expressions "they may possess" (v.12), "they shall rebuild the ruined cities and inhabit them" (v.14) and "I will plant them upon their land" (v.15) in the salvation oracle in 9:11-15 are embedded in the land promise and giving tradition.

[261] Gray V. Smith, "Continuity and Discontinuity in Amos' Use of Tradition", *JETS* 34/1 (1991) 39-40.

[262] Paul, *Amos*, 25.

[263] Andersen and Freedman, *Amos*, 869.

[264] Mays, *Amos*, 159; Smith, "Continuity and Discontinuity in Amos' Use of Tradition", 39-40.

As Yahweh restores Israel "in that day" (v.11), he will even restore the land and its blessings back to Israel, which is expressed in terms of agricultural bounty (v.13) repossession of the land, rebuilding the cities and inhabiting the land. The tripartite relationship is thus explained by embedding the land promise and giving tradition in 9:11-15.

3.11.1. Translation on Amos 9:11-15

11 On that day[a] I will raise up the Succoth of David[b] that is fallen[c], [d]and repair its breaches, and raise up its ruins, and rebuild it[d] as in the days of old;

12 in order that they may possess[a] the remnant of Edom and all the nations upon whom my name is called[b], says Yahweh who does this[c].

13 Behold in the coming days[a], says Yahweh, when the one who plows shall overtake the one who reaps, and the treader of grapes the one who sows the seed; the mountains shall drip sweet wine, and all the hills shall flow with it.

14 I will restore the fortunes[a] of my people Israel, and they shall rebuild the ruined cities and inhabit them; they shall plant vineyards and drink their wine, and they shall make gardens and eat their fruit.

15 I will plant them upon their land, and they shall never again be plucked up out of the land that I have given them, says Yahweh your God.

3.11.2. Text Critical Comments on Amos 9:11-15

V11a: Cripps argues that ביום ההוא "on that day" does not provide any connection in the present unit and considers it to be a work of a later editor.[265] However, judging from the form critical analysis, ביום ההוא in the present case introduces the salvation oracle and does not necessarily indicate any editorial or redactor role[266] (cf. Isa. 11:10, 11; 12:1; 27:2; Zeph. 3:16).

V.11b: סכת דויד is generally interpreted as "booth" or "hut" of David. Harper, Wolff, and Cripps understood סכת as referring to the "dynasty" of David,[267] while Engnell, Hammerchaimb and Mays understood it as "kingdom or empire" of David.[268] H. Neil Richardson raised objection to such interpretations by arguing that סכת suggests the name of a city, Succoth.[269] He argues that during David's military expeditions, Jerusalem was a military base to protect his empire from the attack of the Philistines, Edomites, Moabites and Ammonites. However, to

---

[265] Cipps, *A Critical and Exegetical Commentary on the Book of Amos*, 270.

[266] Paul, *Amos*, 290.

[267] Harper, *Amos and Hosea*, 198-200; Wolff, *Joel and Amos*, 353; Cripps, *A Critical and Exegetical Commentary on the Book of Amos*, 270-271; BDB, 697.

[268] I. Engnell, *A Rigid Scrutiny* (Nashville: Vanderbilt University, 1969), 238; E. Hammerchaimb, *The Book of Amos: A Commentary* (Oxford: Blackwell, 1970), 140. Mays, *Amos*, 164.

[269] H. Neil Richardson, "*SKT* (Amos 9:11): "Booth" or "Succoth"?," *JBL* 92/3 (1973) 376.

expand the territory beyond Transjordan, David could not operate solely from Jerusalem. Thus, David established a second military base at Succoth, a strategic place for territorial expansion.[270] It was located at a major crossroads on the east side of the Jordan Valley, opposite to the Ephraimite heartland. Richardson thus concludes that "Succoth became a city associated with David's victories and the development of his empire and may be said to have been a "city of David" almost as much as Jerusalem was."[271] Richardson's proposal appears plausible, since the biblical tradition celebrates David's victories in close association with Succoth (cf. Ps. 60:5-9; 108:7-8). However, to render סכת as Succoth would have to read MT סֻכַּת as סֻכֹּת, while Succoth is regularly written as סכות. Richardson further explains that סכות is a *scriptio defectiva*, which was originally written as סכת as in Amos 9:11.[272] If Richardson's argument can be sustained, then reading סכת as city of Succoth would render better interpretation. See the following tradition and theological comments for further discussion.

V. 11c: The Qal active participle נפאת, can be translated in a perfect tense, "fallen". The "fallen" here refers to Succoth city, which is in a state of ruins due to the destruction by the Hazael's Syrian armies (2 Kgs 10:32–33).[273]

V.11d-d: The MT version contains three inconsistent suffixes, feminine plural, masculine singular and feminine singular that refer back to the phrase "Succoth of David". The LXX reads all these suffixes in the third feminine singular form (*τα πεπτωχοτα αυτης; τα ξατεσξαμμενα αυτης; ἀοιξοδμησω αυτην*), which have been followed by many scholars as more original reading.[274] Such reading along the LXX has been challenged by James D. Nogalski by arguing that it does not represent original text rather it is an attempt of the LXX to explain away the problematic suffixes.[275] In any case, the theme of Yahweh's act of restoration and rehabilitation of his people back to the land remain unchanged.

V. 12a: The LXX reads *εκζητησωσιν* perhaps erroneously reading the MT rendering of יירשו (they will posses) as ידרשו (they will seek). יירשו "the will posses" appears in the sense of subduing the surrounding nations.[276]

---

[270] Stuart, *Hosea-Jonah*, 398. David established it as a military headquarters to expand the territory of Transjordan to the east and south. Succoth was also politically a stable place as the inhabitants there were loyal to David's rule. Economically the provision of food, water and the repair and maintenance of weapons were close at hand at Succoth. It provides an important link road from Jerusalem and Shecehm to Syria. Cf. Richardson, "*SKT* (Amos 9:11)", 378-379.

[271] Richardson, "*SKT* (Amos 9:11)", 379.

[272] For a detail discussion on the city of Succoth, see Richardson, "*SKT* (Amos 9:11)", 376-378.

[273] Stuart, *Hosea-Jonah*, 398.

[274] See James D. Nogalski, "The Problematic Suffixes of Amos ix 11" *VT* 43/3 (1993) 412.

[275] For the detail discussion on the problem of three different suffixes, see Nogalski, "The Problematic Suffixes of Amos ix 11", 411-417.

[276] Cripps, *A Critical and Exegetical Commentary on the Book of Amos*, 273.

V.12b: The phrase נקרא שמי עליהם "my name is called upon them" refers to a legal act of ownership and possession.[277]

V.12c: עשה זאת "who does this" reassures Israel that Yahweh who announces the restoration will also act upon the promises he announces.

V.14a: Since the idea of restoration of the captives is associated with שבות, some suspect this passage to be a post-exilic addition.[278] However, following Rudolph[279], Paul argues that such expressions of restoration can be traced back to pre-exilic times as seen in the documents of the eighth century Aramaic inscription from Sefire (III 24-25): "אלהן שיבת ב [ית אבי] וכעת השבו ("But now, the gods have brought the return of the hou[se of my father…]."[280] In the present context, the term is used to convey the idea of restoration of the land and agricultural blessings, which was earlier cursed with ruins, blight and mildew (cf. 4:9), thus the meaning of "fortune" better suits the interpretation.

3.11.3. Form Critical Comments on Amos 9:11-15

9:11-15 is an oracle of restoration, which consists of two small subunits: vv.11-12 and vv.13-15. The first subunit begins with the introductory formula ביום "in that day" and concludes with the concluding formula נאם־יהוה "says Yahweh" (v.12). The formula of ביום "in that day" "signal the period of restoration for Israel that will occur after a refining judgment."[281] ביום in v.11 announces the future restorative act of Yahweh upon Israel.[282] Unlike the judgment oracles, which normally predicate punishment on covenant disobedience, the salvation oracle in v.11 predicates the blessings entirely on the favorable act of Yahweh[283] who will restore and rebuild the ruined city in the future. The earlier occurrences of למען "in order that" formula (cf. 2:16; 8:3, 9, 13) takes only the form of judgment oracle but למען in v.12 takes a form of salvation oracle assuring Israel of re-conquering back their former possession of the land. The concluding formula "says Yahweh who does this" further asserts the certainty of Yahweh's act and marks the end of a subunit within the larger pericope of vv.11-15.[284]

The second subunit begins with הנה ימים באים "behold in the coming days" (v.13) and ends with the concluding formula אמר יהוה אלהיך "says Yahweh your

---

[277] Cf. Deut. 28:10; 2 Sam. 12:28; Isa. 4:1; Jer. 7:10; 15:16. Paul, *Amos*, 292; Jeremias, *The Book of Amos*, 167.

[278] Cf. Sweeney, *The Twelve Prophets*, 274.

[279] Rudolph states that the expression is in any case a pre-exilic. Cited in Paul, *Amos*, 294.

[280] Paul, *Amos*, 294.

[281] Cf. Isa. 4:1,2; 10:20,27; 12:1,4; 25:9; 26:1; 28:5; Ezek. 29:21 Hos. 2:16 [MT 2:18]; Joel 3:18 [MT 4:18]; Mic. 4:6. See, Finley, "Amos", 322.

[282] Mays, *Amos*, 163; Stuart, *Hosea-Jonah*, 397.

[283] Stuart, *Hosea-Jonah,* 397.

[284] Claus Westermann, *Prophetic Oracles of Salvation in the Old Testament,* trans. by Keith Crim (Edinburgh: T&T Clark, 1987), 116-117.

God" (v.15). הנה ימים באים appears in 8:11 in a form of judgment speech that Israel will face famine of the word of the Lord but the same introductory formula in 9:13 takes a different form that speaks of the promises of restoring the blessings back to Israel and the land. As a result of restoration and resettlement in vv.11-12, there will have a plantation of vineyard and garden with bountiful agrarian produce (v.13), and the exiles will return back and reoccupy the land (vv.14-15). In short, the restoration oracle in 9:11-15 can be outlined as follows:

Announcement of Salvation:	On that day (v.11a)
Assurance:	I will raise up the Succoth of David that is fallen, and repair its breaches, and raise up its ruins, and rebuild it as in the days of old (v.11b).
Portrayal:	in order that they may possess the remnant of Edom and all the nations upon whom my name is called (v.12a).
Assurance:	says Yahweh who does this (v.12b).
Announcement:	Behold in the coming days, says Yahweh (13a).
Portrayal:	when the one who plows shall overtake the one who reaps, and the treader of grapes the one who sows the seed; the mountains shall drip sweet wine, and all the hills shall flow with it (13b).
Assurances:	I will restore the fortunes of my people Israel, and they shall rebuild the ruined cities and inhabit them; they shall plant vineyards and drink their wine, and they shall make gardens and eat their fruit. I will plant them upon their land and they shall never again be plucked up out of the land that I have given them (vv.14-15a).
Assurance:	says Yahweh your God (concluding formula) v.15b.

Since the entire unit talks about the restoration[285] and incorporates certain expressions that appear to be of post exilic thought,[286] some scholars think that Amos would not have written 9:11-15.[287] However, recent studies have shown several compelling reasons to consider the unity and authenticity of 9:11-15.[288] These include some verbal links: "פּיץ" which appears as "breaks in the wall", through which the women of Samaria would leave in 4:3, appears once again in 9:11 where Yahweh himself will do the work of repair; the overthrown cities in 4:11 will be rebuilt in 9:11; the houses in which no one lived in 5:11 will be lived in again in 9:14. All these point to connection between Amos' earlier oracles with 9:11-15. Moreover, the alleged expression such as, "as in the days of old" and "behold the days are coming" in vv.11, 13 do not necessarily indicate the work of redactors, as Amos employs the same formula in his earlier oracle of judgment (8:3, 9, 13 cf. 2:26; 3:14; 8:11).[289] Thus, we consider 9:11-15 to be authentic Amos' oracle of salvation.

3.11.4. Tradition and Theological Comments in the Light of Tripartite Relationship

The oracle of restoration in 9:11-15 is rooted in the land giving and promise tradition.[290] The phrase, "mountains shall drip sweet wine" (v.14) recalls the tradition of land promise in which the land is describes as flowing with "milk and honey."[291] Yahweh's promise, "I will plant them in the land" in v.15 recounts the promise of the land at the beginning of Israel's history (cf. Ps. 80:8).[292] In the land giving and promise tradition, the tripartite relationship is established based on Yahweh's promise to give Israel the land as inheritance. Land is seen as a focal point for the outworking of Yahweh's plan to restore and reverse the fortune of the Israelites. The Israelites were the people of landlessness; however, Yahweh's promise of land reversed their fortune by giving them a fertile land and with a

---

[285] Cripps argues that the salvation oracle in 9:11-15 is incongruous with Amos' earlier message of judgment. See, Cripps, *Amos*, 69-71.

[286] The phrase כימי עולם (as in the days of old) in v.11; הנה ימים באים (behold the days are coming) in v.13 are considered to be late.

[287] Harper, *A Critical and Exegetical Commentary on Amos and Hosea,* 195-96, Cripps, *A Critical and Exegetical Commentary on the Book of Amos,* 67-77; Mays, *Amos,* 165; Wolff, *Joel and Amos,* 113, 352, Robert B Coote, *Amos among the Prophets: Composition and Theology* (Philadelphia: Fortress Press, 1981), 120-126; Claus Westermann, *Prophetic Oracles of Salvation in the Old Testament,* trans. by Keith Crim (Edinburgh: T&T Clark, 1991), 102.

[288] See, Paul, *Amos*, 288-290; Stephen J. Bramer, "The Structure of Amos 9:7-15", *Bibliotheca Sacra* 156 (1999) 272-281.

[289] Bramer, "The Structure of Amos 9:7-15", 277.

[290] For the discussion on the origin of the promise of land, see Ruprecht, "Vorgegebene Tradition Und Theologische Gestaltung in Genesis 12:1-3", 186-188.

[291] Cf. Deut. 8:7-10.

[292] Westermann, *Prophetic Oracles in the Old Testament*, 117.

promise to make them a preeminent people among the surrounding nations.[293] In the land giving and promise tradition Israel remembered that they did not build the cities or houses neither plant the vineyards nor olive trees but all these were understood as given "נתן" gift to Israel.

Using this land giving and promised tradition, Amos states in v.15 that Israel will again be planted in "their (Israel's) land" (אדמתם), which is further explained as the land "I (Yahweh) give to them" (נתתי להם). This indicates that in Amos' understanding the restored land in the future is likewise understood as a given or gifted land (נתתי "I give").[294] In affirming the land as a "gift" from Yahweh, as Martens argues, Amos affirms that Israel through her occupation of the land, has her attention called to Yahweh.[295] By employing the land promise and giving tradition, Amos announces Yahweh's restorative act, which includes the reoccupation of the land, reconstruction of the ruined cities, cultivation of the farmland and vineyards with bountiful harvest (vv.11-15). All these are attributed to Yahweh's act by asserting that it is "Yahweh who does this".

"In that day" Yahweh will also "raise up" the "Succoth of David". The verb √קים "to raise up" is in hiphil form, which indicates a causative action of Yahweh. Succoth, as argued in the TCC on 9:11b, is the military headquarter from where David launched his policy of territorial expansion. Since the boundaries of land Yahweh promised Israel[296] was finally fulfilled in its entirety during David's rule, and since such territorial expansions were associated with Succoth, the reference to the restoration of David's Succoth could refer to the extent of political territory that Israel would reoccupy during the time of her restoration.

Israelites, who had been sentenced to swords, defeats, and alienation from the land due to their covenantal infidelity (vv.8-10) is now assured of restoration back to the land. Yahweh announces that he will "repair its breaches" (וגדרתי את פציהן) probably referring back to the "breached" (ופרצים) wall in 4:3, from where the Samarians were taken as captives. The expressions "I will raise its ruins" (והרסתיו אקים) and "I will rebuild it" (ובניתיה) recalls Israel's ruined or overthrown cities mentioned in 4:11. The earlier expressions, such as, the breached walls and the ruined cities (4:3, 11) appear in the context of exile and the fall of Israel kingdom as political nation. Therefore, Yahweh's restoration here, which recounts the

---

[293] Cf. Deut. 6:10-11; Num. 24:17-19.

[294] Martens explains how the land gift tradition underscores some theological points for the understanding of the land in Israel: i. as gift, Israel's merit of acquiring land is precluded; ii. Israel did not received the land by her strength to overpower or acquire the land, she possessed the land as gift from Yahweh (Num. 14:39-45); iii. as gift from Yahweh, Israel received the land as an inheritance, as such; no one can be alienated forcibly from the land that which is given by Yahweh. Martens, *God's Design*, 110-112.

[295] Martens, *God's Design*, 119.

[296] For the discussion on the description of the boundaries of promised land, see. Jeffrey L. Townsend, "Fulfillment of the Land Promise in the Old Testament", *Bibliotheca Sacra* (1985) 324-329.

destruction of Am 4:3, 11, probably refers to the resettlement and reoccupation of Israel in the land as in the days of old (כימי אולם). In this case, the idea of land as political territory is emphasized here in the message of Yahweh's restoration.

למען "in order that" (v.12) indicates the result of former action.[297] It connects Yahweh's act of restoration of the exiles to the reassertion of Israel's authority over the nations. In other words, as a result of Yahweh's restoration, Israel will again rise to preeminence among the nations that were formerly under Israel's suzerainty. The "remnant (rest) of Edom" (שארית אדום)[298], which Israel will posses implies that part of Edom was already in Israel's possession. Paul thus states that perhaps there is a political-historical allusion "to the regaining of part of Edom, the port of Elath, which was incorporated during the reign of Uzzaiah (2 Kgs 14:22; 2 Chr. 26:2) but was subsequently lost by Ahaz (2 Kgs 16:6)."[299] The remnant will yet again be possessed by the reemergent Israel.[300]

After restoring back to the land and reclaiming Israel's past territorial domain, Yahweh will also ensures the restoration of agricultural blessings (v.13). The harvest will be abundant that even before the reaper (קוצר) could complete the harvest, the plowmen (חורש) will draw near. The ploughing and reaping describe the two agricultural periods, which normally consists of about half a year.[301] In other words, the period of ingathering of crops will be extended due to the abundant harvest that even before the harvest[302] is completed the time of ploughing will begin.[303] Likewise, before the pressing of the grapes ends, the time of sowing will arrive.[304] Due to the enormous yielding of grapes, the mountains where the vineyards are usually cultivated, will drip with sweet wines (ההרין עסים והטיפו), a picture that recalls Yahweh's promise of land that flows with "milk and honey" (Ex. 3:17; 13:5). The announcement of restoration of blessings thus brings hope to the exploited poor peasants, who due to the poor harvest were

---

297 Paul, *Amos*, 291.

298 Gerhard Hasel points out that Amos employed the "remnant" theme in a threefold usage: (1) "... to refute the popular remnant expectation which claimed all of Israel as the remnant" (Amos 3:12; 4:1-3; 5:3; 6:9-10; 9:1-4, all of which were bleak descriptions of doom with little hope for Israel); (2) "... to show there will indeed be a remnant from Israel"([Amos 5:4-6, 15, an eschatological sense); and (3) "... to include also the 'remnant of Edom' among and with the neighboring nations as a recipient of the outstanding promise of the Davidic tradition" (Amos 9:12)." G. Hasel, *The Remnant* (Berrien Springs: Andrews University, 1972), 393-394.

299 Paul, *Amos*, 291.

300 Paul, *Amos*, 292.

301 Paul, *Amos*, 292.

302 In Palestinian region, harvest usually begins in April/May. See, Wolff, *Joel and Amos*, 354.

303 The time of ploughing begins only after the first autumnal rainfalls on October/November. See, Wolff, *Joel and Amos*, 354.

304 The grapes pressing season starts in August/September while the sowing of seeds commences in November/December. Paul, *Amos*, 293.

forced to borrow by mortgaging the land, which consequently led to the lost of their cultivable land to the money lenders. This is how Yahweh will restore the "fortune" of the people. The fortune "ושבתי שבות" appears frequently in the OT as "a formula for Yahweh's act of changing the circumstance of the life of the people and even an individual (Job 42:10)."[305] As mentioned in the above FCC, the earlier curse "you planted pleasant vineyards, but you shall not drink their wine" (5:11) will be reversed to "they will plant vineyards and drink their wine" (9:11); the gardens and vineyards that once laid waste due to blight, mildew and locusts (4:9) will be reversed to fruitful gardens and shall eat of its fruits (9:14); the overthrown cities (4:11) and the houses in which no one lived (5:11) will be rebuilt and will be lived in again (9:14). Yahweh's restoration in vv.13-14 thus includes Israel and her habitable and cultivable land.

V. 15 further announce the promise of Yahweh to reverse the fortune of Israel. Yahweh will "plant" (נטע), a metaphorical expression to refer to the resettlement of Israel after the captivity,[306] his people back to the land אדמה.[307] Israel, who was earlier destined to fall and not to rise again from the land (אדמה) in 5:2 will now be planted and shall never be plucked off from the land (אדמה). Yahweh asserts categorically that the land where he plants his people is "given" land (the land which I give them, אדמתם אשר נתתי להם). Land is thus asserted as a gift (נתן) of Yahweh to Israel.

Yahweh's plan of restoration and Israel's repossession of the land is the central theme of 9:11-15. In this unit, land is understood in three different meanings: First, land is understood as a territory for political dominance, in which the emphasis is stressed on Israel repossessing the entire land as in days of David. Second, land is understood as a place of habitation, in which the emphasis is put on the rebuilding, occupying and inhabiting the cities. Third, land is also understood as an agricultural and cultivable space in which the emphasis is placed on the fertility and bountiful crops of the land. The descriptions of land, Israel's relationship to the land, and Israel's survival in the land are expressed in the first person singular "I" of Yahweh indicating that the reestablishment of the tripartite relationship is purely based on Yahweh's kind initiative. In this salvation oracle, the restored tripartite relationship will drive Yahweh to favorably restore Israel back to the land and the land will also respond favorably to Israel's cultivation. Such restored tripartite relationship will usher Israel's secured existence in the land.

---

[305] Mays, *Amos*, 167.

[306] Cf. Is 40:21; Jer. 31:28; 32:41. See, Cripps, *A Critical & Exegetical Commentary on the Book of Amos*, 276.

[307] The term אדמה appears twice in v.15, which usually refers to the cultivable land. Perhaps the term is employed here to suit the agricultural picture of planting back the people.

3.12. Amos' Theology of Land

Based on the foregoing exegesis, Amos' understanding of land can be stated as follows:

1. *Meaning of the Term Land*

According to Amos, the term "land" conveys at least four different meanings: First, "land" refers to the entire earth in cosmological sense. Such references appear particularly in the doxological hymns (9:5-6; cf. 4:13 and 5:8f) that praise the majesty of God's creation while affirming Yahweh as the creator of the entire earth. The earth in its entirety is seen as Yahweh's creation. This implies that, as creator, the earth belongs to Yahweh and as owner he apportions separate territory to each political nation as a place of existence (9:7). As a giver of land, Yahweh holds the sovereign authority upon every nation of the earth. As such, all nations are held accountable before Yahweh and come under the jurisdiction of his judgment (1:3-2:16). As creator Yahweh is also portrayed as the controller of nature (4:6-9, 13; 5:8; 9:5-6) who directs the entire cycle of nature upon the earth. As such, cultivations and the success or failure of the produce of the land are attributed to Yahweh's favorable responses to the nature. In such understanding of land as the entire world, land is seen as the arena where Yahweh appears and demonstrates his power and authority. The earth is also understood as the place where humanity exists and survives as place of habitation.

Second, Amos understood land in the sense of territory for political nation such as (the land of) Israel, Judah, Philistines, Moab, Ammonites, Tyre, Egypt and so on, which appears mostly in the judgment oracles (for instance, 1:9-10; 11-12; 2:4-5; 2:6-11; 3:1; etc). In the understanding of Amos, as Yahweh delivered Israel from Egypt and placed them in Canaan, Yahweh also delivered other nations and placed them in their designated territories. This means, Amos sees each political nation as given land by Yahweh (9:7). Thus, Yahweh is portrayed as the one who exercises his authority over the nations and acts as ultimate observer of the affairs of the political history of every nation. As such, interpersonal relation between individuals in the society and political relations between the nations are judged by Yahweh (1:3-2:16). Yahweh is not only portrayed as the observer, he is also depicted as the controller of the destiny of every political nation as such, unfair and unjust acts in social and political relations propel Yahweh to pronounce judgment upon the people and the land. The judgment upon the people is mostly pronounced in the form of defeat, captivity and alienation from their political land and their conquered land would remain devastated. However, the political nation that suffers exile and the land that remained devastated will also be restored by Yahweh by bringing back the inhabitants and reoccupying the land in the coming days of restoration. Thus, in Amos' understanding, land as political nations presents a constant tension. As much as Yahweh forewarns the destruction of the land, Yahweh also announces the restoration and reconstruction of the land. Between the tension of destruction and reconstruction, land remains precarious to the whimsical relationship of Israel with her covenant God, Yahweh.

Third, Amos understood land in the sense of the agricultural and cultivable space that produces crops and sustains human lives on earth (4:6-9; 5:16-17. Cf. 9:11-13). As such, Amos sees the arable land as an important source of economic engagement upon which the life of humanity depends. Thus, attempt to transfer the cultivable land from the original owner is understood as a denial of survival means to others. This is considered as an act of violation "פשע" (2:6). Though humans' survival depends on the produce of the land; the yielding of the crops of the land in turn depends on Yahweh who controls the cycle of nature, such as, rain, fertility and climactic changes upon the earth (4:7-9; 5:8). For Amos, if Israel sins against Yahweh either in the form of going astray from God or in the form of causing injustice against fellow human beings, Yahweh is compelled to execute justice in the form of causing the drought, agricultural failures and thereby famine and plagues upon the inhabitants of the land (4:6-9). Amos thus shows that the response of the cultivable land to Israel's needs depends on the response of Israel to Yahweh, the God who controls the cycle of nature for the cultivation of the land. Though the cultivable land suffers barrenness, infertility and drought as a result of Israel's sin, Yahweh will also restore back the fertility and fecundity of the land. This appears in the restoration oracle (9:13) in which Yahweh announces bountiful crops harvest and favorable cultivations of vineyards and gardens.

Finally, land is also referred to as place of habitation or a living space. Such reference to land appears both in the judgment and restoration oracles. As a place of habitation, "land" remains devastated due to Israel's failure to return to Yahweh and for the failure to maintain justice in the society. The ruin of the cities (living space) for Israel is closely connected with the defeat in the battle, alienation from the land, and exiles to other nations. However, in the restoration oracle, Yahweh again promises to "raise up" and "rebuild" the ruined cities so as to enable his restored people to dwell and occupy the cities once again.

2. *Tripartite Relationship*

The above four levels of meaning show us that land appears to be in constant tension between the precarious judgment of destruction and the future announcement of restoration. The tension appears because of the uncertain and unstable relationship between Yahweh and Israel. Yahweh, Israel and land (tripartite relationship) are thus inseparably presented in Amos' understanding of land.

Amos expressed the relationship between Yahweh and Israel by making constant reference to land. In the oracle of judgment, when Yahweh pronounces judgment upon Israel for their infidelity, Yahweh mentions that the land will also be devastated, cities and houses will be ruined and cultivations of the land will be failed. This indicates that in Amos' understanding, the land also suffers consequences as and when Israel bears Yahweh's punishment (4:7, 9, 11; 5:27).

Likewise, when Israel will be restored in the future, the land will also be restored, cities and houses will be rebuilt, and cultivation of crops will be bountiful (9:11-15). This is how Amos explained and mediated the relationship between Yahweh and Israel through the prism of land. If Israel alienates herself from Yahweh, she finds herself forfeited of the gift and produce of the land and finally alienated herself from their land. Likewise, if Israel's relationship with Yahweh fails, Israel's relationship with the land also fails, which is expressed in terms of agricultural loss or exiles and alienation from the land. However, if Israel's relationship with Yahweh remains proper, Israel's relationship with land also remains stable. Thus, in the understanding of Amos, the tripartite relationship of Yahweh, Israel and land remains like a tripod stand. If relationship with the one fails the relationship with the other fails too.

3. *Traditions*

Such understanding of tripartite relationship is based on various historical and religious traditions of ancient Israel, which are discussed below. Amos skillfully interweaves various traditions to examine the tripartite relationship and to articulate his theological message for the prevailing issues related to land.

To show how an improper relationship between the nations provoked Yahweh's anger against the nations and how it leads to the loss of land, Amos employed the *Brotherhood and Kinship traditions*. The tradition of brotherhood is one of the bases of Amos' understanding of an independent existence of each political nation in its own territorial land. Since this tradition advocated the harmonious existence between the nations by promoting the economics of sharing and politics of solidarity, Amos sees the danger of acting contrary to this tradition. With the breakdown of the tradition of the brotherhood covenant, there was military attack against the other nation, loss of land and alienation of people from their homeland (1:10-11). Amos also employs the kinship tradition, which encourages tolerance between the nations (Edom and Israel/Judah), respect for territorial boundaries and reminded that the land of each political territory is the gift of God. However, such tradition of forbearance was violated as Edom perpetually attempted to destroy the land and annihilate the population of her uterine brother. The breach of both the brotherhood and kinship traditions also affects the tripartite relationship. In breaking the traditions, the victimized nation, against whom the traditions were not upheld, lost their land and their population were alienated from the homeland. On the other hand, the violators of the traditions also suffered the loss of their political territory as Yahweh intervenes in judgment and devours the guilty nations by fire. Moreover, the breaching of the traditions is an act of violation amounted to the completion of sin against Yahweh. This is stated to be the reason of Yahweh's judgment that would consequently lead to the devastation of their political land.

To explain that the disloyalty to Yahweh's command and occupation of the land are mutually exclusive, Amos utilizes the *Torah tradition*, which obligates Judah to live by its stipulations. Torah as an embodiment of the covenant between Yahweh and Israel, its stipulations are meant to govern the life style of the people in the land. The tradition of Torah affirmed that Israel/Judah lived in the land gifted by Yahweh and so in order for them to live continually in the given land, Israel/Judah were expected to live according to the stipulations codified in the Torah. As Judah failed to live by the Torah, Yahweh announces the destruction of their land (2:4-6). Thus, according to Amos, rejection of the statutes of Torah amounts to the rejection of Yahweh's commands that govern the life in the land. Amos sees such rejection to be the reason of breaking the relationship between Yahweh and Judah and consequently with the land. As Judah failed to live by the tradition of Torah, she went astray from Yahweh and she finally lost her strongholds, that is, her political land (2:4-5).

Amos also uses the interrelated *traditions of Exodus, Wilderness and Conquest* to stress the tripartite relationship. The Exodus tradition that remembers Israel's deliverance from Egyptian's slavery and the Wilderness tradition that recount the way Yahweh sustain his people while the conquest tradition that affirmed Yahweh's intervention on Israel's behalf and the giving of the land to Israel. By employing these traditions Amos affirms that Israel's occupation and survival in the land is the result of Yahweh's action, which also serves as rationale for Yahweh's demand for righteousness and loyalty from Israel. By using the Exodus tradition, Amos presents Yahweh as a liberator who delivers people of different ethnic origins and designate them a particular territory of land to live (9:7). This means, for Amos, first, Israel cannot claim special status because other nations also have their history of exodus. Second, whether other nations realize it or not, their exodus is authored by Yahweh and he place them into the land he designates. Thus, the land of each political nation is ultimately understood as a "given" land and that the ethnic groups are the occupants of a "given" land (9:7). Yahweh thus exercises the owner's prerogatives of expelling the people from the land and leaving the land vacant from its occupants (2:14-16; 4:11; 5:27). Amos employs the conquest tradition to remind Israel that she defeated the unconquerable Amorites solely because of Yahweh's act. It also warn Israel that just as Yahweh sent off the former inhabitants of the land of Canaan because of their sins, Yahweh would also sent off Israel from the land of Canaan for their sins. By embedding these traditions, Amos shows that Israel's settlement in the land is primarily Yahweh's achievement and that Israel owes an allegiance to Yahweh for his kind act.

While explaining the failure of agricultural land, loss of political land and exile in the coming days, Amos employed the *Covenant tradition*. Covenant tradition, whether between the nations or between Yahweh and his people, appears significantly in Amos' oracle. The crimes and atrocities committed between the nations without any regard for the covenant (1:9; 11) aroused Yahweh's anger to judge the nations in the form of the loss of the political land. Amos thus interprets the consequence of covenantal disloyalty in terms of the destruction of and alienation from the land. Yahweh demands that the covenant relationship among the nations should be honored at all cost. Despite the fact that Yahweh has given the land to Israel, the occupation of or settlement in a given land depends on the conditions of the covenant. Therefore, when Israel fails to fulfill the covenantal obligations Yahweh chastises Israel by withholding rain, causing corps damage and alienating the people from the land. In using the covenant tradition, Amos emphasizes that Israel's alienation from Yahweh consequently alienates Israel from her land as well. Thus, Amos shows that alienation from and survival in the land depends on the condition of the covenant. Israel's relationship with the land is inseparably connected with the covenantal loyalty to Yahweh. Israel only remained qualified to dwell in the land if she lives according to the qualities of life envisaged by the covenantal norms. In other words, Israel's relationship with the land either stands or falls based on her commitment to the covenant stipulations.

Amos emphasized the *theophany and creation traditions* to elucidate Yahweh's majestic power and sovereign authority over the entire earth. By using theophany tradition, Amos shows that the earth is an arena where Yahweh appears in majesty. The consequent responses of the nature to Yahweh's appearance such as, the quaver of the earth, the rise and sink of the river (9:5) confirms Yahweh's sovereign power over the entire earth. In the creation tradition, Amos presents the entire earth as Yahweh's creation (9:5-6; cf. 4:13; 5:8f) as such, land ultimately belongs to Yahweh as creator. As ultimate owner, Yahweh apportioned a land to each nation as a separate territory for existence (9:7). By employing the theophany and creation traditions, Amos shows Yahweh's power over nature and thereby his sovereign power and authority over the affairs of humanity on entire earth.

Though Amos sees the failure of agricultural land and the loss of political land due to the breach of the traditions, Amos also gives hope of future restoration. Such restorative message is based on the land promise and giving tradition. Just as Israel possessed the land of Canaan with vineyards and gardens which they did not cultivate and cities which they did not build, Amos sees the coming restorative act of Yahweh wherein Yahweh would bring back his people to repopulate and reoccupy the land with bountiful blessings of crops. In short, for Amos, the relationship between Israel *vis-a-vis* the land is always seen in relation with Yahweh.

Chapter 4

The Understanding of Land in the Book of Hosea

4.1. Hosea, the Prophet

Nothing much is known about Hosea, except his father's name Beeri (1:1; 2a), his unfaithful wife, Gomer, his three children (chs. 1-3) and his prophetic activity in the Northern kingdom. The place he lived in is not mentioned but frequent references to places in the north, such as, Samaria, Ephraim, Bethel, Gilgal and Shechem (6:10; 5:15; 8:5; 6:9) suggest that Hosea lived and prophesied in the northern kingdom.[1]

The book also does not provide any information on his profession. Ch. 3 provides some clues about his economic status. When Hosea had to pay the money for his wife (3:2), half of the price he paid in silver and the other half with a homer and a skin of wine (ch.3). Probably Hosea had insufficient money to pay the entire amount in cash so that he paid the remaining in kind namely in barley and wine. This suggests, according to Miller, that Hosea was probably a small farmer.[2] Miller also suggests that Hosea probably comes from a levitical priesthood lineage because of his in-depth understanding of Deuteronomy. Both Deuteronomy and Hosea see Israel as people related to Yahweh by a covenant (Deut. 5; Hos. 8:1-3; 12:14); both point to the Decalogue as the basic outline of what Yahweh requires of his covenanted people (Deut. 5:1-22; Hos. 4:1-3); both stress knowing Yahweh and not forgetting his laws (Deut. 4:9; 6:6-13; Hos. 4:6); both stress that to forsake Yahweh's covenant by breaking the law will have disastrous consequences (Deut. 28:15-68; 31:1-9; 33:10; Hos. 4:6; 8:12).

---

[1] John W. Miller, *Meet the Prophet: A Beginner's Guide to the Book of the Biblical Prophets* (New York: Paulist, 1987), 68.

[2] Miller, *Meet the Prophet*, 69.

Miller thus suggests that Hosea probably comes from the disestablished levitical priesthood.[3] However, such view is not widely held in the recent scholarship and even the late seventh century dating of Deuteronomy is dismissed in recent scholarship, the debate of which does not need to detain us here.[4] It would suffice to say here that Hosea probably had been a small time farmer as indicated by his linguistic affinities with the cultivation of land (2:6-13; 16-23; 14:4-7). He was also well aware of the Deuteronomic tradition and its covenant requirements for Israel to live as the people of God in the land.

Scholarly consensus is divided as to whether Hosea's marriage was literal or allegorical. Abraham Ibn Ezra, David Kimchi, Hengstenberg, Kiel and others consider Gomer as unfaithful Israel personified and Hosea's marriage is understood as pure allegory, parable, vision or dream.[5] However, since the name Gomer and Deblaim are personal names and not a sign-language, other scholars agree that Hosea literally married Gomer, who later proved to be unfaithful.[6] In any case, the important theological significance that the book of Hosea seeks to convey is that the marriage that is supposed to be characterized by loyalty is instead marred with unfaithfulness. It seeks to convey that Israel is supposed to remain faithful to her covenant God, Yahweh; however, Israel became unfaithful to her covenant God. Hosea's prophetic ministry seeks to address such issue of covenantal infidelity in the Northern kingdom, Israel.

4.2. Historical Context of Hosea

According to the superscription (1:1), the historical setting of Hosea's ministry is placed during the reigns of Uzziah (787-756), Jotham (756-741), Ahaz (741-725), and Hezekiah (725-697) in the South and Jeroboam ben Joash (786-746) in the North (Hos.1:1).[7] These kings reigned during the time of growing affluence and looming political uncertainty in the eighth century BCE. Since the Assyrian conquest of Samaria in 721 BCE is not mentioned, Hosea's ministry might have ended sometime before the fall of Samaria. The political, socio-economic and religious conditions of Israel during the period of the above mentioned kings are as follows:

---

[3] Miller, *Meet the Prophet*, 70-71.

[4] For our present purpose here, it would suffice to mention here that the view that Deuteronomy was written by disestablished northern Levites is not widely held by the scholars. See, Gordon McConville, *Deuteronomy,* Leicester Apollos; Downer's Grove, IVP, 2002. Even the view that Deuteronomy comes late after the seventh century has been convincingly refuted recently. See Gordon Wenham, "The Date of Deuteronomy: Linch-pin of Old Testament Criticism", *Themelios* 10/3 (1985) 15-20.

[5] C.L. Seow, 'The Book of Hosea,' in David Noel Freedman and others (eds), *The Anchor Bible Dictionary,* vol. 3, (New York: Doubleday, 1992), 292, also see, 291-297.

[6] James Luther Mays, *Hosea: A Commentary*, OTL (Philadelphia: Westminster, 1969), 23.

[7] Hans Walter Wolff, *Hosea*, trans. by Gray Stenser (Philadelphia: Fortress Press, 1974), 4-6.

4.2.1. Political Context

Hosea's ministry began in the reign of Jeroboam II (786-746) who brought enormous prosperity and enlarged Israel's boundary from Hamath to the sea of the Arabah (2 Kgs 14:25, 28). However, after Jeroboam II's death, Israel's political situation sank into chaos with constant bloodshed, revolts and assassinations in the palace. Jeroboam's son and successor, Zechariah reigned for only six months and was assassinated by Shallum, who took over the throne but Shallum could reign for only one month as he was also assassinated by his military commander, Menahem (748-736 BCE). After Menahem took over the throne, he immediately submitted himself to Tiglath-Pileser III of Assyria and agreed to pay one hundred talents of silver and became Assyria's vassal (2 Kgs 15:19-20).[8] Pekahiah succeeded his father Menahem but he could rule for only two years before he was assassinated by his commander, Pekah who seized the throne (738-737) and formed an anti-Assyrian alliance with Syria, known as the Syro-Ephraimite coalition.

In 733 BCE Tiglath-Pileser III, also known as Pul, rose against the Syro-Ephraimite coalition and ravaged the land of Israel, deported much of its population, annexed most of Israel's territory, and considerably reduced the kingdom of Israel. Only the capital Samaria and the hill country of Ephraim remained under king Pekah of Israel.[9] Hoshea ben Elah overthrew Pekah by assassinating him and took over the throne of Israel with Assyria's approval. He surrendered, paid huge tribute and became a vassal king of Assyria (Hos. 5:13; 8:9f). After Tiglath Pileser III was succeeded by Shalmaneser V (ca. 727-722), Hoshea withheld tribute to Assyria and sought Egypt's help to overthrow Assyria's yoke. This was a political misadventure of Israel with disastrous consequences that finally led to the capture of king Hoshea (Hos. 13:10-11). Though Shalmeneser V died soon, his successor Sargon II completed the conquest of Samaria and deported the entire population to Assyria in 722 BCE.[10] Israel's political situation was thus marred with bloodshed, assassinations, political coups and the looming invasion from the neighboring nation to put Israel's independent political existence as a nation to an end.

4.2.2. Socioeconomic Context

The above political context shows that after the reign of Jeroboam II, the Israelite society was enmeshed with revolts and bloodshed, which caused social unrest and miseries upon the people. As stated above, both the Israelites' population and her territory had been reduced significantly by the time of Pekah. This probably weakened the Israelites' economic and military strength considerably. However, despite the declining socioeconomic conditions, it was probably not at its lowest

[8] Thomas O. Hall, "Introduction to Hosea", *Review & Expositor* 54/4 (1957) 507.

[9] Mays, *Hosea*, 4.

[10] Bruce Birch, *Hosea, Joel and Amos*, Westminster Bible Companion (Louisville, Kentucky: Westminister John Knox Press, 1997), 10.

ebb since Israel continued to pursue her self-serving agenda. For instance, Hosea indicts Israel's for building "palaces" in 8:14, which indicates a palatial structure that stood as a symbol of prosperity in Hosea's time. If, as Premnath argues, the term "treaty" in 12:1 is understood in the context of procuring military tools, then Israel was probably in a good economic position to upgrade her military strength. On the other hand, if "oil" refers to the tribute paid to the foreign nation in 12:1, then we can see the overtone of exploitation in the society as "carrying oil" could mean extracting agricultural surplus from the peasants in order to bear the brunt of royal expensive undertakings through a system of taxation.[11] Premnath further demonstrates the socioeconomic situation of Hosea's time by stating that the phrase, "You have loved a prostitute's pay on all threshing floors" (9:1), can be understood in the harvest context as referring to the share of agricultural produce taken away as rent in kind by the rich money lenders.[12] Corruption also appears to be rampant in the market places as Hosea states, "A trader, in whose hands are false balances, he loves to oppress" (12:7 [RSV]). In other words, Hosea's indictments include the elite's prosperity which is rooted in oppression of the peasants in their cultivable land and their market places. These instances show that Israel society was on decline and the prophet Hosea forewarns that Israel would be soon defeated, devastated and deported to other nation as a judgment from Yahweh.

4.2.3. Religious Context

Hosea mentions different forms of religious expressions prevalent in Israel: divination (3:4; 4:12), hilltop shrines under trees (4:13), temple prostitution (4:14), worship of calves and making of molten image (8:5-6; 13:2) and multiplication of altars (3:4; 10:1).[13] These references point to a widespread syncretistic form of worship in Israel, which was probably accentuated by the fusion of Yahwism and Baalism. Such syncretistic form of religion was demonstrated by the archeological findings as John Bright states, "It is significant that the Samaria Ostraca yield almost as many names compounded with "Ba'al" as with "Yahweh."[14] Hosea indicts Israel of these forms of syncretistic worship, which is considered as improper with the covenant form of worship. Such worship is understood to be an act of unfaithfulness to her covenant God, Yahweh just like Gomer acted unfaithfully with her husband, Hosea (chs 1-3).

Reference to Baal is mentioned several times (2:8, 13, 17; 11:2; 13:1) and once the Baal of Peor in 9:10 (cf. Num. 25). Baal ("lord or owner") is the title

---

[11] D.N. Premnath, "Amos and Hosea: Sociohistorical Background and Prophetic Critique", *Word & World* 28/2 (2008) 129.

[12] Premnath, "Amos and Hosea", 130.

[13] Graham I. Davies, *Hosea*, (Sheffield: JSOT, 1993), 41.

[14] John Bright, *A History of Israel*, 4th edn. ((Louisville, Kentucky: Westminister John Knox Press, 2000), 260.

associated with the Canaanite male deity, whose response to land is considered to be the main reason for successful cultivations. For the Canaanites, the cultivation of land and the worship of Baal were inseparable. As the Israelites learned cultivation from the Canaanites, probably the Israelites were influenced by the Canaanite lore of the land and started to worship Baal. On different occasions Hosea mentions how Israel worshipped or gave credit to Baal for the agricultural productivity (2:5; 4:12; 13; 7:14; 9:12). Various rites and ceremonies of Baal religion were observed to ensure the good will of the fertility deities, Baal. One of the practices includes sexual participation with the cult prostitutes. The Baal religion teaches that fertility of the land is dependent upon Baal's sexual relations with his consorts. It was believed that the worshippers can, by engaging into sexual act with cultic prostitutes, arouse the desire of the fertility gods to have sex and thereby the productivity of the land could be ensured.[15] The religious issue Hosea addresses is that of syncretism. Israel while worshipping Yahweh has also turned to the other form of pagan worship. Hosea sees such syncretism to be a betrayal of Israel's exclusive loyalty to Yahweh within the covenant relationship.

Amidst the above mentioned socio-economic corruption and religio-political apostasy, Hosea announces that because of Israel's covenantal infidelity manifested through various socioeconomic and religiopolitical offences, Yahweh would intervene in judgment. The result, Israel would be handed over to defeat and exile and would lose both the produce of the land and her land as political territory. Such tripartite relationship is expressed in Hosea's understanding of land. The following exegeses consider some relevant texts to expose the tripartite relationship of land theology in Hosea.

4.3. Covenant and Creation Traditions (Hosea 2:2-13 [MT 2:4-15])

The metaphorical expression, "she is not my wife and I am not her husband" (v.2) speaks of the broken covenant relationship indicating that there is an underlying Covenant Tradition behind 2:2-13. In response to Israel's (wife) unfaithfulness, Yahweh threatens to take back the gifts of land: "*my* grain," "*my* new wine," "*my* wool," and "*my* flax", which stress Yahweh's control over nature. This indicates that the Creation Tradition is used in sentencing Israel for covenant violation. By employing the Covenant Tradition, the strained relationship between Yahweh and Israel is explained and by employing the Creation Tradition Yahweh's control over nature and his withdrawal of the gifts of the land is explained indicating that the tripartite relationship in 2:2-13 is explicated by employing the Covenant and Creation Traditions.

[15] Stephen Winward, *A Guide to the Prophets* (London: Hodder & Stoughton, 1968), 50.

4.3.1. Translation on Hosea 2:2-13

2 [a] Contend with your mother[a], contend for she is not my wife, and I am not her husband[b]. Let her put away her [c]promiscuity from her face, and her adultery from between her breasts[c],

3 least I will strip her naked and expose her as in the day she was born, and will set her as in the desert[a], and will set her as in the parched land[b], and kill her with thirst[c].

4 Upon her children also I will have no pity, because they are children of whoredom.

5 For their mother was promiscuous; she who conceived them has acted shamefully. For she said, "I will go after my lovers[a] who provide me [b]my bread and my water, my wool and my flax, my oil and my drink[b]."

6 Therefore behold[a] I will hedge up[b] your way with thorns; and I will build a wall against her, so that she cannot find her paths.

7 She shall pursue[a] her lovers, but not overtake them; and she shall seek[b] them, but shall not find them. Then she shall say, "I will go and return[c] to my first husband, for it was better with me then than now".

8 She did not know that it was I who gave her the grain, the wine, and the oil, and who lavished upon her silver and gold that they made into Baal.

9 Therefore I will take back my grain in its time, and my wine in its season; and I will take away my wool and my flax, which were to cover her nakedness.

10 Now I will uncover her shame in the sight of her lovers, and no one shall rescue her out of my hand.

11 I will put an end to all her merry making, her festivals[a], her new moons, her Sabbaths, and all her appointed festivals.

12 I will lay waste her vines and her fig trees, of which she said, "These are my pay, which my lovers have given me". I will make them a forest, and the wild animals shall devour them.

13 I will punish her for the festival days of the Baals, when she offered incense to them and decked herself with her ring and jewelry, and went after her lovers, and forgot me, says Yahweh.

4.3.2. Text Critical Comments on Hosea 2:2-13

V.2a-a: LXX renders *κριθητε* and Aquila and Symmachus read *δικασασθε*, which basically mean "judge." The MT version ריב refers to pleading, contending, raising complaints or attacking with protests, which calls the accused for an account from the plaintiff in the court (cf. Gen. 31:36; Judg. 6:32; Jer. 25:31).[16] The same term appears in 4:1 in the context of Yahweh's controversy with the inhabitants of the land. In 2:2, the verb ריב is followed by the preposition ב, which denotes a striving

[16] Derek Kidner, *The Message of Hosea,* BST (Leicester, England/Downers Grove, Illinois: IVP, 1981), 27; James Luther Mays, *Hosea: A Commentary* (Philadelphia: Westminster John Knox Press, 1969), 37.

with words or remonstration.[17] Since the following clause states the accusation, "for she is not my wife and I am not her husband", ריב can be understood as applying to the legal connotation in the court context. This remonstration is sometimes interpreted as a declaration of divorce,[18] however Mays and Stuart have pointed out that there is no corroborating evidence in the Israelite law to consider this expression as a legal divorce formula.[19] The purpose of this accusation is to reclaim the wife as indicated by the following jussive form "let her" (ותסר) which expresses purpose or wish that the wife would mend her ways. The goal of accusation is thus for restoration of relationship rather than retribution.

V.2b: the negatives לא אשתי (not my wife) and אישה לא (not her husband) appear parallel to the second and third child with negative names (לא־רחמה "no compassion" and לא אמי "not my people" cf. 1:6, 9). Since the text seeks to make an analogy between Hosea's relationship to Gomer and Yahweh's relationship to Israel, the doubly negative couplet in 2:2 should be seen in relation to 1:9. As there is no provision stated in the covenant for dissolution of it rather only the punishments are enlisted to enforce the covenant, the negative couplets in 1:9 and 2:2 cannot be interpreted as the formal announcement of the dissolution of the covenant (divorce),[20] but a "dissolving of the close relationship between Yahweh and the people"[21] temporarily in view of the situation.

V.2c-c: Wolff states that the terms זנונים and נאפופים are the objects placed at the face or breast probably headbands, belts, rings, necklaces or similar jewelry used by the participants of Canaanite sex cult or these terms could also refer to the scratches on the breasts resulting from ecstatic frenzy.[22] Sweeney states that "her harlotries" and "her adulteries" refer to some jewelry that signifies the harlotry status. Such explanation would suggest Gomer's role as cultic prostitute. However, Gale A. Yee opines that rendering זנונים as "whore or prostitute" is misleading by arguing that although the prostitutes were marginalized; the practice of prostitution was tolerated in Israelite society, while adultery and promiscuity

---

[17] Macintosh, *Hosea*, 39.

[18] Cf. R. de Vaux, *Ancient Israel*, 35. Cited in Mays, *Hosea*, 37.

[19] Mays, *Hosea*, 37; Stuart, *Hosea-Jonah*, 47.

[20] Francis I. Andersen and David Noel Freedman, *Hosea*, AB 24 (New York: Doubleday, 1980), 221. The terms used in Hosea, such as, "not my wife", "not her husband", "not my people" and "not loved" reflect the language of rejection. Melanchton opines that in the Hebrew Bible rejection motif is prominent, which constitutes of "dissolving of the close relationship between Yahweh and the people". However, she understood rejection to be temporal in view of the prevailing situation since Israel's election is not finally abolished. See, Monica J. Melanchton, *Rejection by God: The History and Significance of the Rejection Motif in the Hebrew Bible,* SBL 22 (New York: Peter Lang, 2001), 79.

[21] Monica J. Melanchton, *Rejection by God: The History and Significance of the Rejection Motif in the Hebrew Bible,* SBL 22 (New York: Peter Lang, 2001), 79.

[22] Wolff, *Hosea*, 33-34.

would never be.[23] Yee's argument can be sustained since such rendering of the term expresses the gravity of Israel's infidelity against Yahweh. Thus, we interpret the expression "זנוניה מפניה ונאפופיה מבין שדיה" as "promiscuity from her face, and her adultery from between her breasts".

V.3a: כמדבר literally "like in the wilderness". Two possible interpretations underlie here. First, it could refer to the husband's (Yahweh's) threat that the consequences of infidelity will make her life (land) כמדבר "like in the desert", indicating that the arable land, which Israel inhabits, will loose its fertility as in a desert. Second, it could refer to putting the wife (Israel) back to the condition of her excruciating desert experience during the Exodus journey. Since the desert experience is understood as the stage of discipline on Israel's way to the Promised Land and since the husband's (Yahweh) accusation is not for divorce but to woo the wife (Israel) back, the second interpretation fits more in the context. It is thus interpreted as "as in the desert."[24]

V.3b: כארץ ציה (as the parched land) does not appear in the Pentateuch but in the poetic tradition of the Psalms and the prophets, the term ציה appears fifteen times while the phrase ארץ ציה nine times. In these occurrences Israel's memory of the desert experience and Yahweh's definitive dealing with them is evoked.[25] The phrase כארץ ציה "as the parched land" appears in the context of announcing the judgment; as such it could refer to reverting Israel back to desert stage, that is, to send out Israel from the Promised Land (alienation).[26] ארץ in this sense refers to the political territory of Israel.

V.3c: "kill her with thirst" is exactly the same expression that appears in the complaints of the Israelites' wilderness journey (cf. Ex. 17:3; 32:12) in which Israel protests against Yahweh for bringing them up from Egypt to kill them "with thirst". Andersen and Freedman state that the threat to kill with thirst applies to people and not to the land.[27] Zvi, however, rejects such proposal since killing the wife by thirst is not a mode of execution of "wayward" wife in any of ANE culture.[28] If Zvi's proposal could be sustained then the pronoun "her" could refer to the land and "thirst" probably refers to the drought. In this case, "wife" metaphorically represents here the land unlike in v.2 where wife represents Israel. The wife is thus used interchangeably in vv.2-3 (see also the following discussion on Tradition and Theological comments).

V.4a: The phrase upon her children I will have "no pity or compassion" (בניה לא ארחם) reflects God's rejection of Israel. The rejection motif is already

[23] Gale A. Yee, "She is not my Wife and I am Not her Husband": A Materialist Analysis of Hosea 1-2", *Biblical Interpretation* 9/4 (2001) 371.

[24] Andersen and Freedman, *Hosea*, 226.

[25] Andersen and Freedman, *Hosea*, 226.

[26] Andersen and Freedman, *Hosea*, 226.

[27] Andersen and Freedman, *Hosea*, 226.

[28] Zvi, *Hosea*, 68.

communicated by Yahweh when he calls Israel "not pitied" and "not my people" in 1:6, 9.

V.5a: The plural form אהבי "my lovers" indicates a plurality of adulterous relationships. Two possible meanings of "lovers" can be observed here. First, traditionally, "lovers" is understood as referring to "the Baals" (vv. 8, 13).[29] Baal worship and idolatry aroused in Israel as Israel sought to correctly understand the Canaanites' concept of land and agriculture. It was a historical reality among the surrounding nations of Israel to know the lore of the land and worship the god of the conquered land to live a secured life (cf. 2 Kgs 17:26).[30] Likewise, Israel was also probably tempted to understand the lore of the land of Canaan, which may have induced her to Baal worship. Second, a recent study by Gale A. Yee has shown that "the lovers" (v.5, 7, 10) can also be referred to "the nations" as Hosea identifies the "lovers" as "nations" in 8:9-10 with whom Ephraim wrongly allied herself with.[31] See the following discussion on Tradition and Theological comments.

V.5b-b: "bread... water...wool... flax... oil... drink" are the basic commodities of life. Water and bread, the basic necessities of daily diet are associated with Baalism. Baal is understood as the storm deity who provides rain and thereby ensures fertility and the growth of new crops and his father "Dagad" as the god of grain. Baal and Dagad are thus worshipped as a means to obtain water and bread. However, the fallacy of such worship will be proved when Yahweh kills her (the land) with thirst (drought, cf.v.3).[32] Wool is used for warm clothing (Job 31:20) and flax for cool clothing (Ezek. 44:17f), both of which are used by the Israelite women (Prov. 31:13) as main fabrics for garments in Israel. On the other hand, oil was commonly used for anointing, for cultic rituals ad cooking as well.[33] All these items are necessary to sustain life, which Israel (wife) thought is provided by her lovers (Baals).

V.6a: לכן "therefore" appears four times in Hosea (2:6; 9, 14 [Heb 2:8, 11, 16]; 13:3) to introduce a formal declaration of the divine intention while הנני "behold" coupled with a participle announces a threat. By employing "therefore/behold" Hosea let his audience anticipate what was coming: God's response to Israel's sin.[34] Yahweh's intention introduced by "therefore" in v.6

---

[29] Most scholars identify the lovers with "Baal". Cf. Mays, *Hosea*, 39; Sherwood, *The Prostitute and the Prophet*, 215-235; Gunenther, *Hosea-Amos*, 60-63; Derek Kidner, *The Message of Hosea*, BST (Leicester, England: IVP, 1981), 29; Macintosh, *Hosea*, 48; Mays, *Hosea*, 49; Willis, "I am your God", 296.

[30] Macintosh, *Hosea*, 49.

[31] Yee, "She is not my Wife and I am not Her Husband", 376.

[32] Andersen and Freedman, *Hosea*, 323.

[33] Macintosh, *Hosea*, 48; Mays, *Hosea*, 48.

[34] Stuart, *Hosea-Jonah*, 49.

follows the expressed intention of the mother in v.5.[35] לכן in v.6 is first of the three announcements of husband about the measure he intends to take against his erring wife. The following clause הנני שׂך (v.6) states the husband's intention to preserve the marriage and to bring an end to the wife's adultery.

V.6b: "hedge" refers to a barrier of thorns or a fence of stones that are put up around the field to keep the animal in or out, which according to Andersen and Freedman analogously refers to Yahweh's act to "prevent his apostate people from making their usual pilgrimages to the Baal shrines."[36] However, such literal understanding of preventing the way to Baal's shrine does not seem to be the intention of Yahweh since according to vv.7, 9-12, Yahweh's intention is to demonstrate the futile result of Israel's Baal worship for agricultural prosperity.

V.7a: ורדפה, from √רדף "to pursue", is a Piel intensive verb, which demonstrates Gomer's passionate and determined action of pursuing her lovers.

V.7b: ובקשׁתם "and seek them" appears frequently in connection with attendance to religious cults to gain the divine favor."[37] ובקשׁתם appears here in connection with seeking Baal.

V.7c: the phrase "I will go and return" indicates the idea of repentance, since ואשׁובה "I will return" means "to enter once again into the original relation."[38] This expression appears in contrasts with the earlier statement "I will go after my lovers" in v. 5.

V.11a: חג "festival" is a collective noun, which probably refers to the three annual pilgrimage festivals: Passover, Weeks, and Booth (cf. Ex. 23:14; Num. 22:28, 32f).

4.3.3. Form Critical Comments on Hosea 2:2-13

The form of 2:2–13 is that of the lawsuit as indicated by ריב "to contend" and the particle כי "for/that" in v.2 which specifies the act of wrong doings. The entire speech in this unit is drawn from the legal setting for which reason the accused wife is addressed in the third person singular except in v. 8 where the third person plural עשׂו "they made" occurs.[39] The husband is presented as Yahweh, Israel's first husband (v.9) and Israel as Yahweh's wife. Yahweh (the husband) accuses Israel (the wife) of adultery (Israel's apostasy, cf. vv. 5, 7, 10, 12). Despite warnings from the accuser (Yahweh), the defendant (Israel) remained adamant in her adulterous way. Thus, Yahweh the prosecuting attorney and judge pronounce judgment to withhold all the produces of the land from Israel.

---

35 Macintosh, *Hosea*, 50.

36 Andersen and Freedman, *Hosea*, 326-237.

37 Andersen and Freedman, *Hosea*, 239.

38 Mays, *Hosea*, 40.

39 Hans Walter Wolff, *A Commentary on the Book of Hosea* (Philadelphia: Fortress Press, 1974), 32.

In a normal court setting of Israel, the elders of the city assume the role of judge (Deut. 22:15) while the "men of the city" act as the executors of punishment (Deut. 22:21). However, in 2:2-13, Yahweh changes his roles as plaintiff, judge, arbitrator, and executor of punishment. Despite Yahweh's changing roles, the unit maintains the same legal overtones throughout. Thus, the passage can be considered as a unit bound together by the legal setting of the court. Since the salvation oracle begins in1:10 and ends in 2:1 and since a new unit of restoration begins at 2:14 with direct address, "therefore I will allure her", 2:2-13 is clearly demarcated as a separate unit, which can be outlined as follows:

Accusation:	Contend with your mother... she is not my wife and I am not her husband (v.2a)
Admonition:	Let her put away her... promiscuity... adultery (v.2b)
Threat of punishment:	I will strip her naked and expose her... set her in the desert ... ... kill her with thirst... (vv.3-4).
Further accusations:	For their mother was promiscuous... acted shamefully. For she said I will go after my lovers... (v. 5).
Announcement of judgment:	Therefore (v.6a)
Description of judgment:	I will hedge up your way with thorns; and I will build a wall against her, so that she cannot find her paths. (v.6b-7).
Further accusations:	She did not know that it was I who gave her the grain, the wine, and the oil, and who lavished upon her silver and gold that they made into Baal (v.8).
Announcement of judgment: Description of judgment:	Therefore (v.9a) I will take back my grain... My wine ...wool and my flax... I will uncover her shame... no one shall rescue her out of my hand. I will put an end to all her merry making, her festivals, her new moons, her Sabbaths, and all her appointed festivals (vv.9b-11).

In using the lawsuit of marriage metaphor, Hosea portrays Yahweh as the prosecutor and the judge, who undertakes a legal action against Israel for her covenantal infidelity, cf. vv. 8, 13. Yahweh is not only portrayed as Israel's first husband but also as the only provider of the gift of the land. Israel's unfaithfulness is portrayed as an intentional disloyalty to the covenantal stipulations, which is described as the reason of breaking the tripartite relationship as Yahweh's invocation of judgment affects the relationship not only between Yahweh and Israel but also with the land (see the discussion on Tradition and Theological Comments in the following).

Precise historical setting is difficult to determine, however, prophetic utterances within 2:4-13 indicate some possible historical settings. Since the lavish use of wine, oil, silver, and gold (vv.5 and 8) indicate a prosperous economic situation and also a growing fertility cult in vv. 11, 13, the setting seems to point to the untroubled times. Probably the oracle could be dated during the early part of Hosea's ministry or during the last part of Jeroboam II's reign of national prosperity ca. 750 BCE, when the Assyrian military assault still lay in the future.[40]

4.3.4. Traditions and Theological Comments on the Tripartite Relationship

The unit of 2:2-13 is generally identified as the Yahweh-Israel marriage metaphor. The broken relationship between Hosea and Gomer is understood as referring to the broken relationship of the covenant between Yahweh and Israel. Cook has demonstrated recently that the present unit is rooted in the Sinai Covenant Tradition.[41] The covenant nuances are made clear in 1:9 where the birth of the son לא עמי (not my people) is announced to state the broken covenant between Yahweh and Israel. A few other expressions, which show covenant overtones, include: "she is not my wife" (v.2), which expresses the disintegration of marriage, symbolizing the breaking of the covenant. Moreover, the threat "to strip naked" in v.3 expresses a common metaphor of punishment for breaking a treaty or covenant in the ANE.[42] This suggests that the underlying tradition here is the covenant tradition. Hosea's point of emphasis in using this marriage metaphor is to underscore the exclusive relationship Israel had with Yahweh that was forged at Sinai (cf. 9:10; 12: 9[10]; 13:4-5).[43] (For the discussion on how the tripartite relationship was established in the Sinai covenant, see the Tradition and Theological Comments on Amos 4:6-13). In describing the judgment for covenant violation, Hosea employs the Creation Tradition to assert Yahweh's control over nature. This is explained by the repeated use of first person singular construct "my" (6 times) indicating that all the gifts of land belong to Yahweh as creator. As such, Yahweh pronounces the judgment of alienation from the land (v.3a), turning the cultivable land into a dry parched land (v.3b), withholding the fecundity of the land (v.9), and destruction of the produce of the land (v.12). Covenant unfaithfulness is thus seen to be the reason for affecting the tripartite relationship within the covenant and creation traditions.

Since our focus is on what transpires from the text concerning the relationship between Yahweh, Israel and land, we need not discuss the contentious issue of whether the marriage is literal or allegorical. Based on the textual-metaphorical expressions, as stated in the TCC on v.3c, it appears clear that the "husband"

---

[40] Stephen L. Cook, *The Social Roots of Biblical Yahwism* (Atlanta: SBL, 2004), 87.

[41] Cook, *The Social Roots of Biblical Yahwism,* 87-88.

[42] Mays, *Hosea*, 38.

[43] Yee, "She is not My Wife and I am not Her Husband", 379.

(vv. 2, 7) represents "Yahweh" and the "wife" represents both "Israel" and "land". As mentioned in the above FCC, Hosea employs here the court language and metaphorically portrays Israel's covenant disloyalty through the picture of Gomer's infidelity. Hosea accuses his wife of promiscuity and admonished her to mend her ways least she be punished (v.2). Gomer's paramour is identified as "lovers" (v.5, 7). As mentioned in the TCC on v.5a, "lovers" can have two possible interpretations. First, traditionally, "lovers" is understood as referring to "the Baals" (vv. 8, 13). Second, "lovers" can also be referred to "the nations" as Hosea identifies the "lovers" as "nations" in 8:9-10 with whom Ephraim allied herself.[44] If these two possible meanings could be taken into consideration, then the land issue becomes more prominent. First, the peasants were in a condition to pay enormous rent/taxes to the ruling class in the form of crops while the ruling class had also intensified the cultivation to maximize the agribusiness. In such a context of agricultural intensification, to meet the demand of taxation and commerce, the Baal religion that focused on the fertility of the land appealed to both the peasants and the ruling class who craved for bountiful harvests. Second, Israel relied on the allies of foreign "nations" to protect herself from the possible attack of the surrounding nations by the end of Jeroboam II's reign. Israel sought political alliances with other nations who in turn demanded heavy tribute as protection money from Israel. During such trivial time, the monarchy imposed an economic burden upon the peasants' class by forcing them to escalate the production of wine, oil and grain so as to appease the aggression of these nations through tribute of cash crops.[45]

In both the above instances, Hosea sees the danger that directly affects the land use pattern in Israel. On the one hand, following the Baalism form of fertility cult posed the danger of appropriating the Canaanite system of land use, which viewed the land as property that can be acquired, purchased and alienated from the prior owners.[46] As such, there was a looming danger of reducing the traditional pattern of inalienability of land to alienability. On the other hand, the prophet also sees the danger of Israel allying with other nations (lovers) for political agenda (12: 1[2]) in which the monarchy shifted the economic burden to the peasants who were already laboring under financially reduced and agriculturally precarious conditions.[47] The consequences of this are the transition from the traditional

[44] Yee, "She is not My Wife and I am not Her Husband", 376.

[45] Yee, "She is not My Wife and I am not Her Husband", 362.

[46] Dearman, *Property Rights*, 13.

[47] Yee, "She is not My Wife and I am not Her Husband", 362.

mode of familial production[48] to a tributary mode of production[49] in which the surplus crops of the peasants went into the hands of the wealthy elite and the manipulative land use projects and exploitation of the peasants became rampant.

Both the worship of Baal and the alliance with other nations are contrary to the covenantal norms envisaged in the Sinai covenant. This, according to Hosea, is a willful act of breaking the covenant with Yahweh, which he pictured through the metaphor of sexual promiscuity. In the Israelite matrimonial culture, a wife is economically dependent upon her husband and restricts her sexual attachment exclusively to her husband. Any form of illicit relationship was considered a disgraceful act. In drawing this imagery, Hosea underscores an important theological point that Israel's existence and survival in the land as a nation lies in the exclusive relationship with Yahweh and that her allegiance to Baals and alliances with the nations amount to dishonoring Yahweh, just as a wife's infidelity dishonors her husband. Yahweh, thus, warns Israel to reform her way with a threat (vv.2b-3). In threatening Israel, the term פשט is used, which appears in the context of forceful and violent stripping of a person's garment (cf. Gen. 37:23). In the Israelite tradition, stripping and humiliation of an adulteress served as a prelude to the execution before being burnt or stoned to death (Gen. 38:24; Lev 21:9; Deut. 22:23-24. cf. Ezek. 16:39f).[50] Since in the ANE treaty context, the threat "to strip naked" expresses a metaphor of punishment for breaking a treaty covenant, the term indicates an overtone of punishment for breaking the covenant.[51] As mentioned in the above TCC on v.3d the wife represents both the people and the land of Israel,[52] as such the phrase "I will strip her naked" refers to the looming exile as indicated by the ANE practices of leading the conquered peoples into exile, naked and bound[53] while at the same time it expresses the coming drought that would render the land infertile and barren.

Israel is accused of her determined action to go after her lovers (v.5). The cohartative אלכה "I will go" preceded by אחרי "after" conveys a firm, willful and blatant resolution of Israel to go after her paramour.[54] As mentioned in the above TCC on v.5b and v.5c-c, erroneously Israel thought that the produce of the land

---

[48] In the familial mode of production, the peasants "practiced a mixed, village-based agriculture that distributed risk of crop failure… villagers retained their "surplus" income and resources". Yee, "She is not My Wife and I am not Her Husband", 347.

[49] Under the tributary system, the patrimonial system of land holding became latinfundia into a few wealthy landlords. In order to use land, the peasants paid heavy taxes and rent in the form of cash crops, thus, turning their surplus to the landholders. Yee, "She is not My Wife and I am not Her Husband", 347.

[50] Stuart, *Hosea*, 48; Macintosh, *Hosea*, 43.

[51] Mays, *Hosea*, 38; Allen R. Guenther, *Hosea, Amos* (Scottdale, Pennsylvania/Waterloo, Ontario: Herald, 1998), 59.

[52] Wolff, *Hosea*, 34.

[53] Guenther, *Hosea, Amos*, 59.

[54] Macintosh, *Hosea*, 48; Mays, *Hosea*, 39.

(bread, water, wool, flax, oil and drinks) comes through her "lovers", that is, through the Baalist form of fertility cult and through her commercial and political alliances with the nations. For such willful act of infidelity, Yahweh pronounces judgment (vv. 6-9). לכן "therefore" in v.9 introduces what Yahweh would do against Israel. In a series of first person pronominal suffixes, "I will take back.., I will take away…, I will uncover…, I will put to an end…, I will lay waste…, I will make them…, and I will punish (vv. 9-13), Yahweh successively announces his impending judgment, which clearly speaks of the consequences upon the land as a political nation and as a cultivable portion. The first person singular suffix "my" in v.9, "my grain, my wine, my flax and my wool (the representatives of all the produce of the land)" indicates that all the produces of the land comes from Yahweh and not from Israel's "lovers". Since Israel forsakes Yahweh, the provider, he will now take away these benefits from the land of Israel. Thus, Israel as a nation will also be deprived of her joy and festivity (v.11), the arable land that generates the crops will also become barren/parched land (v.3) and the wild animals would devour the land (v.12), indicating that the land would remain barren and become inaccessible for cultivation. Such withdrawal of land blessings is not only a punishment to chastise Israel but also to serve a pedagogical purpose that Israel would recognize Yahweh as the sole bestowal of the blessings of the land.

In the covenant tradition, the withdrawal of agricultural products of the land is the result of Israel's covenant infidelity (Deut 28:29-30, 51). Such understanding of the tradition appears to be the basis of Hosea's metaphorical message of the relationship between Yahweh, Israel and land. In the above exegetical comments, the idea of land as a political nation and a space for cultivation of grain, wine, flax, oil and wool upon which the survival of the Israelites depends, appear prominent. The land also appears to be an arena of struggle between Yahweh and Israel. Yahweh's pronouncement of judgment against Israel affects the land and its cultivation severely on the one hand while the land's bearing of Yahweh's judgment affects the lives of the Israelites on the other hand. Israel broke her relationship with Yahweh and Yahweh withholds all the benefits of the land thereby the survival of Israel is severely affected. Israel's departure from Yahweh not only alienates her from the blessing of the land, but Israel would also be finally removed from the land as indicated by the looming judgment of exile. However, the cyclical effect of such tripartite relationship eventually seeks to teach Israel to realize that Yahweh is the only provider and the only way back to the life of blessing on the land is to reaffirm her allegiance to Yahweh.

4.4. Covenant Tradition (Hosea 2:16-23 [MT 18-25])

The term ברית "covenant" appears (v.18) in close connection with the expression, "my people" and "my God" (v.23), which indicates that the covenant tradition is embedded in the present text. Israel reaffirms Yahweh as "my husband/God" and

Yahweh reciprocates Israel's affirmation by favorably answering to Israel's need for peace and agricultural bounty in the land. The tripartite relationship is thus reaffirmed based on the covenant tradition in 2:16-23.

4.4.1. Translation on Hosea 2:16-23

16 And it shall be, in that day[a], says Yahweh, you will call me[b], "My husband"[c], and no longer will you call me, "my Baal"[c].

17 For I will remove the names of the Baals from her mouth, and they shall no longer be mentioned by name.

18 I will make for you a covenant[a] on that day with the wild animals of the field[b], the birds of the air, and the creeping things of the ground; and I will cause to break[c] the bow, the sword, and war from the land[d]; and I will make you lie down in safety.

19 And I will betroth[a] you to me forever; I will betroth you to me in righteousness and in justice, in steadfast love, and in mercy.

20 I will betroth you to me in faithfulness; and you shall know Yahweh[a].

21 On that day I will answer[a], says Yahweh, I will answer the heavens and they shall answer the earth;

22 and the earth shall answer the grain, the wine, and the oil, and they shall answer Jezreel;

23 and I will sow her for myself in the land. And I will have pity on Lo-ruhamah, and I will say to Lo-ammi, "You are my people;" and he shall say, "You are my God".

4.4.2. Text Critical Comments on Hosea 2:16-23

V. 16a: ויום-ההוא "and in that day" appears in 2:16, 18, 21 to introduce a future promise. Unlike 1:5 where ויום-ההוא appears in connection with threat, in v. 16 it points to a new proclaimed confession of Israel, which is followed by the description of Yahweh's restoration. It is difficult to determine what period "in that day" refers to. In view of the preceding judgment against Israel in vv.9-13, we can conjecture that "in that day" could refer to the indefinite future after Israel suffers Yahweh's judgment in proportion to her sin. In any case, "in that day" will be a time to renew the broken covenant between Yahweh and Israel,[55] which will also result in "peace", "safety" (v.18) and prosperity of the agricultural produce in the land (vv.21-23). The reestablished tripartite relationship is thus envisaged in the future "in that day".

V.16b: תקראי "you will call me" is rendered in LXX as *καλέσει* (3rd fem. sg) "she will call," likewise the Syriac and Vulgate versions renders 3rd fem. sg.[56] Stuart argues that "The suff[ix] of the MT may reflect an original object suff[ix], which

[55] Mays, *Hosea*, 47.

[56] Stuart, *Hosea-Jonah*, 55-56.

in poetry can (rarely) take the form of the poss suff: "She will call me."[57] Though it is difficult to determine whether the 2 fem. sg or 3 fem. sg is original, in any case what appears clear is that the reference here is to the wife (Israel) who will affirm her loyalty to her husband (Yahweh).

V.16c-c: Both איש and בעל can be generally interpreted as "husband" yet there is a subtle difference. אישי "my husband" is a personal, endearing and intimate expression (cf. Gen. 2:23; 3:6, 16), which conveys "the husband as one who belongs to and who enjoys a deep personal relationship with the 'wife' אִשָּׁה"[58] On the other hand, בעלי "my Baal" conveys the meaning of "to own", and "have rights over", and tends to emphasize the husband's legal rights as a possessor of the woman" (cf. the legal texts such as, Ex. 21:3; 22; Deut. 22:22; 24:4).[59] Thus, in using this distinctive term "my husband" in v.16, Hosea seeks to convey Israel's total devotion and commitment to Yahweh as a wife would to her husband who loves her and not just because she is legally bound to him.[60]

V.18a: Covenant (ברית) appears five times (2:18; 6:7; 8:1; 10:4; 12:2) in Hosea out of which four of its occurrences mention Israel as one of the parties involved in the covenant but 2:18 appears to be different as the covenant is made here not with Israel but yet for Israel. The phrase וכרתי להם ברית "I will cut a covenant with them" clearly identifies who establishes the covenant with whom and for whom. The first person pronominal suffix "I" stresses Yahweh to be the initiator of the covenant and the other party with whom the covenant is made is referred to as the "wild animals of the field". The making of this covenant serves two purposes: first, the covenant will pacify the wild animals that had earlier threatened Israel's survival (v.12).[61] Second, the covenant will put the fear of war, exile, defeat and bloodshed to an end.[62] Such understanding of freedom from the ravaging wild animals and freedom from enemies' attack upon the land are understood in the covenant tradition to be the result of covenantal faithfulness, which Hosea has recast in a marriage metaphor. Israel's security in the land is seen to be contingent upon her covenant relation with Yahweh and that the harmonious tripartite relationship is envisaged within the covenant faithfulness.

V.18b: Since חית refers to "wild animals", the term השדה "the field", which is stated here as habitat of these wild animals, refers not to a cultivable land but an uncultivated country side where the untamed wild animals live.

---

[57] Stuart, *Hosea-Jonah*, 56.

[58] Wolff, *Hosea*, 49.

[59] Mays, *Hosea*, 48.

[60] Mays, *Hosea*, 48.

[61] Citing D. R. Hillers, Stuart states that "In the ancient Near Eastern treaties, attacks from wild animals and destruction from war were two prominent motifs employed in the curse-threats appended to the treaty stipulations. D. R. Hillers, *Treaty-Curses*, 54-56. Cited in Stuart, *Hosea-Jonah*, 59.

[62] Stuart, *Hosea-Jonah*, 58; Andersen and Freedman, *Hosea*, 280-281.

V.18c: The Hiphil form אשבור "I will cause to break" is closely linked with 1:5 as usage of the term in both the verses appears in the context of the future, "in that day" and in connection with breaking the bow. However, the difference is that in 1:5 "breaking of the bows of Israel" represents the final defeat of Israel's army at the valley of Jezreel while in 2:18, the expression refers to the cessation of warfare so as to usher in a new age of hope and security for Israel.[63] Andersen and Freedman thus state that "It could mean to break the threat of a foreign invader, and so give the nation safety."[64]

V.18d: Andersen and Freedman think that "If הארץ refers to the land of Israel, rather than the earth, then the divine action would involve the enemy, whose weapon will be shattered in their defeat. The land will be free of threats, and there will be no further need of armaments…".[65] הארץ is mentioned as a safe place to reside as wars will cease, which indicates that it refers to the political territory of Israel (cf. 1:2; 4:1, 3; 9:3; 10:1).[66]

V.19a: Basically the verb ארשׂ "to betroth" refers to an engagement prior to the actual marriage (Deut. 20:7; 28:30), which was the ancient Israelite practice of settling the marriage contractually by the groom's payment of the bride-price to the bride's father."[67] Betrothal was a final step in the Israelite matrimonial process that was equivalent to the status of marriage legally in the court (Deut. 20:7; 22:23-29; Ex. 22:16-17). "To betroth" appears repeatedly (3 times in vv. 19-20). It indicates that the relationship is solemn and emphatic. Such intimate relationship is further expressed by the preposition לי "to me", which emphasizes that it will be very personal. The verbal syntax indicates Yahweh's initiating relationship with Israel, which is described not only as intimate but also as permanent (עלולם) and will be characterized by the qualities of righteousness, justice, steadfast love, mercy and faithfulness (vv.19-20).

V. 20a: and you shall know Yahweh (וידעת את-יהוה) reverses Yahweh's accusation "she forgot me" (שׂכחה) in 1:13. The covenant connotation expressed √ידע "to know" and שׂתיךְ "to betroth" in v. 20 convey the understanding of the covenant that is further explicated by the attributes of covenant: righteousness, justice, steadfast love, mercy and faithfulness in vv. 19-20. ידע in most of its Old Testament occurrences has sexual overtones, which indicates that the covenant between Yahweh and Israel will be a deep and intimate relationship.

V.21a: √ענה is commonly interpreted as "to answer". It frequently appears in a legal context as testimony or answer to certain action (cf. Ex. 20:16; Deut. 5:20; 31:21; 1 Sam. 12:3; Isa. 3:9; Mic. 6:3; Job 9:14, 15; 15:6).[68] The invocation

[63] Andersen and Freedman, *Hosea,* 282.

[64] Andersen and Freedman, *Hosea*, 282.

[65] Andersen and Freedman, *Hosea*, 282.

[66] Mays, *Hosea*, 49.

[67] Stuart, *Hosea-Jonah*, 59.

[68] Sweeney, *The Twelve Prophets*, 37.

of heavens and the earth "to answer" is a common summons in legal covenant making in the Israelite and ANE traditions. Thus, the expression here can be understood as a binding covenant relationship between Yahweh and Israel.[69] Yahweh's entry into the covenant with Israel will once again have a significant bearing on the land since, as a result of that covenant, the heavens will respond to earth and the earth will respond to the agrarian products such as grain, wine, and oil (v.22). The fecundity of the land is stated here to be the result of the faithful covenant relationship between Yahweh and Israel. הארץ in vv.21-23 appears in the context of Yahweh's favorable response to the crops of the field and to the crops and Jezreel-a crop centre of the North that stands for all Israel agriculturally,[70] which indicates that הארץ here refers to the cultivable land of Israel.

4.4.3. Form Critical Comments on Hosea 2:16-23

Ben Zvi argues that the concluding formula "says Yahweh" in v.13 shows that the preceding unit ends there and a new unit begins with "therefore" in v.14.[71] Wolff, Mays, and Stuart argue differently and consider vv.16-23 to be a separate unit since, unlike vv.2-15, a new unit begins with "On that day,"[72] marking a new unit of salvation oracle in v. 16 and concludes with a renewal of covenant in v.23. Moreover, unlike vv.2-15, the form of "court lawsuit" is no longer employed in vv.16-23.[73] Thus, we consider vv. 16-23 to be a separate unit.

Within the unit of vv. 16-23, there appears a frequent change of personal pronouns referring to Israel as "you" 2 fem. sg (v.16); "her" (v.17); "them" (v.18); "you" (v. 19); and "her" (v.23).[74] Such inconsistent use of personal pronouns suggests that the material is probably a collection of the prophet's sayings but connected together by a theme of restoration "in that day."[75] The successive formulas "on that day" and "says Yahweh" in vv. 18, 23 suggests that the oracle is future oriented and anticipates the transformation of the Yahweh-Israel relationship and the establishment of harmony with nature and the nations.[76] The consistent use of first person throughout indicates that all these promises are the singular act of Yahweh, which seeks to reverse the threat of punishments announced earlier in 2:2-13. As mentioned in the above TCC on v.18a, the earlier threat of sending the wild animals to devour (v. 12) is now reversed to living with the wild animals in safety (v. 18); instead of taking away the produces of the land

---

[69] Sweeney, *The Twelve Prophets*, 37.

[70] Stuart, *Hosea-Jonah*, 61.

[71] Ehud Ben Zvi, *Hosea,* FOTL 21A (Grand Rapids, Michigan/Cambridge, UK: William B. Eerdmans Publishing Company, 2005), 64.

[72] Wolff, *Hosea*, 47; Mays, *Hosea*, 46-47; Stuart, *Hosea-Jonah*, 56.

[73] Stuart, *Hosea-Jonah*, 56.

[74] Mays, *Hosea*, 47.

[75] Mays, *Hosea*, 46-47.

[76] Andersen and Freedman, *Hosea*, 276.

(v. 9), Yahweh will now supply them (v. 22); Yahweh's anger expressed through the symbolic names Lo-ruhamma (not pitied, v.6) and Lo-ammi (not my people, v.8) will now be reversed with "You are my people (v.23).[77] In other words, the form of salvation oracle in vv.16-23 portrays Yahweh as the God who restores the fortunes and reverses the circumstances of his people.

The setting of this oracle is difficult to determine, since it can hardly be related to specific events and circumstances.[78] Since v. 23 mentions "Lo-ruhamah" and "Lo-ammi", the children of Hosea, we can assume, as Mays and Stuart argue, that at least five years could have been elapsed since the beginning of Hosea's public activity.[79] Since Hosea's early part of ministry is placed around 750 BCE (see the form critical comments on 2: 2-13), the elapse of about five years would fit the oracle to post 745 BCE, probably soon after Jeroboam II's reign. Such dating would be plausible since after Jeroboam II's period, social and political instability slowly became the order of the day. The message of hope and restoration (vv.16-23) would be more credible to such a period of instability.

4.4.4. Tradition and Theological Comments in the Light of Tripartite Relationship

The covenantal relationship between Yahweh-Israel continues in a marriage metaphor in 2:16-23. According to Mordecai A. Friedman behind the marriage proposal by God to Israel and the latter's response in v.16, there is a tradition of Yahweh's entering into the covenant with Israel at Sinai in Ex. 19:5-6, 8, "If you obey my covenant, you shall be my treasured possession ... you shall be unto me a kingdom of priests and a holy nation... and all the people responded as one...". He further states that the covenantal response in Deut. 26:17-19, "You have *declared* the Lord, this day, to be your God... and the Lord has *declared* you, this day, to be His treasured people", is seen by Hosea as a marriage between Yahweh and Israel and thereby he spoke of it as a covenant.[80] Though Mordecai's proposal can still be debated, it cannot be dismissed easily as the later prophets, namely, Ezekiel and Malachi also use the marriage metaphor to convey the idea of covenant (Ezek 16:8; Mal. 2:14). The use of the marriage metaphor to convey the covenant was not unknown among the prophets of Israel. What appears significant in the (re)establishment of the covenant in 2:16-23 is the restoration of the tripartite relationship. As mentioned in the TCC on v.21a, Yahweh's entry into the betrothal relationship with Israel not only restores Israel's relationship with Yahweh (v.16) but it also restores Israel's sociopolitical circumstances by

---

[77] Andersen and Freedman, *Hosea*, 264.

[78] Stuart, *Hosea-Jonah*, 57.

[79] Mays, *Hosea*, 47; Stuart, *Hosea-Jonah*, 57.

[80] Mordecai A. Friedman, "Israel's Response in Hosea 2:17b: "You are My Husband", *JBL* 99/2 (1980) 202.

abolishing war and ushering peace and security upon the land (v.18a) and by bestowing fertility and fecundity in the land (vv.21-22).

The restoration of Israel is announced with a prophetic formula "in that day" (vv.16, 18, 21). It introduces a future hope of restored covenant relationship between Yahweh and Israel. The restored relationship is expressed through a covenant formula: "you [Israel] will call me [Yahweh] "My husband" and no longer..."My Baal" (vv.16-18). As mentioned in the TCC on v.16c-c, the term "my husband" (unlike "my Baal") conveys Israel's total devotion and commitment to Yahweh as a wife would to her husband. Israel's affirmed loyalty to Yahweh as "my husband" is preceded by the initial act of Yahweh's reconciliatory action, "I will entice her... take her... speak to her... give her vineyard..." (vv.14,15). As stated in the TCC on v.18a, the repeated use of first person "I" in Yahweh's speech (vv.14-15, 17-24) conveys that it is Yahweh who initiated the step of restoration. In other words, the restoration of blessings from the offended one (Yahweh) to the guilty party (Israel) resulted in restoration of the covenant, which consequently leads to the harmonious relationship between Yahweh, Israel and the land. This tripartite relationship is expressed in v.18b in which Yahweh promises to abolish war and to bring safety in the *land* as a result of *Israel's* affirmed loyalty to *Yahweh*. Israel's affirmation of Yahweh as "my husband" (v.16) not only leads to the covenant relationship between Yahweh and Israel but such affirmed loyalty also leads Israel to freedom and rest upon הארץ (the land) in v.18. הארץ in this sense refers to the land of Israel as a political nation and that בטח "safety" refers to the security in the land both from attack of the wild animals and foreign nations.

The covenantal relationship is further emphasized in vv.19-20 using a marriage terminology (וארשתיך) "I will betroth you". As mentioned in the above TCC on v. 19a, "to betroth" conveys an intimate, personal and permanent relationship, which is further characterized by righteousness, justice, steadfast love, mercy and faithfulness in vv.19-20. As stated above, such reestablished relationship between Yahweh and Israel would drive Yahweh to make covenant with nature and the nations for Israel's safety in the land (v.18). It also ensures the fertility upon Israel's arable land (vv. 21-23). This is repeated by the term ענה "to answer" (vv. 21-22), which indicates Yahweh's firm resolution to restore back the agricultural bounty to Israel. Yahweh assures that the heavens will "answer" the earth (הארץ) and the earth will "answer" the grain, wine and oil (vv.21-22) and Jezreel (a crop centre of the North that stands for all Israel agriculturally).[81] The bountiful blessing of the land envisaged here is stated to be the result of Yahweh's answer to the land in response to Israel's affirmative response to him as "my husband". In this sense, הארץ "the earth" in vv.21-22 refers to the agricultural land that will prosper Israel in the coming days of restoration. In affirming Yahweh's promise to "answer" the heavens, earth and crops of the field, Hosea portrays Yahweh (not Baals) as the God who controls the nature. Yahweh's

[81] Stuart, *Hosea-Jonah*, 61.

ענה (answer) to agricultural bounty in vv.21-22 follows Israel's positive "answer" ענה to Yahweh in v. 15. This means, in Hosea's understanding, the restoration of land blessing is a result of reciprocal response to the covenant relationship between Yahweh and Israel. Wright thus rightly asserts that for Israel to return to the land, she must first return to God, and then only Israel can be restored back to the land.[82]

In short, the above exegesis has shown that the tradition of the Sinai covenant has shaped Hosea's understanding on the relationship between Yahweh, Israel and land in 2:16-23. Yahweh's unconditional restoration of blessings to the guilty Israel is seen to be a decisive factor in leading Israel back to Yahweh. This (re)establishment of the covenant between Yahweh and Israel is seen to be the only alternative for Israel's safety and security in the land (הארץ). Hosea expresses the hope of a restored tripartite relationship by employing a salvation oracle in which he envisaged that the land as a place of habitation will be safe as the threat of animals and wars will come to an end and also the land as a place of cultivation will be fertile and prosperous. Thus, Israel's social, economic and political threats will be removed "in that day". All these blessings are attributed to Yahweh and to the result of her covenantal loyalty. Israel's identity as a nation and her safe survival in the land depend on her constant reference to Yahweh and her loyalty to the covenant.

4.5. Covenant Tradition (Hosea 4:1-3)

In 4:1-3 Israel is accused of cursing, lying, murder, stealing and adultery, which is the vocabulary of the Decalogue of Sinai covenant. Such covenant violations not only affect the relationship between Yahweh and Israel but they also affect Israel's life upon the land along with the entire creation. 4:1-3 thus presents how the tripartite relationship is affected because of Israel's failure to honor Yahweh's Decalogue.

4.5.1. Translation on Hosea 4:1-3

1 Hear the word of Yahweh, O people of Israel, surely[a] Yahweh has complaint against the inhabitants[b] of the land. There is [c]no trustworthiness, no loyalty[d], and no knowledge[e] of God in the land.

2 Cursing, lying, and murder, and stealing and adultery break out[a], bloodshed follows bloodshed.

3 Therefore the earth withers[a], and all who live in it languish; together with the wild animals and the birds of the air, even the fish of the sea are perishing.

[82] Wright, *God's People in God's Land*, 9.

4.5.2. Text Critical Comments on Hosea 4:1-3

V.1a: כי is normally translated as "for/because". However, since כי appears in the beginning of the sentence, it conveys an asseverative force, "surely" or "certainly."[83]

V.1b: The generic term "inhabitants" includes priests, prophets, men, women and living creatures. In other words, the entire Israel is addressed here as the inhabitants of the land.[84]

V.1c: The thrice repeated אין "there is no" emphasizes a complete lack of trustworthiness, loyalty and knowledge of God in the land. Since in Hosea אמת appears only in this verse, it is difficult to determine its meaning. Elsewhere in the Bible אמת refers to reliability of a person's speech and action in discharging his responsibilities with others. For instance, Proverbs 29:14 states that a king's throne is secured if he judges "in/with truth" באמת; Exodus 18:21 reads, אנשי אמת צנאי בצע "men of integrity who hate bribe" can assist Moses in his public administration.[85] אמת in these instances describes a responsible interpersonal relationship that is characterized by integrity and honesty. In 2:20 [MT. 2:22], אמת is used to describe Yahweh's faithfulness by which he is committed in his covenantal relationship with Israel. The negation אין (there is no) of אמת thus describes that "Israel has not reciprocated the trust God has shown"[86] neither by living truthfully with her God nor by relating honestly among themselves in the society.

V.1d: חסד "loyalty" describes the action of a person who undertakes social responsibility with love and trust so as to avoid bitterness and live harmoniously in the society (Gen. 21:23; 24:49). חסד is an essential characteristic of solemn covenantal loyalty and relationship (1 Sam. 20:8).[87] Lack of חסד among the people results in oppression of poor and needy people (Ps. 109:16-17). In 10:12 Hosea uses חסד in relation to seeking Yahweh. In these instances, חסד refers to the loyalty between the Israelite people and Israel's covenant loyalty to Yahweh. As indicated in the above occurrences, חסד describes the ideal relationships that are applied both to Israel's relationship to God and between the members of Israel in society. חסד describes the ideals of loyalty that are essential to maintain and sustain the relationship both between God and Israel and between the people themselves. Using the negative charge אין, Yahweh accused Israel of omitting covenantal loyalty in her relationship with God as emphasized in the marriage metaphor (2:2-13) and in her relationship with fellow members of society as indicated by the following crimes: murder, lying, stealing and adultery, v.2.

---

[83] Macintosh, *Hosea*, 127.

[84] H.D. Beeby, *Hosea: Grace Abounding* (Grand Rapids, Michigan: William B. Eerdmans Publishing Company, 1989), 48.

[85] Macintosh, *Hosea*, 127.

[86] Birch, *Hosea, Joel and Amos*, 47.

[87] Macintosh, *Hosea*, 127.

V.1e: "knowledge" and "to know" occur repeatedly in Hosea (2:8, 20; 4:1, 6; 5:3-4; 6:3, 6; 8:2-4; 9:7; 11:3; 14:9). Since the verb "to know" is associated with sexual intimacy, the knowledge of God refers to intimate and personal relationship with God.[88] In this sense "knowledge of God" refers to involving and doing what Yahweh desires for Israel. It is thus not just a cognitive recognition of the requirements of the covenantal stipulations but it is also an activity for Israel to act upon. The absence of trustworthiness and loyalty has its root cause in the absence of "knowledge of God". The knowledge of God is the embodiment of the will of God for Israel. It describes what Yahweh expects from Israel in her relationship to God and in her relations with fellow members of the society. Each of these is a relational quality, which is essential to maintain a healthy relationship both with God and with the fellow members of the society.

V.2a: The LXX adds ἐπὶ τῆς γῆς "in the land", which is absent in the MT. Wolff and Stuart think that the phrase "in the land" was once present in v.2 but it might have missed out as a result of "haplogr via homoiotel."[89] We have not added the so called missing phrase in our translation; instead we have retained the present form as appears in the MT.

V.3a: √אבל can mean both "to mourn" and "to dry up". Since Hosea employs the imagery of drought and withering in 2:3, "I will make her ... like a wilderness, and turn her into a parched land, and kill her with thirst", אבל can mean "to dry up". By using אבל Hosea emphasizes that the entire natural world faces the consequences of Israel's failures to remain faithful to her covenanted God.[90]

4.5.3. Form Critical Comments on Hosea 4:1-3

Scholars disagree whether the unit ends with v.3,[91] or continues in vv.4ff.[92] Vv. 1-3 directs the speech specifically to the land and its inhabitants unlike vv.4ff, which addresses the priests and prophets. Thus, we consider vv.1-3 to be a separate subunit. We notice the vocabulary of Yahweh's indictment in vv.1-3 continues in vv.4ff, such as, "knowledge" (4:1. cf. v.6); "adultery" (4:2. cf. v.13) and "swearing" (4:1. cf. v.15). Even the theme of indictment and court trail continues in vv.4ff. Thus, vv.4ff cannot be entirely delineated from vv.1-3. We consider that 4:1-3 is a self-contained unit of indictment, but it also serves to introduce the judgmental

[88] Birch, *Hosea, Joel and Amos*, 47-48.

[89] Wolff, *Hosea*, 65; Stuart, *Hosea-Jonah*, 72.

[90] Jeffrey H. Hoffmeyer, "Covenant and Creation: Hosea 4:1-3", *Review and Expositor* 102 (2005) 145.

[91] Mays, *Hosea*, 62; Hoffmeyer, "Covenant and Creation: Hosea 4:1-3", 144.

[92] Gray W. Light, "The New Covenant in the Book of Hosea", *Review & Expositor* 90 (1993) 221.

section of 4:4-13:16.[93] For our exegesis we limit ourselves to vv.1-3 as a self-contained unit.

The general consensus among scholars is that vv.1-3 belong to the form of lawsuit.[94] Using the form of "covenant lawsuit"[95] (cf. "complaint" in v. 1), Hosea portrays Yahweh as God who goes to the court against his people Israel in the roles of plaintiff, prosecuting attorney, and judge. This is indicated by the following unit of court speech as Brueggemann demonstrates:[96]

Summon to hear:	Hear the word of Yahweh (v.1)
Name of the accused:	O people of Israel… inhabitants of the land (v.1)
Name of accuser:	Yahweh (v.1)
Announcement of trail:	has a complaint (v.1)
General accusation:	There is no trustworthiness, no loyalty, and no knowledge of God in the land (v.1)
Specific indictment:	Cursing, lying, and murder, and stealing and adultery break out, bloodshed follows bloodshed (v.2).
Formula of announcement:	Therefore (v.3)
Description of penalty:	the earth withers, and all who live in it languish; together with the wild animals and the birds of the air, even the fish of the sea are perishing (v.3).

In the above structure, Yahweh summons Israel to hear the complaint. First, he indicts Israel for the sins of omission in which Israel is accused of the absence of relational qualities of the covenant: "There is no trustworthiness, no loyalty, and no knowledge of God in the land" (4:1). Second, Yahweh indicts Israel for the sins of commission in which Israel is accused of "cursing, lying, murdering, stealing, and adultery" (4:2). Based on these indictments, Yahweh pronounces judgment against Israel that consequently affects the land and the living creatures upon it (v.3).

Due to the absence of any clear historical event, scholars find it difficult to precisely locate the historical setting of the oracle. Since the present unit announces the disaster of drought, Wolff thinks that the oracle might have originated from the early period of Hosea's ministry.[97] According to van Gelderen and Duane A.

---

[93] Cf. Carl J. Bosma, "Creation in Jeopardy: A Warning to Priests (Hosea 4:1-3)", CTJ 34 (1999) 64.

[94] Mays, *Hosea,* 61; Wolff, *Hosea*, 66; Bruce C. Birch, *Hosea, Joel, and Amos* (Louisville, Kentucky: Westminister John Knox Press, 1997), 46; Walter Brueggemann, *Tradition in Crisis: A Study in Hosea* (Richmond, Virginia: Westminister John Knox Press, 1968), 70-71; Gray W. Light, "The New Covenant in the Book of Hosea", *Review and Expositor* 90 (1993), 221; James A. Wharton, "Hosea 4:1-3, Interpretation", 32/1 (1978) 78.

[95] Mays, *Hosea*, 61.

[96] Brueggemann, *Tradition in Crisis*, 71.

[97] Wolff, *Hosea*, 66.

Garrett, the reference to "bloodshed follows bloodshed" in v.2 could refer to the setting of post Jeroboam II's period (746 BCE). This was the period of quick succession of kings in the Northern Kingdom during which revolts, assassinations and palace coups followed successively.[98] Probably the "bloodshed" mentioned in v.3 could reflect such historical situation.

4.5.4. Tradition and Theological Comments in the Light of Tripartite Relationship:

Hosea's indictment in v. 2 reflects the Decalogue language of Sinai covenant: cursing (Ex. 20:7; Deut. 5:11), lying (Ex. 20:16; Deut. 5:20), murder (Ex. 20:13; Deut. 5:17), stealing (Ex. 20:15; Deut. 5:19), and adultery (Ex. 20:14; Deut. 5:18).[99] Such terminology indicates that Hosea's judgment speech has its root in the covenant tradition of the Decalogue. We have noted earlier that in the covenant tradition Yahweh and Israel entered into a covenantal relationship at Sinai in which Yahweh gave Israel the provision of laws to sustain the covenant relationship between Yahweh and Israel. One such provision includes the Decalogue and following its commandments was set as the condition for Israel both to sustain her relationship with Yahweh and to dwell in the land. However, Israel had failed to keep the Decalogue norms of life for which reason Yahweh pronounces covenant judgment upon Israel. In pronouncing the judgment sentence, Hosea states that not only had the land withered on account of Israel's failure, even "the beasts of the field", "the birds of the heavens", and "the fish of the sea" (v.3) were affected.

Hosea summons Israel to hear Yahweh's complaint (v.1). The accused Israel is indentified here as "the inhabitants of the land" (יוֹשְׁבֵי הָאָרֶץ). הארץ, in its two occurrences in v.1, appears in connection with "the sons of Israel" and also in relation with what Israel lacks, which indicates that הארץ here refers to the land of Israel in a sense of political territory. הארץ is also associated with Israel as the יוֹשֵׁב "inhabitants" of the land. Since in 9:3 הארץ is described as Yahweh's land,[100] יוֹשְׁבֵי הארץ "inhabitants of the land" identifies Israel as the recipient of God's gift of land.[101] Yahweh summons the Israelites, the beneficiary of Yahweh's gift of land, to hear his ריב "complaint/dispute". ריב is used here in a forensic sense[102] with which Yahweh establishes evidence to indict Israel.

---

[98] C. Van Gelderen and H.W. Gispen, *Het Bock Hosea*, COT (Kampen, 1953), cited in Wolff, *Hosea*, 68; Duane A. Garret, *Hosea, Joel*, New American Commentary (Broadman & Holman, 1997), 28.

[99] Richard D. Patterson, "Portraits From a Prophet's Portfolio: Hosea 4", *Bibliotheca Sacra* 165 (2008) 304.

[100] Mays, *Hosea*, 62.

[101] Cf. Wolff, *Hosea*, 67.

[102] Macintosh, *Hosea*, 127.

As mentioned in the above FCC, Yahweh's charge against Israel includes general indictment on the absence of trustworthiness, loyalty and knowledge of God (v.1). These covenantal virtues (trustworthiness, loyalty and knowledge), as stated in the TCC on v. 1c, 1d and 1e, are essential qualities in the context of covenant relationship between Yahweh and Israel (cf. 2:18-20 [20-22]. However, the absence of these covenantal virtues created an ethical vacuum in which the crimes mentioned in v.2 filled the society. In a series of five infinitive absolutes, cursing, lying, murder, stealing and adultery, Yahweh indicts Israel of specific crimes. These sins are offences committed against the neighbor that are categorically forbidden in the apodictic stipulations of Yahweh's covenant ratified in the Decalogue of Sinai covenant.[103] In Judg. 17:2 אלה "cursing" appears in the context of pronouncing a curse in connection with the name of Yahweh. Such idea of curse by using Yahweh's name appears to be the meaning of אלה in v.2.[104] Invoking curse improperly in God's name amounts to a misuse of God's name. This is prohibited by the apodictic law (Ex. 20:7). The second crime כחש "lying" is a forensic term that refers to an act of perjury, which is prohibited in the ninth commandment (Ex. 20:16). In Gen. 18:15; Lev. 19:11 and Josh. 7:11, the term implies deception with an intention to cheat and defraud others, which is linked with robbery and oppression (Lev. 19:11).[105] It was a particular problem in Israel's practice of trade (cf. Deut. 25:13) and judicial system (cf. Am. 5:12; Ex. 20:16; 23:1-3, 7). רצח refers to premeditated murder, which is prohibited in the sixth commandment (Ex. 20:13), while גנב refers to "stealing", which is prohibited in the eighth commandment (Ex. 20:15). In Ex. 21:16, גנב is used for kidnapping, which is punishable by death. נאף "adultery" is forbidden in the seventh commandment (Ex. 20:14).

Two observations can be made on the above indictments. First, the juxtaposition of the absence of trustworthiness, loyalty and knowledge of God (v.1) establish a causal relationship with v.2 of the presence of all vices.[106] In other words, Hosea articulates an intractable connection between Israel's (im)proper relationship to God and (mis)conduct in the society. Mays, thus, concludes that "social ethics and theological orthodoxy are inextricably interdependent". Second, the indictments are based on the stipulations of the covenant to which Israel gave her unanimous consent at Sinai (Ex. 24:3, 7). Thereby Hosea establishes Israel's breach of the covenantal stipulations. Israel, therefore, is proven guilty and deserves the covenantal curses which enforced its integrity.

Based on the above charges and evidences a sentence is proclaimed (v.3) by using the judgment announcement formula על-כן "therefore". על-כן is an inferential

---

[103] Carl J. Bosma, "Creation in Jeopardy: A Warning to Priests (Hosea 4:1-3)", *CTJ* 34 (1999) 96.

[104] Cf. Macintosh, *Hosea*, 64.

[105] Bosma, "Creation in Jeopardy", 98.

[106] Bosma, "Creation in Jeopardy", 100.

conjunction, which establishes a dynamic act-consequence correspondence between the twofold indictments in vv.1-2 and the tragic sentence announced in v.3. As a result of Israel's failures in her covenant with Yahweh, the entire natural world remained affected. The earth (הארץ) mourns (אבל). Though הארץ in v.1 refers to the land of Israel, in v.3 הארץ is used in connection with "all who live in it" including the wild animals, birds of the air and the fish of the sea, which, in the creation narrative (cf. Gen 1:26), refers to the entire world. In other words, the entire world is in the state of תאבל "dries up or withers". Whether or not תאבל refers to "mourning" or "withers,"[107] or whether or not the verb is in present tense or future, in any case תאבל states the consequence of the land due to Israel's covenant disloyalty to Yahweh. The consequence upon the land is not just described as drought but a "terrible diminution of all life-forces"[108] as the entire vitality of the land is lost, such as, the wild animals, birds of the air and the fish of the sea. Such catastrophes are all attributed to Israel's failure to live according to the covenant of Yahweh.

The above discussion shows that הארץ first refers to the land of Israel, which Israel inhabits as her territory as a political nation. In this understanding of political nation, Israel's inhabitation (יושב) in the land is understood in terms of God's gift of land. Second, הארץ refers to the entire earth in a cosmic sense, in which the condition of the land and all its vitality is inseparably linked with the quality of life lived in relation to the covenantal norms of Yahweh. In both the usages, Hosea shows how the relationship between Yahweh, Israel and land are intertwined and how this tripartite relationship is affected. Yahweh vouchsafed the land to Israel on the condition that Israel's lifestyle is confirmed to the ethical standard of Yahweh's teachings (Num. 35:33-34).[109] Since Israel failed to live according to her covenant with Yahweh, the judgment is pronounced that affects all the vitality of the entire land. Israel's estranged relation with Yahweh jeopardized Israel's life in the land and all the vitalities of the land were also endangered because of Israel's covenant disloyalty to Yahweh. In sum, covenantal disloyalty is seen as the reason of destabilizing the tripartite relationship. The land הארץ is thus portrayed as an inseparable feature that serves a significant role between the relationship of Yahweh and Israel.

4.6. Covenant Tradition (Hosea 5:8-11)

Though the term covenant does not appear in 5:8-11, the judgment of defeat from enemies, ailments of physical decay, attack from wild animals and desolation of the land echo the tradition of covenant curses. Also, the charge of removing the boundary mark (v.10b) indicates that the following judgment oracle is embedded

---

[107] For the issue on the interpretation problem of this verb, see Bosma, "Creation in Jeopardy", 102ff.

[108] Mays, *Hosea*, 65.

[109] Macintosh, *Hosea*, 128.

in the covenant tradition (see the TCC on 5:10a). The breaking of the tripartite relationship in 5:8-11 is stated in terms Yahweh's judgment against Israel and Judah for the violation of the covenant, which leads to the desolation of the land.

4.6.1. Translation on Hosea 5:8-11

8 Blow[a] the horn in Gibeah[b], the trumpet in Ramah[b]. Sound the alarm at Beth-aven[b]; behind you is Benjamin[c]!

9 Ephraim shall become a desolation in the day of punishment; among the tribes of Israel I declare what is sure.

10 The princes[a] of Judah are indeed those who remove[b] the landmark; on them I will pour out my wrath like water.

11 Ephraim is oppressed, crushed in judgment[a], because he was determined to go after futility[b].

12 I am like pus[a] to Ephraim, and like rottenness[a] to the house of Judah.

13 When Ephraim saw his sickness, and Judah his wound, then Ephraim went to Assyria, and sent to the great king[a]. But he is not able to cure you or heal your wound.

14 For I will be like a lion[a] to Ephraim, and like a young lion[a] to the house of Judah. I, I[b] myself will tear and go away; I will carry off, and no one shall rescue.

15 I will return again to my place until they acknowledge their guilt and seek my face. In their distress they will beg my favor:

4.6.2. Text Critical Comments on Hosea 5:8-11

V.8a: The Qal imperative תקעו "blow" indicates the alarm of the approaching enemies. It is the role of a watchman posted at a watch tower or vantage point atop a strategic hill to see advancing enemies and blow a horn or trumpet to warn the population so that people could run to the fortified cities for safety. By employing this term, Hosea speaks as a watchman and warns the people of the looming military attack of the enemies.[110]

V.8b: LXX renders בגבעה "in Gibeah" as *επι τους βουνους* as "upon the hills"; ברמה "in Ramah" as *εν τω οικω* "upon the heights" and אחריך בנימין "behind you is Benjamin" as *εξεστη βενιαμειν* "Benjamin is astonished."[111] We have retained the MT's version of these terms since each of these cities remained historically and geographically significant for Israel and Judah. Gibeah was the capital city of Saul, located about three miles north of Jerusalem (1 Sam. 10:26; 11:4), Ramah was the place where Samuel anointed Saul. It was situated about five miles north of Jerusalem (1 Sam. 9:1-10:16) and Beth-aven, meaning "house of iniquity" (a derogatory substitute name for Bethel, cf. 4:15) was the site of a

---

110 Mays, *Hosea*, 88.

111 Macintosh, *Hosea*, 199.

royal sanctuary of the Northern kingdom, Israel. Thus, historically these cities were of important significance and geographically the cities were of "enormous strategic importance as they controlled the northern approach to Jerusalem."[112] Because of such historical and geographical significance, there was constant warfare between Israel and Judah to gain control over these cities. Originally these cities belonged to the Benjamites (cf. Josh. 18:25-28), but the ownership of these territories changed frequently. During the early part of the ninth century, Abijah had captured these cities for Judah (cf. 2 Chr 13:19). Later, king Baasha captured Ramah and the surrounding cities for the North (cf. 1 Kgs 15:16–22). By the eighth century, as a result of king Jehoash's successful attack upon Jerusalem, these cities were brought under Israelite control (ca. 798–782 BCE; cf.2 Kgs 14:11–14).[113] According to Martin Noth, these cities were a recent acquisition of the Northern kingdom during the Syro-Ephriamite war (2 Kgs 16:5; cf. Isa. 7:6).[114] Hostilities between the North and South frequently redrew the territorial boundary that ran through these cities of Benjamin's land. Hosea's reference to these cities assumes significance as it shows centuries of warfare between the two kingdoms to control each others' territory.

V.8c: Scholars have proposed several emendations of the MT's אחריך בנימין literally "after/behind you, Benjamin". The LXX reads אחריך as *εξεστη βενιαμειν* "Benjamin is terrified". Macintosh states that LXX reading is more likely an attempt to make sense of אחריך to be a derivative from חרד "to terrify". Following LXX usage, Wellhausen and Wolff interpret it as "terrify Benjamin."[115] Stuart emends אחריך as אחרי כי, a construct form אחרים of "descendants" and interprets it as "descendants of Benjamin".[116] The MT's rendering of אחריך "behind you" is a problematic term, which is understood differently as a shout of ancient tribal war cry, or a warning to Benjamin that the enemies are after him, or a warning that the attack of Benjamin is after Israel.[117] The MT's preposition "behind you, Benjamin" can be retained, which could be understood as verbless clause, that is, "Behind you is Benjamin."[118]

V.10a: Andersen and Freedman argue that "king" is not mentioned in v.10 but only שׂר "princes" because the terminology is drawn from the period of the Judges.[119] Wolff, however, argues that שׂר includes "military leaders" (cf. 7:16) as well as "administrative officials (13:10), who are not to be separated from the king

---

[112] Macintosh, *Hosea*, 195.

[113] Cf. Martin Noth, *The History of Israel*, trans. by Peter Ackroyd (New York: Harper & Row, 1958), 216, 236ff.

[114] Noth, *The History of Israel*, 259; Stuart, *Hosea-Jonah*, 102.

[115] Wolff, *Hosea*, 104, no. a.

[116] Stuart, *Hosea-Jonah*, 98.

[117] Harper, *Amos and Hosea*, 274.

[118] Andersen and Freedman, *Hosea*, 407.

[119] Andersen and Freedman, *Hosea*, 408.

(7:3; 8:4; 13:10).[120] Likewise, Stuart also argues that שׂר identifies the indicted people as the military and palace officials.[121] Their crime is defined as גבול, which is not simply a "boundary", but a boundary stone or marker. The legal tradition of the covenant (Deut. 19:14-21:23) forbids impinging on the borders or property of others.[122] Removing or altering boundary mark is considered as a serious crime in the Wisdom teachings (Pro. 22:28; 23:10; Job 24:2).[123] The identification of the princes of Judah as violators of boundary markers serves as a reason of for Yahweh's judgment against them.

V.10b: Gordis understood the preposition כ as asseverative, which positively and seriously declares Judah's crime. If כ is asseverative, as Gordis argues, then the phrase היו שׂרי יהודה כמסיגי גבול in v. 10 can be interpreted as "The princes of Judah are indeed those who remove the landmarks."[124] We have retained כ as asseverative in our interpretation.

V.11a: The LXX reads *κατεδυναστευσεν* ... *κατεπατησεν το κριμα* perhaps to harmonize with Am. 4:1 where the two verbs "oppress" and "crush" appear. To the active participle verb *κατεδυναστευσεν* (oppress), the accusative object *τον ἀντιδικο αυτου* (his opponents) is added and this makes a parallel reading with מִשְׁפָּט (*κριμα*). Thus, LXX interprets "Ephraim oppress his opponent, and has trampled upon justice."[125] Matri and Harper contend that since the passive participles do not go along with the imperfect tenses of the preceding verbs, the passive participle עָשׁוּק "to be oppressed" be emended to active participle עוֹשֵׁק "one who oppresses"[126] as rendered in the LXX. However, these proposals for emendations are not necessary since such usages are not uncommon (cf. Deut. 28:33). We have retained the MT version as both the verbs (עשׁק and רצץ) denote cruel oppression.

V.11b: צו is a problematic word. Matri proposed that צו is a shortened from of שׁוא "vanity", which he thinks is corrupted in the MT.[127] Duhm and Alt propose צרו "enemy" and understood it to be referring to Syria (Aram) who was historically Israel's enemy but with whom Israel had allied.[128] It is also proposed that צו refers to רצון "Rezin", the Syrian king of the Syro-Ephramite alliance. Against these proposals, Driver points out that the MT's rendering צו has its cognate in the Arabic *sww* "empty" and *swwt* "echoing sound", which refers to "vain follies" or

[120] Wolff, *Hosea*, 62.

[121] Stuart, *Hosea-Jonah*, 104.

[122] Sweeney, *The Twelve Prophets*, 1:65.

[123] Mays, *Hosea*, 90.

[124] R. Gordis, "The Asseverative *Kaph* in Ugaratic and Hebrew", *JAOS* 63 (1943) 177.

[125] Cf. Wolff, *Hosea*, 104; Macintosh, *Hosea*, 206.

[126] Harper, *Amos and Hosea*, 275-276; Matri cited in Macintosh, *Hosea*, 206.

[127] Matri, cited in Macintosh, *Hosea*, 205.

[128] Cited in Macintosh, *Hosea*, 205.

"futility."[129] We retain MT's rendering and consider the meaning of צו as "futility" as proposed by Driver, which refers to the "futility" of Ephraim's political alliance with Rezin. The term appears in Isa. 28:10, 13 to describe the shouts of the drunkards of Ephraim.

V.12a: עשׁ is generally translated as "moth" and linked with destructive activity. Wolff, Rodolph and Driver have raised doubt over the term "moth" since moth only destroys clothes, not people.[130] Driver argues that עשׁ probably belongs to II עשׁ, which means "pus."[131] Wolff supports Driver's proposal since the expressions, "wounds", "sore" in v.13 supports the understanding as "pus."[132] רקב "rottenness" refers to that which affects people by damaging the bones (cf. Prov. 12:4; 14:30; Hab. 3:16). These terms expressed a metaphor that is extremely abrasive and shocking as they convey that Yahweh will be like "pus" to Ephraim that would cause rottenness not only to cause decay and putrefaction but would also affect the bones in the body of the people.

V.13a: According to Wolff, the phrase מלך ירב "the great king" refers to the sacred name of the Assyrian king after the letters of the original expression רב מלכי.[133] The Akkadian equivalent of the phrase is *šarru rabū* "the great king."[134]

V.14a: שׁחל is a poetic term for lion. Apart from this passage and in 13:7, שׁחל also appears in Job, Psalms and Proverbs. כפיר refers to "young lion" but one that is old enough to hunt prey.[135] Using the metaphor of lion ready for its prey, Yahweh asserts that it is he who causes the entire catastrophe. This is indicated by the repetition of pronoun אני אני "I and I", which emphasizes that the agent of the coming destruction is Yahweh himself. Since the affliction is of divine origin, appellation to powerful forces on the earth would be of no avail.[136]

4.6.3. Form Critical Comments on Hosea 5:8-11

The alarm war cry in 5:8 marks a new beginning of unit. Until 5:7 Hosea's accusation mostly concerns the cultic apostasy of Israel but in 5:8 the focus shifts to political apostasy of Israel and Judah.[137] Following Albrecht Alt, most scholars have generally recognized that the events referred to in 5:8ff belonged to the

---

[129] Driver, cited in Macintosh, *Hosea*, 204.

[130] Wolff, *Hosea*, 104, 115; Macintosh, *Hosea*, 207.

[131] G.R. Driver, "Difficult Words in the Hebrew Prophets", in H.H. Rowley (ed.), *Studies in Old Testament Prophecy* (Edinburgh: T&T Clark), 66f.

[132] Wolff, *Hosea*, 104; 115.

[133] Wolff, *Hosea*, 104.

[134] Macintosh, *Hosea*, 209.

[135] Harper, *Amos and Hosea*, 279.

[136] Harper, *Amos and Hosea*, 278.

[137] Mays, *Hosea*, 86.

history of the Syro-Ephraimite War (735-732 BCE).[138] The Syro-Ephriamite war was prompted by combined alliance of the Aramean king, Rezin and the Israelite king, Pekah, to fight against the rising Assyrian threat. The king of Judah, Jotham, and later his son Ahaz refused to join the Aram-Israel alliance. This prompted the Syro-Ephraimite coalition to fight against Judah so as to overthrow Ahaz and replaced him with a compliant ruler Ben Tabeel (cf. Isa. 7:6). Instead of succumbing to the pressure of the Syro-Ephriamite coalition, Judah appealed to Tiglath-Pilesar III of Assyria for military assistance. Assyria intervened and destroyed Damascus and killed Rezin. By 733 BCE most of Israel's territory in Trans-Jordan, Galilee, the Jezreel Valley and coastal plain was captured and brought under Assyria's control. Eventually, Hoshea ben Elah assassinated Pekah and took over the throne in Israel. Immediately he surrendered to the Assyrian King, paid tribute and became Assyria's vassal state. Alt argues that Judah attacked Israel during this time in conjunction with the Assyrian invasions and that Hosea 5:8 expresses the alarm felt in Benjamin as the Judean army moved northward.[139]

The style and form vary in 5:8-15and does not seem to represent a single oral unit but is connected together by focusing on Israel's alliances with foreign nations and its common historical setting of the Syro-Ephraimite context.[140] Since 6:1 clearly marks a new unit of a call for repentance, "Come, let us return to Yahweh", we confine the present unit to 5:8-15. Vv.8-9 is a prophetic saying in which Hosea appears as a watchman. V.8 sounds the alarm at the invasion into Israelite territory by Judah. V.9a depicts Ephraim, the heartland of Israel, in desolation. V.9b declares that the proclamation of desolation is certain. Vv. 10-15 consist of two judgment speech followed by indictment and announcement of judgment. Variations on the form of judgment speeches appear in the prophetic oracles and one such variation from the regular pattern is seen in this unit. This is shown in the following structure of the unit:

I. A watchman's warning of the looming military disaster in Ephraim, vv. 8-9
II. The judgment speech against Judah, v.10
    i. Name of the accused: Princes of Judah, v. 10a
    ii. Indictment: (they) remove the landmark, v.10b
    iii. Sentence: I will pour out my wrath like water, v. 10c
III. The judgment speech against Ephraim, v.11
    i. Name of the accused: Ephraim, v.11a
    ii. Sentence: is oppressed, crushed in judgment, v. 11a

[138] Albrecht Alt, "Hosea 5,8-6,6. Ein Krieg und seine Folgen in prophetischer Beleuchtung", *Kleine Schriften* (Muchen: C.H. Beck, 1964) II: 163-168. Cited in Sweeney, *The Twelve Prophet*, 1: 60; Mays, *Hosea*, 86-87; Macintosh, *Hosea*, 194-195; Wolff, *Hosea*, 111; Birch, *Hosea, Joel and Amos*, 63-64.

[139] Alt, cited in Sweeney, *The Twelve Prophets*, 1: 60.

[140] Mays, *Hosea*, 87.

iii. Indictment: because he was determined to go after futility, v 11b

IV. The announcement of judgment against Ephraim and Judah, vv. 12-15
 i. Sentence against Ephraim: I am like pus for Ephraim, v.12a
 ii. Sentence against Judah: and like rottenness to the house of Judah, v.12b

V. Further indictment against Ephraim and Judah: When Ephraim saw his sickness and
Judah his wound, then Ephraim went to Assyria… But he is not able to cure you or heal your wound (v.13)

VI. Judgment against Israel and Judah: For I will be like a lion to Ephraim… I myself will tear and go away… I will carry off, and no one shall rescue…In their distress they will beg my favor (vv.14-15).

4.6.4. Tradition and Theological Comments in the Light of Tripartite Relationship

Though the term covenant does not appear in 5:8-15, the indictment on the removal of the boundary marker (v.10)[141] and the curses, such as, the theomorphic curses of a lion (v.14),[142] oppression[143] (עשוק) and crushing[144] (רצוץ) from enemies (v.11) are the language of the covenant curses. In other words, in his judgment speech against Israel and Judah, Hosea employs the tradition of covenant enforcing curses in 5:8-11. In the covenant tradition, Yahweh's protection of Israel and Israel's secured existence in the land are tied up with Israel's covenant faithfulness to Yahweh. The covenant stipulations also warned that Israel's unfaithfulness would not only strain her relationship with God but it will also affect her relationship with the land. Such warnings include, defeat from enemies' attack, ailments that cause physical decay, attack from ferocious wild animals and alienation from the land. Hosea employs all these images in his judgment speech against Israel and Judah indicating that the covenant has been broken and that Yahweh enforces the curses according to the covenant stipulations. In this judgment speech, the tripartite relationship is portrayed as broken, in which Yahweh withdrew from Israel (v.15), Israel and Judah were alienated from the land (I will carry off, v. 14) and their land remains in desolation (v.9).

Hosea takes the role of a watchman and warns Ephraim of the impending invasion. As mentioned in the TCC on v.8b, Gibeah, Ramah and Beth-aven are

---

[141] Cf. Deut 27:17; 19:14. Stuart, *Hosea-Jonah*, 104.

[142] Cf. Deut 28:26; 32:24. Stuart, *Hosea-Jonah*, 105-106.

[143] Cf. Deut 28:29, 33; cf. Lev 19:13; Deut 24:14; Hos 12:8.

[144] Cf. Deut 28:33; cf. Amos 4:1.

located militarily in a strategic territory for which reason these cities became the bone of contention for Israel and Judah. As mentioned in the above FCC, during the Syro-Ephraimite war along with the coalition army Pekah, the king of Israel attacked Judah and annexed these cities. However as the Assyrians intervened and attacked Israel from the north, Judah also counter-attacked Israel from Israel's southern boarders. Possibly Hosea's war cry in v.8 announces such attack against Israel from both Assyria in the north and Judah in the south and that the certainty of desolation of the land announced in v.9 speaks of Israel's defeat and loss of her land. If the historical setting of Syro-Ephraimite coalition could be sustained, then two observations stand out as the reason for Hosea's alarm cry against Ephraim. First, Hosea warns Israel of her violent foreign alliance with the Arameans. Second, Hosea warns Israel of her aggressive territorial expansion toward Judah, her covenant brother, with the help from Aram.

Not only Ephraim, Judah is also indicted for removing the boundary mark (v.10). Scholars understand the phrase, "removing the boundary mark" as referring to Judah's literal annexation of Benjamin's territory.[145] According to Mays the context of v.10 appears to be the aftermath of Syro-Ephraimite war, the argument of which can be sustained.[146] The counter attack, which Hosea announced in v.8, would have taken place and Judah's military officials (שׂר) had probably annexed Gilead, Ramah and Beth-aven and expanded further into Israelite territory. If this argument can be sustained, Judah's offence lies in her invasion on the Northern territory and thereby violating the boundary mark between the two nations. According to the covenant stipulation, the boundary mark is a sacred institution of Yahweh[147] and therefore territorial encroachment was strictly forbidden. Judah's removal of boundary mark thus amounts to covenant violation of the divine territorial allocations. For such territorial encroachment, Judah remains guilty before Yahweh. Thus, Yahweh pronounced judgment against Judah that she would suffer "wrath" that is poured like water (v.10c). In the later prophets both ברה "wrath" and פך "pouring" appear in the contexts of divine destruction (cf. Zeph 1:14–18). Such meaning of divine destruction of land may be the emphasis of God's wrath against Judah in v.10.

The judgment speech in vv.11-15 continues to indict and sentence Ephraim and Judah. Israel's present condition, "oppressed, crushed in judgment" (v.11a) refers to the aftermath of Tiglath-Pileser's conquest.[148] As mentioned in the FCC on 5:8-11, Israel's territory of Gilead, Jezreel and Galilee have already been annexed by Assyria in the north, while Judah has also impinged into Israel's territory

---

[145] Gale. A. Yee, "The Book of Hosea: Introduction, Commentary, and Reflection", in Lender E. Keck and others (eds), *The New Interpreter's Bible*, vol. vii (Nashville: Abingdon Press, 1996), 248.

[146] Mays, *Hosea*, 89.

[147] Cf. Deut. 27:17, cf.19:24.

[148] Wolff, *Hosea*, 114; Mays, *Hosea*, 90.

from the southern side. Thus, the expression, "oppressed, crushed in judgment" conveys the victimization of Ephraim of her territorial borders.[149] The language that describes Ephraim's present state, עשוק "oppressed" and רצוץ "crushed" belong to the language of covenant curse, which indicates that Yahweh has enforced covenant judgment against Israel. The reason is introduced by כי "because" Ephraim has gone after "futility" (צו). As stated in the TCC on v.11b, "futility" refers to the alliance with Rezin, which Israel pursued by betraying her covenant brother, Judah.[150] In other words, Israel's political security is not determined by her coalition partners with other nations, which in fact is futility. Instead, her existence and security as a political nation is dependent upon her relationship with her covenant partner, Yahweh. Ephraim's futile alliance with Rezin shows her lack of faithfulness to trust the basic covenant promise that "Yahweh will grant that the enemies who rise up against you will be defeated before you. They will come at you from one direction but flee from you in seven."[151]

Both Israel (v.11) and Judah (v.10) have violated the covenant stipulations as a result of which Yahweh pronounces his sentence by employing a simile of putrefaction (v.12). Yahweh declares that he now acts like a עש "pus" and רקב "rottenness" to Israel and Judah respectively. Both the terms describe the decay of dead bodies (cf. Job 13:28). The description represents the war images of physical wounds and hurts inflicted by the enemies in the aftermath of the military defeat and devastation. Such description of sickness is prominent in the covenant curses (cf. Deut. 28:21–22, 27, 35, 59–61; 32:24), as such, the similes of "pus" and "rottenness" in vv 13–14 bear implicit reference to the broken covenant. It is Yahweh, not Assyria, who is the cause of their wound.

Hosea further indicts Israel and Judah (v.13) since instead of realizing that Yahweh is enforcing his covenant curses for their disloyalty and return to him, both Israel and Judah sought Assyria's help to find answer to their national imbroglio. King Ahaz of Judah appealed to Assyria after the Syro-Ephraimite coalition attacked Judah in 734 BCE (2 Kgs 16:10). By 732 BCE even Ephraim under king Hoshea yielded to Tiglath-Pileser III for peace (2 Kgs 15:30ff).[152] However, neither Ephraim nor Judah found answer to their national disaster by appealing "to Assyria" (v.13). The plural suffixes כם "you" in v 13b refer to both Israel and Judah.

Yahweh again pronounced judgment against Israel and Judah in vv.14-15. Using the metaphor of שחל "lion" and כפיר "young lion", Yahweh describes the looming destruction that would violently tear up the two kingdoms. The verb מציל from √נצל means "to carry off /take away" and indicates the idea of exile. Since the repetition of first person pronoun, אנכי, אני, אני in v.14 emphasize that

[149] Sweeney, *The Twelve Prophets*, 1: 66.

[150] Cf. Wolff, *Hosea*, 114; Mays, *Hosea*, 90; Birch, *Hosea, Joel and Amos*, 65.

[151] Deut. 28:7 [RSV].

[152] Macintosh, *Hosea*, 211.

Yahweh himself causes the destruction against Israel and Judah, the emphasis of v.14 conveys that Yahweh himself will exile and alienate Israel and Judah from their land. The theomorphic curses that invoke harm inflicted by wild animals[153] and the destruction caused by lions in v. 14 yet again emphasizes that the issue here is the violation of the covenant.

In the above passage, Hosea does not employ any particular land terminology; however, the terms Assyria, Ephraim, and Judah speak of land in the sense of political nations. Two observations can be made on the above exegesis that seems to have broken the tripartite relationship in 5:8-15.

First, alliance with foreign nations is seen as an expression of a lack of faith in Yahweh, the covenantal God. In the covenant tradition, trusting Yahweh and obeying his commands are set as condition for Israel to live a secured existence in the land (Deut. 28:7). The tradition also warns that disobedience to Yahweh and to his covenantal stipulations will cause defeat and destruction of the land (Deut. 28:25). Since faithfulness to the covenant with Yahweh demands loyalty only to Yahweh, Israel and Judah's alliances with and loyalty to foreign nations are considered as a violation of the covenant terms. As such, Yahweh decreed judgment that both Israel and Judah will be defeated, their land will be desolated, and the people will be carried off from the land (v.14).

Second, intruding into each other's territory is seen as a violation of the covenant stipulations. The covenant tradition warns that removing the boundary mark is a serious offence before Yahweh. Both Israel and Judah engaged in war to annex each other's territory, which is considered as a violation of the covenant. As such, Yahweh decreed that Israel and Judah would be oppressed, crushed and suffer decay and putrefaction.

Israel and Judah's secured existence as a political nation cannot be determined by their political alliances with foreign nations, apart from Yahweh. Israel and Judah's territorial annexations cannot offer them any secured political dominance. All these attempts are considered as "futility."

4.7. Covenant, Torah and Exodus Traditions (Hosea 8:9-13)

In Hosea's usage "lovers" (v.9) metaphorically refers to the breach of covenant relationship, which speaks of the Covenant Tradition while the reference to the rejection of Yahweh's instruction (v.12) speaks of the Torah tradition and the sentence to send Israel back to Egypt (v.13) indicate Exodus Traditions. The Covenant, Torah and Exodus are interrelated traditions, which Hosea employs to speak of the tripartite relationship. Instead of coming to Yahweh, Israel went after her lovers and rejected Yahweh's instructions, which result in Yahweh's punishment against Israel by sending them back to Egypt (alienation from the land). 8:9-13 thus speaks of how the relationship between Yahweh, Israel and land remain affected.

[153] Lev. 26:22; Deut. 28:26; 32:24.

4.7.1. Translation on Hosea 8:9-13

9 Indeed[a] they have gone up to[b] Assyria, a wild ass[c] wandering alone; Ephraim hired the lovers[d].

10 Even if they hire with the nations, I will now gather them up[a] and they shall soon writhe under the burden[b] of kings and princes.

11 When Ephraim multiplied altars to expiate sin, they became to him altars for sinning.

12 Though I write for him the multitude of my instructions[a], they are regarded as a strange thing.

13 Though they offer choice sacrifices, though they eat flesh, Yahweh does not accept them. Now he will remember[a] their iniquity, and punish[a] their sins; they shall return to Egypt[b].

4.7.2. Text Critical Comments on Hosea 8:9-13

V.9a: כי according to Wolff has a deictic-emphatic sense with a contradictory, scornful undertone that can be interpreted with exclamation "indeed!", "verily!" "that's it!"[154]

V.9b: Andersen and Freedman opine that probably עלו "they have gone up" points to the officials of Menahem who went up to pay a huge tribute to Assyria (ca. 738 BCE, cf. 2 Kgs 15:19-20).[155] Macintosh, on the other hand, argues that it refers to Hoshea's payment of tribute to Assyria to secure his throne after he deposed king Pekah in 732/1 BCE.[156] In the light of v.8 where Israel is portrayed as already "swallowed" and now remains "a useless vessel", Macintosh's argument can be sustained. This means, "they have gone up to Assyria" most likely refers to Hoshea's attempt to pacify Tiglath-Pilesar III after he attacked and annexed some of Israel's territory in Trans-Jordan, Galilee, the Jezreel Valley and coastal plain.

V.9c: פרא "wild donkeys" usually lived in herds and were always wary of humanity (Job 39:5-8). Mays states that פרא is used here to point to Israel's willful stubbornness in not remaining in the company of Yahweh.[157] According to Szabo, פרא expresses the metaphor in which wild animals were domesticated. He states that after the wild asses are caught they were loaded with heavy burdens to domesticate them. The metaphorical indication he sees in the term "wild donkeys" is that Israel will groan under the burdens of the king of Assyria.[158]

V.9d: By employing the term אהבים "lovers", Hosea picks up the metaphor of adulterous love affairs to describe Israel's alliance with the foreign nation, Assyria. The image recalls the breach of covenant relationship in which Israel shifts her

---

[154] Wolff, *Hosea*, 90, 135.

[155] Andersen and Freedman, *Hosea*, 505.

[156] Macintosh, *Hosea*, 318.

[157] Mays, *Hosea*, 121.

[158] Szabó, "Textual problems in Amos and Hosea", 515.

loyalty to Assyria, while the covenantal requirements demand Israel's exclusive loyalty to Yahweh as her husband.

V.10a: The term אקבצם "I will gather them" is understood differently. LXX renders it as *εισδεξομαι αυτους* "I will admit, receive them."[159] Rashi's interpretation closely follows LXX as he sees the term expresses a future redemptive activity of Yahweh.[160] However, such interpretation is unlikely since the literary context does not suggest any promise of redemption. Since Ephraim is not yet largely scattered, Rudolph argues that "gathering" is inappropriate. Instead he proposes that אקבצם "I will gather" should be emended to אקצבם "I will cut them off."[161] Citing the occurrence of קבץ in 9:6, which appears in parallel to קבר "to bury", that is, to come to an end, Macintosh argues that אקבצם can be interpreted as "I shall make an end of them."[162] Quite distinctively, Wolff states that the present passage employs a form of messenger speech to convey the threat. As such, he argues that אקבצם refers to "gathering together for judgment."[163] Likewise, Mays and Stuart also argue that the term describes the divine punishment.[164] Since the context of the passage appears to be an indictment for making alliances with nations, אקבצם mostly likely conveys the idea of judgment.

V.10b: LXX renders *του ξριειν* on the basis of which Gratz and Marti proposed ממשׁח "they grow weary of."[165] MT renders it as מִשׂא, literally "load or burden", which can be retained here since the context seems to suggest that the tribute and taxation are indicated. In other words, the term conveys that Ephraim will soon begin to writhe under the taxation burden of the kings and princes.

V.12a: The term תורה "instructions" is stated as אכתב "I write", which means something already fixed in writing and since the list of the Decalogue sins is mentioned in 4:2ff, Mays is probably right to argue that תּורתי "my instruction" indicates that Hosea knew a written form of *Torah*.[166] Since the early copy of the covenant book (Deuteronomy) was found and the reading of which shocked Josiah when it was read to him (2 Kgs 22:11-13),[167] we can assume that the written form of some portions of the Torah was already in existence. The content of the Torah, as Hosea understood, appears in close association with the covenant (8:1), the Decalogue of Sinai (4:2), and the priestly responsibilities (4:6).[168] However,

[159] Macintosh, *Hosea*, 322.

[160] Rashi, cited in Macintosh, *Hosea*, 320.

[161] Rudolph, cited in Macintosh, *Hosea*, 320.

[162] Macintosh, *Hosea*, 320.

[163] Wolff, *Hosea*, 143.

[164] Mays, *Hosea*, 121; Stuart, *Hosea-Jonah*, 135.

[165] Cited in Macintosh, *Hosea*, 323.

[166] Mays, *Hosea*, 122.

[167] *Hosea-Jonah*, 136.

[168] For the discussion on the existence of the written word of God in the Northern kingdom as the Torah, see Frank Crusemann, *The Torah: Theology and Social History of the Old Testament Law*,

the instructions of Yahweh were considered as foreign (זר) because the priest and prophet were negligent in exposing the Torah among the people (cf. 4:5, 6), and thus it became a "foreign" thing to the people.

V.13a: Both the verbs √זכר "to remember"[169] and √פקד "to punish"[170] can have the sense of "paying attention to," or "acting upon" and both appears in the contexts of dealing with legal matters,[171] with a strong forensic sense. In employing these legal forensic terms, Yahweh is portrayed as the judge who has proven the indictment and pronounces the sentence upon the guilty.

V.13b: Egypt appears thirteen times in Hosea in which five of its occurrences recall the beginning of salvation history (2:15; 11:1; 12:9, 14; 13:4); in other five occurrences, Egypt appears in parallel to Assyria (7:11; 9:3; 11:5, 11; 12:2), while in the remaining three "Egypt" appears alone (7:16; 8:13; 9:6).[172] In 12:9 [MT. 10] and 13:4, the Exodus tradition appears with explicit reference to Yahweh as Israel's God, "I am Yahweh your God from the land of Egypt", which recalls the revelation of Yahweh's name to Moses (Ex. 3:4). In 12:9 [10], the Exodus tradition appears to convey that Yahweh will act to bring back Israel to the wilderness state of poverty so that Israel will not depend on their affluence, but on Yahweh. On the other hand, in 13:4, the Exodus tradition is recalled to express that no other God has acted as powerfully as Yahweh did for Israel. A similar expression appears in 12:13 where the Exodus tradition is employed to remind Israel that through his prophet, Yahweh brings out Israel from Egypt and he continues to preserve Israel through his prophet, yet because Israel continued to provoke Yahweh, Israel will have to bear the punishment (12:13).[173] In these references, the Exodus tradition is employed to explain Israel's historical identity in relation to Yahweh's kind act. Based on the act of Yahweh in the Exodus, Yahweh is vindicated to proclaim his instructions to Israel and to determine his course of judgment for Israel's failure to live according to his expressed will. In other words, the Exodus tradition appears in Hosea mostly to justify the coming judgment for Israel's failure to reciprocate Yahweh's kind act.

The present occurrence of the Exodus tradition in v. 13 also appears in the context of judgment. Mays argues that the punishment "they shall return to Egypt" can be explained in connection with the expression "return to Egypt", which appears in parallel to the threat of Assyria in 9:3 and 11:5. He thus argues that the punishment here refers to either Israel's surrender to Assyria's deportation or to flee to Egypt as refugees.[174] In a little distinctive line, J. Lundblom sees the

---

trans. by Allan W. Mahnke (Edinburgh: T&T Clark, 1996), 18-20.

[169] זכר, Gen 40:14; Lev 26:45; Amos 1:9.

[170] פקד, Exod 32:34; Lev 18:25; Isa 13:11; cf. Hos 1:4; 9:9b.

[171] Stuart, *Hosea-Jonah*, 136-137.

[172] Wolff, *Hosea*, 145.

[173] Steve McKenzie, "Exodus Typology in Hosea", *Restoration Quarterly* 22/1-2 (1979) 102.

[174] Mays, *Hosea*, 123.

reference to "Egypt" in v.13 as an inclusio by tying it together with "Assyria" in v.9 and argues that "return to Egypt" actually refers to the deportation to Assyria. Lundblom thus sees that Assyria to whom Ephraim turned for an alliance in v.9 is metaphorically another "Egypt."[175] This means, according to Lundblom, just as the messengers have gone to Assyria with their tribute money, they will later be forced to travel this same road again when Israel is taken into captivity. For further discussion, see the tradition and theological comments in the following section.

4.7.3. Form Critical Comments on Hosea 8:9-13

Freedman proposes that Hos. 8:9-13 is a unit of poetry, which can be isolated on the basis of the inclusio:[176] behold they have gone up to Assyria (v. 9); behold they will return to Egypt (v.13). Following Freedman's proposal, Lundblom demonstrates how 8:9-13 forms a separate unit of poem by pointing out the parallel couplets in the unit: the repetition of "behold" (מהה v.9 and מהה in v.13); pairing a perfect and an imperfect in typical poetic style עלו "they have gone up" (v.9) and הבהבו "they shall return" (v.13), and using אשור "Assyria" and מצרים "Egypt" as a fixed pair (v.9, cf. v. 13).[177] Though such poetic parallelisms in 8:9-13 appear convincing, there is also a clear reference to indictment against the sins of a political alliance v.9 and heterodox religious practices (vv.11-13a) and the pronouncement of judgment (v.10, 13b). Thus, we consider vv.9-13 to be a unit of judgment speech, which can be outlined as follows:

Name of the Accused:	They (Ephraim) v.9
Indictment (against political alliance):	have gone up to Assyria…Ephraim hired the lovers (v.9).
Sentence:	… I will now gather them up and they shall soon writhe under the burden of kings and princes (v.10)
Indictment (against cultic practices):	… Ephraim multiplied altars … I write for him the multitude of my instructions, they are regarded as a strange thing… (vv.11-13a.)
Sentence:	Now he will remember their iniquity, and punish their sins; they shall return to Egypt (v.13b).

The aftermath of the Syro-Ephraimite War is the most likely setting for the present oracle. Scholars have found the common setting of 5:8-7:16 and ch.8 as

---

[175] J. Lundblom, "Poetic Structure and Prophetic Rhetoric in Hosea", *VT* 29 (1979) 307.

[176] David Noel Freedman, "Prolegomenon", in George Buchanan Gray, *The Forms of Hebrew Poetry* (New York, 1972), xxxvi-xxxvii.

[177] Lundbom, "Poetic Structure and Prophetic Rhetoric in Hosea", 300.

belonging to the period of military and political turmoil.[178] Tiglath-Pilesar III's military campaign had successfully neutralized Northern Israel, while Hoshea ben Elah had dethroned Pekah and immediately paid tribute to Assyria in 732/1 BCE with an intention of securing his throne and to stop total conquest of Israel by Tiglath-Pileser III (cf. 7:8–12). This is most likely to be the reference of "they have gone up to Assyria" in v.9 and the worsening political situation described in vv. 9-10. In this case, we can date the passage to the period of king Hoshea, probably ca. 732 and 725.[179]

4.7.4. Tradition and Theological Comments in the Light of Tripartite Relationship

The term covenant is not explicitly mentioned in the present unit. However, as mentioned above, in Hosea's usage "lovers" (v.9) metaphorically speaks of the breach of covenant relationship. "Lovers" is used here to indict Israel for shifting her allegiance from Yahweh to Assyria. Hosea sees Israel's going after her lovers to be a violation of her covenantal relationship with Yahweh (see the discussion below). The Israelites also set up multiple altars after the Canaanite practice, which is a violation of the covenant stipulation of a single sanctuary (Deut. 12:4-5, 11, 14).[180] Such covenantal violations are seen to be the basis of Hosea's indictment.

Hosea mentions "Torah" to indict Israel in v.12. The Torah tradition contains Yahweh's instructions in matters related to a special relationship between Yahweh and Israel in which Yahweh is seen as "Israel's God" and Israel as Yahweh's "treasured possession". To regulate that relationship, the instructions of law were given to Israel, which became the tradition of Torah. In the Torah tradition, Israel's obedience to the Torah is envisaged as a guarantee to secure her life in the land while disobedience would lead to punishment that would affect Israel's survival in the land. In 8:9-13 Israel's failure to abide by the law of Torah is stated to be the reason for affecting the tripartite relationship. In v.12 Israel's disobedience is served as the basis of Yahweh's indictment for which judgment is announced in v.13b. In announcing Yahweh's judgment, Hosea employs the Exodus tradition, "they will return to Egypt" (v. 13b). In the Exodus tradition, Egypt is remembered as a place of Israel's enslavement before Yahweh's deliverance of and covenant with Israel. However, Hosea's use of the Exodus tradition here is different in that unlike the early Exodus where Yahweh delivers the enslaved Israelites, Yahweh will now reverse Israel's destiny by reverting Israel back to her former misery and affliction as in her Exodus slavery.

Israel is indicted for seeking Assyria's help in v.9f. As mentioned in the above FCC, המה "they" refers to the accused who are identified as "Ephraim" (v.9). Yahweh's indictment against Israel is that המה "they" (Ephraim) have gone

[178] Wolff, *Hosea*, 136-137; Stuart, *Hosea-Jonah*, 130.

[179] Stuart, *Hosea-Jonah*, 130.

[180] Stuart, *Hosea-Jonah*, 135.

up (עלו) to Assyria. The verb עלו, as argued in the TCC on v.9b, refers to Hoshea's emissary who went to Assyria on behalf of Israel's king to pacify and to pay tributary taxation to Tiglath-Pilesar III to save the kingdom of Israel from further Assyrian's invasion. Since the pronoun המה "they" (Ephraim) is in emphatic mood, it is probably right to state that המה emphasizes Israel's willful scheme to offer a tribute to Assyria.[181] If this argument can be sustained, then the point Hosea emphasizes is that Israel has willfully chosen to seek Assyria's help for her political security instead of Yahweh's. Israel's political alliance with Assyria is castigated by using the terms פרא "wild ass" and אהבים "lovers". Wild asses are always suspicious of men and live away from civilization. By comparing Ephraim with a wild ass, Hosea points out that Israel has chosen to stay away from the company of Yahweh. The image of "lovers", as stated in the above TCC on v.9d, recalls the breach of covenant relationship in which Israel sought help and pledged her loyalty to Assyria for her safety instead of seeking and trusting Yahweh's help as the covenant requirements demand Israel's exclusive trust upon Yahweh for her security. Hosea thus sees Israel's alliance with Assyria as a violation and mistrust of her covenant relationship with Yahweh. In such covenant context of Israel as a political nation, Hosea understood Israel's existence as a political nation not in terms of absolute independence but in terms of subordination to Yahweh's sovereign authority. As such, going after Assyria for her own political advantage is understood as a direct challenge to Yahweh's sovereign authority.

Based on the indictment regarding Israel's infidelity in v.9, the sentence is pronounced in v.10. In the judgment, Yahweh declares that he will "gather" Israel and they shall "writhe" under the "burden" of the kings and princes. Attempts have been made to emend MT's קבץ and read "disperse" "scatter" so as to convey an idea of exile (see also the TCC on v.10a). However, such emendation may not be necessary, since קבץ "gather" describes the gathering up for judgment of the accursed,[182] while חיל "writhe" describes the context of political danger.[183] Thus, whether we emend אקבצם "gather" to favor the reading of exile or not, we see that "to gather" in the context of looming political danger echoes the coming exile in which Israel will be taken away and will remain as the subject to the dominion of her enemies.[184] Such expression is a kind of judgment specified in the covenant curses (cf. Deut. 28:36). משא "burden" refers to tribute or taxation. Since "kings and princes" is cited in some ancient texts as the title for the king of Assyria,[185] we can probably construe that it is Assyria who will burden Israel of tributary taxation under which Israel will suffer with writhing. Though Assyria is seen as the instrument of destruction, the first person singular verb אקבץ "I will gather"

[181] Wolff, *Hosea*, 142.

[182] cf. Joel 4:2 [3:2]; Zeph 3:8; cf. Hos 9:6. See, Stuart, *Hosea-Jonah*, 135.

[183] Cf. Mic. 4:10; Jer. 4:19; 51:29; Ezek. 30:16. See, Wolff, *Hosea*, 144.

[184] Mays, *Hosea*, 121; Stuart, *Hosea-Jonah*, 135.

[185] Birch, *Hosea, Joel and* Amos, 81; Macintosh, *Hosea*, 321; Mays, *Hosea*, 121.

attributes the action to Yahweh. In other words, it is Yahweh himself who will cause Israel's debacle.

Israel is indicted again in vv. 11-13a for its their cultic practices. First, the castigation is directed to Israel for the multiplication of altars. As mentioned above, the setting up of multiple altars was a Canaanite practice, which is a violation of the covenant stipulation of a single sanctuary (Deut. 12:4-5, 11, 14). Since an altar was meant for sacrifices for the atonement of committed offences, more altars were erected in Israel to expatiate the sins (חטא). However, the altar sites became places of false worship, places to satiate their gluttony, drunkenness, and to worship other gods.[186] Instead of expiating their sins, altars thus became places to accumulate more sins. Second, Israel is accused of disregarding תורה "the laws or instructions" (v 12). As mentioned in the TCC on v.12a, תורה refers to the disclosure of Yahweh's will concerning the covenant stipulations (8:1), the Decalogue of Sinai (4:2), and the priestly teachings and responsibilities (4:6). However, the Torah, which is supposed to maintain and preserve the covenant relationship between Yahweh and Israel, became a strange thing (זר) to Israel.

Israel's multiplication of sins (v.11) and their disregard of Yahweh's instructions (v.12) are served as the basis of Yahweh's judgment (v.13b). Yahweh announces that he will "remember" (זכר) Israel's guilt and "punish" (פקד) her for her sins. As stated in the TCC on v.13a, both the verbs have forensic sense of legal setting, which indicate that the judge, Yahweh has established Israel's offence. The punishment is made clear in the final sentence, "behold they will return to Egypt". What punishment "return to Egypt" means is difficult to determine. Whether "return to Egypt" refers to the deportation to Assyria and be enslaved like in their old Exodus or whether "return to Egypt" refers to the escape to Egypt in the aftermath of Assyria's attack remains a contentious issue. In any case, (whether enslavement to Assyria or escaping to Egypt) the theological significance of "return to Egypt" speaks about the looming exile, which will alienate the people of Israel from their political land. The sentence will thus reverse Israel's salvation-history and Israel will once again be alienated from their land, and will be enslaved and oppressed in a foreign land. Israel's departure from the teachings of Yahweh's Torah will alienate Israel from political land.

Scholars have noted a close affinity between Hosea and Deuteronomy. One such instance is in 8:9-13. One the one hand Deuteronomy 17:16 warns that the Israelite kings should not look unto Egypt, and by extension of its meaning other nations, for aid, because Yahweh warned, "You shall never return that way again" and on the other hand, Deut. 12: 4-5, 11, 14, 30-31 warns Israel to offer sacrifices only in a sanctuary that Yahweh designates. The debate of whether the book of Deuteronomy is early or late is briefly discussed in the Historical Background. Though most critical scholars believe that Deuteronomy comes later than Hosea, recent scholars like Gordon McConville, Gordon Wenham, Peka Pitkanen

[186] Sweeney, *The Twelve Prophets*, 91.

and others have convincingly argued for the early date of Deuternomy.[187] This contentious issue need not detain us here. However, for our present purpose it needs to be mentioned similar ideas and beliefs found in Deuteronomy could have shaped Hosea's thinking. Deuteronomy helps us understand Hosea's text better today. In the light of Deut 17:6 and 12:4-5,11ff, cited above, we can state that in turning to an other nation for help and in setting up the multiple altars, Israel had violated the covenant stipulations. Thus, Hosea announces that the gift of the land will be taken back, and the people will return to Egypt in exile, a forfeiture of the land.[188]

Based on the above exegesis, we can make a few observations. First, an important theological significance in relation to tripartite relationship is that for Israel to depart from Yahweh is to arrive at the loss of her land and nation. Hosea expresses this by portraying Israel's willful departure from Yahweh to seek Assyria's help for her survival. However, Israel would instead be burdened with taxation and deportation. The emphasis is that apart from Yahweh, Israel's dependence on nations cannot grant her a political security. Second, rejection of Yahweh's Torah and existence in the land as an independent political nation are mutually exclusive. Hosea explains this by stating that Israel has regarded the teachings of Torah as a strange thing and likewise, Yahweh destined Israel to a strange land, "they shall return to Egypt". The emphasis is that for Israel to exist as an independent political nation is to live according to the covenant and the instructions of the Torah. Israel's failure to live accordingly became the reason for Yahweh to sentence Israel to punishment, which includes the threat of war, exile and deportation from their political land. In other words, Israel's willful disregard of the covenant and Yahweh's instructions appear to be the reason of jeopardizing the tripartite relationship. In such description of jeopardized tripartite relationship, Israel would neither have a stable political nation nor would Israel exist as a politically independent nation as Israel willfully departed from Yahweh and rejected his instructions. In describing Israel's relationship with Yahweh and the precarious political situation of Israel, Hosea did not employ any technical land terminology. However, the use of terms such as "Israel", "Assyria" and "Egypt" express the territories of political land. Thus, the idea of land as political nation appears prominently in Hosea's oracle in 8:9-13.

4.8. Covenant-Torah Tradition (Hosea 10:13b-15)

Though Torah in not mentioned in 10:13b-14, the reference to "Your (Israel's) ways" (v.13b) appears in sharp contrast and opposition to Yahweh's way indicating that Israel has rejected the Torah Tradition. For trusting in their ways instead of

---

[187] The view that Deuteronomy was written late is not widely held by the scholars. See, Gordon McConville, *Deuteronomy,* Leicester Apollos; Downer's Grove, IVP, 2002; Wenham, "The Date of Deuteronomy: Linch-pin of Old Testament Criticism", (1985) 15-20.

[188] Steve Mckenzie, "Exodus Typology in Exodus", *Restoration Quarterly* 22/1-2 (1979) 104.

Yahweh's, the covenant curse punishment of defeat from enemies, annihilation of people, alienation from and destruction of the land are invoked (vv.14-15). This indicates that the Covenant Tradition is employed to explain how the tripartite relationship is severed because of forgetting the Torah Tradition in 10:13b-15.

4.8.1. Translation on Hosea 10:13b-15

13b Because you have trusted in your way[a] and in the multitude of your warriors,

14 therefore the tumult of war shall rise against your people, and all your fortresses shall be destroyed, as Shalman[a] destroyed Beth-arbel on the day of battle when mothers were smashed in pieces[b] with their children.

15 Thus, it shall be done to you, O Bethel[a], because of your great wickedness[b]. At dawn[c] the king of Israel shall be utterly cut off.

4.8.2. Text Critical Comments on Hosea 10:13b-15

V.13ba: The MT's בדרכך, literally "in your way" is rendered in the LXX as *τοις αρμασιν* "chariots" perhaps to harmonize or to make parallel with גבוריך "warriors". Following the LXX, Wellhausen, Wolff and Mays emend MT's בדרכך to ברכבך "chariots."[189] Instead of emending the MT's rendering, S. Bartina attempts to compare דרך with Ugaritic *drkt*, meaning "dominion", "power", and argues that such meaning is possible here. Macintosh, however, rejects this view on the ground that there is no clear parallel or support in the tradition.[190] Instead of emending בדרכך to ברכבך to convey a war context, we can retain MT's בדרכך "your ways" and still retain the context of war since we see military implication of Israel's "ways" in the light of the term "warriors". דרכך "in your way" can refer to "the course of life", "actions" and "undertakings"[191] assuming that Hosea indicts Israel for following its own way or course of life apart from Yahweh. דרכך appears here in a negative sense, which appears in opposition to Yahweh's way.[192]

V.14a: Scholars have proposed two possible interpretations of שלמן "Shalman". First, it is understood to be a corrupted or abbreviated name of Shalmaneser V, king of Assyria (727-722 BCE), who is believed to have invaded and destroyed Israel in his military camping against Samaria (724 BCE). It is believed that he died soon after the conquest of Samaria and his successor Sargon II claimed credit for the conquest.[193] Second, it is understood to be a reference to Salamanu, the Moabite king who is mentioned among the listed names of kings who paid tribute to Tiglath-Pilesar III of Assyria. In any case, the reference of Shalum in relation to cruel slaughter points to past collective memory in

[189] See, Wolff, *Hosea*, 181; Mays, *Hosea*, 147.

[190] Macintosh, *Hosea*, 425.

[191] Andersen and Freedman, *Hosea*, 569.

[192] Zvi, *Hosea*, 222.

[193] Sweeney, *The Twelve Prophets*, I: 111.

which Israel suffered a gruesome atrocities and Hosea warns that Bethel will suffer similar fate because of her wickedness.

V.14b: The LXX reads *ηδαφισαν* "they dash to the ground", a third plural active instead of the MT's passive. רטשׁ "to dash into pieces" is used to describe the wounds inflicted by arrows (Isa. 13:18), hurling of children against the solid rock (Ps 137:9)[194] and dropping the children from a height or smashing the children's skull.[195] The picture here is of cruelty in murdering the children in front of their parents and killing the parents thereafter in a manner of wholesale extermination.

V.15a: Following the LXX rendering of *οικος του 'Ισραηλ* "house of Israel", most scholars emend MT's בית־אל "Bethel" to בית־ישׂראל "house of Israel" on the ground that Hosea refers to Bethel pejoratively as בית-און "Beth-aven" (cf. 4:15; 5:8; 10:5).[196] Macintosh however, argues that though Hosea uses Beth-aven as a derogative term to Bethel, in the present case Bethel can be retained as the characteristic wickedness of Bethel is expressed in the following "because of your great wickedness" and it may have been unnecessary to use the pejorative term.[197] He concludes that "Bethel" represents the site of national cult while "king of Israel" in the following clause represents the royal house of Israel.[198] We follow Macintosh's proposal and retain MT's rendering of בית־אל as referring to Bethel.

V.15b: רעת רעתכם literally "wickedness of your wickedness", which is a Hebrew style of superlative expression.[199] It is translated as "great wickedness" to express the intensity and the outrageous wicked action.

V.15c: בשחר "at dawn" refers to the instant moment of the battle as soon as the troops took the battle field. Probably it predicts a short encounter.[200]

4.8.3. Form Critical Comments on Hosea 10:13b-15

Scholars have noted a break of unit in v.13a and see a new unit in v.13b, which ends with v.15.[201] Vv.13b-15 consists of a distinct theme and structure. Unlike vv.11-13a where the theme of agriculture is employed, כי in v.13b shifts to a theme of war and ends with the destruction of the Israelite kingdom in v.15.[202] The present unit is a prophetic speech of judgment against Israel with indictment for trusting

---

194 Macintosh, *Hosea*, 428.

195 Andersen and Freedman, *Hosea*, 571.

196 Wolff, *Hosea*, 181; Mays, *Hosea*, 148; Stuart, *Hosea-Jonah*, 167.

197 Macintosh, *Hosea*, 433.

198 Macintosh, *Hosea*, 433.

199 Wolff, *Hosea*, 181.

200 David Allen Hubbard, *Hosea*, TOTC (Leicester, England: IVP, 1989), 184.

201 Harper, *Amos and Hosea*, 356; Wolff, *Hosea*, 183; Mays, *Hosea*, 148; Birch, *Hosea, Joel and Amos*, 95.

202 Birch, *Hosea, Joel and Amos*, 95.

in military power rather than in Yahweh (v.13b) and the judgment sentence in vv.14-15. The structure of the present unit can be outlined as follows:

Indictment:	... you have trusted in your way and in the multitude of your warriors (v.13b).
Formula of judgment:	therefore (v.14).
Sentence:	the tumult of war shall rise... your fortresses shall be destroyed, as Shalman destroyed Beth-arbel on the day of battle when mothers were smashed in pieces with their children... it shall be done to you... the king of Israel shall be utterly cut off (vv.14-15).

Wolff argues that the change of second person plural (vv.11-13a) to singular "your warriors", "your people", "your fortresses" (vv.13b-14) suggests that royal representatives of Samaria were present at the scene (at Samaria).[203] Mays argues that the reference to Israel's growing confidence in military strength (v.13b) probably reflects the setting of the period of Hoshea ben Elah, who was beginning to revolt against his Assyrian masters just before the end of Tiglath-Pilesar's reign.[204] After the political debacle in 732/1 BCE, though Israel was reduced to Assyria's vassalage, she began to strengthen her military strength (v.13b). Seizing the opportunity of political transition in Assyria from Tiglath-Pilesar III to Shalmaneser V, probably Hoshea ben Elah attempted to throw off Assyria's yoke by putting his confidence in the growing military strength (2 Kgs 17:4). Probably Hosea's oracle in vv.13b-15 reflects such setting of military preparations.

4.8.4. Tradition and Theological Comments in the Light of Tripartite Relationship

As stated in the above comments, the term "Torah" does not appear here but the indictment of trusting "in your ways" is contrasted with Yahweh's way, which indicates that Yahweh's indictment is based on the rejection of Yahweh's way (Torah). The Torah tradition, though not explicit, is embedded in the indictment. Also, the term covenant is absent, but the punishment mentioned in 10:14-15 is rooted in the covenant curse tradition.[205] The sentence to destruction of Israel's מבצר "fortification" recalls the covenant curse of Deut. 28:52, "They shall besiege you in all your towns, until your high and fortified walls, in which you trusted, come down". The reference to the horrors of war and the destruction of both the population and city like Bethel recall the covenant punishment reserved for Israel's rebellion, "Your land will be laid waste and your cities will lie in ruins"

[203] Wolff, *Hosea*, 183.

[204] Mays, *Hosea*, 148.

[205] Yee sees that the particle כי reveals the covenantal violation that instead of trusting Yahweh, the covenanted God, Israel relies in her own power and strength. Yee, "The Book of Hosea", 275.

(Lev 26:33, cf. Deut 32:25; 28:34, 53–57; Lev 26:33, 37). Contrary to the covenant, Israel had adopted the covenant-shattering domestic and international policies for which Yahweh indicts and sentences Israel to judgment that will lead to the final destruction and loss of political nation.

כי "because" introduces Yahweh's indictment in which Israel is accused of trusting in her "ways" and "warriors" (v.13b) instead of trusting Yahweh. As mentioned in the TCC on v.13ba, בדרכך "your ways" refers to the course of life, action or policy Israel had undertaken apart from Yahweh. Probably the indictment of trusting in "your ways" refers to Israel's confidence in her military strength as the theme of the passage moves to war and the military machinery of Israel. This reading is further supported by another military term "warriors" in v.13b. The evidence of Israel's military strength of the eighth century BCE is found in the *ANET* in which a mention is made about King Ahab's two thousand chariots.[206] At the time of Samaria's fall in 721 BCE, Sargon II of Assyria had claimed that he had captured fifty chariots from Israel.[207] Israel thus had a history of accumulating chariots and strengthening military forces to defend herself from external attacks. After Assyria crushed the Syro-Ephraimite coalition ca. 733 BCE, probably Israel would have strengthened her military forces to break loose from Assyria's tyranny (2 Kgs 17:4), which could be the background of Hosea's indictment against Israel's trust in her "ways" and "warriors". In any case, the offense lies not in the possession of warriors, but in trusting (בטח) in and relying on military prowess, which is understood as an offense against Yahweh in the writings of the eighth century prophets (cf. Am. 6:13; Isa. 31:1). In the covenant relationship, Yahweh is understood as the God who emancipates and protects Israel to exist as a nation and therefore acquisition of horses and chariots for military purpose is forbidden in the covenant stipulations of Deuteronomy (Deut. 17:16). Hosea sees Israel's trust in her military tactics (her ways) to be a misplaced confidence and thereby a rejection of the way of Yahweh, which in fact amounts to the violation of the covenant trust (relationship).

Based on the above indictment of Israel's misplaced confidence, the judgment is announced in v.14 about the brutalities of war that will bring the nation of Israel to destruction. This is described by employing the term שאון "tumult", which refers to the roaring and terrifying commotion of combat[208] that shall destroy Israel's fortress. The looming destruction will not only strike the military structures (fortress), but it will also strike the common people (women and children, cf. v.14) like Shalman destroyed Beth-arbel. Several proposals have been made concerning the reference of Shalman (see the above Text Critical Comments in 10:14a). The reference is obscure as this event is not found in

---

[206] J.B. Pritchard (ed.), *Ancient Near East Texts* (Princeton: Princeton University Press, 1954), 279.

[207] Pritchard, *Ancient Near East Texts*, 284.

[208] Stuart, *Hosea-Jonah*, 171.

any literature, Israelite or otherwise. However, this historical event must have been infamous among the Israelites of Hosea's day,[209] to which Hosea appeals to convey that the destructions of Israel will be like Shalman's destruction of Beth-arbel. In the manner of battles fought to exterminate a population by wantonly murdering even the mothers and children (2 Kgs 8:12; Isa 13:16; Nah 3:10; Ps 137:9; cf. Hos 13:16), Israel would experience brutality. Such suffering of the brutalities of war is predicted in the covenant stipulation as a punishment for Israel's rebellion against Yahweh (cf. Lev 26:37; Deut 32:25; 28:34, 53–57).

Further descriptions of destruction are associated with Bethel and the king of Israel (v.15). Bethel, as a site of the "calf of Samaria" is the national cultic place (cf. 8:5f) in which the first commandment of the Decalogue covenant, "you shall not have other gods" is violated. On the other hand, the king, as leader of the nation to whom the Israelite' army belongs, perpetuated the way of autonomy by trusting in military machinery instead of trusting Yahweh. Yahweh considers such mistrust and violation of the covenant stipulations as an act of "wickedness". Thus, "ככה" (v. 15) brutalities of war will soon bring annihilation. As mentioned in the TCC on v.15c, בשחר "at dawn" conveys the immediacy and speed with which the cruel battle will bring Israel's religious centre (Bethel), military machinery (fortress), population (women and children) and political kingdom (the king) to a miserable and cruel ending.

In the above exegesis, the term land does not appear however, the idea of land as political nation appears prominently, which is expressed in terms of destruction of fortress and cutting off its population from their political land. In the covenant tradition, the special relationship envisaged between Yahweh and Israel resulted in Yahweh's intervention on Israel's behalf to occupy the land. Israel's existence as a distinct political nation is understood to be the result of Yahweh's kind act. Yahweh is, therefore, a trusted covenanted partner of Israel's existence and security. To perpetuate this covenant relationship and to ensure Israel's security, the Torah was given as Yahweh's way of life for Israel. However, instead of trusting Yahweh's directed way of life (Torah), Israel trusted in her ways thereby rejecting the way of Yahweh (Torah). For such misplaced and misdirected trust of Israel, Yahweh invoked the covenant curse against Israel that includes the massacre of Israel's population, destruction of their land and alienation (cut off) from their land. The tripartite relationship is thus explained in terms of strained relationship due to the rejection of the Torah and Israel's alienation both from Yahweh and the land as a form of covenant punishment.

4.9. Covenant Tradition (Hosea 14:4-7 [MT. 14:5-8])

In Hosea's usage, אהב "love" (v.4) expresses loyalty and faithfulness in the relationship between Yahweh and Israel while שוב "return" (v.7) speaks of the

[209] Robert D. Bergen, "Calling Forth Yahweh's Curses: Hosea's Judgment of Israel in 8:1-10:15", *Criswell Theological Review* 7/1 (1993) 50.

reunion of relationship. In both cases, the relationship is linked with covenant faithfulness. This indicates that the Covenant Tradition is embedded in 14:4-7. Yahweh's free love for Israel and Israel's return to Yahweh reunites the covenant relationship which in turn ushers Yahweh's blessings for Israel upon the land. The tripartite relationship is thus explained within the covenant tradition in 14:4-7.

4.9.1. Translation on Hosea 14:4-7

4 I will heal their disloyalty[a]; I will love[b] them freely[c], for my anger has turned from them.

5 I will be as the dew[a] to Israel; he shall blossom as the lily, and he shall strike root[b] like a tree of Lebanon[c];

6 his shoots shall spread out; his beauty shall be like the olive, and his fragrance like Lebanon.

7 They shall return in his shadow, they shall flourish as a garden; they shall blossom as the vine, their fragrance shall be like the wine of Lebanon.

4.9.2. Text Critical Comments on Hosea 14:4-7

V.4a: The Targum reads, "I will accept them in their repentance", which conveys forgiveness as a condition to repentance.[210] The MT's משובתם "their disloyalty or apostasy" is rendered in the LXX as *τας κατοικιας αυτων* "their dwellings" perhaps the LXX mistakenly assumes the root to be ישב "to dwell". The MT's "disloyalty" is retained in the light of a call to "return" to Yahweh in v.1, which presupposes Israel's disloyalty.

V.4b: אהב "love" appears frequently in Hosea in close connection to covenant relationship. In 3:1 אהב "love" describes a husband's (Yahweh) act of winning back the wayward wife (Israel) despite the wife's love for her friend (adultery). In 11:1 אהב describes a spontaneous fatherly help and care for a child.[211] In both occurrences, אהב denotes Yahweh's act of restoring Israel back in relationship with him. אהב in v.4 appears in the context of Yahweh's healing of Israel's disloyalty, which presupposes Israel's unfaithfulness to the covenant that Yahweh seeks to heal.

V.4c: The LXX reads MT's נדבה as *ομολογως* "openly or confessedly", which does not make much difference in interpretation. נדבה is a term used to describe "free will or voluntary offering" or "offering made out of generosity" (cf. Deut. 12:6, 17; Am. 4:5). It is used here as an adverbial accusative to describe the nature of love.[212] It is interpreted here as "freely", which reverses the earlier threat of punishment, "My God will cast them off" (9:16).

---

[210] Kevin J. Cathcart and others (eds), *The Targum of the Minor Prophets: Translated, with a Critical Introduction, Apparatus and Notes*, vol. 14 (Edinburgh: T & T Clark, 1989), 61.

[211] Wolff, *Hosea*, 60.

[212] Macintosh, *Hosea*, 568.

V.5a: טל "dew" is a night-mist or vapor, which comes in the summer with the west wind and counteracts much of the disastrous effect wrought by the sirocco or east wind.[213] Yahweh is compared here figuratively with "dew" for the land of Israel. The imagery of "dew" recalls the wonder of the Palestinians' agricultural image. In Israel's topography, after long dry months without rain, spring would blossom up and the grapes would sprout amidst a dry land only because the dews moisturize the ground and sustain the growth of vegetations. In using this imagery, Hosea nullifies and counteracts Baal's effectiveness as Baal's worshippers consider that "dew" or "water" to be of Baal's activity to moisturize the earth to flourish. Baalism expresses this concept in sexual terms in which dew or rain is understood as Baal's semen to impregnate the consort Asherah or the earth for fertility.[214] By employing this image of "dew", Hosea not only illustrates the efficacy of God's salvation for Israel,[215] but also affirms Yahweh as God who controls the course of nature.

V.5b: The MT's verb ויך is from √נכה meaning "to strike" not in a sense of causing injury but in a sense of taking root. The term שרש "root" appears in Am. 2:9 in which Yahweh asserts that his action on Israel's behalf is the only reason for Israel's existence in Canaan. שרש "root" thus conveys the idea of (re) settlement in the land where Israel will again take her root. Such understanding of (re)settlement is expressed in the Targum where the MT's ויך שרשיו "and he shall strike root" is read as "and they shall dwell in their fortified land" (the Targum).[216] Israel's taking root in the land (ויך שרשיו) in v.6 makes a contrastive relation with the earlier punishment in which Ephraim is "stricken" and their root "dried up" (9:16).[217]

V.5c: "like a tree in Lebanon" is conjectured as כלבנה "like a poplar."[218] Such emendation is not necessary since Lebanon is, in other instances, associated with the prophetic predictions of restored covenant blessings (cf., Am. 9:13-14; Mic. 7:14; Isa. 55:13),[219] and since the present unit speaks of the future restoration of Israel, metaphorically expressed like a tree in "Lebanon" לבנון, better fits the message of restoration.

---

[213] Harper, *Amos and Hosea*, 413.

[214] Sweeney, *The Twelve Prophets*, 1: 140.

[215] Hans Walter Wolff, "Guilt and Salvation: A Study of the Prophecy of Hosea", *Interpretation* 15/3 (1961) 278.

[216] Cathcart and others (eds), *The Targum of the Minor Prophets*, 61.

[217] Ben Zvi, *Hosea*, 297.

[218] Those scholars include, Koehler-Baumgartner, *Hebraisches und aramaisches Lexicon Zum AT* (Leiden, 1953), E. Sellin, *Das Zwolfprophetenbach*, KAT 12/1 (Leipzig, 1929), Th. Robinson and F. Horst, *Die Zwolf Kleinen Propheten*, HAT 1/14 (Tubingen, 1964), A. Weiser, *Das Bauch der Zwolf Kleinen Propheten* ATD 24 (Gottingen, 1949), Cited in Wolff, *Hosea*, 232.

[219] Stuart, *Hosea-Jonah*, 215.

4.9.3. Form Critical Comments on Hosea 14:4-7

Unlike a prophetic exhortation in vv.1-3 [MT. 2-4], the divine speech in vv.4-7 employs the first person for Yahweh while the Israelites are addressed in the third person. This indicates that 14:4-7 is a divine speech that consists a separate unit. Vv.4-7 is an oracle of salvation that announces a future restoration and blessing to Israel.[220] Yahweh announces to heal Israel (v.4), which Israel had been seeking desperately but vainly (6:1) from her "lover" Assyria (5:13). Yahweh who is earlier portrayed as a lion, leopard and bear (5:14; 13:7) who laid waste the vineyard (2:12 [14]) is now compared with "dew" that promotes life and growth of vegetation.[221] Also the rejection motif expressed earlier, "not my people" and "no compassion" (1:6, 9; 2:4) is reversed to "how can I give up Ephraim… I will not destroy Ephraim (11:8-9), which express Yahweh's acceptance of Israel. Yahweh's acceptance of Israel in 11:8-9 is connected with Israel's repentance in 14:1-2, which promises Yahweh's blessings to Israel that will once again she will be rooted in the land and grow like cedar and olive trees and blossom like vine in 14:7. In other words, the form of salvation oracle announced in vv.4-7 reverses the earlier pronouncements of judgment to a future promise of restoration. The pattern of oracle includes an introductory messenger formula characterized by the divine "I" and Yahweh's prediction of future restoration.[222] V.4 asserts the future action of Yahweh to heal and to love Israel freely. Vv. 5-7 portray a description of a new situation of salvation, which resulted because of Yahweh's act of salvation.[223]

Following Westermann's scheme, Brueggemann considers that the salvation oracle in 14:4-7 consists of "announcement" (v.4) and "portrayal" (vv.5-7),[224] as follows:[225]

Announcement:	I will heal their apostasy; I will love them freely, for my anger has turned from them. I will be as the dew to Israel (vv.4-5a);
Portrayal:	he shall blossom as the lily, and he shall strike root like a tree of Lebanon; his shoots shall spread out; his beauty shall be like the olive, and his fragrance like Lebanon. They shall return in his shadow, they shall flourish as a garden; they shall blossom as the vine, their fragrance shall be like the wine of Lebanon (vv.5b-7).

---

[220] Salvation oracles, following messages of judgment addressed to Israel, are found in Hosea 1:10-2:1; 2:14-23; 3:5; 11:8-11; and 14:4-8. See Westermann, *Prophetic Oracles of Salvation in the Old Testament,* 113-118.

[221] Wolff, *Hosea*, 236.

[222] Charles H. Silva, "Literary Features in the Book of Hosea", *Bibliotheca Sacra* 164 (2007), 44.

[223] Brueggemann, *Tradition for Crisis*, 72, 152. no. 29.

[224] Claus Westermann, "The Way of the Promise Through the Old Testament", in Bernhard W. Andersen (ed.), *The Old Testament and the Christian Faith* (New York: Harper and Row, 1963), 200-224.

[225] Cf. Brueggemann, *Tradition for Crisis*, 72.

The passage does not provide us any direct clue to ascertain the date. Stuart contends that the theme of repentance has an overtone of a parting word of hope to Israel who would be exiled so that they would take with them the word of hope of restoration and communicate to their children (cf. Deut. 30:2, 6) and that their God has not forever abandoned them (Lev 26:44). Thus, Stuart presupposes that the present unit is spoken in the context of imminent destruction probably during the last months of the siege in 722 BCE or immediately after the fall of the Northern Kingdom.[226]

4.9.4. Tradition and Theological Comments in the Light of the Tripartite Relationship

Covenant tradition seems to be the basis of Yahweh's act of restoration. Prosperity predicted through abundant vegetation in 14:4-8 is the language of the covenant restoration blessings (Deut 30:9 cf., Am. 9:13-14; Mic. 7:14; Isa. 55:13). Other key terms that express the promise of future restoration include אהב "love", שׁוב "return" and אף "anger", which are all the primary covenant terms. In the covenant tradition, אהב "love" expresses the notion of loyalty and faithfulness between the covenant partners[227] (for the discussion on "love" as a technical term of covenant, see the Traditions and Theological Comments on Amos 1:9-10). The verb שׁוב "to return" appears in a covenant context and a key term in Hosea's hortatory vocabulary (cf. 2:9[7], 11[9]; 3:5; 6:1; 7:10, 16; 12:7[6]; 14:2[1]). Stuart rightly points out that אף "anger", which Yahweh has withdrawn from Israel, appears as a precursor to the covenant punishments in the covenant tradition.[228] In other words, the basis of tripartite relationship in which Yahweh restores his relationship with Israel and the subsequent blessings upon the land in 14:4-8 is rooted in the covenant tradition.

Yahweh announces to heal Israel's disloyalty (משׁובתם), which is a key issue in Hosea. To seek security, Israel left her husband (Yahweh) and went after her lovers (chs 1-3). Such disloyalty, however, brought agricultural failure (2:9[11]), political chaos, military defeat and deportation (5:8-15; 8:9-13). Disloyalty is thus understood to be a root cause of breaking the tripartite relationship in that disloyalty not only alienates Israel from Yahweh but it also alienates Israel from her political land. However, in v.4 Yahweh announces that he will withdraw his anger and instead offer his healing and love to Israel. As a result of Yahweh's healing, there will have a renewed relationship between Yahweh, Israel and the land. The renewed tripartite relationship is portrayed by employing the agricultural images in which Israel's prosperity and stability in the land is depicted by using the images of "tree" that takes its "root" in Lebanon (v.5). As argues in the TCC on v.5b, שׁרשׁ "root" in the eighth century prophets (cf. Am. 2:9) appears to convey the idea of

[226] Stuart, *Hosea-Jonah*, 212.

[227] Stuart, *Hosea-Jonah*, 214-215.

[228] Deut. 29:19, 22, 23, 26, 27; 31:17; 32:22. Stuart, *Hosea-Jonah*, 215.

(re)settlement in the land. In the judgment speech in 9:16-17, "root" appears in the context of exile to cut off Israel from the land, but in the salvation oracle in v.5 "root" makes a contrastive relation to convey the idea of resettlement, which is expressed in the Targum, "and they shall dwell in their fortified land."[229] As a result of renewed relationship that is characterized with unconditional love (אהב) in v.4, Israel will "return" to Yahweh and shall dwell in the "shadow" of Yahweh. The "return" שׁוב can refer either to a return to Yahweh or return from exile. The latter is dependent on the former and most likely both senses are intended here.[230] In any case, one important point in terms of the tripartite relationship is that "return" to Yahweh is inseparably linked with the prosperity of the land as expressed in the metaphor that Israel will flourish like a "garden", blossom like "the vine" and shall be fragrant like "the wine of Lebanon" (v.7). In other words, as Carol J. Dempsey concludes, "there is an intricate link between the redemption of humanity and the restoration of the natural world."[231]

Restoration in 14:4-7 is primarily stated in terms of the restored covenant relationship between Yahweh and Israel. The restored relationship between Yahweh and Israel will invariably lead to the restored relationship between Israel and land in which Israel will receive abundant yields of the land and dwell safely in the land. This means restoration here deals with the re-establishment of the tripartite relationship. The basis of this restoration is stated as Yahweh's love (אהב), which he freely bestows on Israel. As a result of restoration, Israel would return back to the relationship with her covenantal partner, Yahweh and would enjoy the covenant blessings of the land. For Israel, prosperous existence and secured survival in the land depend on her right relationship with her God, Yahweh.

4.10. Hosea's Theology of Land

Based on the foregoing exegesis, we now summarize Hosea's understanding of land as follows:

Meaning of the Term Land

1. First, ארץ "land" appears to convey a *cultivable land* that produces its yields for the physical sustenance of Israel. References to land in the sense of agricultural plot appear in the judgment speech (2:2-13) in which Yahweh announces to withhold the productivity and fecundity of the cultivable land by causing drought (2:3). Failure of the cultivable land is attributed to Yahweh's causative action because of Israel's failure to live in faithful relation to her covenanted God. Both האדמה and ארץ appear in the salvation oracle (2:16, 21, 23 [18, 23, 25]) to refer to the cultivable land in which Yahweh is portrayed as a God who bestows fertility upon

[229] Cathcart and others (eds), *The Targum of the Minor Prophets*, 61.

[230] Stuart, *Hosea-Jonah*, 215.

[231] Carol J. Dempsey, *The Prophets: A Liberation-Critical Reading* (Minneapolis: Fortress Press, 2000), 159.

the land as a blessing of his restorative act. In the salvation oracle in 14:4-7 [5-8], the idea of a cultivable land appears in the form of an announcement of future blessings of fertility and abundant crops. In these oracles of judgment and salvation, no other forces but Yahweh alone is seen as the ultimate controller of nature and earth. Israel's prosperity and physical nourishment is stated in connection with the produce of the land and the response of land to these needs of Israel is stated to be dependent upon Yahweh's favorable response to the land. Yahweh's response to the land, either favorably or unfavorably, is in turn conditional upon Israel's faithfulness or faithlessness to Yahweh.

2. Land is understood in terms of a *living space or habitation.* "ארץ" is stated as a living place in which Israel is described as its inhabitants "ישׁב" and for the Israelites to inhabit the land "ארץ" is inseparably connected with the ethical life envisaged in the Decalogue (4:1-3). In the judgment oracle, names of the cities, such as, "Gibeah", "Beth-aven", "Ramah", "Jezreel" and so on are mentioned, which are understood as a divine allotted places for habitation. These places are mentioned in conjunction with the judgment of destruction in which Israel's place of habitation is sentenced to desolation along with the annihilation of the population (5:8-8, cf. 1:4-5). In the salvation oracle in 2:16-23 [18-25], הארץ is stated to be a safe place of habitation for Israel (v.18) as a result of Yahweh's restorative act. While referring to a habitation for the animal kingdom, the term שׂדה "field" is used to refer to an open and uncultivable land where wild animals reside (2: 18 [20]). Yahweh is thus seen as a God who designates a different living space both for humans' habitation and the animal kingdom. As such, land as a place of habitation conveys the idea of Israel as recipients of Yahweh's gift of land. Therefore, the lifestyle of Israel as inhabitants of Yahweh's gift of land is demanded to confirm to the standard of Yahweh's law.

3. Hosea understood land in a sense of *territory for political nation.* ארץ in the judgment oracle refers to the land of Israel as a political nation that will be defeated and sent to exile (2:3). In such context, defeat and exile are connected with the annihilation of the population, alienation from the land and loss of political land (2:2-13; 10:13b-15). Land as political nation also conveys an understanding of a separate political territory allocated by Yahweh. As such, encroachment into the boundaries of other nations is considered an act of violation against Yahweh's territorial allocation. In such understanding, the demand of respect for territorial boundaries of other nations are implied though not stated explicitly (5:10f). In Hosea's understanding, the land of Israel and Judah as separate political entities are not considered to be totally independent so as to carry out their own political interests, rather their existence as nations are always subordinated to the sovereign authority of Yahweh. As such, seeking an alliance with nations apart from Yahweh is considered to be defying the sovereign authority of Yahweh (8:9-13; 10:13b-15). Security on land as a political nation is ensured by Yahweh alone and not by possessing military might (10:13b-15). Hosea begins to convey his understanding

of the land as political nation with the threat of looming exile and loss of land (2:2-13). However, he ends his oracle with a future hope and glory in which the land as a political nation will once again be prosperous and will be rooted in their land. In the context of future hope, the reconstruction and rebuilding of Israel's political land is associated with the restorative act of Yahweh's redemption (14:4-7 [5-8]).

4. Hosea also employs "land" to refer to *the entire earth.* ארץ appears in connection with "all who live in it" including the birds of the air, fish of the sea and animals upon the land (4:3). In this instance, ארץ encompasses the entire earth in a cosmological sense. In such cosmological understanding, the vitalities of ארץ are inseparably connected with the qualities of humans' ethical standard lived in relation to one another in the society (4:1-3).

Tripartite Relationship

The above four levels of meaning of land in Hosea show the land to be in constant tension between the precarious judgment of destruction and the future announcement of restoration. Between these tensions, Israel's relationship with Yahweh is seen to be a determinant factor either for the loss, destruction of and alienation from the land or the prosperity of and secured existence in their own political land. Land thus appears to be *an arena of struggle* in the relationship between Yahweh and Israel. Yahweh's judgment against Israel affects the land, such as, the loss of fertility of land, wastage of crops and vineyards and destruction of their political land. On the other hand, the land's bearing of Yahweh's judgment affects the lives of the Israelites in which the loss of fertility and crops of the land severely affected Israel's economy while the destruction of their political land brought innumerable damage of property, loss of human lives and alienation from their own homeland. In this tripartite relationship, land refuses its blessings to Israel when Israel breaks her relationship with Yahweh. Israel's departure from Yahweh is understood as a departure from all the blessing of the land.

In the salvation oracle, the re-establishment of relationship between Yahweh and Israel eventually leads to the favorable condition of the land. As Israel responds to Yahweh's call, the land in return responds to Israel's need in terms of the fertility and fecundity of the land (2:16-23). The renewed covenant between Yahweh and Israel will eventually reestablish the relations between Israel and land in that the land will return all its yields to Israel and Israel will return back and take root in the land. Israel's return to the land and the land's return of fertility to Israel is the result of the return to the covenant relationship between Yahweh and Israel (2:16-23; 14:7-8). In this inseparable tripartite relationship between Yahweh, Israel and land, Yahweh is presented as the God of creation who controls the cycle of nature for vegetation and the destiny of every nation. Israel is portrayed as the recipient of Yahweh's blessings with the land as an agent of either blessing or curse for Israel depending on her constant reference and loyalty to Yahweh.

Traditions

Such understanding of land in relation with Yahweh and Israel seems to be based on historical and religious traditions of ancient Israel, which are summarized as follows.

By employing the *creation tradition* (2:3-13), Hosea shows how Israel's moral failures before Yahweh affect the entire land (cf.4:3). The creation tradition affirms that Yahweh is the God who controls nature and bestows all the vitalities and life forces upon the earth. Contrary to the creation mandate for humanity to multiply upon the earth, Israel instead engaged in murder and bloodshed (cf.4:2). Such vices are clear violation of the creation mandate to bless and to take care of God's creation. Hosea employs the creation tradition to show how Israel's behavioral vices affect the very creation of Yahweh. Cosmic diminution of life forces and the declining vitality of the land are connected with Israel's failure to live up to the ethical standard of Yahweh.

Hosea employs the *Torah tradition* (8:9-13; 13b-15) to assert that Israel's disobedience to the commandments of Yahweh leads her to exile and alienation from the land. The Torah tradition contains Yahweh's instructions to regulate Israel's existence in the land and to direct Israel's relationship with Yahweh. However, as Israel regards the Torah as strange things (8:12), Yahweh also decrees that Israel will be exiled to a strange land in Egypt. Israel also rejected the Torah and instead trusted in its own ways (10:13b). Israel's failure to abide by the law of Torah thus affects the tripartite relationship in which departure from Yahweh's instruction leads them to depart from their homeland to exile in foreign nation (8:12-13; 10:15). For Israel to dwell in the land is to live according to the Yahweh's Torah.

Hosea employs the *Exodus tradition* to affirm that Israel's occupation of the land is an exclusive act of Yahweh. Yahweh is thus portrayed as God who is capable to deliver Israel from any political predicament and destruction of the land. However, instead of trusting and depending on Yahweh, Israel allied herself with foreign nations to defend her land from possible attack. Such political move of Israel is considered as an affront to Yahweh's salvation history in Exodus. Thus, Yahweh pronounces to reverse the Exodus in that Israel will revert to her former misery and affliction as in her Exodus slavery (8:13). As Israel's messengers have gone to Assyria for alliance, Israel will be forced to travel this same road but to captivity.

Covenant tradition appears more prominently in Hosea to convey the relationship between Yahweh, Israel and land. By using covenant tradition Hosea shows how Israel's loyalty to Yahweh causes plentiful blessings upon the land while disloyalty bring desolation upon the land and causes miseries upon Israel. By employing the marriage metaphor, Hosea shows Israel's inclinations towards Baal and nations as an act of violation of covenant relationship with Yahweh (cf. 9:10; 12: 9[10]; 13:4-5). To implement covenant regulations, Yahweh summons Israel and as found guilty, Israel was sentenced to punishment, namely, the withdrawal of land produce and the looming exile and alienation from their land (2:3, 9).

Covenantal norms of ethics in the interrelationship between the people of Israel *vis-a-vis* Yahweh are considered to be the condition for living in the land. Violations of the covenantal ethics in interpersonal relationship wither the earth and the entire living species (4:1-3). Secured existence in the land is tied up with Israel's commitment to covenant faithfulness. Such faithfulness includes adherence to the Decalogue ethics and respect for the territorial integrity for each other nations (4:1-3; 5:10). Failure to adhere to the Decalogue ethics and an act of encroachment into others territory is considered to be a violation of covenant relationship with Yahweh. As a result, Yahweh announces the desolation of the land, deportation to a foreign nation and suffering of putrefaction (5:8-15). Hosea reiterates covenant tradition to convey how Israel's self confidence in her military power and in her political alignment with foreign nations amount to the violation of covenant relationship and thereby Israel forfeited its claim to reside in the land. In the covenant tradition, it is Yahweh's interference that made Israel's occupation in the land of Canaan possible. Yahweh is, therefore, a trusted covenanted partner for Israel's existence and security. However, instead of trusting Yahweh, Israel trusted in Assyria and in her military strength to secure her political territory from impending chaos (8:9; 10:13b), which is an act of utter mistrust on Yahweh. Such misplaced trust will lead to the displacement of the entire population from the land. Yahweh is thus portrayed as God who alone can secure Israel's existence as a nation (8:9-13; 10:13b-15).

However, just as covenant tradition is predominantly employed as the basis of judgment, it is also used as the basis of restoration for Israel. In the salvation oracle, the re-establishment of the covenant relationship between Yahweh and Israel leads to the restoration of the tripartite relationship. As Israel return to Yahweh, the land is also restored back to Israel along with the gifts that the land produces as a form of covenant blessing to Israel (2:16-23). Restored relationship between Yahweh and Israel will invariably lead to the restored relationship between Israel and land in which land yields abundant fruits for Israel and Israel is restored back to the land as safe place for existence. The basis of this restoration is Yahweh's love (אהב), which he freely bestows on Israel (14:4-8). For Israel, prosperous existence and secured survival in the land depends on her covenant faithfulness with her God, Yahweh.

Chapter 5

The Understanding of Land in the Book of Micah

5.1. Micah, the Prophet

Micah, whose name means "who is like Yahweh?", carried out his prophetic ministry in the south. Except for his name and hometown, his personal background is not known much. He comes from Moresheth that is identified as Moresheth-Gath (1:1, 14, cf. Jer. 26:18), about twenty miles south-west of Jerusalem, which was fortified by Rehoboam as part of the defense system to guard the western approaches to Jerusalem.[1] Since there is no mention of Micah's call to prophetic ministry and since he uses the terms "rulers", "judges" and "heads" instead of "kings" (3:1,9,11), Wolff argues that Micah was not a prophet but a clan elder from Moresheth who perpetuated the wisdom traditions and administered justice.[2] Wolff's proposal of Micah as "clan elder" is well recognized by scholars but his dismissal of Micah as prophet is criticized by most scholars who place Micah firmly among the prophets.[3] Citing evidence from the later prophet Jeremiah who mentions that Micah had prophesied (Jer. 26:16-20), Mason concludes that the prophetic tradition remembered Micah as a prophet.[4] It is believed that Micah fled from Moresheth to Jerusalem as a result of the invasion of Assyria's king Sennacherib in 701 in which forty six cities and numerous villages of Judah were captured. In any case, his references to social injustice (2:1-2; 3:1-12), threat

[1] James Luther Mays, *Micah*, OTL (Philadelphia: Westminster John Knox Press, 1976), 15.

[2] Wolff even considered the prophetic formula, which appears rarely (2:3; 3:5), as redactorial additions. Cited in Mason, *Micah, Nahum, Obadiah*, 24.

[3] These scholars include, Weiser, van der Woude and Mason. Cited in R. Mason, *Micah, Nahum, Obadiah* (Sheffield: JSOT, 1991), 25.

[4] Mason, *Micah, Nahum, Obadiah*, 25.

of external terror and looming exile (2:8, 12-13; 3:12) point to his first-hand information and to the tumultuous period in which he carried out his prophetic activities.

5.2. Historical Context of Micah

According to the superscription (1:1), Micah proclaimed his oracles concerning Samaria and Jerusalem in the last half of the eighth century BCE during the reigns of Jotham (ca. 756-741), Ahaz (ca. 741-725) and Hezekiah (725-697),[5] which dates him as Isaiah's contemporary (cf. Isa.1:1). Scholars disagree whether Micah began his ministry as early as Jotham's reign or during Hezekiah's period.[6] Based on Jer. 26:18 where Micah's ministry is dated to the reign of Hezekiah and the reference, "I will make Samaria a heap of ruin" (1:6) most scholars consider that Micah began his ministry at the time of Hezekiah and before the fall of the Northern kingdom (722 BCE).[7] Though such dating is agreeable, it is not impossible to date Micah's ministry back to Jotham's period as mentioned in the superscription (1:1). Arguing that the reference to "horses" and "chariots" in 5:10 indicates a period of prosperity, an early period of Jotham that immediately followed the great days of his father Uzziah, Leon J. Wood argues that Micah was active by Jotham's period.[8] In any case, whether or not Micah's ministry can be dated back to Jotham's period, what appears clear is that Micah came after Uzziah's death (Jotham's father), which ushers the period of decline for Judah and well before the fall of Samaria in 722 BCE. This indicates that Micah proclaimed his oracles during the tumultuous period of threat and insecurity in Samaria and Jerusalem during the last half of the eighth century (see the following discussion).

5.2.1. Political Context

After 745 BCE, the unprecedented period of peace, prosperity and territorial expansion for Israel and Judah ended with the deaths of Jeroboam II and Uzziah. To restrain the rise of Assyria, the allied nations Israel and Syria formed a Syro-Ephraimite coalition in which Judah was forced to join. Determined not to join the coalition, Judah appealed for Assyria's help from the threat of the coalition. Two significant historical turns of events can be noted here. First, with Assyrian's intervention (734-732 BCE), most of Israel's territories, such as the Transjordan, Galilee and coastal plains were stripped off from the Northern kingdom. Second,

---

[5] Wolff, *Hosea*, 4-6.

[6] For a summary discussion about various views of scholars on Micah's period, see C. Hassell Bullock, *An Introduction to the Old Testament Prophetic Books* (Chicago: Moody, 1986), 106-108.

[7] Georg Fohrer, *Introduction to the Old Testament,* trans. by David E. Green (Nashville, New York: Abingdon Press, 1968),444; Homer Hailey, *A Commentary on the Minor Prophets* (Grand Rapids, Michigan: Baker, 1972), 187; Werner H. Schmidt, *Old Testament Introduction* (Bombay: St. Paul, 1992), 255.

[8] Leon J. Wood, *The Prophets of Israel* (Schaumberg, Illinois: Regular Baptist, 1979), 310.

as a result of Assyria's help, Judah not only paid tribute to the Assyrian king, Tiglath-Pilesar III but also became a vassal of Assyria (cf. 2 Kgs 16; 2 Chro. 28).[9] After the destruction of Samaria in 722 BCE, Sargon II of Assyria came to Judah in 720 BCE and again in 714-711 BCE[10] and moved on to the coastal plain of Philistia probably to prevent any Egyptian assistance.[11] Later in 701 BCE, Sennacherib threatened to totally destroy Jerusalem with his 185,000 troops (cf. Isa. 36-38; 2 Kgs 18-19; 2 Chro. 32). Micah expresses the apprehension of the Jerusalemites about the presence of the enemy's army surrounding Jerusalem to desecrate it (4:11). Amidst such political turmoil in the context of Assyrian's territorial expansion, there was a threat of destruction, the loss of political nation and alienation of the people of Judah from the land.

5.2.2. Socioeconomic Context

Out of many issues related to the socioeconomic condition, two pertinent problems need special mention. First, the prosperity ushered in during the preceding years of King Uzziah largely profited the ruling officials (see the historical context of Amos) who became extremely rich while the common people did not get any benefit and remained poor. Such disparity in the economic distribution created a social division between the elite-ruling class and the poor peasant-landholders. With money in their hand and power within their reach, the elite ruling class began to seize, evict and foreclose the land of the economically vulnerable people (2:1-3; 8-9; 3:1-3, 9-10; 7:2–6). The poor victims could not get justice since the judge, priests and prophets alike abhorred justice (3:9) and were interested in bribery (7:3) to adjudicate the case. Amidst such socioeconomic chaos and judicial failure, the majority poor and vulnerable became landless while the minority ruling elite became owners of large landholdings.

Second, the tribute demanded by Assyria, in the aftermath of the Syro-Ephraimite war, forced Ahaz to strip the temple of its gold and emptied the treasury (2 Chro. 28:5-8, 17-21), which destabilized the socioeconomic condition of Judah considerably.[12] The burden of taxation was passed on to the poor peasants who were forced to produce more to pay the tax. Such demand of taxation and the means to pay it became a conflicting option for the peasants as their cultivable land had either shrunk or been seized forcefully due to encroachment and forceful foreclosure by the ruling elite (2:1-2). Producing agricultural yields to pay heavy taxation with small or no land become a suicidal option. Moreover, to free from Assyria's vassalage and to protect Jerusalem from external attack, Hezekiah introduced a policy of corvee to engage the common people in the work of the

---

[9] Gary V. Smith, *An Introduction to the Hebrew Prophets: The Prophets as Preachers* (Nashville, Tennessee: Broadman & Holman, 1994), 100-101.

[10] Smith, *An Introduction to the Hebrew Prophets*, 101.

[11] Sweeney, *The Twelve Prophets*, vol. 2, 341.

[12] Smith, *An Introduction to the Hebrew Prophets*, 101.

national defense system, such as, the construction of the water supply system, expansion of royal buildings and fortification of cites (2 Kgs 20:20 and 2 Chro. 32:27ff).[13] This also caused adverse impact on the socioeconomic condition of the day. On the one hand they were forced to till more land for higher production to pay tax and debts but on the other hand they were forced to labor for the government projects thereby forcing them to neglect their private cultivation. In such a suicidal socioeconomic condition, the peasants find no survival option. The references to "who eat the flesh of my people" (3:3), "who build Jerusalem with bloodshed and violence" (3:10) reflect Micah's criticism against such socioeconomic problems created by the ruling officials who have failed to consider the welfare of the people.

5.2.3. Religious Context

Alongside the deteriorating political and socioeconomic condition, the religious activities also started to decay in Judah. Micah did not speak as much as Amos and Hosea did, yet if Micah's ministry can be dated to Ahaz's reign as stated in the superscription (1:1), we can notice the prevalent apostasy in Judah. After the deliverance of Judah by the Assyrians from the Syro-Ephraimite coalition, Ahaz went to Damascus to pay homage to Tiglath-Pilesar from where he made a replica of the Assyrian's bronze altar and set it up at Jerusalem (2 Kgs 16:10-18).[14] Syncretistic worship thus crept into the Jerusalem temple. Despite Hezekiah's zeal for Yahwistic faith (2 Chro. 29-31), his religious reform could not bring a lasting spiritual transformation. This is indicated by Micah's accusation against the priests and prophets who lead the people "astray" and proclaimed "peace" in the land for material gain, which Micah considers as a perversion of worship practices (1:7; 3:5–7, 11; 5:12–14 [11–13]). Such misconception of peace amidst turbulent socioeconomic and political setting was partly contributed to by their misconstruction of Zion theology, which affirmed that Yahweh has chosen Zion as his dwelling place and it will be protected from their foes (3:11). The political territory of Jerusalem was thus seen as inviolable. Such misplaced faith blinded their faith to perceive how socioeconomic injustice and religious apostasy would lead them to the forfeiture of land as envisaged in the covenant faith at Sinai.

With the above historical background in mind, the following section exegetes some key texts in Micah that describe and explain the tripartite relationship.

5.3. Theophany Tradition (Micah 1:2-7)

Yahweh's "coming down" on the earth and the consequent turbulences caused by his presence upon the land speak of the Theophany tradition. Yahweh's manifestation upon the earth causes unrest upon Israel and disturbs life on the

[13] Mays, *Micah*, 89.

[14] John Bright, *A History of Israel*, 4th edn. (Louisville, Kentucky: Westminister John Knox Press, 2000), 277.

land. Disturbance of the tripartite relationship is thus expressed through Yahweh's intervention on earth as occasioned by Israel's transgression.

5.3.1. Translation on Micah 1:2-7

2 [a]Hear, you peoples, all of you; pay attention, O earth[a], and the fullness of her; and let the Lord Yahweh be a [b]witness among you[b], the Lord from his holy temple.

3 For behold[a], Yahweh is setting out of his place, and will descend and will trample upon the high places of the earth.

4 And the mountains will melt under him and the valleys will be cleft, like wax before the fire, like waters poured down a steep place.

5 All this is for the rebellion of Jacob and for the sins of the house of Israel. What is the transgression of Jacob? Is it not Samaria? And what is the sin of the house of Judah? Is it not Jerusalem?

6 [a]Therefore I will turn[a] Samaria a heap of ruin, the field to vineyards plantings; and I will pour down her stones into the valley, and uncover her foundations.

7 All her images shall be beaten[a] to pieces, all her hires shall be burned[a] with fire, and all her idols I will lay waste; for from the hire of a harlot she gathered them, and to the hire of a harlot they shall return.

5.3.2. Text Critical Comments on Micah 1:2-7

V.2a-a: The imperative שמעו "hear" is a common introductory call to hear. In all its six occurrences in Micah (3:1, 9; 6:1, 2, 9), שמעו is used to accuse and condemn the leaders of Israel in the presence of global or cosmic observers and adjudicators.[15] Here Yahweh stands as the Lord of all the nations of the earth.[16] The setting of the entire earth in v.2 is indicated by the following phrase ארץ ומלאה "earth and the fullness of her". By comparing with the original command מלאו את-הארץ "fill the earth" in Gen. 1:28, Andersen and Freedman maintain that the earth's "fullness" in v.2 includes the population of all the living creatures and not just humans.[17] If such comparison could be sustained, ארץ ומלאה "earth and fullness of her" convoys a cosmic understanding of the earth in the sense of the entire world. The command שמעו "to hear" is thus set in a cosmic setting, which is addressed to עמים "peoples" and ארץ "earth" that embraces the entire population of the world as indicated by כלם literally "all of them". The third person plural following the

---

[15] Francis I. Andersen and David Noel Freedman, *Micah: A New Translation with Introduction and Commentary*, AB 24E (New York: Doubleday, 2000), 138.

[16] Juan I. Alfaro, *Justice and Loyalty* (Grand Rapids, Michigan: William B. Eerdmans Publishing Company, 1989), 14.

[17] Andersen and Freedman, *Micah*, 152.

vocative is not ungrammatical (cf. 1 Kgs 22:28).[18] Yahweh's summons of all the people of the earth is to set them (peoples) as participants in his trial against Israel and Judah. ארץ thus refers to the entire earth. Andersen and Freedman point out that the term appears about fifteen times in Micah with clear grammatical distinction. When ארץ is used in a cosmic sense the definite article is omitted even though the noun is definite (cf. 1:2, 3; 5:3; 6:2; 7:17, the exception is 4:13). To refer to a particular political nation ארץ is used with definite article ה (sometimes with pronoun suffix), such as, "the land of Egypt" (6:4; 7:15), "the land of Assyria (Nimrod, 5:5)" and "the land of Israel" (5:4, 5[with pronominal suffix]; 7:2, 13[definite article]).[19]

V.2b-b: עד "witness" designates Yahweh's role as one who testifies in the court. עד draws the imagery of a "courtroom or a legal setting in which a witness is required to testify concerning the wrongdoing of the accused or the legality of an action (cf. Num. 5:13; Josh. 24:22; 1 Sam. 12:5)."[20] עד is preceded by בכם, which, according to Willis, means "against you."[21] It is incongruent to render בכם as "against you", which would suggest that the accusation is directed against the nations. V.5 states that Yahweh accuses only Samaria and Jerusalem (v.5) and not the nations. We consider בכם as "among you", which would grant the "peoples" and "earth" a role of witness in the trial proceedings while Yahweh plays the role of accuser and judge against Samaria and Jerusalem.[22]

V.3a: BHS for metrical reason emends הנה יהוה "behold Yahweh", but MT's rendering הנה should be retained as it provides continuity with v.2 and "marks the onset of predictive narrative."[23] כי "for" logically introduces the reason for summons in vv.3-7 (for further discussion, see the following FCC). "Behold" is followed by participial construction "sets out" (יצא), which suggests a military connotation and the consecutive perfect verbs "and will descend and trample" (וירד, ודרך) describe the result (judgment) that follows the coming of Yahweh upon the earth.

---

[18] Charles S. Shaw, *The Speeches of Micah: A Rhetorical-Historical Analysis*, JSOTSS 145 (Sheffield: JSOT, 1993), 32.

[19] Andersen and Freedman, *Micah*, 138.

[20] Marvin A. Sweeney, *The Twelve Prophets*, Berit Olam, vol. 2 (Collegeville, Minnesota: Liturgical, 2000), 349.

[21] Cf. Ex. 20:16; Num. 5:13; Deut. 17:7; 19:15; 31:19, 26; Josh. 24:22; 1 Sam. 12:5; Prov. 24:28; 23:18; Ps 27:12. John Willis, "Some Suggestions on the Interpretation of Micah 1:2", *VT* 18 (1968), 372-379.

[22] In his form critical analysis, Wright has demonstrated how "heaven" and "earth" are appointed as witnesses in the lawsuit. A similar idea is echoed here. Cf. G.E. Wright, "The Lawsuit of God: A Form Critical Study of Deuteronomy 32", in Bernhard W. Anderson and Walter Harrelson (eds), *Israel's Prophetic Heritage: Essays in Honor of James Muilenburg* (New York: Harper, 1962), 26-67.

[23] Andersen and Freedman, *Micah*, 161.

V.6a-a: the waw-relative ושׂמתי can be appropriately rendered as "I will turn", linking a logical consequence after the accusation in v.5.

V.7a-a: The verbs יכתו and ישׂרפו "beaten and burned" describe what the Israelites should do to "images" and "idols" according to the covenant stipulations (Deut. 7:5). Instead the Israelites perpetuate the idols and images. Micah states that Yahweh will now do what Israel has failed to do.

5.3.3. Form Critical Comments on Micah 1:2-7

Jan A. Wagenaar argues that v.2 is a proclamation of judgment against the nations while vv.3-5a (theophany) is directed against Israel. He further argues that vv.5b-7 is not a continuation of vv.3-5a since the names "Jacob" and "Israel" in v.5a refer to the people of Jerusalem/Judah (also in 3:1, 8, 9), while in v.5b "Jacob" and "Israel" refer to both the political entities of the Northern and Southern kingdoms.[24] Wagenaar thus concludes that vv.2-7 is not a literary unit. Though it appears like a different group of people are addressed, such as, "nations", "Israel" and also "Israel and Judah" in vv.2-7, trifurcating the unit based on such supposition appears to be artificial. Close examination of the text reveals a connection of vv.2-7. In a kind of cosmic law court, Micah calls the earth to "hear" that Yahweh as "witness" brings a lawsuit against his covenanted people (v.2). Vv.3-4 are linked with v.2 by a connective phrase כי־הנה (See the above TCC on v.3a). Micah invites Israel to "behold [הנה]" God's coming in judgment from heaven upon the earth (v.3) and the resultant convulsion upon the earth (v.4). V.5 states the reason of this judgment as "Jacob's transgression" and "the sins of the house of Israel", while vv.6-7 portray the description of judgment upon Israel.[25] Nogalski observes that the reference to "valley" in v.4 corresponds to the "valley" in v.6 and in both the cases "fire" is mentioned as an element of destruction. As such he rightly concludes that Micah takes up the images of destruction in vv.6-7 takes up from v.4 and applies them to the destruction of Samaria.[26] Despite differences among the critics, most scholars agree that vv.2-7 can be read intelligently as a coherent unit.[27]

Based on the above discussion, we consider vv.2-7 as a unit of judgment oracle against Israel expressed through the imagery of a court setting. Yahweh is portrayed as plaintiff and judge who calls the cosmos to hear as witness in his lawsuit against his people (v.2). Yahweh's coming to take the case is described in the image of theophany that results in the convulsion of the earth (vv.3-4).

---

[24] Jan A. Wagenaar, *Judgment and Salvation: The Composition and Redaction* (Leiden: Brill, 2001), 54-55.

[25] John A. Martin, "Micah", in John F. Walvoord and Roy B. Zuck (eds), *The Bible Knowledge Commentary* (Colorado: David C. Cook, 1983), 1477-1478.

[26] James Nogalski, *Literary Precursors to the Book of the Twelve* (Berlin: de Gruyter, 1993).

[27] Rudolph, *Micah*, 42-43; Hillers, *Micah*, 22-23; F.W. Dobba-Allsopp, *Weep, O Daughter: A Study of the City-Lament Genre in the Hebrew Bible*, Biblica et Orientalia 44 (Rome: Pontificio Instituto Biblico, 1993), 134.

Samaria is accused of transgression and sin (v.5) and based on this accusation, the verdict is pronounced against Samaria (vv.6-7). Vv.2-7 can be outlined as follows:

Introductory call to hear:	v.2a
Peoples and earth appointed as witness:	v.2b
Theophany: Call to witness Yahweh's coming on earth:	vv.3-4
Indictment against Samaria (and Jerusalem):	v.5
Declaration of sentence (loss of political land):	vv.6-7.

W. Boyd Barrick argues that the theophany, which results in convulsion of the earth and the devastation of the land, is "prophetic hyperbole, probably inspired by a tremor of extraordinary severity during Uzziah's reign (ca. 760) which damaged Samaria to some extent and which left a profound mark on the popular imagination."[28] On the other hand, by arguing that the phrase "for I will pour down" in v. 6 refers to the conquering invader, Waltke argues that it refers to Yahweh who uses Shalmanaser V's Assyrian army against Samaria (2 Kgs 17:3-6) and that that the literal event signified in the present unit is Shalmeneser V's invasions against Hoshea of Israel.[29] Since Hoshea's reign is dated ca. 732-724 BCE,[30] if Waltke's argument can be sustained, vv.2-7 can be dated sometimes before the fall of Samaria. The argument appears plausible since the text suggests that the oracle antedates the fall of Samaria to the Assyrians in 722 BCE.[31]

5.3.4. Tradition and Theological Comments in the Light of Tripartite Relationship

The description of Yahweh's "coming down" and "treading upon" the earth and the consequent convulsion of the nature expressed by the terms, "melt", "wax", and "poured water" recalls the language of theophany (vv.2-4).[32] Beyerlin maintains that "the theophanic motifs in the book of Micah, and especially in 1:3, are grounded in the traditions of the Sinai theophany."[33] In the Sinai theophany (Ex.19:16-20), Yahweh's arrival was occasioned by Israel's affirmed allegiance

---

[28] W. Boyd Barrick, *BMH as Body language: A lexical and Iconographical Study of the Word BHM When Not a reference to Cultic Phenomena in Biblical and Post-Biblical Hebrew* (New York/ London: T&T Clark, 2008), 51.

[29] Waltke, *A Commentary on Micah*, 47-48, 50.

[30] Cf. Sweeney, *The Twelve Prophets*, Vol. 2, 347.

[31] Leslie C. Allen, *The Book of Joel, Obadiah, Jonah and Micah*, NICOT (Grand Rapids, Michigan: William B. Eerdmans Publishing Company, 1976), 268.

[32] Van Gemeren, *Interpreting the Prophetic Word* (Grand Rapids, Michigan: Zondervan, 1990), 152-153.

[33] W. Beyerlin, *Die aramaischen Israels in der Verkundigung des Propheten Mica.* FRLANT 72 (Gottingen: Vandenhoeck & Ruprecht, 1959), 29-42. Cited in Andersen and Freedman, *Micah*, 158.

to Yahweh and preceded by Yahweh's promise to make Israel a nation (nation presupposes a territory of land, cf. Ex.19: 5-6, 8). The Sinai theophany thus seals the tripartite relationship between Yahweh and Israel in which the promise to make Israel a nation and by extension of its meaning, the territory of land, became an important aspect. Micah employs the Sinai theophany tradition in vv.2-7 and recasts it in a little different way to suit his message of judgment that announces the break of tripartite relationship. In Micah, the theophany is not occasioned by Yahweh's promise to rescue his people from distress as in the past occasions (Judg. 5, cf. Isa. 64; Hab. 3) but to bring judgment that includes the loss and destruction of land.[34] It is occasioned by Israel's "transgression" and "sin" and therefore the theophany is not to establish the covenantal tripartite relationship like at Sinai (Ex.19), but to enforce the covenant punishment that would break the relationship between Yahweh and Israel and the loss and devastation of land.

As mentioned in the FCC on 1:2-7, Micah's judgment oracle employs the form of lawsuit in which he calls the attention of all that fills the earth (ארץ), which includes the population of all the living creatures along with the peoples. As argued in the TCC on v.2b-b, ארץ in v.2 refers to the earth in cosmic a sense. The arbitration of the case is thus set in a cosmic setting and the peoples and everything upon the earth are called in to witness Yahweh's judgment against Israel.

Yahweh's judgment against Israel is described in terms of his personal intervention upon the earth. In v.3 Micah draws the attention of his audience to Yahweh with the exclamation "behold." Two characteristic elements are mentioned in the description of theophany: first, the coming of Yahweh from his place and second, the consequence of Yahweh's manifestation upon the earth. The theophany tradition is remembered in terms of Yahweh's irresistible intervention against enemies for the deliverance of Israel (cf. Judg. 5:4ff; Pss 18:8-16; 68:8-9; 77:17-20). Micah reinterprets Yahweh's manifestation upon the earth by affirming that Yahweh's coming is not to deal with Israel's enemies[35] but to deal with the Israelites themselves for their "transgression" and "sins" (cf.v.5). The verb יצא "to set out", which describes Yahweh's coming, refers mostly to "going forth" for a particular task especially in the setting of war against the enemies.[36] In other words, Yahweh now turned to Israel with the judgment of destruction like he turned to destroy Israel's enemies in the past. The relationship between Yahweh and Israel

[34] James Limburg, *Hosea-Micah*, Interpretation (Atlanta, Georgia: Westminister John Knox Press, 1988), 166.

[35] Theophany tradition is associated with Yahweh's march against the nations with whom Israel fights. The idea of theophany in the ANE is commonly associated with the deity fighting against the enemies' nations, for instance, the god Assur splits the mountains; Adad shakes the earth; Martu causes fire to rain and Ishtar causes herself to rain as fire upon the land. Cf. Hans Walter Wolff, *Micah: A Commentary* (Augsburg/Minneapolis: Fortress Press, 1990), 55.

[36] Mays, *Micah*, 43.

is thus seen to be jeopardized in which even the land remained precarious to melting and tearing apart like wax in the fire and waters that pours down in a steep place. Though v.5 states that it is because of their "transgression" and "sins" (see the following discussion), the reference to "high places" in v.3 indicates some aspects of religious apostasy in Micah's charge against Israel. The "high places" in the prophetic criticism refer to illegitimate worship sites that mostly involve idolatry.[37] Israel is thus charged with abandoning Yahweh and thereby breaking her relationship with Yahweh. Such a case of indictment justifies Yahweh's act to punish Israel and ruin her land as a political nation. The tripartite relationship is thus severed because of Israel's disobedient act against Yahweh expressed in terms of idolatry.

The consequence of Yahweh's coming upon the earth is described by employing a waw-relative clause ונמסו "and will melt". The "high places" (v.3) are identified here as "mountains", which will be melted away while the "valley" will be split at the time of Yahweh's intervention. According to Wolff "mountains" are the foundations of the earth that represent endurance, height and majesty (cf. Pss 90:2; 95:4), while the "valleys" or "the plains" stand for the favored fruit bearing areas where humans live.[38] These terms represent the entire surface of the earth encompassing the whole topography. In other words, even the strongest of the earth's foundation cannot withstand Yahweh's judgment and even the most arable land will become like cleavages. This means even the strong foundation and fecund portion of the land will become a devastated and uninhabitable land. Survival upon the land will thus become difficult at the time of Yahweh's intervention.

Such massive destruction of land is based on Yahweh's accusation against Israel (v.5). This is expressed by a causal force כל־זאת "all this", which is connected with פשע "rebellion" and חטא "sins". As mentioned in the TCC on Am. 1:9b, פשע is a willful criminal infraction of the covenant, especially an act related to property offence, while חטא refers to an objective deviation from the covenant stipulation.[39] What appears clear in the usages of these terms is that Israel (and Judah) has disregarded the covenant stipulations that include the infraction of property (land, fields, and houses cf. 2:2 and 3:9-11) and idolatry ("images" and "idols" and "high places" cf. vv.2, 7). As a result of such ethical and theological deviations from Yahweh's covenant stipulation, the Israelites have fallen out of her relationship with Yahweh. By raising a rhetorical question, הלוא "is it not?", Micah "prepares his audience to agree with him that the two capital cities are in fact the covenant breakers worthy of Yahweh's judgment.

Based on the indictment in v.5, the judgment is pronounced in vv.6-7. Two descriptions of Samaria's destruction are noted here. First, the city will become a

[37] Sweeney, *The Twelve Prophets*, vol. 2, 350.

[38] Wolff, *Micah*, 56.

[39] Waltke, *A Commentary on Micah*, 50.

heap of ruin "עי" and it will revert to field (השדה) for "planting vineyard" (כרם למטעי). Whether or not Samaria would become a place of cultivation as a result of enemies' annihilation and/or alienation of its population is not clear. In any case, it speaks of the depopulation of Samaria and destruction of its political kingdom. The terms "field" and "vineyard" (השדה, כרם) to describe Samaria speak of arable land. In other words, Samaria will revert to its formerly unsettled situation as before Omri acquired the site.[40]

Second, the "stones" in Samaria will be "poured down" into the valley (v.6). As mentioned above, prior to the establishment of Samaria, it was uninhabitated hill unsuitable for vineyard cultivation.[41] The hill of Samaria was acquired by Omri ca. 880 (2 Kgs 16:24) and made into a fortress, which was later converted to the city by Ahab. Omri and Ahab used stone masonry for advanced architectural buildings of palaces and defense walls at Samaria.[42] This is proved by the archeological excavation at Samaria that has shown "the strong and well-crafted walls that defended eighth century Samaria."[43] Micah's reference to "stones" pouring down the valley could refer to such monumental palaces and fortifications of defense walls. Since in the ancient world cities were commonly built atop hills or tells above the valley, the phrase "pour down the stone into the valley" suggests the collapse of a city and its wall. It is a description of the total destruction of Samaria, where the stone erected buildings and defense wall atop the hill will be hurled into the valley. In other words, Samaria, a metonymy of the Northern kingdom will fall and Jacob referring to Northern Israel, a political nation, will suffer destruction and annihilation. The destruction of the nation is further emphasized by שממה "waste" in v.7, which applies to a land or a city, never to an object.[44] The agent of such destruction is stated as "fire" (אש), which was a common military tactic in the ANE to destroy the enemies' cities (see the TCC on Am.1:10a). The features of the destruction of Samaria are thus portrayed in a graphic picture of military conquest.

The above exegesis has shown us that ארץ refers to the earth in cosmic sense. The cosmic earth is portrayed as an active participant witnessing Yahweh's judgment and serve as an arena for Yahweh's lawsuit against his offenders. "Samaria", on the other hand, is a synecdoche to refer to the land or territory of Northern Israel as a political nation, while the terms "plains" and "valley" refer to land as living space and an arable land. All these nuances of land will be affected in the following ways: the cosmic earth will be melted away; the political nation and city of habitation will be razed and the plain cultivable land will be like a cleft. Such consequences upon the land are attributed to Israel's disloyalty to the covenant

---

[40] Waltke, *A Commentary on Micah*, 52.

[41] Wolff, *Micah*, 57.

[42] Andersen and Freedman, *Micah*, 178.

[43] Sweeney, *The Twelve Prophets*, vol. 2, 352.

[44] Andersen and Freedman, *Micah*, 182.

relationship with Yahweh that is expressed through Israel's transgression, sins and idolatry. As a result, Israel's relationship both with Yahweh and land comes to a state of precariousness. In other words, the message of breaking the tripartite relationship is expressed in terms of theophany in which Yahweh's intervention to deal with Israel's sin and transgression is seen as the reason of causing great damage upon the land making the inhabitants difficult to survive upon the land. The break of tripartite relationship is expressed through sins and transgressions against Yahweh.

5.4. Sinai Covenant Tradition (Micah 2:1-5)

Condemnation on coveting and seizing land in 2:1-5 is embedded in the prohibition of the Sinai Covenant Tradition on covetousness (the Decalogue). Violation of this covenant tradition results in Yahweh's judgment against Judah and the loss of land. The tripartite relationship is therefore jeopardized because of the covenant violation in 2:1-5.

5.4.1. Translation on Micah 2:1-5

1 Woe[a] to those who plan iniquity[b] and work evil[b] upon their beds! When the morning dawns, they perform it, because it is in the power[c] of their hand.

2 They covet fields[a], and seize[b] them; and houses[c], and take them away[b]; they oppress a man[d] and his house, a man and his inheritance[e].

3 Therefore thus says Yahweh, Behold, against this family I am devising evil, from which you cannot remove your necks; and you shall not walk haughtily, for it will be an evil time.

4 In that day they shall take up a taunt song against you, and wail with bitter lamentation, and say, "We are utterly ruined; he changes the portion of my people; how he removes it from me! Among our captors he divides our fields".

5 Therefore you will have none to cast the line by lot in the assembly[a] of Yahweh.

5.4.2. Text Critical Comments on Micah 2:1-5

V.1a: Westerman argues that ארור "curse" in Deut. 27 appears syntactically similar with הוי as both deals with the covenant curses against social morality sins and he concludes that the prophetic הוי "woe" had its origin in the covenant curses.[45] Clifford, however, argues that since the funeral lament is the only attested nonprophetic use of הוי (1 Kgs 13:30), he considers that funeral lament is the origin of הוי.[46] Though the origin of הוי remains debatable, in any case, the eighth century prophets mostly employ הוי to announce the punishment against a guilty

[45] Claus Westermann, *Grundformen prophetischer Rede* (Munich: Kaiser-Verlag, 1960), 137-140. Cited in R.J. Clifford, "The Use Of Hoy In The Prophets", *CBQ* 28 (1966) 458.

[46] Clifford, "The Use of Hoy", 459.

party for a certain kind of action (cf. Am. 5:18-20; Isa. 1:4; 3:11). Normally הוי is followed by the participle that specifies the people to whom the doom is announced. In v.1, they are identified as the land grabbers who scheme evil plots to acquire and seize the lands. Micah uses הוי to describe a lamentable fate and situation in store for those accused land grabbers.

V.1b-b: און "iniquity" refers to actions "which are destructive of community's well being."[47] Following R. Knierim, Mays states that און "identifies an act as the expression of a power intent on the violation of an order set by God to preserve and augment the life of an individual or their social group."[48] Similarly, Kenneth L. Baker and Waylon Bailey point out that "iniquity" here refers to "abuse of power in illegal and unethical machinations, resulting in social injustice."[49] In other words, the term refers to an act through which the accused schemes to expropriate others' land that is understood as a violation of the set order of God for the community's well being.

V.1c: כי יש-לאל ידם literally "because their hand is god". This suggests that the perpetuators exercise their absolute power to do whatever they want to do as they have the power to do so.[50] The power is linked with the encroachment of landed properties, fields and inheritance.

V.2a: שדה "fields" in Isa. 5:8-10 refers to a cultivable plot as it appears in the context of the vineyard cultivation. Since there is a linguistic and thematic affinity between Is. 5:8 (the vineyard song) and Mic. 2:2, we assume that שדה in v.2 also refers to the cultivable land.

V.2b: גזל "to seize" and נשא "take away" emphasize physical violence and forceful eviction. In Gen. 21:15 גזל describes the seizing of immovable properties like fields and well. Such idea of tearing a person away from their property and forceful eviction from their patrimonial lands are intended here. The verbs גזל and נשא indicate the dispossession and eviction of the man and his family. The forceful eviction is described by another term עשק "to oppress" and refers to denying people that which is rightfully theirs by taking something away forcefully through the advantage of power.[51]

V.2c: In a more common usage of the term בית refers to "house" in a sense of living space or residential plot. However, there is another aspect of meaning of the term בית as demonstrated by Marvin Chaney and W. Moran. In his study on the term בית, Chaney establishes that בית in the Decalogue originally refers to the neighbor's plot of arable land held in redistributional domain by an

---

[47] Mays, *Micah*, 63.

[48] Mays, *Micah*, 63.

[49] Kenneth L. Baker and Waylon Bailey, *Micah, Nahum, Habakkuk, Zephaniah*, NAC 20 (Nashville, Tennessee: Broadman, 1999), 63.

[50] C.F. Keil, *Minor Prophets*, vol. 10 (Grand Rapids, Michigan: William B. Eerdmans Publishing Company, 1982), 439.

[51] Cf. Shaw, *The Speeches of Micah*, 80; Mays, *Micah*, 63.

Israelite extended family.[52] Similarly, after extensive study of the Accadian *bitu* in Ugaritic documents from the second millennium, which deals with the transfer of immovable property, Moran concludes that property in these texts is referred to as house *(bitu)*, field *(eqlu)*.[53] We consider that בתים "houses" in v.2 can mean a living, residential plot or/and arable land.

V.2d: גבר according to Wolff refers to a citizen capable of military service and who possesses full legal rights and obligation.[54] Micah uses this term to describe that the right and freedom to property has been violated by the rich oppressors. Arguing along Alt's proposal that there was a long-standing animosity between the citizen-farmer of Judah and the royal officials of Jerusalem, Andersen and Freedman infer that the oppressors here are the court officials and military commanders appointed from Jerusalem.[55] This view is plausible since in 3:1, 9 the perpetrators of injustice are identified as "rulers". If the argument on גבר as referring to citizen-farmers and the accused as royal officials can be sustained, then it would suggest a prevailing struggle on the land use patterns between the old covenant tradition, which sees land as inalienable inheritance and the Canaanites' pattern of alienable land imitated by the rulers of Jerusalem (cf. 3:1, 9).[56]

V.2e: There is no consensus among the scholars about the term נחלה. Wright, Brown and others interpret it as "inheritance",[57] which Dybdahal considers as misleading since in most of its occurrences נחלה does not appear in the context of "death or to the passing on from one member to the family of another" but נחלה often refers "to a part/share or portion of land."[58] Dybdhl's position may be right in the context of its occurrences in Joshua and Numbers where נחלה appears to refer to the entitlement or rightful property but not to refer to land passed on to generations. However, the distributed land during the settlement era had over the period of years been divided into smaller allocations with the growth of family members. Such portion of land passed on the existing generation has been considered as נחלה "inheritance" (cf. 1 Kgs 21). In any case, נחלה is understood as rightful share and entitlement to land and property.[59]

---

[52] M. L. Chaney, "You Shall Not Covet Your Neighbor's House," *Pacific Theological Review* 15 (1982) 6.

[53] W. Moran, "The Conclusion of the Decalogue (Ex. 20:17= Dt 5:21)," *CBQ* 29 (1967)549-52.

[54] Wolff, *Micah*, 8, 78.

[55] A. Alt, *Kleine Schriften zur Gischichte des Volkes Israel*, Vol. 3 (Munchen: Beck'sche Verlagsbuchhandlung, 1959), 373-381. Cited in Andersen and Freedman, *Micah*, 273.

[56] Andersen and Freedman, *Micah*, 273.

[57] Wright, *God's People in God's Land*, 19; Arthur M. Brown, "The Concept of Inheritance in the ld Testament", Ph.D diss. (Columbia University, 1965), 8ff. cited in Habel, *The Land is Mine*, 33.

[58] Jon Dybdhal, "Israelite Village Land Tenure: Settlement to Exile", Ph.D diss. (Fuller Theological Seminary, 1981), 54, 59. Cited in Habel, *The Land is Mine*, 33-34.

[59] For detail discussion see, Habel, *The Land is Mine*, 33-35.

V.5a: קהל יהוה "assembly of Yahweh" is a designation of the sacred assembly of Israel (cf. Deut. 23:3; Num. 16:3; 20:4; 1 Chro. 28:8; Neh. 13:1). קהל is the assembly where tribal allotment and settlement were determined in ancient Israel (Deut. 33: 4-5, 21). It was also a place that preserves integrity of the tribal territory and adjudicates boarder disputes (Josh. 22-23). Though קהל appears mostly in the exilic literature, its usage in Micah does not necessarily suggest a post exilic work; rather by using this term Micah intents to evoke the memories of past days[60] where integrity of the boundaries were maintained.

5.4.3. Form Critical Comments on Micah 2:1-5

The opening statement with הוי (v.1) implies the beginning of a new unit. However, scholars disagree on the issue of continuity between vv.1-3 and vv. 4-5. Robinson sees discontinuity between vv.1-3 and vv.4-5 by arguing that v.4 is a fragment to which an editor had added a prose (v.5). V.4 is seen as the lament of the Judean farmers whose lands have been seized by the conquerors.[61] Smith also separates v.4 from vv.1-3 by arguing that v.4 is a mock lament by an unnamed foe (but understood as the Assyrians) who sang dirges at their defeat of Judah, while v.5 is also considered to be separated from v.4 as it lies outside of poetical form and does not connect with the reproach of the enemies in v.4.[62] Rudolph, however, contends that the lament in v.4 is the cry of the oppressors who are accused in vv.1-2 and warned in v.3. He emends לך in v.5 to לכם as haplography of ם in order to harmonize with על-כם in v.4. and argues that those who mourn in v.4 are none other than those who are threatened in v.5, namely, the oppressors of vv.1-3.[63] Rudolph thus sees the continuity of vv.1-3 with vv.4-5. Following Rudolph, most scholars have favored the unity of vv.1-5, which is bound together by a common theme of land and its foreclosure.[64]

2:1-5 is a unit of prophetic accusation and judgment against those who seize others' land.[65] It consists of woe speech directed against the greedy people who amassed the land (vv.1-2), which serves as the basis of judgment connected by "therefore" in v.3. The temporal clause "in that day" in v.4 connects with v.3 "it will be an evil time". The direct speech in v.4 continues with the quotation of a lament song using poetical terms which the addressees would sing and then picks

[60] Andersen and Freedman, *Micah*, 290.

[61] T.H. Robinson, *Die Zwolf Kleinen Propheten* (HAT, Tubingen, 1964), 133-134. Cited in William McKane, "Micah 2:1-5: Text and Commentary", *JSS* 42/1 (1997) 14.

[62] J.M.P. Smith, *A Critical and Exegetical Commentary on Micah, Zephaniah, Nahum, Obadiah, Joel,* ICC (Edinburgh: T&T Clark, 1911), 58-59.

[63] Rudolph cited in McKane, "Micah 2:1-5", 16.

[64] McKane, "Micah 2:1-5", 14; Leslie C. Allen, *The Book of Joel, Obadaiah, Jonah and Micah*, NICOT (Grand Rapids, Michigan: William B. Eerdmans Publishing Company, 1976) 286; Hillers, *Micah*, 31-33.

[65] Wolff, *Micah*, 72.

up again the punishment theme. "Therefore" in v.5 further mentions the element of the looming punishment.[66]

There is no particular historical allusion in the text. However, the state of affairs described in the text shows a slow disintegration of the society of Judah: seizure of houses and foreclosing of land by the plutocrats from the vulnerable owners (v.2). Alt argues that Micah's polemic reflects the consequences of the relationship between the Davidic kings and the city-state of Jerusalem and territory of Judah. The Davidic kings made grants of land to Jerusalem notables in their entourage and later these notables, driven by economic motives, started evicting the peasants and drove out the farmers from their homestead and land.[67] Quite distinctively Bardtke argues in his comments on Isa. 5:8-9, which also has a bearing in Mic. 2:1-2, that the protest raised here is related to the danger faced by the Judean state. He argues that there was an influx of refugees from the Northern Kingdom, traders of Canaanite extraction who use to buy town houses and agricultural land. With the growth of the numbers of family or clan, the land was allocated in smaller portions to each of its members. The traders bought such land in its entirety and thereby added field to field for cultivation. Judeans' peasants were employed as farm laborers, became landless and displaced persons. All these were done with the encouragement of the Judean state, since it helped to fill its war coffer in the face of the Assyrian threat and since efficient farming created wealth that is needed to pay the demands of Assyrian tribute. Bardtke thus sees the prophetic interventions of Isa. 5:8-9 and Micah 2:1-2 as a reflection of this temporary period in the history of Judah, the sharp danger represented by the Assyrian threat and the social dislocation which it produced.[68]

Alt and Bardtke's proposals appear convincing but such views remain hypothetical in the absence of any evidence. In any case, forceful acquisition of others' patrimonial inheritance during the mid eighth century was not uncommon. The example can be found in 1 Kgs 21 where Naboth refused to sell his patrimonial inheritance but Ahab carried out a criminal plot against Naboth and unlawfully evicted him and his household (2 Kgs 9:26) from their patrimonial land. Such instances of forceful eviction of the poor peasants from their patrimonial land are echoed in the eighth century prophets' literature (cf. Isa. 5:8-24; Am 2:6-8; 8:4-6).[69] In other words, the indictment on the acquisition of land by a few plutocrats in vv.1-2 reflects Judah's social conditions during Micah's time.

---

[66] Mays, *Micah*, 61.

[67] A. Alt, "Micah 2:1-5. *ΤΗΣ ΑΝΑΔΑΣΜΟΣ* in Judah", in *Interpretationes as Vetus Testamentum pertinentes Sigmundo Mowinckel sepsuagenario missae* (Oslo: Forlaget Land og Kirke, 1955), 13-15. Cited in McKane, "Micah 2:1-5", 12.

[68] H. Bardtke, "Die Latifundien in Juda Wahrend der Zweiten Halfte des Achten Jahrhunderts v. chr", *Hommages a Andre Dupont-Sommer* (Paris 1971), 244-50. Cited in McKane, "Micah 2:1-5", 12.

[69] Sweeney, *The Twelve Prophets*, vol. 2, 361.

5.4.4. Tradition and Theological Comments on Tripartite Relationship

The charge of wrong doings described as "covet", "seize", and "oppress" in v.2, which appears contrary to the covenant stipulation for right conduct call for Yahweh's judgment. חמד "to covet" is the word of the Decalogue, "you shall not covet" (Ex. 20:17; 34:24; Deut. 28:32). The covenant tradition instructs Israel about the property rights[70] in which covetousness is considered as violation of the commandment. עשק "to oppress" in v.2 appears in the covenant tradition that forbids "oppression,"[71] which is also warned by the teachers.[72] The phrase יהיה לך-לא in v.5 translated here as "you will have none" is also the beginning statement of the first commandment. Micah's indictment echoes the language of the violation of the Decalogue of Sinai covenant. Since the covenant tradition warns that disloyalty will lead to the forfeiture of the land, Micah sees the violation of the covenant norms (vv.1-2) to be the reason of breaking the tripartite relationship: Judah violates the covenant and Yahweh enforces his covenantal curse upon his people (v.3) that in turn affects the people of Judah since Yahweh's judgment brings the loss of and alienation from the land.

Micah's condemnation begins with הוי, which expresses the tragic situation that would befall upon those land hungry people who devise wicked plans (v.1). The identity of "those who plan iniquity" is not explicitly stated but they are characterized as people with "power in their hand" (כי יש-לאל ידם, v.1). These people covet, seize and take away "the fields, houses and inheritance", through land foreclosure,[73] which rightfully belong to others as inherited patrimonial lands (v.2). Micah sees such acquisition of land as a blatant violation of the covenant instructions on property rights. Micah sees here that "power" coupled with "covetousness" leads to the wicked and evil act of violence and such diabolical act is described by the terms גזל "to seize", נשא "take away" and עשק "to oppress" (see the TCC on v.2b). But how do the accused seize land and oppress the victims? Scholars do not agree on the nature of forceful land acquisition by the powerful people. Mays, Hillers, Allen and others suggest that the oppressors seize land through the imposition of debt and usury.[74] Shaw rejects such interpretation and argues that the modus operandi of land seizing has been through harassment and acts of violence achieved through the use of military force.[75] In any case, whether the seizing of land is carried out through debt servitude and usury or through the force of military action, what appears significant in Micah's accusation is that land

---

70 Bruce Waltke, *Obadiah, Jonah, Micah*, TOTC (England: IVP, 1988), 635.

71 Cf. Lev. 5:21; 19:3; Deut. 24:14.

72 Cf. Prov. 14:31; 22:16; 28:3. Mays, *Micah*, 63.

73 Ben Ehud Zvi, *Micah*, FOTL 21 B (Grand Rapids, Michigan/Cambridge, UK: William B. Eedrmans Publishing Company, 2000), 44.

74 Mays, *Micah*, 64; Hillers, *Micah*, 33; Allen, *Micah*, 298.

75 Shaw, *The Speeches of Micah*, 81.

which belongs rightfully to others has been forcefully taken away. This means, the issue that Micah addresses here is about a forceful alienation of people from their inheritance and property. Verbs uses here, as mentioned in the TCC on v.2b, emphasize a physical violence and forceful eviction of others from their land, house and fields through the advantage of power.

Land and land ownership, in the covenant tradition, ultimately belongs to Yahweh and the Israelites are just the recipients of Yahweh's gift of land as his tenants (Lev. 25:23). The covenant law thus prohibits any kind of permanent sale or transfer of land outside the family circle. Even in the case of extreme poverty that may force a fellow Israelite to sell his land, the jubilee law envisages that at the end of forty nine years the land be reverted to the original owner (Lev. 25; Deut. 15:1-11). Besides, the inheritance right of the first born (Deut. 21:15-17) and the Levirate marriage (Num. 27:1-11; 36:1-12) also protect the line of inheritance to ensure that the land remains within the family. Against such instructions on the land usage pattern, the powerful ones seized the landed property either by military force or in lieu of the unpaid debt and foreclosed the homestead and fields of the poor peasants. Such tactic of land acquisition, according to Micah, is an act of iniquity, evil and oppression (v.2).

Based on the above indictment (vv.1-2), v.3 introduces a divine sentence. The judgment formula לכן "therefore" announces Yahweh's counterplot: "I am devising evil" (v.3). This refers to Yahweh's "plans" to harm "those who plan" to harm others (v.1).[76] Yahweh's plan to bring harm is linked to a yoke on the neck, which is a metaphorical expression of servitude to conquering enemies[77] (cf. Isa. 9:4; 10:27; 47:6). The identity and the agent to carry out the punishment are not mentioned. In any case, it will humiliate the powerful to equally suffer the helplessness in a way that they caused other to suffer.[78] In other words, the perpetrators who schemed evil and took away others' land will find its fitting judgment as the conqueror will take away the land from them (v.4, cf. 1:16).

Because of the oppressive subjugation and the loss of land, there will be a bitter lamentation: "we are utterly ruined", "he changes the portion of my people", "removes it from me", and "he parcels out our fields" (v.4). These cries talk about the loss of land and the annexation of their political nation, Judah. לכן "therefore" in v.5 further states the consequence of the loss of land, namely, the dispossession, "you will have none to cast the line by lot in the assembly". "The casting of lot" was applied to apportion land during the period of settlement (Josh. 15:1; 18:6; Num. 26:55; 36:2),[79] while "assembly" was an institution where tribal territories were allocated and border disputes settled. By employing the language of ancient land allocation, Micah underscores his emphasis on the loss of land that "what

[76] Brown, "Micah 2:1-11", 418.

[77] Cf. Kimichi. Cited in McKane, "Micah 2:1-5", 14.

[78] Mays, *Micah*, 64.

[79] Sweeney, *The Twelve Prophets*, Vol. 2. 362.

was done by Joshua at the birth of the nation will be now be undone."[80] "To cast off" משליך from the assembly of Yahweh means to be expelled from the land and become landless.[81] V. 5 thus predicts that in the future there will be a reversal of land distribution history in which Judah will lose the land and will lose the privilege to participate in the assembly to distribute the land, because the people would have been carried off to exile and the conquerors of Judah will share the land among themselves.

The above exegesis shows Micah's understanding of land as an arable or cultivable plot (שׂדות, בתים), a living and residential plot (בתים), a patrimonial inheritance as rightful entitlement (נחלה) and a portion or territory of allotment (חלק). Micah's usages of these terms not only suggest his understanding of land as a survival means for cultivation and existence but these terms also show land as an inalienable and rightful share of all people of Judah as members of the assembly of Yahweh. However, with covetousness in their heart and power in their hand the rich people started dispossessing and evicting others from their rightful land. Such practice of land grabbing is against the covenant instructions on the land use and violation of the Decalogue. Micah sees these acts as violations of the covenant and calls for the covenant judgment of defeat at the hands of enemies, destruction of the land and exile in humiliation to a foreign land. In other words, because of the violation of the covenant, Judah alienated herself from Yahweh's covenant instructions and as a consequence Judah will now be alienated and exiled from her land. Micah thus presents the break of tripartite relationship between Yahweh, Judah and land expressed in terms of Judah's violation of the covenant.

5.5. Zion Tradition (Micah 3:9-12)

Yahweh is "in the midst of us, no evil will come upon us" (v.11) speaks of the inviolability of Jerusalem, which is rooted in the Zion tradition. Against such affirmed faith, Micah asserts that Yahweh himself will fight against Zion (which represents Judah's political land/nation) and it will be "ploughed" and "ruined" (v.12) because of the lack of justice (vv.9-11). The tripartite relationship affirmed within the Zion tradition is explained to be void if unaccompanied by the practice of social justice.

5.5.1. Translation on Micah 3:9-12

9 Hear this, you [a]heads of the house of Jacob and rulers of the house of Israel[a],
who abhor justice[b] and cause all the straight[c] crooked,
10 who build[a] Zion with blood and Jerusalem with violence.

---

[80] Daniel J. Simundson, "The Book of Micah: Introduction, Commentary and Reflection", in Leander E. Keck, *Introduction to Apocalyptic Literature, Daniel and Twelve Prophets*, NIB 7 (Nashville: Abingdon Press, 1996), 550.

[81] Andersen and Freedman, *Micah*, 290.

11 her [a]heads give judgment for a bribe[b], her priests teach[b] for price, her prophets divine for money; but they lean upon Yahweh[c] and say, "Is not Yahweh in the midst of us? No evil shall come upon us".

12 Therefore[a] because of you[b] Zion shall be plowed as a field[c]; Jerusalem shall become a heap of ruins, and the mountain of the house a wooded height[d].

5.5.2. Text Critical Comments on Micah 3:9-12

V.9a-a: "heads of Jacob...rulers of Israel" refer to royal officials of Jerusalem as indicated by the association of their crimes with Zion and Jerusalem. In the LXX, the MT's "rulers" is rendered as "remaining ones", which is difficult to explain. Following Hillers' comments, Shaw states that the LXX's rendering is probably influenced by the remnant theme in 2:12-13.[82] Micah frequently employs these titles in his prophetic speech (1:5; 3:1, 9). ראש "heads" and קצין "rulers" are synonymous title associated with the administration of justice (3:1, 9, 11). The earliest usage of ראש is Ex. 18:25 where the title is attributed to those appointed to serve as judges for Israel. Mays states that in the rural villages, the presiding over the court remained the responsibility of the elders but in Jerusalem and fortified cities, the officials appointed by the kings served as judges (cf. 2 Chro. 19:4-11; Deut. 16:18-20). קצין appears in the premonarchical life of Israel to refer to the military leaders (Josh. 10:24; Judg. 11:6, 11) and in proto Isaiah and Micah to refer to the officials of Judah.[83] Following Dearman's comments, Shaw reaffirms that the only other occurrence of the pair קצין/ראש is in reference to Jephthah's role as military leader.[84] Shaw thus concludes that probably the leaders indicted here are the "military leaders who are royal administrative appointees and who probably had the power to settle disputes."[85] By employing קצין/ראש, Micah fixes the officials' identity and places their obligations to make right decisions and to implement justice which go with their position in ancient Israel tradition of social order.[86]

V.9b: משפט here refers to the established social norms for protecting the legal right of the innocent in disputed matters on life and property. Covenant faithfulness to Yahweh demanded the upholding of the rights of the poor and weak, which are considered as an act of justice (Ex. 23:1-3; 6-8; Deut. 16:19; Lev. 19:13, 15).[87] In 3:1 Micah reminded the chiefs or rulers of their responsibility to know משפט "justice" and in v.9, he reprimanded them for making contempt of justice by accepting bribery (v.11) and perverting what was straight (right).

---

[82] Cf. Hillers, *Micah*, 42; Shaw, *The Speeches of Micah*, 97. no. 2.

[83] Mays, *Micah*, 78.

[84] Dearman, *Property Rights*, 50. no. 1; Shaw, *The Speeches of Micah*, 110.

[85] Shaw, *The Speeches of Yahweh*, 110.

[86] Mays, *Micah*, 88.

[87] Mays, *Micah*, 88.

V.9c: כל is in a construct state and with the article denotes the entirety, "all". ישרה is a genitive of measure, and according to Waltke, in all Semitic languages, the feminine form of ישרה, which is rare, marks it as an abstract noun from the adjective ישר.[88] Comparing its occurrence with דרך in 1 Sam. 12:23, Andersen and Freedman argue that the use of the definite article in v.9 suggests that הישרה־כל means "every straight path."[89] Whether or not to assume דרך here is of little significance since the emphasis is on the verb עקש "to pervert or to make crooked". Waltke argues that the root ישר originally had a meaning, "to be straight" but predominantly occurs in metaphorical sense "to be right."[90]

V.10a: The participle here is rendered in the MT as singular, which scholars think should be emended to plural. However, Shaw rightly considers such emendation as unnecessary as it could be understood as a "collective."[91]

V.11a-a: ראשיה "her head" refers to magistrates (see the above notes on v.9a-a), who are characterized as those who "hate good" (v.2), "abhor justice" (v.9) and sell their judgment for a bribe (v.11).[92] The third feminine singular ה states a genitive of relation referring to Zion/Jerusalem, that is, the leaders of Zion/Jerusalem.

V.11b: ירה "to instruct" is the duty of the priests concerning the various instructions for carrying cultic activities as codified in Leviticus and also in matters of complicated legal disputes for instructions from God for their resolution (cf. Deut. 17:8ff). The selling of their instruction refers to the taking of bribe to pervert the rules of religious conduct.[93]

V.11c: שען literally "to lean" as a lame person on a stick is used to state both legitimate trust in and false reliance on God (cf. Isa. 10:20; 50:10).[94] "To rely on Yahweh" is an expression for dependence on divine help (Isa. 10:20; 2 Chro. 13:18; 14:20; 16:7ff). It is a confidence drawn on the basis of Israel's relationship with Yahweh.[95]

V.12a: The almost verbatim parallel is found in Jer. 26:18 except with a minor addition of "thus says Yahweh of host". Perhaps to harmonize with Jeremiah, Budde and Sellin add "thus says Yahweh" in v.12.[96] Wagenaar, however, argues that the absence of "thus says Yahweh of host" does not imply that the announcement

---

[88] Waltke, *A Commentary on Micah*, 177.

[89] Andersen and Freedman, *Micah*, 381.

[90] Waltke, *A Commentary on Micah*, 177.

[91] Shaw, *The Speeches of Micah*, 99.

[92] For further discussion see, J.R. Bartlett, "The Use of the Word ראש as a Title in the Old Testament", *VT* 19/1 (1963) 1-10.

[93] J. Weingreen, "The Title Moreh Sedek", *JSS* 6 (1961) 162-174.

[94] Andersen and Freedman, *Micah*, 384.

[95] Mays, *Micah*, 90.

[96] Dilbert R. Hillers, *Micah,* Hermenia (Philadelphia: Fortress Press, 1094), 47.

of judgment was not from Yahweh or inauthentic.[97] לכן "therefore" is a logical participle linking the sentence to the accusation.

V.12b: בגללכם "because of you" is a frozen prepositional compound consisting of inseparable ב and the noun גלל and second masculine plural pronominal suffix כם, which according to Waltke, attributes the fall of the city not to the impotence of Yahweh but to the קחין/ראש.[98]

V.12c: שׂדה "as a field", according to Waltke, is not an accusative of result to translate as "into field" but it is an accusative of state that specifies that Zion will be in a state of being a field.[99]

V.12d: במות "high places" throughout the Bible refers to the places that were used for illegitimate worship of Yahweh or foreign gods."[100] The parallel term עיין "ruin" suggests that a physical destruction is intended here.

5.5.3. Form Critical Comments on Micah 3:9-12

The introductory call to attention "hear this" in v.9 demarcates a new unit. V.12 apparently ends the unit with judgment against Jerusalem since "it shall come to pass" in 4:1 marks a transition of new unit.[101] Vv.9-12 is a unit of judgment speech in which Micah calls for attention to listen to the charges against the accused, which is followed by the pronouncement of judgment based on the accusations.[102] The unit can be outlined as follows.

Introductory Call to Attention:	Hear this (v.9a)
Name of the Accused:	...heads ... and rulers of the house of Israel (v.9b)
General Indictment:	who abhor justice and cause all the straight crooked (v.9c)
Specific Indictment:	...build Zion with blood and Jerusalem with violence... judgment for a bribe... teach for price ...divine for money; but they lean upon Yahweh and say, "Is not Yahweh in the midst of us? No evil shall come upon us" (vv.10-11).
Messenger Formula:	Therefore (v.12a)
Announcement of Judgment:	...Zion shall be plowed...Jerusalem shall become a heap of ruins, and the mountain of the house a wooded height (v12b).

[97] Wagenaar, *Judgment and Salvation*, 246.

[98] Waltke, *A Commentary on Micah*, 181.

[99] Waltke, *A Commentary on Micah*, 189.

[100] Sweeney, *The Twelve Prophets*, Vol. 2, 375.

[101] Sweeney, *The Twelve Prophets*, Vol. 2, 373.

[102] Bruce K. Waltke, *Micah*, TOTC (Leicester, England: IVP, 1988), 164.

On the historical setting of the present unit, Mays considers that Micah's accusation of building Jerusalem with violence probably refers to the fortifications and public buildings erected in Jerusalem during Hezekiah's time. Hezekiah sought to liberate Jerusalem from Assyria and started the work of fortifications for national defense. Mays cites the instance where Hezekiah sought to secure Jerusalem's water supply and expanded the royal buildings (2 Kgs 20:20 and 2 Chro. 32:27ff) to prove his case. Arguing that Hezekiah's policy of corvee enforced by his commandeering labor would have been harsh and that the blood of the enslaved labor spilt over what was built cried out to God, Mays contends that Micah's prophecy "who build Jerusalem with bloodshed" (v.10) refers to such events of Hezekiah's period.[103] Sweeney likewise argues that the charges against the heads, prophets and priests (v.9) for bribery refer to "the expectation of the rewards" by making their decision in favor of Hezekiah's preparation to oppose Assyria, while the charge of building Jerusalem with "blood" refers to the animal sacrifices made at the temple as the nation implored Yahweh's help to fight the Assyria.[104]

Quite distinctively, Andersen and Freedman consider that the present unit of Micah's prophecy can most suitably be dated to Ahaz's reign who engaged in rebuilding Jerusalem and that the accusation of building Jerusalem with "blood" refers to Ahaz's sacrifice of his two sons in time of national threat (2 Chro. 28:3). The Syro-Ephraimate invasion is considered to have been a threat to Ahaz, which compelled him to make such offerings thinking that sacrifice of royal sons would avert the danger by bringing the wrath upon enemies.[105] Since both Samaria and Jerusalem were standing intact during the time of Micah's prophecy, Andersen and Freedman conclude that the prophecy could be dated before 724 BCE.[106]

Andersen and Freedman rightly point out that with Hezekiah's reputation on reformation it is unlikely that v.10 is a criticism of Hezekiah's building program,[107] (Hezekiah broke down the altars at high places and removed the syncretistic worship). However, despite his reformation, as Sweeney points out, there was a tension between Hezekiah's religious reforms and his policy to revolt against Sennacherib of Assyria (ca. 705-701),[108] by allying with the Egypt (2 Kgs 18:21ff). In such a setting, probably Micah sees the danger of Hezekiah's revolt and accuses those who give their judgment in favor of armed rebellion to receive royal favor (bribe), which would amount to the accumulation of wealth at the cost of bloody wars. Bloodshed and violence in v.10 could also refer to such

[103] Mays, *Micah*, 89.

[104] Sweeney, *The Twelve Prophets*, vol. 2, 374-375.

[105] Andersen and Freedman, *Micah*, 382-383.

[106] Andersen and Freedman, *Micah*, 387.

[107] Andersen and Freedman, *Micah*, 382.

[108] Marvin A. Sweeney, *Isaiah 1-39*, FOTL 16 (Grand Rapids, Michigan/Cambridge, UK: William B. Eerdmans Publishing Company, 1996), 80.

situation. It is also possible that Micah had in mind the gruesome sacrifice of Ahaz's sons to secure divine help when Judah faced national peril (cf. 2 Chro. 28:3) and that the "bloodshed" mentioned in v.10 could possibly refer to such event and period of Ahaz's reign. Micah's accusation on bloodshed in Jerusalem cannot be restricted to a strict timeline of particular event. Assuming that Micah's prophetic activity covers the reigns of Jotham, Ahaz and Hezekiah of Judah as mentioned in 1:1, we conclude that the historical setting of Micah's prophecy in 3:9-12 covers the accumulated offence of bloodshed and violence since the time of Ahaz and Hezekiah's reign.

5.5.4. Tradition and Theological Comments in the Light of Tripartite Relationship

The expression that Yahweh is "in the midst of us, no evil will come upon us" (v.11) reflects Zion tradition. Zion tradition affirms the inviolability of land based on the belief that Yahweh's presence is in Zion. Yahweh's presence is symbolized by the presence of the ark and temple. Whereas, the presence of ark, Jan Dus argues, is associated with Yahweh as the "conqueror" and "owner" of the land (Jos. 3:11-13; 22:19),[109] Jerusalem's temple symbolized the presence of Yahweh in Zion as Yahweh's dwelling place (Pss 9:12; 74:2); Yahweh's holy mountain (Pss 2:6; 87:1; 99:9); the home of his holy house (Pss 5:7; 27:4.).[110] Based on such understanding of the ark and temple in Zion, Zion is believed to be inviolable and divinely protected.[111] The "heads,, "rulers," "priests" and "prophets" affirm Zion's inviolability because of Yahweh's presence amidst them. However, they failed to attach any ethical obligation and instruction to such affirmed faith. Micah employs the Zion tradition that was popularly held among these officials to counter their belief by showing the reversal motif in this judgment oracle. The officials who arrogantly trust in Zion's inviolability, "Is not Yahweh in the midst of us, no evil shall come upon us" (v.11. cf. Pss 46; 48; 76), will see the base of that trust false, "Zion will be ploughed" (v.12).[112] Micah picks up the Zion tradition and reinterprets it by asserting that Yahweh himself will fight against Zion and reduced it to destruction.

Micah's judgment oracle begins with a call to attention "hear this", which is addressed to the "heads" and "rulers." These leaders hold the responsibility to

---

[109] For detail discussion on the link between the ark of God and Yahweh as the land conqueror and landowner, see, Jan Dus, "Der Beitrag des benjaminitischen Heidentums zur Religion Israels" *Communio Viatorum* 6/1 (1963) 67-72.

[110] Cf. Richard S. Hess and Gordon J. Wenham (eds), *Zion: City of our God* (Grand Rapids.: Michigan, 1999), 6-8. Detailed discussion on the Zion tradition and its symbols and significance are discussed by Ben C. Ollenburger, *Zion the City of the Great King: A Theological Symbol of the Jerusalem Cult*, JSOTSS 41 (Sheffield: JSOT, 1987), 13-19, 53-76.

[111] John H. Hayes, "The Tradition of Zion's Inviolability", *JBL* 82/4 (1963) 421.

[112] Marrs, "Back to the Future", 83.

administer justice (cf. v.1) but they are characterized here as abhorrers and perverters of justice (v.9). The accused are indicted of building Jerusalem by bloodshed and violence (v.10). "Bloodshed" in v.10 could refer to a wide range of meanings: the shed blood of the sacrifice of Ahaz's children (Andersen and Freedman); the blood of the enslaved labors (corvee) during Jerusalem's fortification under Hezekiah (Mays); the blood of the animal sacrifices at the temple to implore Yahweh's help (Sweeney). All these are all part of the historical events during the period of Micah (see the above FCC). Micah sees the bloodshed and violence in Judah to be a result of perversion of justice.

Along with the above possible meaning, bloodshed is also closely linked with unjust acquisition of land. Citing 1 Kgs 21; Am. 5:11; Hos. 4:2 and Isa. 1:15, Abraham argues that the shedding of blood condemned in v.10 refers to "the confiscation of the property of the innocent condemned to death."[113] Abraham's argument is plausible in the context of Micah's accusation against the greedy land grabbers who "oppress" and "take away" the victims' land by perverting justice (cf. 2:2, 9). Though there is no verifiable historical event within in the present text, such instance of forceful accumulation of land through bloodshed did happen during the monarchical period as mentioned in Ahab-Naboth incident (1 Kgs 21). Ahab shed Naboth's blood with an intention to take away Naboth's land. Such historical precedent of forceful acquisition of land could have become the pattern of unjust accumulation of wealth and properties by those who had power.[114] The reality of crimes associated with land and properties in the eighth century Israel and Judah is echoed in several texts of the eighth century prophets. The lavish palaces, summer and winter houses and houses of hewn stones (Am. 3:10, 15; 5:11; Hos. 8:14) are linked with the blood and iniquity by spoliation and expropriation of the small land holders.[115] As Waltke argues, Micah used the term "blood" in v.10 as "the synecdoche for the life of the defenseless victims who, having been "murdered" in a villainous court, lost property."[116] Such act of unjust acquisition, according to Micah, is עולה "violence," which refers to violent deeds, such as murder (cf. 2 Sam. 3:34).[117]

The accused are identified as "heads" and "rulers" (v.9) while v.11 names another accused group, "priests" and "prophets". In other words, the victims suffer rampant injustice between the nexus of two power structures: civil- "heads" and "rulers" and religious- "priests" and "prophets."[118] The unjust deeds of these

---

[113] A. T. Abraham, "Three Bible Studies on Struggle for Social Justice", *Religion and Society* 22 (1975) 4.

[114] Mays, *Micah*, 88.

[115] Goldman, "Micah", 168.

[116] Waltke, *A Commentary on Micah*, 178.

[117] Waltke, *A Commentary on Micah*, 179.

[118] Rick. R. Marrs, "Back to the Future: Zion in the Book of Micah", in Bernard F. Batto and Kathryn L. Roberts (eds), *David and Zion: Biblical Studies in Honor of J.J.M. Roberts* (USA:

accused leaders are propelled by greed for "money" and "bribe" (v.11), which results in the perversion of justice (cf. v.9). Micah sees that such unjust ethical practices are rooted in a wrong theological construction: "Yahweh is in the midst of us, no evil will fall on us" (v.11). In other words, the leaders express their relation with Yahweh as chosen people and hold that Yahweh's presence is in their midst, thus their temple and city cannot be destroyed. However, Micah sees such theological affirmation to be void of morality as justice is perverted, bloodshed is prevalent and bribery became the basis of judicial decision among the civil and religious leaders. The Zion tradition that clung to the protective presence of Yahweh and the security of the nation is inconsistent to the tripartite relationship envisaged in the covenant in which the practice of justice is stated as the way of life.

לכן "therefore" in v.12 states the consequences of indictment and concludes the prophetic announcement of judgment. The leaders build Zion with blood but now Yahweh counters them by turning Zion to rubble. "Because of you", namely, the heads, prophets and priests, Zion will be ploughed; Jerusalem will become a heap of ruins and the mountain of the house a wooded height (v.12). Such expression, according to J.R. Wood, is "in accord with Sumerian imagery expressing the destruction of cities and temples."[119] The description of Samaria's devastation by an enemy in 1:6-7 appears to be similar in tone and motivation with the destruction of Jerusalem mentioned here. These instances of destruction indicate that Jerusalem's devastation is envisioned here, probably indicating a looming military destruction. The beautiful houses and estates they acquired with unjust means will now be a heap of ruins and the city, which they thought to be inviolable, will be ploughed. In other words, Zion's beautiful paved court, which they built with bloodshed, will be turned into an uninhhabitable place. The judgment envisaged in 3:9-12 is the loss of land that include a living space (destruction of houses and fortifications), and a political nation and even a loss of privilege to worship Yahweh as the temple itself would become a wooded height. In other words, people will be alienated from the homeland, their land as place of habitation will become an uninhabitable and even the privilege of worshipping Yahweh will be lost with the destruction of the temple, which would become a wooded height. The tripartite relationship would thus be severed because of the perversion of justice in Judah.

5.6. Torah-Zion Tradition (Micah 4:1-5)

Descriptions of Zion as "the house/mountain of Yahweh" (v.1) and "the house of the God of Jacob" (v.2) recount the tradition that affirms Zion as Yahweh's dwelling place. From his dwelling place, Zion, Yahweh teaches "his ways", adjudicates "justice" and sends forth his "word and law" speaking of the Torah tradition

Eisenbraums, 2004), 83.

[119] Joyce Rilett Wood, "Speech and Action in Micah's Prophecy", *CBQ* 62 (2000) 658.

(vv.2-3). As people respond to Yahweh by walking in his ways, Yahweh ceased war upon the land and envisaged peace among the nations and secured cultivable land for every man (v.4). Using the Torah-Zion tradition, Micah explains the reestablished tripartite relationship in terms of people's walk in Yahweh's ways/ path, which results in secured existence upon the land.

5.6.1. Translation on Micah 4:1-5

1 It shall come to pass in the latter days[a] that the mountain of the house of Yahweh[b] shall be established[c] as the highest of the mountains, and shall be raised up above the hills; and peoples shall flow[d] to it,

2 and many nations shall come, and say: "Come, let us go up to the mountain of Yahweh, to the house of the God of Jacob; that he may teach us his ways[a] so that we may walk in his paths."[a] For out of Zion shall go forth the law and the word of Yahweh from Jerusalem.

3 He shall judge[a] between many peoples, and shall reprove[b] for strong nations afar off; and they shall beat[c] their swords into plowshares, and their spears into pruning hooks; nation shall not lift up sword against nation, neither shall they learn war any more;

4 but they shall sit[a] every man under his vine and under his fig tree, and none shall terrify them; for the mouth of Yahweh of hosts has spoken.

5 For all the peoples walk each in the name of its god, but we will walk in the name of Yahweh our God for ever and ever.

5.6.2. Text Critical Comments on Micah 4:1-5

V1a: Waltke states that והיה "and it shall come to pass" has a "deictic temporal formula" while היה has an active sense "to happen."[120] והיה is specified by the temporal adverbial prepositional phrase באחרית הימים "in the latter days", a formula, which introduces the prophecy of the future.[121] The LXX renders it as *και εσται εσχηατον τον εμερον* "and it shall come to pass in the end of days", which is understood as a reference to the eschatological end of time.[122] Due to LXX's *εσχατον* traditionally באחרית הימים is understood in an eschatological sense. However, by comparing the phrase with the Akkadian *ina ahrat umi* (in future days), Sweeney argues that באחרית הימים merely refers to a time in the future and not to the eschatological end of time.[123] The phrase refers to a future that is not presently discernable but points to "the goal or outcome toward which an event is striving."[124] It will be a time in the future that will paradoxically reverse the present situation.

---

[120] Waltke, *A Commentary on Micah*, 192.

[121] Gen. 49:1; Num. 24:14; Deut. 4:30; 31:19; Hos. 3:5.

[122] Sweeney, *The Twelve Prophets*, Vol. 2, 378.

[123] Sweeney, *Isaiah 1-39*, 99.

[124] Waltke, *A Commentary on Micah*, 193.

V.1b: The centre of the event to unfold "in the latter days" is הר בית-יהוה "the mountain of the house of Yahweh, namely, Jerusalem where the temple is located. In the ANE, the temple mountain symbolized several theological concepts, such as, a symbol of god's victory over chaos, a doorway to heaven and a symbol of god's presence.[125] In the present text, the summit of the divine mountain is elevated higher than other mountains to show that Yahweh's rule extends throughout the world.

V.1c: The Niphal singular participle נכון "established" is connected with יהיה to state that the founding is designated as permanent and established by Yahweh.[126]

V.1d: The verb ונהרו "and shall flow" is a cognate of the noun "river". The image of flowing river in connection with Zion appears frequently in the Old Testament (cf. Ps. 46:4[5]; Isa. 8:6). Probably the figure was based on the actual canal of the water of Gihon that flowed to the city toward the south. The usage here figuratively describes the pilgrimages of the nation to mount Zion.

V.2a-a: The מ in מדרכיו "in his way" is ablative, while the third singular pronominal suffix ו is a genitive of possession which shows that the learning originates and derives from דרכיו "his [Yahweh] way". דרך is a metaphor used to express God's gracious act in history and his requirements for his people (cf. Pss 18:22-23[21-22]; 25:4).[127] The preposition ב in בארחתיו "in his path" indicates a sphere in which they walk, that is, within the teaching of Torah. Since conjunctive waw with Qal first common cohortative expresses purpose, ונלכה is translated as "so that we may walk". הכך "to walk" indicate the ethical resolve to live according to the teachings of Yahweh. Twice הכך is used concretely while the third occurrence appears figuratively in v.2. Unlike 3:9-12 where the "heads", "priests", and "prophets" dichotomized Zion tradition from morality of justice and equity, in 4:2 Micah integrates Zion tradition with the ethics of Torah by employing הכך "walk", meaning to "walk" as prescribed by the teachings of the Torah.

V.3a: שפט "to judge" "appears in the patriarchal tradition in which Yahweh is ascribed as "judge of all the earth" (Gen. 18:25). The title השפט appears in Judges in which Yahweh is ascribed as an arbitrator in international disputes (Judg. 12:27).[128] The court office of the "heads" and "rulers" of people "perverted" justice, which Yahweh takes over to arbitrate for the whole earth.

V3b: ותוכיח "and he shall reprove" is from the root יכח, meaning "to establish what is right". It appears often in parallel with שפט "to judge" (cf. Isa. 11:3,

---

[125] For further discussion on the ANE religious concept of mountain, see Waltke, *A Commentary on Micah*, 195.

[126] C.F. Keil, *Minor Prophets*, vol.10 (Grand Rapids, Michigan: William B. Eerdmans Publishing Company, 1982), 456.

[127] Waltke, *A Commentary on Micah*, 198.

[128] Andersen and Freedman, *Micah*, 405.

4; Job 22:4; 23:4). והוכיח is a *waw*-relative signifying the results of judging by Yahweh.[129]

V.3c: וכתתו "and they shall beat" swords into ploughshares and spears into pruning hooks introduces international peace and demilitarization as a result of Yahweh's judgment. Waltke considers וכתתו as resultative Piel with לגוים/עמים רבים עצמים as its subject.[130] The verb comes from the root כתת "to beat/hammer". The military tools "swords" and "spears" that destroy lives will now be hammered out (converted) to agricultural tools "ploughshares" and "pruning hooks" to cultivate the land for sustenance.

V.4a: The *waw*-relative ו and Qal third plural of ישב in וישבו "and they shall sit" introduces a consequence that results from converting the war equipments to agricultural tools and as a result war will cease. The verb ישב shifts the scene of the people from moving into Jerusalem to learn, walk in the path of Yahweh and going out from Zion to a more settled place. The peasant farmers whose land and houses have been forcefully taken away (2:1) will no longer be terrified "מחריד" by anyone but would securely dwell in their own property and enjoy the labor of their works undisturbed.

5.6.3. Form Critical Comments on Micah 4:1-5

The historical setting and composition of the passage eludes consensus as a parallel text appears in Isa. 2:2-4.[131] Mays, Sweeney, Kaiser and others maintain that the passage points to the setting of an exilic or post exilic time.[132] Sweeney reconstructs the historical setting of 4:1-5 to the time of King Cyrus who gave freedom to the Jews to return to Jerusalem and rebuild the temple.[133] He argues that the passage appears to have been composed in relation to the rebuilding of the temple in the late sixth century.[134] Scholars who attribute the unit to a post-exilic redactor also argue that neither Micah nor Isaiah or any other earlier prophet was the author of the present passage since the parallel "Jerusalem-Zion", and the phrase "end of the days" is a typical eschatological term of the post-exilic time.[135] However, such post exilic argument appears to be unconvincing as Roberts has demonstrated that the motifs of the divine mountain, the defeat of the nations and the pilgrimage

---

[129] Waltke, *A Commentary on Micah*, 199.

[130] Waltke, *A Commentary on Micah*, 200.

[131] For a detailed overviews on the history of scholarship, see, Marvin A. Sweeney, "Micah's Debate with Isaiah", *JSOT* 93 (2001) 111-124; Wlatke, *Micah*, 170-175.

[132] Mays, *Micah*, 94-96; Ronald E. Clements, *Isaiah 1-39*, NCB (London/Grand Rapids, Michigan: Marshall, Morgan & Scott/Eerdmans, 1980), 39-40; Otto Kaiser, *Isaiah 1-12: A Commentary* (OTL; Philadelphia: Westminster John Knox Press, 1983), 49-52; Hans Walter Wolff, *Micah: A Commentary*, Continental Commentary (Minneapolis: Augsburg, 1990), 116-18.

[133] Sweeney, *Isaiah 1-39*, 99.

[134] Sweeney, *The Twelve Prophets*, vol. 2, 337.

[135] E. Cannawurf, "The Authenticity of Micah 4:1-4", *VT* 13/1 (1963) 32.

of the nations are quite ancient. Further, he argues that the exilic ruins and post-exilic restoration can hardly provide a plausible background for a development of traditions like Zion.[136]

von Rad argues that the Zion hymn of unsuccessful attack on Jerusalem is "certainly of very much earlier origin" and that the prophet "makes the old tradition into something entirely new."[137] Arguing along the line of von Rad and others, Willis states that the tradition incorporated in 4:1-5 was pre-Israelite, which the Israelites borrowed from the time their conquest and settlement of Jerusalem.[138] A similar argument is put forward by A. Kuhrt, who maintains that the old Babylonian tradition on Ziggurat Entemenaki (Babylonian throne) as the centre for divine rule and peace for the earth apparently influenced this passage.[139] Whether or not Ziggurat Entemenaki influenced the present passage remains debatable. In any case, it shows that the idea of divine a centre for the world is very much old in ANE tradition. Willis argues further that both Isaiah and Micah quoted the Zion hymn that was familiar among the audience to assure them of future promise. Along the line of Cannon's argument, Willis maintains that since the Assyria's invasion drew closer, the prophet conveys a hope to people by quoting this song and embedded promises with it.[140] If the argument on the pre-Israelite tradition in 4:1-5 could be sustained as argued by the above scholars, we may plausibly consider Willis' position in our investigation.

Willis demonstrates some striking contrasts between 3:9-12 and 4:1-5, which perhaps shows that the two units are placed in the present positions intentionally. "The mountain of the house" of Yahweh that would become a wooded height in 3:12 will be established as the highest mountains in 4:1. Zion that would be ploughed as field and become a heap of ruins in 3:12 would be raised above the hills in 4:1. In 3:11 the priests teach for bribe but in 4:2 Yahweh himself would "teach" the people to walk in his ways. In 3:9, 11 the "heads" and "rulers" abhor and pervert justice for bribe but in 4:3 Yahweh himself would judge between people and nations that would bring peace.[141] Following B. Wiklander's analysis of Isaiah 2:2-4, Willis opines that Micah 4:1-5 is "a literary unit consisting of originally self contained speeches."[142] The destroyed Zion, which caused

[136] Roberts, "The Davidic Origin of the Zion Tradition", 329-344. Scholars who argue for a pre-exilic dating include: A.S. Kapelrud, "Eschatology in he Book of Micah", *VT* 11 (1961) 392-405; Hillers, *Micah*, 52; Brueggemann, "Vine and Fig Tree", 189; Allen, *Micah*, 325.

[137] von Rad, *Old Testament Theology*, vol. 2 (Edinburgh: Oliver & Boyd, 1965), 157.

[138] Willis, "Isaiah 2:2-5and the Psalms of Zion", 313. Cf. von Rad, *Old Testament Theology*, vol. 2, 155-69; Wildberger, "Die Volkerwallfahrt zum Zion", 68-67; Hays, "The Tradition of Zion's Inviolability", 419-216.

[139] A. Kuhrt, "The Cyrus Cylinder and Archaemenid Policy", *JSOT* 25 (1983), 69-72.

[140] Willis, "Isaiah 2:2-5and the Psalms of Zion", 313.

[141] Willis, "Isaiah 2:2-5and the Psalms of Zion", 307-308.

[142] Willis, "Isaiah 2:2-5and the Psalms of Zion", 307.

disillusionment in the judgment oracle (3:9-12) is rebuilt again bringing hope for the people in the salvation oracle (4:1-5). This shows a close link between 3:9-12 and 4:1-5. Judging from such thematic connection, we consider that the passage fits well in its present position and most probably comes from Micah himself.[143] We consider that 4:1-5 is a unit of salvation oracle that promises universal hope for the nations. The structure of the passage can be outlined as follows:

Announcement (v.1a)
The Elevation of Zion and the Pilgrimage of nations (vv.1b-2)
Peace and Security in the Land (vv.3-4)
The Liturgical Response (v.5)

5.6.4. Tradition and Theological Comments in the Light of Tripartite Relationship

Zion is portrayed as "the house of Yahweh", "the mountain of Yahweh" (v.1), and "the house of the God of Jacob" (v.2), which recounts the tradition that affirms Zion as "your house" (Pss. 65:4[5]; 68:29[30]), "the house of Yahweh" (Pss. 122:1; 122:9). In Zion tradition, Jerusalem temple and the mountain on which it is built is affirmed as Yahweh's dwelling place and Yahweh is extolled as the God who protects Zion and delivers his people from certain defeat.[144] Micah utilizes the Zion tradition by affirming Yahweh's presence in Zion from where he adjudicates and teaches justice as the way of life. This is different from the priests and prophets who construed Zion theology by deemphasizing justice (cf. 3:9-12). Micah reinterprets the same tradition by incorporating justice and the Torah of Yahweh as a central ethical aspect to the Zion tradition and thereby he makes the Zion passage in 4:1-5 a message of comfort and hope for the dispossessed and disadvantaged peasants.[145] By embedding the central issue of justice, which forms a core teaching of the Torah, Micah shows a reestablished tripartite relationship. Yahweh teaches his way and the nations respond to his teachings by walking in his way and as a result of following Yahweh's instruction; war comes to an end and existence in the land becomes secure.

The oracle begins with a prophetic announcement, "in the later days", which refers to a future time that will be beyond the present possibilities when "God will

---

[143] Scholars who takes this position include, J. Havley, "Le Livre de Michee", *RevSem* 13 (1904), 4; A. von Hoonacker, *Les douze petits Prophetes* (Paris: Gabalda, 1908), 345; C. von Orelli, "Micah", *ISBE* 3 (1960), 2046. Cited in Willis, "Isaiah 2:2-5and the Psalms of Zion", 311. See also, Walter Brueggemann, "Vine and Fig Tree": A Case Study in Imagination and Criticism", *CBQ* 43 (1981), 189.

[144] John T. Wallis, "Isaiah 2:2-5and the Psalms of Zion", in Craig C. Broyles and Craig A. Evans (eds), *Writing and Reading the Scroll of Isaiah Studies of an Interpretive Studies*, vol.1 (Leiden: Brill, 1997), 295-316.

[145] Marrs, "Back to the Future", 95, no. 55.

intervene decisively to bring history toward his intended goal."[146] It will be the time when present social malaise of injustice that victimizes the poor, forceful acquisition of land that dispossess peasants from their land and tragic warfare that destroys and alienates people from their homeland will come to an end.

In those coming days, Mount Zion that is earlier turned into "plowed field" and "wooded height" because of the enemies' destruction (3:12) will be "established" again above all the mountains (v.1) and make itself visible as centre of the world. As noted above in the TCC on v.1c, the participle נכון "established" is connected with יהיה, which states that the establishment of Zion is Yahweh's act and it is permanent. Though the imagery is cultic in nature as it deals with the temple in Zion, the overarching prediction of Micah sees a future possibility that is beyond the present predicament. The present destruction will in fact usher a future reconstruction. The nation of Judah as a whole is threatened by a looming Assyrian invasion on the one hand while the peasants are already in a precarious state due to the forceful seizure of their land but amidst their present precariousness, Micah still see hope in the coming "latter days".

Nations themselves will see Yahweh's involvement and will call Zion "the mountain of Yahweh" and "the house of the God of Jacob", and will make pilgrimage to Zion to learn Yahweh's Torah (תורה). Hans Wildberger thus rightly comments that Yahweh is portrayed as the universal Lord of the peoples of the world.[147] Torah is an instruction of Yahweh, which calls for response and results in a new way of living for those who hear it. Torah appears in parallel with walking in his way and path (דרך, ארח cf. v.2). As argued above, דרך "way" is used to express God's gracious act as well as his requirements for his people while its parallel ארחתיו "his path" with preposition ב indicates a sphere in which they walk. In other words, by seeing Yahweh's deeds, nations will be motivated to seek him and will be propelled to learn his requirements with a purpose, "so that we may walk" (ונלכה) according to the teachings of Yahweh. Nations will make strong ethical resolve to make the content of Yahweh's torah their prescribed way of life.

The centripetal movement to Zion לכו ונעלה "come let us go" finds a reversed centrifugal movement תצא "shall go forth" from Zion (v.2). Between the coming in and going out to/from Zion, the emphasis is stressed on the Torah and its instruction as the way of life. As much as the desire to learn the Torah leads nations to centripetal movement to Zion, it is the motivation of the teaching of Torah that results in centrifugal movement from Zion. In other words, Micah sees the teaching of Torah, which is inseparably rooted with the practice of social justice (v.3, cf. 3:1, 9, 11), to be relevant and authentic in a universal context. As a result of the fascination of Yahweh's Torah, judgment and reproof, nations will take their destructive tools (military instrument of "swords" and "spears") and transform them to survival tools (agricultural implements of "plowshare"

[146] Waltke, *A Commentary on Micah*, 208.

[147] Hans Wildberger, "Die Völkerwallfahrt zum Zion: Jes 2:1-5", *VT* 7/1 (1957) 78.

and "pruning hooks", v.3). The expression "swords" and "spears" in v.3 reflect a paroxysm of war and violence developed in the eighth century BCE.[148] Judah as well as other nations sought to pursue their security by engaging in war and defend their territory by "spears" and "swords". However, Micah sees the transformative power of Torah and its teaching as a leeway to resolve conflicts and ensure peaceful and secured existence of each nation. Micah conceives the era of peace as possibility in relation to the Torah. The security for the land as political nation lies not in the military strength but in the righteous conduct of the people as envisaged by Yahweh in his instruction.

Micah also brings the hope of universal peace down to individual human terms: "they shall sit every man under his vine and under his fig tree, and none shall terrify them" (v.4). The image of "vine" symbolizes Yahweh's blessing (Hos. 2:14[12]; 17[15]) and a source of income (1 Kgs 21:1-4). Citing Wolff, Waltke states that "grapes and figs are the most costly fruits of the land", as such, they "depict every person enjoying God's blessing of lasting peace and prosperity in security, without fear and danger" (2 Kgs 18:31; Isa. 36:16).[149] As a result people will enjoy the fruit of his own labor in security.

The above exegesis shows that Micah uses the term Zion/Jerusalem not only as a cultic centre for religious activities but also to show Zion as a political territory of Judah. During Micah's period, Judah continually engaged in warfare that threatened her existence as a nation. At the same time, Judah also continually faced internal violence that jeopardized the peasant farmers, which caused dissatisfaction among the people.[150] Such situation posed the danger of alienating the people from their land and nation. Amidst such context, Micah sees that secure survival in the land is possible only when there is military disarmament and that disarmament is possible only when Judah as well as nations learn to walk in the "way" and "path" of the Torah. By employing the Zion tradition and integrating it with Torah as the way of life, Micah shows how the relationship between Yahweh, Judah as well as nations and the land is reestablished. Judah and nations find security to dwell in the land when they come to Yahweh and learn his way. The tripartite relationship is seen as a leeway to disarmament and peace and to live in the land safely and that tripartite relationship is sustained only when the Torah of Yahweh is made as a way of life. Thus, according to Micah, Yahweh's presence and protection (Zion tradition) upon his people and land (tripartite relationship) can be affirmed if his instruction (Torah tradition) is confirmed as the way of life.

---

[148] Claude F. Mariottini, "Joel 3:10 [H 4:10]: 'Beat Your Plowshares into Swords'", *Perspectives in Religious Studies* 14 (1987) 125-130.

[149] Waltke, *A Commentary on Micah*, 202.

[150] Cf. Claude F. Mariottini, "Warfare in the Eighth Century: Swords into Plowshare", *Biblical Illustrator* 12 (1986) 11.

5.7. Zion Tradition (Micah 4:11-13)

The idea that nations are against Zion (v.11) but Yahweh will thwart their plan (vv.12-13) speaks of Yahweh's surreptitious intervention for Jerusalem, which is rooted in the Zion tradition. In 4:11-13 the tripartite relationship is reaffirmed in which Yahweh is portrayed as the God who defends his people and protects the land from certain destruction. The tripartite relationship thus envisaged safety for his people to dwell in the land.

5.7.1. Translation on Micah 4:11-13

11 Now[a] great nations[b] are assembled against you, saying, "Let her be profaned[c], and let our eyes gaze upon Zion".

12 But they do not know the thoughts of Yahweh, they do not understand his plan, surely he has gathered them as sheaves to the threshing floor.

13 Arise[a] and thresh, O daughter of Zion, for I will set up your [b]horn iron and I will set up your hoofs bronze[b]; you shall beat in pieces many peoples, and shall devote their gain[c] to Yahweh, their wealth to the Lord of all the earth[d].

5.7.2. Text Critical Comments on Micah 4:11-13

V.11a: The coordinating עתה "now" introduces a new oracle of salvation. According to Waltke ועתה in v.11 refers to "Micah's own time" when Judah faced distress "at the hand of the Assyrians and her deliverance from the siege."[151] Waltke's proposal can be sustained if the historical setting of the oracle in vv.11-13 belongs to the period of Assyria's (Sennacherib) invasion in 701 BCE (see the following FCC).

V.11b: The attributive adjective רבים that follows גוים (nations) can mean "many" or "great". Waltke argues that if רבים precedes the noun it can mean "many" but if it follows the noun it is not necessary to interpret it as "many."[152] Since רבים follows and does not precede the noun גוים "nations", it is interpreted here as "great", which indicates that it is the powerful or great nations that have gathered against Israel. The identity of the "great nations" remains obscure however, since Waltke dates this prophecy to Sennacherib's siege of Jerusalem in 701 BCE, he maintains that "great nations" here refers to Assyria and its international hordes of army (united imperial army) with which Sennacherib invaded Jerusalem in 701 BCE.[153] Waltke's argument appears plausible since J. Lindblom by comparing Isa. 22:6; 29:7 (cf. Hos. 10:10) has also demonstrated that there were various national units that made up Assyria's imperial army.[154] Probably because of the presence of a vast cosmopolitan army at his disposal, Sennacherib calls himself "king of the

[151] Waltke, *A Commentary on Micah*, 250.

[152] Waltke, *A Commentary on Micah*, 197.

[153] Waltke, *A Commentary on Micah*, 250 and 258.

[154] J. Lindblom, *Micah literarisch unterscht* (Helsinki: Abo, 1929), 91-97. Cited in Waltke, *A Commentary on Micah*, 250.

world."[155] Such a vast army from different nationalities led by their local princes for the service of Sennacherib could represent many nations. However, since such cosmopolitan army that represents many nations remained under the solo control of Sennachreb that make his military strength invincible, we consider גוים רבים as "great nations".

V.11b: Elsewhere תחנף "profaned" expresses the defiling of land due to bloodshed (Num. 35:33), child sacrifice (Pss 106:38), violation of the covenant and wrongdoings (Isa. 10:6; 24:5), which sever the relationship with Yahweh unless atonement was made.[156] However, such idea of profanation may not be the meaning here as the term is used by Zion's enemies. K. Seybold notes that חנף in Qal form as here always appears intransitively and for the most part absolutely with "land or earth" as its subject.[157] Following F. Horst who defines חנף as an "act or attitude through which a state of sacral relation to the Godhead is intentionally set aside", Waltke states that the great nations' intention is to profane the sacral relationship between Yahweh and his holy city.[158] The nations' plan to profane the sacral relationship probably involves their attempt to demolish the Jerusalem temple and set up their pagan cults. Desecration of religious places was common in the ANE concept of war where the battle was not only understood as involving the nations but also the pantheons. As such, "the capture of the gods of the nations was a standard procedure in ancient warfare ... [and]... desecrating the shrine of the enemy was one of the chief aims of attacking the capital city."[159] Andersen and Freedman thus conclude that "the language implies that the enemy intended to penetrate the holy precincts and pillage the sacred objects there."[160] Their attempt to profane is thus to devastate Zion and thereby show their power to destroy Zion that is considered as holy abode of Yahweh. Such an act of profanation is an attempt to reveal Yahweh's impotency to save Zion and thereby cast doubt on the sacral relationship between Yahweh and his people. It is thus a serious challenge to the very relationship of Yahweh with Zion and its people.

V.13a: The imperative קומי "arise", recalls ancient Israel's war cry to commence holy war (Num.10:35-36). In the ancient war cry "arise" is uttered by Israel to invoke Yahweh's help in times of war, however, in v.13 it is Yahweh who commands Zion to stand for battle. The divine imperative "arise" also stands in contrasts to nations' vain exhortation to one another to destroy Zion (v.11). Though the nations have come together against Zion, קומי indicates that Yahweh also has come for Zion's victory.

---

155 *ANET*, 288. Cited in Allen, *The Books of Joel, Obadiah, Jonah and Micah*, 338.

156 Hillers, *Micah*, 61.

157 K. Seybold, "חנף", TDOT:5, 38.

158 Waltke, *A Commentary on Micah*, 251.

159 Andersen and Freedman, *Micah*, 451.

160 Andersen and Freedman, *Micah*, 452.

V.13b-b: קַרְנֵךְ "horn", in the ANE literature and iconography, "horn" mostly depicts "power.'[161] The phrase "I will make your horn iron" is "more suggestive of an aggressive aurochs (Num. 23:22; 24:8)."[162] וּפַרְסֹתַיִךְ "your hoof" refers to the threshing heifer. It indicates the strength and might, while נְחוּשָׁה "bronze" speaks of hardness and harshness. Together the image of horn and bronze emphasizes Zion's invincibility both in terms of her power to defend herself and her aggressive action to trash her enemies.

V.13c: והחרמתי translated here as "and you shall devote your gain" is a language of ancient "holy war". Devoting חרם "booty" especially the indestructibility things like silver and gold from the defeated nations were devoted to Yahweh while every animate beings were killed without sparing anyone (Josh. 6:24; 7; 1 Sam. 15).[163] Such an act of devoting the booty to Yahweh is to acknowledge that victory comes from Yahweh.[164]

V.13d: Yahweh is called "the Lord of all the earth" (אדון כל־הארץ) indicating the extent of Yahweh's cosmic Lordship over all the earth. Since ארץ "earth" appears in connection with Yahweh's cosmic Lordship, the term הארץ here refers to earth in a cosmic sense.

5.7.3. Form Critical Comments on Micah 4:11-13

Despite a close link shown by the initial word עתה "now" in vv.9 and 11, most scholars agree that vv.9-10 and vv.11-13 are two different unit.[165] Whereas, vv.9-10 describe the siege, inevitable fall, and the exile of Jerusalem in which the deliverance aspect comes only after the captivity, in vv.11-13 Jerusalem turns against her enemies that confidently come to destroy her. In vv.9-10, the enemies mentioned are the Babylonians, while in vv.11-13 the enemies are the "great nations" (see also the above TCC on v.11a).[166] Moreover the addressee "daughters of Zion" in vv.9-10 refers to the inhabitants of Jerusalem but "Zion" in v.11 refers to the city of Jerusalem itself.[167] Vv.11-13 is thus different in its contents indicating that it is a separate unit.

It is a salvation oracle that deals with how the problem of hostile enemies will be resolved during the time of Yahweh's restoration. It begins with a "now" in v.11, which shows a present predicament on Zion because of the nations' attempt to attack Jerusalem. But v.12 ridicules the destructive plan of the nations for being ignorant about Yahweh's strategy to destroy them. The nations assembled against Zion, but Micah sees such gathering of nations to be an act of Yahweh to prepare

---

161 Waltke, *A Commentary on Micah*, 255.

162 Andersen and Freedman, *Micah*, 454.

163 Hillers, *Micah*, 61.

164 Mays, *Micah*, 111.

165 Mays, *Micah*, 107; Hillers, *Micah*, 60; Mays, *Micah*, 107.

166 Smith, *Micah, Zephaniah, Nahum, Obadiah, Joel*, 97.

167 For further discussion, see Waltke, *A Commentary on Micah*, 250; 257-258.

Zion to defeat her enemies. The enemies' plan to desecrate Zion but reversely Zion will defeat them and consecrate their wealth to Yahweh. Finally, v.13 exhorts Zion with Yahweh's assurance of giving victory to Zion. The salvation oracle in vv.11-13 thus shows that Zion will be restored by reversing her present distress to future victory with the gain of wealth of the nations. The structure of the present unit can be stated as follows.

Present distress of Zion (looming destruction on the land):	v.11a
Enemies' evil plan against Zion (scheme to devastate the land):	v.11b
Yahweh's reversal plan to thwart the enemies:	v.12
Yahweh's encouragement and empowerment to Zion:	v.13a
Yahweh's promise of Zion's victory over enemies:	v.13b

Scholars attribute the present unit to various historical settings. Theodoret, Calvin, Hengstenburg and others assume that the historical allusion of the conflict in vv.11-13 refers to the victory of the Maccabees over the Syrians during the intervening period of the Jews who returned from the Babylonian captivity.[168] The view is rejected on the ground that the Syrian attack on Jerusalem and the Maccabees' victory over them is much too small an event than the description of enemies and subsequent victory of Zion mentioned in vv.11-13.[169] Moreover such historical reconstruction would also place the present unit to the post-exilic setting, which would be untenable. On the other hand, Smith argues that the oracle in vv.11-13 probably belongs to the period of Sennacherib's invasion of Judah in 701 BCE where he stripped bare the land of Judah. It was during this period, Smith argues, Micah encouraged his people who were in a precarious state for he foresees Sennacherib's invasion as only temporary and that Zion would ultimately be victorious.[170] Though there is no direct historical allusion in the text, Isaiah the contemporary of Micah also portrayed Assyria as Yahweh's agent in carrying out his purpose at the time when Assyria was invading Jerusalem (Is. 10:5-19). Similarly, Micah's sees the enemies' threat in vv.11-13 as fulfilling Yahweh's purpose. As such, it may not be wrong to assume that the present unit belongs to the period of Assyrian's invasion in 701 BCE.

5.7.4. Tradition and Theological Comments in the Light of Tripartite Relationship

The whole unit is addressed to Zion and the nucleus is focused on the nations that surround Zion. Scholars have recognized that the phrase "nations are against you" in v.11 is an element of Zion tradition.[171] The expression of enemies

[168] Theodoret, Calvin, Hengstenburg. Cited in Keil, *Minor Prophets*, vol. 10, 473.

[169] Keil, *Minor Prophets*, vol. 10, 473.

[170] Smith, *Micah-Malachi*, 42.

[171] Hillers, *Micah,* 59.

surrounding Zion in a variety of ways and combined with other motifs appears both in prophetic sayings and Zion hymns in Psalms (Isa. 17:12-14; 29:5-8; Pss 46:6; 48:4f; 76:3-6).[172] Stephen L. Cook maintains that the idea of Yahweh thwarting humans' plan and the emphasis of the mystery of Yahweh's purposes in vv.11-13 indicates that the emphasis is on Zion's tradition.[173] Moreover, Yahweh's assurance of victory to his covenant people in their battle in vv.11-13 is central to the covenant texts in Joshua where Yahweh is seen as the warrior who defeats Israel's army. Since vv.11-13 seeks to convey that victory over the enemies is the result of Yahweh's help, Yahweh is seen as the God who defends his covenant people and the land from the attempted desecration from the enemies. It reflects the Zion tradition in which Yahweh is seen as the God who defends his land and people. By employing the Zion tradition the tripartite relationship is reaffirmed in which Yahweh is portrayed as the God who defends his people and protects the land of his people from those who attempt to destroy and devastate the land of Jerusalem and its inhabitants.

As mentioned above in the TCC, ועתה in v.11 refers to a "now" of Micah's period. It was a time of distress for Jerusalem because of the presence of powerful enemies. The enemies who have surrounded Jerusalem are identified as גוים רבים (v.11a). As discussed above גוים רבים means "great nations", which refers to the international hordes of the Assyrian army. Sennacherib's army consists of various nationalities, as such, the Assyrians' army was in itself a conglomerate of many nations. The multinational band of Sennacherib's army assembled against Jerusalem probably in 701 BCE. This caused distress among the people as Jerusalem could find no apparent help or strength to match the invading enemies and only the destruction of land (Jerusalem) and temple became imminent at the hand of Assyria.

First, the assembled enemies expressed their intention to "profane" Zion (v.11b). Two significant exegetical observations can be made on the use of the term חנף. First, though the term ארץ and אדמה do not appear here "Zion" is used here as a synecdoche of the land of Jerusalem. The TCC in v.11b has demonstrated that the term חנף "profane" in Qal form appears mostly with "land or earth" as its subject. As such, the enemies' attempt to "profane" Zion in v.11b most likely refers to their intention to destroy the land of Jerusalem and by metonymy the political territory of Judah. Also, by definition the term חנף refers to an act to profane or to set aside the sacral relationship (see the above TCC on v.11a). Thus, the enemies' scheme to "profane" Zion probably implies their intention to demolish the Jerusalem temple, set up their pagan cults and thereby to profane the sacral relationship of Zion with Yahweh.

Second, the enemies expressed their intention to "gaze upon Zion" (v.11b). Hillers has demonstrated that the phrase "let our eyes gaze upon her" is equivalent

---

[172] Mays, *Micah*, 108.

[173] Cook, *The Social Root of Biblical Yahwehism*, 128.

of ראה ב "to see with joy, victory over one's enemy."[174] If Hillers' position could be sustained, then the expressed intention "let our eyes gaze upon Zion" refers to an act of bringing destruction upon Jerusalem and to joyfully seeing their victory over and the fall of Zion. In other words, the expression points to Assyria's expansionist policy to annex the kingdom of Judah.

The premeditated plan of the nations to "profane" the sacral relationship between Yahweh and his people and to celebrate the fall of Jerusalem, as mentioned above, not only put Zion at stake but it also put Yahweh's commitment and his relationship to Zion at stake at least before the eyes of the nations. The enemies' put the tripartite relationship between Yahweh, people of Judah (Zion) and land into a kind of fiasco in which Yahweh is portrayed as an impotent God because his people and his city of Zion are left helpless. To counteract such misconception, Micah introduces the adversative conjunction ו "but" in v.12 to vindicate Yahweh's inscrutable plan that demonstrates his sovereignty and ability to save his people and land from humans' (enemies of Zion) plan. The "great nations" come to attack and exploit the defenseless Zion "but they do not know the thought of Yahweh" (v.12). The term מחשבות "thought", according to Waltke, consists of the *mem* of abstraction with the root חשב, which means "to plan or calculate creatively and rationally."[175] In other words, Yahweh has a well devised and calculated plan to allow the enemies to assemble against Zion so as to present them as a "sheaves" for Zion to exercise great havoc upon the enemies. By employing the *waw* adversative, Micah shows that evil intention cannot have a final victory against Yahweh's relationship with his people and the land.

Yahweh thus encourages Zion by summoning her to "arise and thresh" the enemies (v.13). The repeated verb אשים "I will set up" stresses "divine agency and empowering" of Zion.[176] With the divine empowerment with "iron horn" and "bronze hoofs", the vulnerable Zion became invincible and the policy of territorial expansion of Assyria was crushed. The great nations gathered against Zion but such a move is stated as Yahweh's plot to gather and bring them to the threshing floor of destruction. As such, in this salvation oracle, Yahweh is portrayed as the God who controls the destiny of history as "the Lord of all the earth". Therefore, as his cosmic Lordship extends to all the earth, Zion's distress will not end up in destruction. Instead, it will lead her to deliverance. Such future deliverance is because of Yahweh's commitment to protect Zion.

In the above exegesis, the occurrences of the terms like "great nations" and "Zion" refer to land in a sense of political territories, while הארץ refers to earth in a cosmic sense upon which Yahweh exercises his cosmic Lordship. By employing the form of salvation oracle, Micah affirms that the powerful nations cannot pursue their tyrannical invasion over the weaker nation because Yahweh's

---

[174] Hillers, *Micah*, 61.

[175] Waltke, *A Commentary on Micah*, 253.

[176] Allen, *The Book of Joel, Obadiah, Jonah and Micah*, 337.

sovereignty extends over all the earth and that the destiny of both the strong and weaker nations lies in the hand of Yahweh. In this salvation oracle, Jerusalem's destiny as a capital city of the nation survived despite Assyria's attempted invasion because Yahweh protects and defends Zion. Such understanding is rooted in Zion tradition in which Yahweh is seen as the God who is committed in his relationship to his people and the land. Yahweh's commitment to such tripartite relationship is served as the basis of his empowerment of Zion and thereby the people of Zion and the land were protected. In this Zion tradition, Yahweh is portrayed as the God who brings victory to Zion on behalf of his people and land.

5.8. Zion and Exodus Traditions (Micah 7:8-20)

Zion's hope "to rise" (v.8) and to "trample" the enemy (v.10) as well as the enemies' mock "where is Yahweh your God" (v.10) are the elements of Zion Hymns. Amidst the gloomy days of destruction of land, Yahweh's intervention is assured, "as in the days when you came out of the land of Egypt" (15), which recall the Exodus tradition. The tripartite relationship is explained in 7:8-20 by affirming that Yahweh will perform his wondrous deeds for Israel, the boundaries of the land shall be extended, exiled people will be back to the land (vv.11-12). These things will happen because Yahweh, in his faithfulness, does not hold Israel's iniquity forever (vv.19-20).

5.8.1. Translation on Micah 7:8-20

8 Rejoice not[a] over me, O my enemy[b]; when I fall, I shall rise[c]; when I sit in [d]darkness, Yahweh will be a light[d] to me.

9 I will bear the indignation of Yahweh because I have sinned against him, until he pleads my case[a] and he will make judgment for me. He will bring me forth[b] to the light; I shall behold his act of vindication.

10 Then my enemy will see, and shame will cover her who said to me, "Where is Yahweh[a] your God?" My eyes will gloat over her; now she will be trodden down like the mire of the streets.

11 A day[a] for the building of your walls[b], in that day the [c]boundary shall be far extended[c].

12 In that day [a]they will come to you[a], [b]from Assyria to Egypt, and from Egypt to the River, from sea to sea and from mountain to mountain[b].

13 But the earth[a] will be desolate because of its inhabitants, for the fruit of their doings.

14 Shepherd your people[a] with your staff, the flock of your inheritance[b] [c]dwelling alone in a forest in the midst of a garden land[c]; let them feed in [d]Bashan and Gilead[d] as in the days of old.

15 [a]As in the days when you came out of the land of Egypt[a] I will show them marvelous things.

16 The nations shall see and be ashamed of all their might; they shall lay their hands on their mouths; their ears shall be deaf;
17 they shall lick the dust like a serpent, like the crawling things of the earth; they shall come trembling out of their strongholds, they shall turn in dread to Yahweh our God, and they shall fear because of thee.
18 Who is a God like you, pardoning iniquity and passing over transgression for the remnant of his inheritance? He does not retain his anger for ever because he delights in steadfast love.
19 He will again[a] have compassion upon us; he will tread our iniquities under foot. You will cast all our sins into the depths of the sea.
20 You will show faithfulness to Jacob and steadfast love to Abraham, as you have sworn to our fathers from the days of old.

5.8.2. Text Critical Comments on Micah 7:8-20

V.8a: לא־תשמחי "do not rejoice" employs the verb √שמח "to rejoice", which often appears in an ode to victory. The Qal jussive second person feminine singular is employed here to personify the enemy, which according to Waltke, is Nineveh, the city of Assyria (for further discussion on Assyria as a possible candidate, see the following FCC).[177]

V.8b: The Qal participle feminine singular איבתי "my enemy" is understood as "the personalization of the corporate identity". Most scholars agree that the speaker is Zion, which represents the community of Yahweh's people (see the following FCC).[178] The identity of איב "enemy" remains obscure, however, by comparing with Isa. 34:8f; Pss 137:7; Obad. 10-15, Mays conjectured that איב refers to Edom who treacherously humiliated Jerusalem after her fall to Babylon.[179] If Mays' proposal is accepted, the text would have to be dated to a late exilic or post-exilic period, which would stretch the argument too far and cannot be sustained (see the FCC on Amos 1:11-12). As Hillers argues, the presence of "enemy" or "enemies" against Zion and the consequent distress caused upon Jerusalem are true at various periods. As such, we can assume that Micah had in mind a long history of enemies' hostility against Zion at different point of time[180] (see the below discussion on FCC).

V.8c: Andersen and Freedman state that קמתי "I shall rise" refers to an action that describes resurrection from the dead (cf. Hos. 6:2), which is used figuratively to refer to the revival of the dead city.[181]

---

177 Waltke, *Micah*, 433.

178 Waltke, *Micah*, 433; Peter C. Craigie, *The Twelve Prophets*, vol. 2 (Louisville, Kentucky: Westminister John Knox Press, 1985), 56; Nogalski, *Literary Precursors to the Book of Twelve*, 146.

179 Mays, *Micah*, 159.

180 Hillers, *Micah*, 89.

181 Andersen and Freedman, *Micah*, 582.

V.8d-d: The paired metaphor "darkness and light", according to Mays, points to Zion tradition. He argues that the expression "sit in darkness" refers to a circumstance of Zion's plight where "the human eyes can see no objective possibility of help" (Pss 35:6; 143:3), while "light" is "visible to the eyes of hope" (Pss 27:1).[182]

V.9a: יריב ריבי "until he pleads my case" is forensic language, which is used in a legal dispute or contention (for the discussion on ריב see the TCC on Hos. 2:2a). The phrase indicates that Zion has proportionately suffered for her sin and that the judge, Yahweh will decide that Zion deserves no further punishment.[183]

V.9b: As a result of establishment of justice by Yahweh in v.9a, Zion will be "brought out" to the "light" (see also the above notes in 8e-e). The verb יוציאני "to bring forth" is a characteristic verb used in the Exodus. This indicates that the future event to behold "light" and "vindication" mentioned in v.9 is understood as a new exodus in which Zion will be led out from darkness and distress to light and light and vindication (deliverance).

V.10a: Renaud and Wolff think that the divine name in the taunt spoken by the enemies is inappropriate and suggest that the divine name here is either a scribal error or a gloss.[184] Shaw, however, thinks that such proposal is speculative and unnecessary and affirms that the MT should be retained.[185]

V.11a: The term יום "day" appears three times in vv.11-12. In its first occurrence, יום is associated with the refortification of "wall", which serves to defend the nation; second, יום appears in connection with the extension of territorial boundaries and finally יום appears to express the return of the exiles from different nations. While each of these occurrences gives a picture of Yahweh's salvation in which the deported people of Zion returned back to their ancestral land and that their resettlement in the land would involve territorial fortifications and expansions. The theological emphasis here is thus on a reestablishment of the tripartite relationship in which Yahweh's people and land would be brought back together as a result of Yahweh's act of salvation. That period is vaguely described as יום "a day" (v.11a) and יום ההוא "that day" (v.11-12), which appears to be a variation of a standard formulaic expression of ביום ההוא "in that day."[186] ויום-ההוא introduces the promise of Yahweh's salvation in the future when Yahweh begin to restore his people (see also the TCC on Am. 9:11a and Hos. 2:16a)

V.11b: As mentioned in the above comments on v.8b, the speaker here is Zion; as such לבנות גדריך "building of your walls" probably refers to the literal rebuilding of the Jerusalem wall. Since the major repair works of the Jerusalem

---

[182] Mays, *Micah*, 159.

[183] Sweeney, *The Twelve Prophets*, Vol. 2, 410.

[184] Hans Walter Wolff, *Micah: A Commentary*, trans. by Gray Stansell (Augsburg: Minneapolis, 1990), 213; Renausd *Formation*, 359. Cited in Shaw, *The Speeches of Yahweh*, 193.

[185] Shaw, *The Speeches of Micah*, 193.

[186] Sweeney, *The Twelve Prophets*, Vol. 2, 410.

wall were carried out during Nehemiah's period in the 5th century BCE, Wolff allocates vv.11-12 to the post-exilic period. However, Andersen and Freedman consider such supposition as unsustainable due to "meager evidence" and also because the Jerusalem wall needed repairs not only during Nehemiah's time.[187] As discussed in the FCC on 4:11-13, Zion was in distress for Jerusalem as the land of Judah was stripped bare during Sennacherib's invasion of Judah in 701 BCE. As such, we consider that the "rebuilding of wall" could be a reference to destruction of the walled cities of Judah in 701 BCE by Sennacherib.[188] In any case, the Jerusalemites understood "wall" theologically in which the razing of the wall was considered as an act of Yahweh's judgment, while the rebuilding of it as Yahweh's salvation.[189]

V.11c-c: חק is rendered here as "boundary" in a sense of territorial limits that Zion will embrace (cf. Is. 5:14; 24:5). Allen argues that such rendering is plausible since the geographical description "from Assyria to Egypt and from Egypt to the river, from sea to sea" in v.12 is the ideal geographical limits of Yahweh's ancient promise of land to Israel.[190] He argues further that since Yahweh's promise of land to Abraham's descendants covers the area "from the river of Egypt to the great river, the river Euphrates (Gen. 15:18) and in line with this promise, later Solomon's empire is said to have extended "from the Euphrates to the Philistine country and to the Egyptian border" (1 Kgs 4:21[5:1]), Allen thus concludes that the reference to "Egypt and Assyria" in v.12 indicates that "Israel's territory was to extend up to the Assyrian border, regarded as the Euphrates, in the northeast and down to the Egyptian border in the southwest. "*From sea to sea*" is evidently a diameter drawn from the Mediterranean to the Persian Gulf, presumably skirting Babylonia."[191] Though the reference to "Egypt", "Assyria", "the River" and "sea" in v.12 is stated in terms of the return from the exiles and not explicitly stated as territorial marks, Allen's argument remains plausible in the light of the reference to these places as territorial boundaries in Yahweh's covenant promise of land to Israel. Assuming such significance, we consider חק in v.11 as referring to "boundary"[192] in a sense of territorial limits. In any case, חק conveys a sense of national security that Zion will enjoy when Yahweh brings into effect her national redemption.

V.12a-a: The identity of "they" in יבוא "they will come" remains obscure since there is no clear indication in the text. Sweeney seems to suggest that "they will come" is an indication of threat that will come from Assyria, Egypt and other

[187] Andersen and Freedman, *Micah*, 585.

[188] Cf. Hillers, *Micah*, 90.

[189] Ps 51:18; 69:35; 102:16; 147:2. Cf. Mays, *Micah*, 161.

[190] Cf. Allen, *The Book of Joel, Obadiah, Jonah and Micah*, 397.

[191] Allen, *The Books of Joel, Obadiah, Jonah and Micah*, 397-398.

[192] Most scholars consider it as "boundary". See Smith, *Micah, Zephaniah, Nahum, Obadiah, Joel*, 149; Andersen and Freedman, *Micah*, 586; Sweeney, *The Twelve Prophets*, vol. 2, 411.

nations against Jerusalem.[193] To understand יבוא as a threat of foreign invasion against Jerusalem is implausible since such reading would be incongruent with the salvation theme of "rebuilding walls" and extension of "boundaries" in v.11. Since Micah's contemporary Isaiah express similarly that Yahweh will gather the people of "Judah" from Assyria, Egypt, coastlands of the sea and other nations (Isa. 11:11-16; 27:12), it is highly possible that יבוא refers to the homecoming of Judah's own people from the exile.[194]

V.12b-b: For the discussion on "Assyria" and "Egypt", see the above TCC on v.11c-c. The phrase "from sea to sea and from mountain to mountain" encompasses the whole world.[195]

V.13a: (For the discussion on the term הארץ "the earth" in Micah, see the TCC on Mic.1:2b-b). Since the context talks about the restoration of Jerusalem (cf. vv.11-12), most scholars agree that הארץ here refers not to the desolation of the land of Israel but the whole pagan nations in a sense of global world.[196] The desolation of הארץ reversely portrays the situation of the enemies' nations like Assyria and Egypt (cf. v.12) in contrast to the circumstances of Jerusalem that will be rebuilding walls and extending her boundaries (cf. v.11).

V.14a: Yahweh is frequently designated as the shepherd of Israel (Pss 23:1ff; 28:9; 80:2), which speaks of the relationship between Yahweh and his people. The shepherd imagery appears at least three times in 2:12; 4:6ff and 7:14. Earlier Israel is portrayed as sheep that would be led away from her land to exile (2:12-13). In the ANE, the king is considered as shepherd of his people who guides, protects and rules the people. By appealing to Yahweh as "shepherd", Yahweh's kingship and authority are recognized and thereby the responsibility to protect and defend his jeopardized people and land are attributed to him.

V.14b: Israel is frequently designated as Yahweh's נחלה "inheritance" (Ps 74:2; 95:7; 100:3), which signifies Israel's special relationship as Yahweh's possession.[197] According to von Rad, נחלה initially "belongs to the sacral body of law dealing with the tenure of land, and originally designated the heritable land allotted by Yahweh to the clan or family."[198] Developing further on the idea of von Rad, Mays contends that in a later stage נחלה "came to be used for the people as the special possession of YHWH, a metaphor of the value of Israel to YHWH created by his election (Pss 33:12; see also Pss 68:9f; 94:5,14; 78:68; 71 etc.)."[199] נחלה expresses an idea of tripartite relationship in which Yahweh's intimate relation with Israel is

---

[193] Sweeney, *The Twelve Prophets,* vol. 2, 411.

[194] Cf.Mays, *Micah*, 162.

[195] Mays, *Micah*, 162.

[196] Keil, *Minor Prophets*, vol. 10, 511; Smith, *Micah, Zephaniah, Nahum, Obadiah, Joel*, 150; Zvi, *Micah*, 177.

[197] cf. Deut. 4:20; 9:26, 29; 1 Kgs 8:51, 53; 2 Kgs 21:14.

[198] von Rad, *Old Testament Theology*, vol. 2, 224.

[199] Mays, *Micah*, 164.

understood in terms of "inheritance" and as Yahweh's inheritance Israel is entitled to inheritance of land from Yahweh.

V.14c-c: Smith interprets the phrase, "dwelling alone in a forest in the midst of a garden land" as a factual statement that describes the returned exiles occupying the hill tops of Judah since access to the surrounding fertile plains, which are in the possession of powerful enemies, is denied to them.[200] Smith's position can be sustained if the text is alluded to post-exilic, which may be untenable here as discussed below. Quite distinctively, Hillers maintains that the state of affairs in v.14 appears similar to Isa. 6:11; 7:21-25 where the empty land rapidly reverts to thorns and briers and animals tread on the land while people, due to impoverishment, revert to hunting in those former cities and vineyards that now turned to scrublands. By comparing these Isaiah texts, Hillers concludes that the description in v.14 is more about the present unfavorable conditions of the people resulting from the destruction of the land, massacre and deportation of the population.[201] Despite the fact that the text remains silent about any specific historical event, by citing C.J. Gadd's findings on a comparable description of the desolation of Babylon in 710-709 BCE in an inscription of Sargon II, Hillers cautiously concludes that the land of Judah or part of it would have experienced the same condition during Micah's time.[202] Though the historical issue remains a conundrum, Hillers' position cannot be easily negated as the resurgent Assyria was already expanding her dominion southward by the time of Micah and several passages in Micah echo the apprehensions of Assyria's invasion (See also the FCC on Mic. 1:6-7; 3:12; 4:11-13).

V.14d-d: Bashan refers to the plains of southwest Syria that overlook the sea of Galilee while Gilead refers on the Transjordan areas belonged to the tribes of Manasseh, Reuben and Gad (Josh. 13). Both Bashan and Gilead were known for their fertility with lush green herbs for the grazing of herds,[203] and both were lost to the Arameans in the ninth century (1 Kgs 22:3). During the reign of Jeroboam II, Israel took back this area under their control. However, after a few decades, by mid eighth century Tiglath-Pilesar of Assyria annexed the area and these Transjordan areas no longer remained Israel's possession (2 Kgs 15:29).[204] Micah's prayer to feed them "in Bashan and Gilead" is a plea for restoration of their lost territories and the blessing of land as in the days of old (כימי עולם) as when they came out of Egypt (cf. v.15).

V.15a-a: The expression כימי "as in the days" points to the historical event of Israel's exodus from Egypt. In the exodus tradition, Israel remembered Yahweh's act as the divine intervention for freedom and the defeat of their enemy, which makes

[200] Smith, *Micah, Zephaniah, Nahum, Habakkuk, Obadiah, Joel*, 153.

[201] Hillers, *Micah*, 90-91.

[202] Hillers, *Micah*, 91.

[203] Num. 32:1-5; Deut. 32:14.

[204] Mays, *Micah*, 165; Sweeney, *The Twelve Prophets*, vol. 2, 412.

possible for the Israelites to possess the land. The miraculous act of exodus is thus associated with the possession of the land in the exodus tradition. Jerusalem was in a precarious state of losing the land due to the looming Assyrian invasion. To assure the threatened Jerusalem, Micah quotes the speech of Yahweh (v.15)[205] that is embedded in the exodus tradition. As Yahweh defeated Israel's enemy on Israel's behalf during the exodus, the encroaching nation Assyria will also be defeated as Yahweh intends to intervene for his people with mighty acts as in the days of Exodus. Thus, the exodus tradition introduced by כימי in v.15 serves as the basis of Yahweh's assurance to bring deliverance for his jeopardized people.

V.19a: Literally "he will return to have compassion on us".

5.8.3. Form Critical Comments on Micah 7:8-20

Scholars are divided as to whether the unit begins with v.7 or with v.8.[206] Though some scholars consider v.7 to be an introduction to vv.8-10, it appears clear that v.7 is syntactically linked closely with vv.1-6, for example: "I will look to Yahweh" in v.7 is linked with "your watchmen" in v.4 in which Assyria's "watch" on Jerusalem for destruction is contrasted with Micah's "watch" for Yahweh for deliverance. Amidst Assyria's threat (vv.1-6), v.7 can be considered as a concluding note of hope for deliverance from Yahweh.[207] As such, we consider v.7 to be an integral part of vv.1-6, while the preceding unit begins with v.8 and ends with v.20.

Despite some differences concerning the beginning of the unit mentioned above, consensus among the scholars is that the unit consists of four smaller parts.[208] First, vv.8-10 is a hymn of trust upon Yahweh in which the prophet expresses his confidence that Yahweh will act and bring deliverance while putting the enemies to shame. Second, vv.11-13 is a salvation oracle addressed to Jerusalem in which the prophet announces the fortification of wall, extension of boundaries, the return of the exiles and the desolation of the enemies' land. Third, vv.14-17 is a hymn in which the prophet appeals to Yahweh's historic relationship with his people and prays for Yahweh's blessing upon his people and defeat for the enemy. Finally, vv.18-20 is a hymn of the assurance of future deliverance in which the

---

[205] Zvi, *Micah*, 178.

[206] Scholars who consider 7:7-20 as a unit include, Hermann Gunkel, "The Close of Micah: A Prophetic Liturgy. A Study in Literary History", in *What Remains in the Old Testament and Other Essays*. Trans. by A.K. Dallas (London: George Allen and Unwin, 1928) 115-1149; Mays, *Micah*, 153; Sweeney, *The Twelve Prophets*, vol. 2, 409; Smith, *Micah-Malachi*, 58-59. Others who consider 2:8-20 as a unit are, Hillers, *Micah*, 89; Allen, *The Book of Joel, Obadiah, Jonah and Micah*, 391-394.

[207] Allen, *The Books of Joel, Obadiah, Jonah and Micah*, 389.

[208] Mays, *Micah*, 153-155; Smith, *Micah-Malachi*, 58; Sweeney, *The Twelve Prophets*, vol. 2, 409; Hillers, *Micah*, 89. Shaw, *The Speeches of Micah*, 196. For detailed discussion on the unity of 7:8-20, see James Nogalski, *Literary Precursors to the Book of Twelve* (New York: Walter de Gruyter, 1993), 168-170.

prophet appeals to Yahweh's forgiveness and his fidelity to his relationship with his people. These four parts are inseparably connected together as unit. Mays has demonstrated that the first part (vv.8-10) speaks of deliverance while the second part (vv.11-13) states the detail of deliverance. The third part (vv.14-17) prays for deliverance and finally the last part (vv.18-20) deals with, what Mays calls, "theology" of the whole stated in terms of "praise of God's forgiveness."[209] The progression of thought between these four parts expressed through the theme of deliverance deals with both the people and the land as a result of Yahweh's intervention. The tripartite relationship can thus be seen as a central factor that connects the four parts as a unit. Based on the above discussion, vv.8-20 can be structured as follows:

1. Present Distress and Future Hope for Deliverance (vv.8-10)
    i. Grief upon the people and the land
    "I fall", "I sit in darkness" (v.8)

    ii. Reason for the present predicaments
    "because I have sinned against him" (v.9a)

    iii. Jerusalem's deliverance and victory over enemy
    "I shall see his deliverance", "she [enemy] will be trodden (v.9b-10)

2. Restoration of Jerusalem and Desolation of the Earth (vv.11-13)
    i. Description of Jerusalem's restoration
    "building of … walls", "boundary… extended" and "they [people] will come to you from Assyria, Egypt, sea and mountain" (vv.11-12)

    ii. Desolation of the earth and its reason
    "the earth will be desolate because of its inhabitants" (v.13).

3. Zion's Prayer of Deliverance and Defeat of the Enemy (vv.14-17)
    i. Prayer for deliverance
    "Shepherd you people… your inheritance… who dwell alone" (v.14)

    ii. Appeal to historic relationship
    "As in the days… came out of the land of Egypt… show them marvelous things (v.15)

    iii. Humiliation of enemy
    "The nations shall see and be ashamed… they shall lick the dust" (vv.16-17)

4. Deliverance Based on Yahweh's Forgiveness (vv.18-20)
    i. Affirmation of God's compassion

---

[209] Mays, *Micah*, 153.

"Who is a God like you, pardoning iniquity... transgression... does not retain anger... [but] delights in steadfast love" (v.18)

ii. Forgiveness as the basis of deliverance
"He will have compassion on us... tread our iniquities underfoot... cast all our sins into ... sea... You will show faithfulness... as you have shown to our fathers (vv.19-20)

No precise reference to any historical time and place is mentioned in the text, which has led scholars to propose several possible settings. It was Gunkel who proposed that the unit is a "liturgy" of penance and confession with liturgies of fast days or the Day of Atonement.[210] On the other hand, as mentioned in the TCC on 7:8b, Mays points to the reference to "enemy" in v.8, which he identifies as "Edom" and argues that it was "enemy" (Edom) who mocked the Jerusalemites at the fall of Jerusalem during the Babylonian invasion. Mays thus suggests that the historical setting suits the aftermath of Jerusalem's fall.[211] Similarly, Smith also argues that the unit belongs to the exilic period, shortly after the fall of Jerusalem. He maintains that the present text may have been used during the exile to offer hope and assurance to the exilic community that Yahweh would restore the fortune of Jerusalem.[212] While it is possible that the present unit, as liturgy, could have a cultic setting (as Gunkel suggests), dating the passage to a later period of Babylonian invasion (Mays and Smith) can be doubted. As mentioned above, in the TCC on vv.8b and 11b, Jerusalem was constantly mocked and attacked by enemies at various periods of time in history. As such, we cannot limit it to Edom's mocking Jerusalem during the Babylonian invasion.

Scholars like Wolff could argue that the reference to "rebuilding wall" (v.11) still indicates that the historical setting belongs to the post-exilic period of Nehemiah (fifth century BCE). However, as discussed above in the TCC on v.11b, Jerusalem's wall needed repairs not only during Nehemiah's time. Even during Hezekiah's time, "rebuilding of the wall" was carried out following a warning that Sennacherib was planning to attack Jerusalem (2 Chro. 32:5).[213] Bo Reicke convincingly argues that such exilic or postexilic setting is untenable since destruction and rebuilding of the land, the city, and the temple was a motif characteristic of ANE lamentations[214] and such ideas originated in the pre-exilic

---

[210] H. Gunkel, "The Close of the Book of Micah: A Prophetic Liturgy" in A.K. Dallas, *What Remains in the Old Testament and Other Essays* (New York: Macmillian, 1928), 115-119. Cited in Zvi, *Micah*, 181.

[211] Mays, *Micah*, 158-159.

[212] Smith, *Micah-Malachi*, 58.

[213] Nogalski, *Literary Precursors to the Book of Twelve*, 167.

[214] Such as, Tammuz liturgies, and 'Al'iyan Ba'al recitatives. Cf. Bo Reicke, "Liturgical Traditions in Micah 7", *HTR* 60 (1967) 363.

literature (Pss. 74:3-8; 79:1-4; Am. 9:1-15).[215] It seems probable that Zion was in distress since Jerusalem and the land of Judah was apparently stripped bare during Sennacherib's invasion of Judah in 701 BCE and that the reference to "fall" and enemy's mockery "where is Yahweh your God" (vv.8, 10) and the "rebuilding of wall" reflect the destruction of the walled cities of Judah in 701 BCE by Sennacherib and that the historical setting of vv.8-20 belongs to the period of the late eighth century BCE (see also the TCC on 7:14c-c).

5.8.3. Tradition and Theological Comments in the Light of Tripartite Relationship

According to Andersen and Freedman, a hymn of trust in Yahweh (vv.8-12) appears similar in thought to the earlier Zion hymn. They argue that the prayer of hope "to rise" (v.8) and to "trample" the enemy (v.10) echo the earlier Zion hymn in ch.4 where fallen Zion is assured to rise up and trample her enemies (4:13). Moreover, the enemies' taunting, "where is Yahweh your God" in v.10 recalls the Zion Hymn in 4:11 where the enemy taunted Zion saying "let her be profaned". Such recurrence of Zion theme, according to Andersen and Freedman, suggest that the subunit vv.8-12 is another poem for Zion.[216] If, as Andersen and Freedman argue, vv.8-12 belongs to the genre of Zion hymn, then the hymn is rooted in Zion tradition and the unidentified feminine speaker (vv.8-12) is Zion. On the basis of the Zion traditions in Micah and from similar imagery in certain Zion Psalms, scholars have identified that the feminine speaker is Zion.[217] In this case, as noted above in the FCC, the description "I fall" and the enemy's taunt "where is Yahweh your God" (vv.8-10) could refer to the setting of Assyria's invasion on Jerusalem in 701 BCE. Amidst Assyria's invasion, Micah employs here the Zion tradition to encourage Zion and to affirm that Yahweh is the God who will defend his people and land from the enemies who have surrounded Zion (cf. Isa. 17:12-14; 29:5-8; Pss 46:6; 48:4f; 76:3-6).

The above Zion tradition that seeks to encourage the jeopardized Jerusalem is further embellished by the use of the Exodus tradition (v.15). As mentioned in the TCC on v.15a-a, the phrase "when you come out of Egypt" recalls Yahweh's intervention on Israel's behalf during their Egyptian slavery. The Exodus tradition remembers Yahweh as the God of liberation who freed the landless slaves of Israel from Egypt in order to give them the land of Canaan. The Exodus tradition of liberation thus inseparably connects Yahweh's redemptive act and his giving of the land to Israel. Since, as stated in the above FCC, the devastation of land was looming around Jerusalem due to Assyria's threat, the use of the Exodus tradition appears germane to assure Zion that Yahweh will bring liberation by subjugating

[215] For more discussion, see Reicke, "Liturgical Traditions", 363ff.

[216] Andersen and Freedman, *Micah*, 577.

[217] Nogalski, *Literary Precursors to the Book of Twelve*, 146.

the powerful nation that is presently threatening Jerusalem as Yahweh did to the powerful nation, Egypt in the past days.

V.8 states that it is because of "sins" Yahweh's anger was aroused and the corollary of נפלתי "I [Zion] fall" is stated to be the result of Zion's "sins" against Yahweh. Therefore to deal with the problem of sin and thereby to restore Yahweh's relationship with Zion and to assure Yahweh's protection of land from the enemy, the Exodus tradition is employed by appealing to Yahweh's nature of forgiveness (v.18). The prayer for forgiveness: נשא עון "pardoning iniquity", ועבר על־פשע "passing over transgression", לא־החזיק לעד אפו "not retaining anger" and חפץ חסד "delights in steadfast love" (v.18) echoes the Exodus vocabulary in which Yahweh is affirmed as a "God merciful and gracious, slow to anger, and abounding in steadfast love and faithfulness, keeping steadfast love for thousands, forgiving iniquity and transgression and sin…" (Ex. 34:6-7). Based on the forgiving nature of Yahweh, the God of Exodus, Zion appeals for the forgiveness of her sins, for the deliverance of her people and land from the looming destruction.

As mentioned above in the FCC, vv.8-10 state the distress of Zion in which she prays to Yahweh for deliverance from her present fiasco. Three descriptions of predicament admit the fall of the nation (vv.8-10). First, Zion is in a state of "fall" (v.8). The verb נפל "to fall" describes war causalities,[218] which indicates that Zion is beginning to feel the pulse of the Assyrian invasion. Second, Zion sits in "darkness" (v.8). חשך "darkness" indicates that amidst Zion's precarious state, she sees no possible help for her deliverance. Third, she is mocked by her enemy who says "where is Yahweh your God" (v.10), which is a usual scornful mock spoken by enemies at times when Zion faces trouble (cf. Pss 42:3, 10; 79:10). Since both the people and land are in a precarious situation, the enemy's mock amounts to affronting the effectiveness of Yahweh's relationship with Zion and his ability to defend the people and land.

While the enemy (Assyria) arrogantly misconstrued Zion's distress to be proof of Yahweh's ineffectiveness and thereby undermined the tripartite relationship, Zion understood her ruin of both the people and land as זעף יהוה "indignation of Yahweh", which she suffers as a result of her sin (חטא) against Yahweh (v.9). In Micah's usage, sin involves deviation from and violation of the covenant norms of life set by Yahweh. It involves the abuse of power in the court and cultic activities that results in social injustice, such as, the expropriation and foreclosure of small peasant landholdings (see the TCC on Mic. 2:1b-b), for which Yahweh announces the evil time of ruin and destruction (cf. 2:1-5). In vv.8-9, we see that Zion is already in a state of ruin. However, after suffering Yahweh's indignation, Zion is confident that she will "rise" and will be in the "light" (vv.8-9). As discussed in the above TCC on v.8, the terms "rise" and "light" not only express the metaphor of Yahweh's deliverance but they also indicate the restoration or rebuilding of Zion (details of restoration is stated in vv.11-12). In other words, the tripartite

[218] Andersen and Freedman, *Micah*, 582.

relationship that was challenged by the enemy at Zion's debacle will be vindicated by Yahweh when he restores Zion and vanquishes the enemy.

Detailed descriptions of restoration (vv.11-13) continue to emphasize on the people, the land or the city. First, v.11a states that "walls" will be rebuilt. As mentioned in the above TCC on v.11b, לבנות גדריך "building of your walls" could be referring to the destruction of walled cities of Judah in 701 BCE when Jerusalem and part of the land of Judah were stripped bare by Sennacherib (see also the above FCC). Jerusalem, a synecdoche for the land of Judah, was thus in a precarious state of losing its land as a political nation. Despite her present ruins, the salvation oracle in vv.11-13 affirms that ruined walls will be rebuilt, which indicates the restoration of the fallen Zion, a metonymy of the nation of Judah.

Second, v.11b states that the "boundary shall be far extended", which again deals with the land as a territorial nation. Though the size of boundary to be extended is not precisely stated, as mentioned in the TCC on v.11c-c, the geographical description "from Assyria to Egypt and from Egypt to the river, from sea to sea" from where people would come (v.12) is the ideal geographical limits of Yahweh's promise of land to Israel (Gen. 15:18; 1 Kgs 4:21). The reference to "Egypt and Assyria" in v.12 thus indicates that the territory to be extended encompasses the ancient boundary ideal stretching from the Assyrian border in the northeast and down to the Egyptian border in the southwest (see the above TCC on v.11c-c).

Third, v.12a states that "they will come", which speaks of the people to return back to Zion. As mentioned in the TCC on v.12a-a, "they will come" from Assyria, Egypt and from the sea and mountain does not refer to the threat of enemies who would come against Jerusalem. Instead the phrase refers to the return of Judah's own people who would come and rebuild the walls and engage in extending their territorial boundaries.

The possibility to rebuild walls, to extend boundaries and to return back to the homeland is further envisaged by the desolation of the earth (v.13). הארץ "the earth" will suffer "desolation" על "because" of its inhabitants (v.13). The idea of the desolation of land because of the inhabitants' sin is common in the prophetic understanding (cf. Isa. 24:5). In the present context, the desolation of the earth "because of its inhabitants" probably refers to the justice to Judah, which entails judgment meted out to the people of the earth.[219] הארץ here appears in contradistinction to Zion, as such, the heathen nations are intended here. As mentioned in the above TCC on v.13a, it refers to the whole pagan nations in a sense of global world. Since the whole pagan nations will be in desolation, it would not be possible for the nations to come and attack Zion. Instead, the global state of desolation would make it possible for Zion to engage in the work of national reconstruction without any external threat.

---

219 W.J. Wessels, "Micah 7:8-20: An Apt Conclusion to the Book of Micah", *Verbum t Ecclesia* 24/1 (2003), 254.

The period of the above details of national reconstruction will happen "that day" or "in that day" (יום הוא, v.11-12), which is a formulaic expression of the prophets to announce the promise of Yahweh's salvation in the future. The formulaic expression "that day" or "in that day" indicates that vv.11-13 is a salvation oracle. Yahweh will bring salvation in which the deported people of Zion would return back to their ancestral land and their resettlement in the land would involve territorial fortifications and expansions. The theological emphasis here is thus on a reestablishment of the tripartite relationship in which Yahweh's people and land would be brought back together as a result of Yahweh's act of salvation.

In vv.14-17, Zion prays to Yahweh for deliverance and for the defeat of enemy. Yahweh is addressed as רעה "shepherd", while Zion is Yahweh's people (עמך) and "inheritance" (נחלתך). However, Zion as Yahweh's people and inheritance now "dwells alone in a forest" (v.14), which probably results from the Assyrians' attack upon the people and land of Zion. By addressing Yahweh as "shepherd" the responsibility to protect and defend the threatened people and land is attributed to Yahweh. Along with the prayer for Yahweh's protection of his people and land from the present threat, Zion's prayer also beseeches Yahweh for the recovery of their ancient ancestral domain. Since Bashan and Gilead belonged to the Northern tribes of Manasseh, Reuben and Gad (Josh. 13), Willis concludes that the origin of the present unit is from the Northern kingdom.[220] However, he has overlooked another significant aspect of Bashan and Gilead. As discussed in the above TCC on v.14, Bashan and Gilead are the Transjordan area of Israel during the united monarchy, which mostly remained under foreign occupation after the divided monarchy. Thus, a prayer to lead them to "Bashan and Gilead" could be referring to restoration of their lost territories and the blessing of land as in the olden days of united monarchy as when they came out of Egypt (cf. v.15).

In the prayer for deliverance, appeal to historic relation is made by recounting the Exodus tradition. The Exodus calls to mind the glorious history of Yahweh's deliverance of Israel from oppression and captivity. As such, despite the present threat from Assyria's invasion both the people and land of Jerusalem will once again see Yahweh's intervention with wondrous miracles as in the time of Exodus. In recounting the Exodus tradition for Zion's deliverance, the focus once again moves to the nations (vv.16-17). When Yahweh intervenes as in the Exodus, the powerful nations will be rendered powerless before Yahweh's wondrous work. Nations will be defeated and humiliated. Their humiliation is described as a crawling snake licking the dust and trembling in fear of Yahweh (vv.16-17).

Zion's hope for deliverance from their distress is not based on their ability to defeat the enemies but it is based on "who Yahweh is" for Zion (vv.18-20). Yahweh is affirmed as the God who forgives (v.18), which is significant in understanding

[220] John T. Willis, "A Reapplied Prophetic Hope Oracle" *VTS* 26 (1974) 64-76.

the tripartite relationship. As stated above, חטא "sin" against Yahweh (v.9) is stated to be the reason of destruction for both the people and land and therefore Yahweh's forgiveness of Zion's sin is seen as the leeway for Zion to save from total destruction. As stated above, the prayer in v.18 of pardoning iniquity (נשׂא עון), passing over transgression (ועבר על־פשׁע), and not retaining anger (לא־החזיק לעד אפו) but delights in steadfast love (חפץ חסד) are the vocabulary of the Exodus tradition (Ex. 34:6-7). Moreover, the image of treading upon the sin and casting of sins into the sea alludes to "an act of deliverance similar to God's salvation from the pursuing Egyptians, when the nation came out of slavery and bondage (cf. Ex. 15:4-5)."[221] Thus, the affirmation of Yahweh's compassion and appeal made to Yahweh for forgiveness is rooted in the tradition of Exodus. The affirmed historic deliverance at the Exodus in which Yahweh brings freedom to the people and gifted them the land of Canaan as a separate and distinct political nation is because of Yahweh's faithfulness and commitment to his promise made to Israel's ancestors (v.20). Because Yahweh remains faithful to his promise, Zion finds hope for the future in Yahweh to experience deliverance for both the people and the land. The tripartite relationship that was severed because of sin (v.9) finds hope of reestablishing it based on Yahweh's forgiveness in vv.18-20.

5.9. Micah's Theology of Land

Based on the foregoing exegesis, we now summarize Micah's understanding of land as follows:

1. *Meaning of the Term Land:*

First, in Micah's understanding ארץ refers to the entire earth in *cosmic* sense, which embraces not only humanity but also every living creature in it. In such understanding, Yahweh is affirmed as the cosmic Lord whose sovereign authority extends to all the earth and everything in it (4:11-13). As cosmic Lord, Yahweh exercises his ultimate authority upon all the earth in which the entire earth (ארץ) participates in Yahweh's trial court as a cosmic arena for judgment (1:2) and as active participant witnessing Yahweh's judgment against his people (2:2). ארץ also responds to Yahweh's manifestation by causing convulsion and chaos upon the earth and thereby affecting the lives of all those who live upon the earth (2:4). Yahweh's arrival on earth for judgment is occasioned by the sins of Samaria and Jerusalem (2:5) and the inhabitants of the earth (7:13). The desolation of the entire earth is thus linked with the inhabitants' relation to the cosmic Lord, Yahweh.

Second, Micah speaks of "land' in a sense of *political territory for nation* in which the term ארץ appears mostly with the definite article ה (and sometimes with pronoun suffix) such as, "the land of Egypt" (6:4; 7:15), "the land of Assyria (Nimrod, 5:5)" and "the land of Israel" (5:4, 5; 7:12). In Micah's usage, land as

[221] Wessels, "Micah 7:8-20", 257.

political nation mostly refers to the land of Israel and Judah in which the capital cities "Samaria" and "Jerusalem" and also "Zion" appear as synecdoche for the Northern and Southern nations respectively (1:5, 6; 3:12; 4:2; 11, 13). The land of Israel and Judah as political nations appear in a constant tension of destruction and exile (1:6, 7; 2:3, 4; 3:12; 7:8, 9) before mighty Assyria who engaged in the policy of territorial expansion. The possibility of peace upon the land as political nations is envisaged only when the nations engage in demilitarization and disarmament (4:3). Demilitarization and disarmament are envisaged as possibilities only when there is willingness to learn to walk in the ways of the Torah (4:2-3). Willingness to walk in the path of the Torah leads to disarmament and international peace in which each person would be able to live securely under his own vine and fig tree (4:4).

Third, Micah uses the term land in a sense of an *arable or cultivable plot.* Terms such as עמק "valley", שׂדות "field" and בתים "house" speak of agricultural land that is considered as inalienable and rightful share for every member of the assembly of Yahweh. The arable plot of land is characterized as נחלה "an entitlement or patrimonial inheritance", and חלק "a portion or territory of allotment" (2:1-5) granted to them as a gift of Yahweh. In such understanding of arable portion, land is seen as survival means of existence and to engage in economic activities. As such, the arable land often became an object of disputation and temptation to possess even with diabolic means (2:1-2; 3:9-11). Micah's accusation against the plutocrats for grabbing the land by dispossessing and impoverishing the peasants are mostly linked with the understanding of land as cultivable portion that is received as inheritance from Yahweh (2:2). By employing the form of judgment oracle, Micah affirms that those who engage in violence, oppression, and injustice to amass the cultivable land (2:1-2) will inevitably be dispossessed by Yahweh of their landed properties just as they have dispossessed the vulnerable people. However in the salvation oracle, after a period of suffering Yahweh's judgment, Micah envisaged that the arable land will be restored back to all the members of Yahweh's assembly (4:4). In the restoration oracle, the enjoyment of the fruits of cultivable land is inseparably linked with peace in the land (4:4). Peace in the land is thus understood to be an essential prerogative for the prosperity of the land (4:4) and such peace, according to Micah, is possible only if people learn to walk in the name of Yahweh (4:5).

Finally, Micah uses the term בתים to speak not only of arable land but also to refer to a *living space or residential plot.* Such understanding of land as residential plot is also understood as נחלה "a patrimonial inheritance or rightful entitlement", and חלק "a portion or territory of allotment" (2:1-5), which the Israelites received as a gift from Yahweh. By amassing unjustly a large portion of agricultural land and the consequent prosperity it brings, the elite class began to invest their money in spacious and palatial buildings by evicting the poor people and their families out of their residential land (2:2). Micah's understanding of land as living or residential space reveals the practice of corruption in which the plutocrats build their palatial buildings by encroaching on into the residential land of the poor while the poor dispossessed were forced out to live in a roofless shelter as they now no longer own even a small portion of residential plot.

2. *Tripartite Relationship*

The above four levels of meaning shows inseparable relationship between Yahweh, Israel/Judah and land. First, in Micah's understanding, the severed tripartite relationship between Yahweh, Israel/Judah and land is explained in terms of "*sins*" in which the earth serves as "witness and arena" for a trial between Yahweh and Israel/Judah. Yahweh coming upon the earth to bring judgment against Israel/Judah is occasioned by "transgressions" and "sins" (1:5). In such understanding of the tripartite relationship, the earth also serves as an agent of Yahweh's judgment by causing convulsion upon the earth (1:4) and by turning the foundations and fortifications of the nation into a heap of rubble (1:6). Existence upon the land thus becomes difficult for Israel and Judah as a result of their sin and transgression against Yahweh.

Second, the tripartite relationship is explained in terms of *Yahweh's Lordship*. Because Yahweh is the Lord, "the Lord of all the earth" (4:13), he holds the sovereign authority over all the earth and that every nation remains accountable before him. Because of the inhabitants of the earth like Assyria who invaded Samaria and Jerusalem and also Judah's officials who encroached on the land and properties of the defenseless people, Yahweh exercises his Lordship by bringing judgment in the form of causing desolation upon the earth (7:13) and by bringing the threat of destruction and exile (1:6,7; 2:3,4; 3:12; 7:8,9). The desolation of the earth is thus attributed to the inhabitants' behavior ("the fruit of their doings", cf. 7:13) before Yahweh. Because Yahweh is the cosmic Lord, the behavior of the inhabitants of the earth comes under his judgment.

Third, the tripartite relationship is explained in terms of *Yahweh's forgiveness and faithfulness*. As a result of sins and transgressions of Israel/Judah, Yahweh announces to bring destruction upon the land and threatened to send Israel/Judah to exile and thereby to alienate them from the land. "Sin" and "transgressions" are thus understood to be the main reasons for breaking the tripartite relationship. However, Micah was confident of Yahweh's forgiveness and faithfulness to his people (7:8-10) to restore the tripartite relationship. As a result of Yahweh's forgiveness, the defeated and the fallen nation of his people will rise up again, the exiles will be brought back to the land, their lost territories will be restored and Yahweh himself will shepherd his people (7:8, 9, 11, 16). This is envisaged in the salvation oracle in which Yahweh's faithfulness to his people is affirmed to be the reason of his restoration. With his forgiveness and faithfulness, Yahweh will again be their shepherd, Judah will be his (Yahweh's) flock and his people would be brought back to the land to enjoy the fertility of the land (7:11,14). In the tripartite relationship, despite the loss of land and the loss of Yahweh's protection, the severance of the relationship between Yahweh, Israel/Judah and land is seen to be temporary. The restoration of the tripartite relationship always remains the hope of the prophetic oracles. Such understanding of the restored relationship is based on several religious and historical traditions, which shaped the prophetic understanding of the tripartite relationship as stated below.

3. *Traditions*

Micah employs a *theophany tradition* to announce the break of the tripartite relationship in 1:2-7. In Micah's understanding, Yahweh's manifestation upon the earth (theophany) is occasioned by Israel's transgression, which jeopardized the relation between Yahweh and Israel. As a result of Israel's transgression, Yahweh intervenes to enforce his punishment against Israel and that punishment is described in terms of the consequences upon the earth that melts and tears apart like wax (1:3-4). As such, the theophany tradition of Yahweh's intervention upon the earth explains how Israel's transgression jeopardized Yahweh-Israel relationship and how that strained relationship put the land of Israel in a precarious state of devastation and loss (1:6-7). Israel's relationship with Yahweh and with the land comes to the state of precariousness. Micah thus succinctly explains the breaking of the tripartite relationship in terms of theophany tradition.

To explain how social oppression and injustice severs the tripartite relationship, Micah employs the *Sinai covenant tradition*. In Micah's understanding, coveting and seizing of land and houses are violations of the Sinai covenant between Yahweh and Israel concerning the pattern of land use and property rights (2:1-2). As such, Micah calls for the covenant judgment of destruction of the land and exile of its population to a foreign land as covenant tradition envisages the forfeiture of land as punishment for covenant violation. In violating Yahweh's covenant, Judah alienates herself from Yahweh and the consequence of which leads to the alienation of Judah from the land. The tripartite relationship is thus broken due to the violation of covenant as Judah is alienated both from her land and her God (2:1-5).

To elucidate how the tripartite relationship is severed and reestablished, Micah employs *Zion traditions*. Unlike the popular understanding of his time that affirms Yahweh's presence and protection without practicing social justice (3:11), Micah conveys that Yahweh is in fact against Zion because of the prevailing injustice. Affirmation of Yahweh's presence and protection (Zion traditions) is nullified if unaccompanied by the practice of justice. Justice is abhorred and perverted, which led to bloodshed and violence and in the process the poor were denied legal protection and deprived of their rights in Zion (3:9-12). Thus, Yahweh will also deny his protection to Zion and the people of Zion will be deprived of their land for the land will be ploughed and ruined (3:12). Injustice is thus seen to be the reason of debarring Yahweh's protection and denial of land to Zion (severing the tripartite relationship) in Micah's usage of Zion tradition in 3:9-12.

While Judah recognized the destruction of her land and the denial of Yahweh's protection upon her people to be the result of her sin (7:9), the nations considered Judah's defeat as Yahweh's inability to defend his people and land (7:10). Yahweh's relationship with his people and land is thus put at stake. To counter this belief, Micah employs the Zion tradition (4:11-13) and asserts that Yahweh will thwart the nations' plans, empower his people and protect their land from certain defeat (4:13). The empowerment and protection of Yahweh (Zion tradition) thus affirms the validity of the tripartite relationship. On what basis the Zion tradition is used to validate the tripartite relationship is unclear in 4:11-13. However, what appears clear is that Micah did not deny the validity of Zion tradition *per se* but what he negates is the absence of the practice of justice in Zion tradition. In 7:9-10, Yahweh's protection of his people and land (tripartite relationship) is envisaged after Zion suffers Yahweh's indignation in relation to her sin. The affirmation that Yahweh will protect his people and land (Zion tradition) in 4:11-13 and 7:8ff from those who attempt to destroy and devastate the land of Jerusalem and its inhabitants once again reaffirms the tripartite relationship between Yahweh, Judah and the land.

Though Yahweh's protection is denied because of the absence of justice in Zion (3:12), his presence is not negated, "let us go up to…Yahweh… that he may teach us" (4:2). Unlike the popular understanding of Yahweh's presence and protection (Zion tradition) without practicing justice (3:9), Micah integrates the Zion tradition with *Torah* in which justice is stressed as the content of Yahweh's teaching (4:1-5). By emphasizing justice, the core teaching of Torah, Yahweh's presence and protection (Zion tradition) is assured and international peace is envisaged (4:1-5). As the nations respond to Yahweh's teachings by walking in his way, war comes to an end and existence in the land become peaceful and secure. This picture of a harmonious relationship between Yahweh, Judah as well as nations and land (the tripartite relationship) is envisaged in the setting of accepting Yahweh's justice as the way of life. In other words, Micah shows that Yahweh's presence and protection (Zion tradition) can be claimed for the people and the land (tripartite relationship) if Yahweh's way (Torah tradition) is practiced in social relations.

Micah employs the *Exodus tradition* to explain that the present state of fall (7:8) does not invalidate Yahweh's relationship with the people of Zion and land (7:15-17). The enemies' presence at Zion brings distress, which is in fact caused by Zion's sin, but the looming defeat and the loss of land is not the end of Zion's fate. By affirming the Exodus tradition, Micah asserts that just as Yahweh brings liberation by subjugating the powerful nation Egypt during the Exodus, Yahweh will act on Zion's behalf and bring liberation to Zion. As the Exodus tradition is linked with the giving of the land to Israel, Yahweh's intervention on Zion's behalf in the future will not only bring liberation of the people but even the land will be restored back to Zion (7:11). Thus, by affirming the Exodus tradition, the reestablished tripartite relationship is once again envisaged in the final section of Micah's oracle. The basis of such affirmed hope on the reestablished tripartite relationship is attributed to Yahweh's faithfulness and steadfast love to the ancestors of Israel (7:20).

Chapter 6

The Understanding of Land in the Book of Isaiah (Chs 1-39)

6.1. Isaiah, the Prophet

The name Isaiah can be translated as "Yahweh is salvation."[1] Nothing much is known about him and his family except his father's (1:1), wife's and children's names (8:3). Isaiah, the son of Amoz and a younger contemporary of Micah, lived in Jerusalem in the second half of the eighth century BCE. Though there is no evidence that Isaiah was born into a noble family of Jerusalem, he certainly was a prominent person who had easy access to the palace, was able to converse with the kings (7:3ff) and other influential people in his community like the high priest (cf. 8:2). According to his personal account, he was called or was given a specific charge to prophecy after the death of King Uzziah (6:1-13). Isaiah married a prophetess (8:3) and had at least two children, Shear-jashub (7:3) and Maher-shalal-hash-baz (8:3). His prophetic ministry was carried out during one of the important periods of transition in the history of Israel and Judah, which is discussed briefly in the following section on the historical context of Isaiah's period.

6.2. Historical Context of Isaiah's Period

Isa. 1:1 places the historical setting of Isaiah's ministry in reigns of Uzziah, Jotham, Ahaz and Hezekiah of Judah (for the discussion of the date of these kings, see the Historical Background of Micah). If the superscription can be taken into consideration, the historical situation from Uzziah to Hezekiah's period would provide a clear picture concerning the issues related to the land. To understand

[1] Otto Kaiser, *Isaiah 1-12*, OTL (London: SCM, 1972), 2.

it clearly, we have briefly discussed various contexts of the period of Isaiah as follows.

6.2.1. Political Context

Famine, revolts and succession problems in Assyria from Shalmaneser IV (ca. 783-773 BCE), Asshur-dan III (ca. 773-754 BCE) and Asshur-ninari V (ca. 754-746 BCE) rendered Assyria weak, which enabled Uzziah to pursue his political and military ambitions successfully. During this second half of the eighth century, Uzziah took control over the land of the Philistines, Meunites, Arabs, Ammonites (cf. 2 Chro. 26:6-8.) and even the port of Elath was brought under Judah's control (cf. 2 Kgs 14:22).[2] These subdued nations paid huge tributes to Judah, which added much wealth to the national treasury. The international political situation was thus conducive for Judah to extend the boarders of her land afar with much success. However, Judah's territorial expansion and its consequent prosperity could not continue for long with a change of political equation in the international arena. With the enthronement of Tiglath-Pilesar III (ca.745 BCE), the Assyrian period of weakness came to an end and Tiglath-Pilesar started to assert Assyrian's hegemony internationally.[3] To contain the rising Assyrian supremacy, Pekah of Israel and Rezin of Syria formed a Syro-Ephraimite coalition and forced Judah to join the same. As Ahaz refused, the coalition armies marched against Judah with an intention to dethrone him and put Tebeel in his place (7:6). The result of the disastrous Syro-Ephraimite war was a partial annexation of the land of Israel especially the northern and eastern provinces (ca. 732) and a subjugation of Judah by Assyria.[4] Thus, both the northern and southern kingdoms became vulnerable to lose their land as political nations at the hand of Assyria. This Syro-Ephraimite coalition provides the background to much of Isaiah's prophecy that is related to land issue.[5]

Despite Isaiah's protest,[6] Hezekiah (715-687), the successor of Ahaz, attempted to break free from Assyria's vassalage by negotiating for Egypt's help (ca.711).[7] This angered Assyria and by 701 Sennacherib's successor, Sargon turned to Judah and according to his inscription, laid waste forty six cities of Judah and carried off 200,000 Judahites.[8] The archeological excavation at Lachish, which was besieged by Sennacherib, reveals some evidence of destruction. The findings have

---

[2] Gary V. Smith, *Isaiah 1-39: An Exegetical and Theological Exposition of the Holy Scripture*, NAC (Nashville, Tennessee: Broadman and Holman, 2007), 27.

[3] David Stacey, *Isaiah 1-39* (London: Epworth, 1993), xxi.

[4] Kaiser, *Isaiah 1-12*, 4.

[5] Stacey, *Isaiah 1-39*, xxi.

[6] Cf. 28:7-13; 14-22; 29:13-14.

[7] Cf. 30:1-5, 6-7, 8-14, 15-17; 31:1-3; 4-5, 8ff.

[8] Marvin A. Sweeney, *Isaiah 1-39*, vol. 16, FOTL (Grand Rapids, Michigan: William B. Eerdmans Publishing Company, 1996), 77.

revealed the remains of fifteen thousand bodies that were dumped in a huge pit and covered with pig bone probably as an act of sacrilege,[9] which is presumed to be the result of Assyrian's ravage. Whether Sargon's claim is exaggerated or not is difficult to determine.[10] In any case, Sargon's inscription speaks of the annexation and destruction of some portions of Judah's land and alienation of some population of Judah from their homeland. Moreover, according to the biblical record, the Syro-Ephraimite coalition killed 120,000 soldiers of Judah (2 Chro. 28:6-8), which reduced her military strength considerably. During this period, the Edomites invaded Judah and carried away captives and the Philistinestook control over Bethshemesh and the Negev of Judah, Aijalon, Gederoth, Soco, Timnah and Gimzo and settled there (2 Chro. 28:17-18). The foregoing discussion on the political situation indicates some major issues related to land that can be seen in the form of territorial expansions, annexations and alienation of people from the land. These issues are dealt with in the following exegeses.

6.2.2. Socioeconomic Context

As mentioned above, the tributes paid to Uzziah by the subdued kingdoms added much wealth to Judah's national treasury. Also, with the control of the port of Elath, which is internationally located in a strategic place, Judah started engaging in business activities that brought huge prosperity to the people. As Judah's economy boomed, Jerusalem and other strategic location were fortified as a symbol of national pride (cf. 2:15; 30:25).[11] Even the real estate development boomed as rich people started investing for large and extravagant houses while evicting the poor from their land (cf. 5:8 "woe to those who join house to house"). Such development is evidenced by the excavations at Tirzah, which show that while in the 10th century BCE houses were of uniform small size but in the eighth century there were both large expensive houses and small huddled houses indicating the contrast of rich and poor people.[12] This archeological evidence bears witness to the growth of real estate development that affects the life of the poor people, especially their land. Also, since the locally produced wine, oil and other agricultural and animal husbandry products were in high demand, there was a large scale cultivation of viniculture and orchards and rearing of livesstock. This led to the growth of massive land acquisition by the rich elites, in which the process the poor peasants were dispossessed of their cultivable land (cf. 5:8-9). Latifundialization process thus crept into the society bringing in its wake the

[9] Cf. Bright, *A History of Israel*, 4th edn., 286.

[10] Stacey, *Isaiah 1-39*, xxii; Joseph Blenkinsopp, *Isaiah 1-39* AB19 (New York, Doubleday: Anchor, 2000), 102.

[11] Cf. Milgrom, "Did Isaiah Prophecy During the Reign of Uzziah?" 164-167.

[12] Mays, *Amos*, 2-3.

practice of injustices and corruption.[13] Isaiah's oracles bear witness to such practices of injustice (3:14-15; 5:7-9).

With the change of international political equations that coincides with the rise of Assyria, Judah's prosperity soon began to decline. Foreign territories gained by Uzziah, which brought huge revenue had been lost in the course of the Syro-Ephraimite war leading to a serious loss of economy for Judah. Moreover, after the Syro-Ephraimite coalition killed 120,000 soldiers, Judah was militarily crippled. The Edomites and Philistines attacked Judah, took away some of her people and occupied portions of her land (cf. 2 Chro. 28:6-8). To protect his land and throne from such political fiasco, king Ahaz of Judah appealed for Assyria's help (cf. 2 Kgs 16:7-9, 17) by paying huge tribute to Tiglath-Pilesar even at the cost of emptying the temple treasury (2 Kgs 18:13-16). This affected Judah's economy severely.

The above discussion points out to us that the growth and decline of the socioeconomic condition of Judah depended much on the political situation of the time. When the political setting was conducive, the territories of Judah were extended and the land enjoyed prosperity. However, with the change of political guards in the international arena, the land of Judah as a political nation remained vulnerable affecting the socioeconomic condition of the people severely as discussed above. Such socioeconomic condition which seems to be a by product of the political situation is again seen to be the rooted in Judah's religious condition. This is discussed in the following section.

6.2.3. Religious Context

The initial political success and socioeconomic prosperity during the middle half of the eighth century are linked with the piety of the nation. Uzziah sought the Lord and he was blessed with success and prosperity (cf. 2 Chro. 26:1-15).[14] Uzziah, however, did not remove the high places where people probably worshipped other gods throughout the nations (2 Kgs 15:4) as indicated by the indictment against the prevailing idols and bowing down "to the work of their hands" (Isa. 2:8, 20) and rejecting the teachings of Yahweh (5:24).[15] The religious condition deteriorated dramatically during Ahaz's reign. He encouraged the worship of Baal by making a molten image, sacrificed his son and followed abominable practices (2 Chro. 28:1-4). In appealing to Tiglath-Pilesar, Ahaz not only signed away his political freedom but also religious liberty. Though there is no precise reference that the Assyrians compelled Judah to follow her gods, scholars argue that it was the policy

---

[13] For further discussion see, D. N. Premnath, "Latifundialization and Isaiah 5:8-10", 49-60.

[14] Gary V. Smith, *An Introduction to the Hebrew Prophets: The Prophets as Preachers* (Nashville, Tennessee: Broadman and Holman, 1994), 118.

[15] Smith, *Isaiah 1-39*, 27.

of Assyrian to force the vassal states to worship Assyrian's gods.[16] This probably explains Ahaz's innovation in the Jerusalem temple (2 Kgs 16:18-20). After he went to meet Tiglath-Pilesar, Ahaz paid homage to the Assyrian gods at the bronze altar, the replica of which he sent and installed in Jerusalem's temple. The worship of other gods began to flourish in Jerusalem with idols and molten images in every corner (Isa. 2:6-8, 20; 8:19).

With such syncretistic tendency mentioned above, Yahwistic religion that demands exclusive worship of Yahweh, social and moral obligations and the practice of justice and righteousness in the society had been largely neglected. Corruption and oppression, which became the order of the day (1:4, 17, 3:14-15; 5:7-9) are linked with religious apostasy (1:3, 4) for which reason Isaiah announced the divine judgment that would destroy both the people and the land (1:7, 20, 24; 3:14-16). The foregoing discussion thus points out to us that the severance of the tripartite relationship between Yahweh, Israel/Judah and land during Isaiah's time is closely linked with apostasy from Yahweh, which leads to the judgment of God to destroy both the people and the land. This issue is discussed in the following exegeses.

6.3. Authorship Debate

Scholarly debate on Isaiah's authorship continues without any consensus.[17] We do not intent to discuss the authorship problem here in detail but only to highlight the issue in order to state the reason of selecting chs 1-39 in our selection of the texts for exegesis. Until the late eighteenth century, authorship of the entire book of Isaiah was largely attributed to the eighth century Judaean prophet (Isaiah). Modern scholars like Harrison, Motyer, Allis and others hold to this view.[18] However, with the publication of Bernhard Duhm's epoch making work on Isaiah,[19] most affirm that the book has three distinct divisions belonging to three major historical periods: chs 1-39 as Proto-Isaiah (pre-exilic), chs 40-55

[16] Cf. M. Cogan, *Imperialism and Religion: Assyria, Judah and Israel in the Eighth and Seventh Centuries BCE* (Missoula, Mont.: Scholars, 1973); J. McKay, *Religion in Judah Under the Assyrian* (London: SCM, 1973); Bright, *History of Israel*, 276.

[17] For the discussion on the problem of authorship see, H.G.M. Williamson, *The Book Called Isaiah: Deutero Isaiah's Role in Composition and Reduction* (Oxford: Clarendon, 1994), 1-29; Blenkinsopp, *A History of Prophecy in Israel*, 98ff; Christopher R. Seitz, *Zion's Final Destiny: The Development of the Book of Isaiah a Reassessment of Isaiah 36-39* (Minneapolis: Fortress Press, 1991), 1-35.

[18] R.K. Harrison, *Introduction to the Old Testament* (London, 1954), 770-771; Motyer, *The Prophecy of Isaiah*, 25-27; O.T. Allis, *The Unity of Isaiah* (Cambridge: Tyndale Press, 1951). See also the defense of unity in Oswalt's introduction.

[19] Bernhard Duhm, *Das Buch Jesaia* (HKAT 3.1; Gottingen: Vandenhoeck & Ruprechet, 1892).

as Deutro-Isaiah (exilic) and chs 56-66 as Trito-Isaiah (post-exilic).[20] Following the historical critical analysis of the book, we consider chs 1-39 as belonging to Proto-Isaiah, which comes from the Isaiah of Jerusalem during the later half of the eighth century. Since the present research deals with the issue of land in the eighth century BCE, we limit our investigation to chs 1-39.

However, even within the corpus of chs 1-39, scholars believe that there is an aggregate of different compilations with different editorial history before incorporating it into the book.[21] Certain sections, namely, chs 13-23 "oracles against the nations" and chs 24-27 "apocalyptic section" are not considered as belonging to Isaiah of Jerusalem.[22] This study does not consider those sections that are not considered to be authentic Isaiah. In short, the following exegetical texts are selected from chs 1-39 but even within this corpus chs 13-27 are not selected for our purpose as the authorship of this section is still debated. Only relevant texts from chs 1-12 and 28-39 considered to be from Isaiah himself are dealt with in the following section.

6.4. Covenant and Remnant Traditions (Isaiah 1:4-9)

The term covenant does not appear here but the description of the desolation of land and cities with fire (v.7) indicates a close link between Isaiah's oracle (vv.4-9) and the tradition of covenant curse formula (Lev.26; Deut.28-29). Despite enemies' destruction (v.7), some survivors continued to live in the land, which is attributed to Yahweh's kind act (v.9) indicating that the remnant tradition is employed in vv.8-9. Judah forsakes Yahweh (v.4), which alienates her from Yahweh and also from the land. This is expressed in terms of the destruction of the land and cities with fire as a form of covenant curse punishment. Yet the remnant remained in the land because of Yahweh's intervention. The break of tripartite relationship and sustenance of it are expressed by employing the covenant curse tradition and the remnant motif in 1:4-9.

6.4.1. Translation on Isaiah 1:4-9

4 Woe[a] sinful[b] nation[c], a people[c] laden with iniquity[b], offspring[c] of evildoers, sons[c] who deal corruptly! They have forsaken[d] Yahweh, they have despised[d] the Holy One of Israel, they are utterly estranged.

5 Why[a] will you still be smitten, that you continue to rebel? The whole head is sick, and the whole heart faint.

[20] Duhm cited in Williamson, *The Book Called Isaiah*, 3; H. Fohrer, *Intoduction to the Old Testament*, trans. by David E. Green (Nashville; Abingdon Press, 1965), 349ff. S.R. Driver, *An Introduction to the Literature of the Old Testament* (Edinburgh: T&T Clark, 1913), 237.

[21] Blenkinsopp, *A History of Prophecy in Israel*, 98.

[22] Hans Wildberger, *Isaiah 13-27*, trans. by Thomas H. Trapp (Minneapolis, Fortress Press, 1997), 1-2.

6 From the sole of the foot even to the head, there is no soundness in it, but bruises and sores and bleeding wounds; they are not pressed out, or bound up, or softened with oil.

7 Your land lies desolate, your cities are burned with fire; in your very presence aliens devour[a] your arable land; it is desolate as overthrown[a] by aliens.

8 And the daughter of Zion is left like a booth in a vineyard, like a lodge in a cucumber field, like a besieged city.

9 If Yahweh of hosts had not left us a few survivors, we should have been like Sodom, and become like Gomorrah.

6.4.2. Text Critical Comments on Isaiah 1:4-9

V.4a: For the discussion on the term הוי "woe", see the TCC on Mi. 2:1. Despite scholarly impasse on the origin of הוי, we have noted that the eighth century prophets mostly employ הוי to announce the punishment against the guilty for wrong actions (cf. Am. 5:18-20; 3:11). As in other occurrences, הוי is here followed by the participle "sinful" (חטא) indicating that the action is continual. The accused nation (גוי) to whom the doom is announced is identified as "sons who deals corruptly", "forsake Yahweh", "despised the Holy One of Israel" and "estranged" from Yahweh. Isaiah's הוי is thus directed against those transgressors (see the comments on v.4b) to describe a lamentable situation in store for them.

V.4b: חטא "sinful" basically means "to miss the mark, to go astray or to fall short."[23] Otto Kaiser states that חטא, when applied to human conduct, refers to "deviation from an ideal order which really requires another way of life (cf. Prov. 9:12)" and, when applied to the religion, it refers to "deviation… against the form of conduct expected and required by Yahweh."[24] In a similar vein Watts explains that חטא more precisely refers to one who has missed the required norm of law both in the society as well as in relation to God,[25] while עון "iniquity" refers to being "crooked"[26] or "a change of movement, in a sense of to 'diverge, run astray, deviate, bend.'"[27] Together the word pair "חטא" and "עון" explains Israel's failed relationship with Yahweh due to her perpetual act of deviation (cf. the participial term) and thereby missed the mark and norm that Yahweh set in his law for her. Such deviation expressed by "חטא" and "עון" is considered as "rebellion" (פשע) in v.2.

V.4c: Poetic parallels that state Israel as גוי "nation", then as עם "large-scale kinship group", then as זרע familial unit and finally as בנים "sons" of Yahweh describe Judah from general to specific descriptions.[28] Such semantic development

[23] cf. Judg.20:16. John D. Watts, *Isaiah 1-33* WBC 24 (Waco, Texas: Words, 1985), 18.

[24] Kaiser, *Isaiah 1-12*, 2nd edn., 19.

[25] Watts, *Isaiah 1-33,* 18.

[26] Watts, *Isaiah 1-33*, 18.

[27] Kaiser, *Isaiah 1-12*, 19.

[28] Blenkinsopp, *Isaiah 1-39*, 182.

on the one hand shows an increasingly intimate relationship of Yahweh with his people and suggests on the other hand that "both the nation corporately and the individuals who comprise it are alike guilty."[29] As the descriptive terms of Judah moves from general to specific, the predicates are also progressively heightened beginning from sin to depravity (estranged).[30] Further discussion on these terms is dealt with in the following section on Tradition and Theological Comments.

V.4d: √עזב "to forsake" appears about twenty- five times in Isaiah to describe the cities and countryside that are abandoned as well as to describe the breach of the covenant by turning away from Yahweh.[31] In Deuteronomic writings, "forsake" appears in parallel to "break my covenant" (Deut. 31:16) and in the light of v.28 where Zion is indicted of "forsaking Yahweh", we can assume that עזבו in v.4 conveys Israel's abandoning of Yahweh for other gods. √נאץ "to despise" is also a covenant term, which conveys a sense of thinking lightly of Yahweh's power and distrusting his ability to fulfill his promise and threat or ignoring the covenant.[32] The piel form of נאץ here indicates that Judah has willfully turned away from God. Both עזבו "they forsake" and נאצו "they despise" speak of Israel's breaking of the covenant and willful turning away from Yahweh to other gods,[33] which in Deuteronomic and prophetic writings serve as the basis of Yahweh's abandonment of his covenant obligation to Israel (Deut. 31:19; Jer.14:21). Williamson rejects such covenant based interpretation by arguing that there is nothing inherently 'covenantal' about either verb since there is no specific allusion to covenant in the passage.[34] However, we have argued in detail in the following Tradition and Theological Comments but it would suffice to say that the picture of Yahweh/ Israel relationship expressed through parent/child imagery as here is rooted in the covenant tradition. We consider that the indictment of forsaking and despising Yahweh thus refers to the violation of the covenant relationship.

V.5a-a: על מה is usually interpreted as "upon what ground?" or "wherefore?", which can be simply rendered as "why?"[35] על מה "why" appears here to reinforce a rhetorical question "why will you be smitten?", which evokes the imagery of a rebellious slave flogged by the master.[36]

---

[29] H.G.M. Williamson, *Isaiah 1-5*, ICC (London: T&T Clark, 2006), 41.

[30] Stacey, *Isaiah 1-39*, 3.

[31] Watts, *Isaiah 1-33*, 18.

[32] Cf. Num. 5:24; 12:5; 14:11,23; 16:30; Pss. 10:3,13; 74:10,18. Watts, *Isaiah 1-33*, 19; George Buchanan Gray, *A Critical and Exegetical Commentary on the Book of Isaiah 1-24*, ICC, vol.1 (Edinburgh: T&T Clark, 1980), 11.

[33] Cf. Judg. 2:12; 10:6,10,13; 1 Sam. 8:8; 12:10. Cf. Watts, *Isaiah 1-33*, 19.

[34] Williamson, *Isaiah 1-5*, 43.

[35] Williamson, *Isaiah 1-5*, 47.

[36] Brevard S. Childs, *Isaiah*, OTL (Louisville, Kentucky: Westminister John Knox Press, 2001), 18; Kaiser, *Isaiah 1-12*, 19.

V.7b: זרים אכלים "your enemy devouring" your land (אדמה), literally "your enemy eating your land" refers to an enemy living on the produce of the invaded or conquered land.[37]

V.7b: ושממה "devastation" which speaks of the destruction of land appears similar to Lev. 26:31-33 where the destruction of land as territory of political nation, as place of habitation and cultivation were envisaged as a consequence of covenant violation. As such, scholars see the description of Jerusalem's destruction here as an outworking of the covenant curses in the law.[38] While the term כמהפכת "overthrow" appears elsewhere to describe the destruction of Sodom and Gomorrah (cf. Deut. 29:22). Isaiah had probably had a similar catastrophe in mind.

6.4.3. Form Critical Comments on Isaiah 1:4-9

Despite some minor differences, most scholars consider vv.4-9 as unit.[39] The initial "woe" in v.4 indicates the beginning of a new unit and the fact that it ends with v.9 is indicated by the new opening unit of introductory call to "hear" in v.10. The inconsistent use of pronouns, such as, third person plural "they" (v.4), second masculine plural "you" (vv.5-8) and first person plural "we" (v.9) raise the issue of whether vv.4-9 is essentially a unit. However, throughout vv.4-9 the prophet addresses the people and moreover, citing Roberts and Hillers, Sweeney states that the vocative character of the woe oracles and the use of first person plural are rhetorical devices by which the prophet identifies himself with the suffering people.[40] Alongside the problematic use of pronouns, Kaiser also challenges the authenticity of v.9, which he considers to be a redactional work because of its change in form and shift in its theme from the preceding vv.4-8.[41] However, the remnant motif in v.9 appears more germane in the present unit, which conveys that "the people would have become like Sodom and Gomorrah had YHWH not allowed a remnant to survive (v.9)."[42] In other words, the inconsistent use of pronouns (vv.4-9) and the remnant motif (v.9) do not necessarily negate the unity of the passage. We consider vv.4-9 to be a self-contained unit.

In this present unit, we see a form of woe speech (v.4), which accuses Judah of wrongdoing and a form of rhetorical speech describes the state of the people and the land. V.4 contains the "woe oracle" to exclaim and mourn the suffering of

---

[37] cf. Gen.3:7; Jer.8:16. Gray, *The Book of Isaiah 1-27*, 13.

[38] Speir, "Zu drei Jesajastellen", 310-311; van Peuursen, "Guarded", 103; Cohen, "Philological Reevaluation", 46-47. Cited in Williamson, *Isaiah 1-5*, 50.

[39] Westermann, *Basic Forms of Prophetic Speech*, 190-194; R.J. Clifford, "The Use of HOY in the Prophets" *CBQ* 28 (1966) 485-466; E. Gerstenberger, "The Woe Oracles of the Prophets" *JBL* 81 (1962) 249-263.

[40] Sweeney, *Isaiah 1-39*, 75.

[41] Kaiser, *Isaiah* 1-12, 18.

[42] Sweeney, *Isaiah* 1-39, 76.

the people who are characterized as "sinful nation", "people laden with iniquity", "offspring of evildoers" and "sons who deal corruptly". By employing the third person plural "they" the people are indicted of forsaking, despising and being estranged from Yahweh. This is followed by a rhetorical question "why will you be smitten?" (v.5a) in which Isaiah employs the second person plural "you" to point to the state of the people and to indicate that the misery they suffer is the result of their misdeeds (vv.5-6). Vv.7-8 portrays the state of the land by portraying enemies' devastation of the land while v.9 describes the aftermath of Sennacherib's invasion, which renders Judah as "remnant" of the land. The unit can be outlined as follows:

Woe Speech	(v.4)
Woe Address	(v.4a)
Accusation	(v.4b)
Rhetorical Speech	(vv.5-9)
The state of people's suffering	(vv.5-6)
The state of the land (destroyed and occupied)	(vv.7-8)
The remnant people	(v.9)

Consensus eludes scholars concerning the historical setting of the present unit. Various historical events have been proposed to connect this passage. Based on 2 Kgs 16:5, which mentions the attack of Rezin (Syria) and Pekah (Israel) against Judah, some scholars consider the Syro-Ephraimite invasion (734 BCE) to be the event of destruction described in this passage. Stacey, however, considers this view as improbable since northern Israel would not be considered as "strangers" (v.7) and that sacking, plundering and destruction of the land of Judah would not have served the Syro-Ephriamite purpose to win Judah as their allies.[43] On the other hand, Kaiser proposed that the destruction of land mentioned in vv.7-8 is connected with the Babylonian siege of Jerusalem in 597-587 BCE.[44] Sweeney, however, considers the Babylonian siege as untenable as the "remnant" imagery in v.9 is appropriate to the context of 701 BCE when Sennacherib claimed to have destroyed forty-six Judean cities and carried off 200,000 Judahites, which certainly renders Jerusalem as a remnants.[45] Similarly, Leclerc also contends that the image of hut and lodge in the vineyard and cucumber field (v.8) is not one of destruction but of survival after the siege. This image, Leclerc argues, is a poignant image of Jerusalem during Hezekiah's time in which Jerusalem was left alone in the land after forty six strong cities and various villages of Judah were plundered

[43] Stacey, *Isaiah 1-39,* 3.

[44] Kaiser, *Isaiah 1-12,* 21

[45] Sweeney, *Isaiah 1-39,* 77.

and destroyed by Sennacherib in 701 BCE.[46] We consider that the passage here fits well with the description of Sennacherib's siege during Hezekiah's reign in 701 BCE.[47]

6.4.4. Tradition and Theological Comments in the Light of Tripartite Relationship

As stated above, the term covenant does not appear in 1:4-9. However, we have argued especially in the TCC on v.4d that the terms such as, √עזב "to forsake", which implies Judah's abandoning of Yahweh for other gods is understood as a violation of the covenant of Sinai Decalogue while נאצו "despised" conveys a sense of undermining and ignoring Yahweh's power and ability to fulfill his covenant promise and threat. Both "forsake" and "despise" speak of Judah's breaking of the covenant by willfully turning away from Yahweh. Moreover, the term "sons" addressed to Judah in v. 4 is rooted in the Yahweh/Israel (Judah) covenant relationship. We consider that the woe speech, indictment and description of destruction of both the people and land are rooted in the covenant curse tradition.

The image of survivors of destruction in vv.8-9 employs the language of the remnant tradition. Hans Wilberger has demonstrated that the idea of remnant employed here had a long history before the time of Isaiah (cf. Josh. 8:22; 10:28-40; 11:8; 2 Kgs 10:11).[48] But Isaiah employs the remnant terminology (הותיר) especially in v.9 to emphasize that there will be escapees though only of small number who will pass through the judgment of destruction because of Yahweh's intervention (for further discussion, see the following exegesis).

Yahweh directly addresses the people by employing the "woe" exclamation to show the depth of sin (v.4). As mentioned in the TCC on v.4a, the woe speech announces a lamentable punishment against the guilty for wrongdoings. The guilty party is identified by employing four nouns: "nation", "people", "offspring" and "sons" (v.4), which refer to the people of Judah as indicated by the phrase "daughters of Zion" (v.8). The four aforementioned nouns show accused Judah's privileged position before Yahweh and how it has contravened such position. In the covenant tradition, the people of Judah (Israel) are called to be a unique and holy nation (Ex. 19:5-6)[49] but now they have become a habitually sinful nation

[46] Thomas Leclerc, *Yahweh is Exalted in Justice: Solidarity and Conflict in Isaiah* (Minneapolis: Fortress, 2001), 185.

[47] Most scholars consider Sennacherib's attack on Jerusalem in 701 BCE to be the appropriate date of this passage. Cf. Gray, *The Book of Isaiah 1-27*, 12; Leclerc, *Yahweh is Exalted in Justice,* 185; Sweeney, *Isaiah 1-39*, 77; A.S. Herbert, *The Book of the Prophet Isaiah Chapters 1-39* (Cambridge: Cambridge University, 1973), 25.

[48] Hans Wildberger, *Isaiah 1-12: A Commentary*, trans. by Thomas H. Trapp (Minneapolis: Fortress Press, 1991), 28-29.

[49] See also the discussion on The Sinai Event and Covenant Making in Chapter Two.

(גוי חטא). The people of Judah who are called "my [Yahweh's] people" (Ex. 6:7-8) in the covenant tradition have now become a people "laden with iniquity" (v.4). Also the terms "offspring" (זרע), which is used to describe Abraham's descendants and "sons" (בנים), which expresses Judah's relation to Yahweh in terms of father-son relationship convey a special position of the people of Judah with Yahweh within the covenant tradition.

However, Judah's privileged position through her relationship with Yahweh was marred as indicated by the four descriptions: "sinful,"[50] "loaded with iniquity", "evildoers" and "deals corruptly" (v.4). These generic descriptions do not specify any sinful act of Judah;[51] however, the indictment of forsaking, despising and being estranged from Yahweh[52] (v.4) indicate that Isaiah is referring to Judah's alienation from the covenant relationship with Yahweh as a sinful act. As stated in the TCC on v.4d √עזב "to forsake" and √נאץ "to despise" are covenant terms that describe Judah's willful breach of the covenant by turning away from Yahweh to other gods, which is further enunciated by the term √נזר "to estrange", meaning alienated from Yahweh. As such, the indictment of forsaking, despising and estrangement from Yahweh in v.4 refers to Judah's violation of the covenant and breaking of her relationship with Yahweh. This appears to be the reason for Judah's present suffering and predicaments in vv.5-9.

The above woe speech is followed by the rhetorical question "why will you be smitten?" (v.5a) in which the second person plural "you" is employed to point out that the misery that Judah suffers is the result of her misdeeds (vv.5-6). The woe speech that laments the pitiful situation of Judah is described in two ways. First, vv.5-6 state the present condition of Judah's physical suffering by employing the image of an injured rebellious slave who has been beaten up by the master inflicting wounds, bruises and stripes (v.6), which causes sickness all over the body (from sole to head, cf. v.6).[53] Second, vv.7-8 state the condition of the land that is destroyed and occupied by aliens. The general consensus among scholars is that the description of the devastated and devoured land, the besieged and burned cities with fire and the presence of aliens (enemies) are the account of military invasion (vv.7-8).[54] Of particular significance here with regard to the hostile military invasion are the terms ארצכם שממה... שרפות אש... אכלים (earth devastated... burned with fire... devoured) in v.7, which, as mentioned in the

[50] Joseph A. Alexander, *The Prophet Isaiah: A Commentary* (Grand Rapids, Michigan: Zondervan, 1978), 82.

[51] Isaiah's list of sinful act in ch.1 includes oppressive treatment of a socially vulnerable widows and orphans (vv.17, 21-23); theft (v.21); murder (v.21); perversion of the course of justice by taking bribe (v.23).

[52] Alec Motyer, *Isaiah*, TOTC (Leicester, England: IVP, 1999), 41-42.

[53] Childs, *Isaiah*, 18.

[54] Blenkinsopp, *Isaiah 1-39*, 183; Watts, *Isaiah 1-33*, 20; Sweeney, *Isaiah 1-39*, 77; Leclerc, *Yahweh is Exalted in Justice*, 30.

TCC on v.7a, appears similar to the warning of covenant curse envisaged in Lev. 26:31-33 in the event of Israel's apostasy from the covenant God. According to Peter Machinist, the image of the devastation of land, the cities burned with fire and the presence of enemies (v.7) appear widely both in the Bible and in the Assyrian annals to describe the destruction of warfare.[55] As such, the image of ruined land and cities by the enemies described in v.7 is the result of the hostile military warfare and as argued in the FCC, such description of military invasion is appropriate to Sennacherib's invasion of Judah during Hezekiah's reign (701 BCE) in which forty-six Judean cities were destroyed and 200,000 Judahites were carried off to Assyria.

Pertinent to our discussion in v.7 are the terms ארצכם "your land", which refers to the territory of Judah as political nation; עריכם "your cities" refers to the place of habitation including towns and villages which people inhabit as their living space while אדמתכם literally "your ground" refers to an arable land where vineyard and cucumber are cultivated (v.8).[56] These terms indicate that the land of Judah as political nation is not only overthrown but even their land as living space is destroyed by fire and their arable land as cultivable portion is devastated by the enemy who are now living on the produce of their land (cf. TCC on v.7a). However, such massive destruction carried out by Assyria is neither a total devastation of Judah's land nor a complete annihilation of her population. This is stated in v.8 where the "daughter of Zion,"[57] which refers to Jerusalem, still remains with a few survivors. Those "remnants" (v.9) who survived the judgment of Yahweh exist because Yahweh spared (הותיר "left") them. Isaiah concludes his oracle with the remnant tradition, which does not emphasize the penitent and purified survivors as developed in the late exilic period. However Isaiah's use of the remnant tradition here shows that complete alienation of people from the land and total extinction of the population as in the case of Sodom and Gomorrah has not happened because of Yahweh's intervention. Isaiah thus emphasizes that Yahweh will continue to remain faithful toward his people for he will not completely abandon or destroy the people and land.

The foregoing discussion has pointed out that the land of Judah as political nation including the cities as place of habitation and arable land as cultivable portion has been devastated by the Assyrians (v.7) Such destruction appears to be the outworking of Yahweh's punishment as envisaged in the covenant curse tradition for the violation of the covenant. Forsaking, despising and being estranged from Yahweh are considered as sin, iniquity and evil, which alienate Judah from Yahweh (v.4). Such willful alienation from Yahweh alienates Judah from the land and its blessing. However, despite enemies' destruction, remnants

---

[55] Peter Machinist, "Assyria and Its Images in the First Isaiah", *JAOS* 103 (1983) 724. no. 25.

[56] See also, Alexander, *The Prophet Isaiah*, 84.

[57] "Cities with their inhabitants are poetically regarded as a woman". Gray, *Isaiah 1-27*, 13.

continued to exist in the land because of Yahweh's kind act (v.9). The break of tripartite relationship is thus explained in terms of covenant curse tradition while sustenance of such relationship is also enunciated by employing the remnant tradition in 1:4-9.

6.5. Torah Tradition (Is. 2:5-9)

The phrase "come let us walk in the light of Yahweh" (v.5) refers to "the teaching of Yahweh" as embodied in the Torah. The indictment against divination and accumulation of horses, silver, gold and chariots (vv.6-8) reiterates the prohibition of the Torah. This indicates that the present oracle (vv.5-9) is based on the Torah tradition. Deviation from the teaching of Torah leads to the practice of idolatry in the land for which the divine punishment of humiliation comes upon the people (v.9). The tripartite relationship is explained in terms of the Torah tradition in which the absence of the Torah ideals is explained by the presence of paganism in the land, which brings humiliation (defeat and loss of land) upon the people (v.9).

6.5.1. Translation on Is. 2:5-9

5 O house of Jacob[a], come, let us walk in the [b]light of the Yahweh[b]!

6 For[a] you have forsaken[b] your people, O house of Jacob. Indeed they are full of diviners[c] from the east and cloud raisers[d] like the Philistines, and they clasp hands[e] with foreigners.

7 Their land is filled with silver and gold, and there is no end to their treasures; their land is filled with horses[a], and there is no end to their chariots[a].

8 Their land is filled with idols; they bow down to the work of their hands, to what their own fingers have made.

9 And so people are humbled, and everyone is brought low-do not forgive them!

6.5.2. Text Critical Comments on Is. 2:5-9

V.5a. Most scholars consider בית יעקב "house of Jacob" to be the work of a redactor(s) that is inserted here to connect with the preceding and the following verses. T.K Cheyne thinks that the "house of Jacob" refers to both houses of Israel and Judah.[58] Citing Amos 3:13; 9:8c; 4:8; 7:2, 5, 7, Davidson argues that prior to 721 BCE, "house of Jacob" or "Jacob" refers to only to the Northern Kingdom.[59]

V.5b-b: "Light of Yahweh" is understood as the instruction of Torah especially in the Psalms. Pss 18:29 states that Yahweh gives light (אור), Yahweh's Torah gives light (Pss 19:9). Pss 119:105 exalts Torah as the light of Yahweh that brightens the path. The verb "walk" used in this connection, as Brueggemann

[58] R. Davidson, "The Interpretation of Isaiah II 6ff.," *VT* 16 (1966) 1.

[59] Davidson, "The Interpretation of Isaiah II 6ff.," 3.

states, bespeaks Torah obedience.[60] See the discussion below on the tradition and theological comments.

V.6a: Instead of rendering כי as assertive, "surely" it is translated here as connecting particle "for", which connects v.5 with v.6 indicating that the unit begins with v.5.

v.6b: נטשתה from √נטש to leave or forsake. Oswalt suggests that the verb "is not used in an absolute sense, but refers to their present condition."[61]

V.6c: BHS proposes מקסם "divination" or קוסמים "diviners/divinations" while Targum reads קוסמים מקדם "diviners from the east." As most scholars agree, מקסם is possibly dropped out probably because מקסם is similar with מקדם "from the east."[62] Delitzsch states that the term מקדם refers to "the source from which a person draws and fills himself, Jer. Li. 34, Ezek xxxii. 6." Thus, he interprets the term as referring to "full of eastern manners and customs, more especially of idolatrous practices."[63]

V.6d: ועננים is translated as "soothsayers" or "cloud raisers." The root word seems to be ענן "cloud" possibly suggesting some magical form of causing the rain. For further discussion, refer to the exegetical comments below.

V.6e: ישפיקו from √שפק, which is interpreted as "to suffice or abound"[64] or to "clap or slap"[65] In other occurrences in the OT שפק is used for a slap on the thigh as a sign of shame or sorrow[66] and for clapping the hands in anger or as mockery.[67] Rogers argues that the term refers to the clapping of hands during the time of coronation. His argument is built on the supposition that the term שפק can be synonymously interpreted in the light of other related cognates used for clapping, such as, נכה, מחא, תקע (cf. 2 Kgs 11:12; Pss. 47:2-3; 98:6,8). Though these terms appear in the context of coronation/enthronement, it remains doubtful whether these terms can be interpreted as cognates of שפק. This cryptic term has generated an unending debate among the scholars. Most likely the term refers to clasping of hands, suggesting the making of political alliances and trade relations with foreign nations. The danger of such alliances involves cultural and religious assimilations. For further discussion, refer to the exegetical comments below.

V.7a: The eighth century prophets consider "horses" and "chariots" as symbols of pride and power (cf. Is. 30:15; 31:1; 43:17; Mi. 5:9). Blenkinsopp

---

[60] Walter Brueggemann, *Isaiah 1-39* (Louisville, Kentucky: Westminster John Knox Press, 1998), 26.

[61] John Oswalt, *The Book of Isaiah Chapters 1-39*, NICOT (Grand rapids, Michigan: William B. Eerdmans Publishing Company, 1986), 119.

[62] Oswalt, *Isaiah 1-39*, 122.

[63] Delitzsch, *Isaiah*, 118.

[64] Jeffrey S. Rogers, "An Allusion to Corronation in Isaiah 2:6, " *CBQ* 51 (1989) 232.

[65] Rogers, "An Allusion to Coronation in Isaiah 2:6", 232-233.

[66] Jer 31:19; Ezek 21:17 (Eng. 21:12).

[67] Num 24:10; Job 27:23; Lam 2:15.

states that being very expensive import items in Israel, a "horse" cost seventy times as much as a sheep and a "chariot' four times as much as a horse.[68] The reference to numerous horses and chariots in the land along with the mention of "silver", "gold" and "treasure" indicate a time of prosperity. Horses and chariots are essential war equipment, which are acquired through political alliances and trade with foreign nations and such treaties brings foreign cults.[69]

6.5.3. Form Critical Comments on Is. 2:5-9

Due to some inherent problem within the text, Duhm considers Isaiah 2 as the most corrupted material of the book.[70] Within vv.5-9 mostly the problem lies in the inconsistent usage of second and third persons, which are considered to be the result of editorial insertion especially v.5 and the phrase "house of Jacob" in v.6a.[71] However, even the second person form in v.6a and v.9b, which appears to be inconsistent with the third person form in vv.6-9, can be understood as the author's attempt, as Sweeney argues, to cast vv.6-9 as an accusation speech against Jacob addressed to Yahweh.[72] Apart from the suspected redactorial works, vv.6-9 is considered to have come from the prophet Isaiah.[73] Despite the scholarly impasse as to whether a subunit begins with v.5[74] or with v.6,[75] we can consider vv.5-9 as a unit of "prophetic announcement"[76] in which v.5 assumes the form of invitation and zooms in the message to the house of Jacob. This is followed by a preposition כִּי "for" in v.6a that introduces the following accusation in vv.6b-8, which leads to the application of divine judgment in v.9. Thus, vv.5-9 as it stands can be considered as a unit, which consists of invitation, indictment and petition.

According to Kaiser, the prophet addressed the "double audience," that is, "God" (vv.6a and 9b) and the "people" (v.10), which indicates that the oracle was delivered during the festal gathering in the temple of Jerusalem. He opines that during the festal occasion, the prophet intended to petition to God on behalf

---

[68] Blenkinsopp, *Isaiah 1-39*, 196.

[69] Blenkinsopp, *Isaiah 1-39*, 196.

[70] Cited in Oswalt, *The Book of Isaiah Chapters 1-39*, 120.

[71] Kaiser, *Isaiah 1-12*, 33; R. Davidson, "The Interpretation of Isaiah II 6ff.," *VT* 16 (1966) 2.

[72] Sweeney, *Isaiah 1-39*, 101.

[73] Sweeney, *Isaiah 1-39*, 103.

[74] Sweeney, *Isaiah 1-39*, 101-102.

[75] Gray, *Isaiah 1-24*, 48; Kaiser, *Isaiah 1-12*, 58; Oswalt, *Isaiah 1-39*, 119-110; Grogan, "Isaiah," in Frank E. Gaebelein (ed), *Isaiah, Jeremiah, Lamentations, Ezekiel* (Grand Rapids, Michigan: Zondervan, 1986), 37; David McKenna, *Isaiah 1-39*, The Communicator's Commentary, vol. 16a (Dallas, Texas: Word Books, 1993), 75.

[76] Cf. Sweeney, *Isaiah 1-39*, 102.

of his people,[77] however, he was so overcome by their sins that what began as a petition became a denouncement.[78] In a quite distinctive line, Jeffrey F. Rogers proposes that the historical setting surrounding the present text is the occasion of the coronation of Pekah as the king of Samaria.[79] He argues that the term שׂפק in v.6 refers to "clapping of hands associated with coronation,"[80] and concludes that there was convocation of royal officials and cultic troops from Aram and Philistia who came to attend the enthronement of Pekah.[81] However, Rogers' view on royal coronation appears unlikely as we have noted in the above TCC on v.6e that שׂפק is instead used in the context of trade and political alliances with other nations. Quite distinctively Sweeney considers that the historical situation appears to be the time of Hezekiah just before Sennacherib's invasion.[82] He argues that the term מקדם in v.6 is used as a reference to Aram in particular and to the territory east of Egypt in general by citing references in 9:11 and 11:14-15 where "east" is used in relation to Aram and to Edom (Moab) and Ammon.[83] Hezekiah not only made financial preparation to revolt against Assyria (v.6) but also pursued political alliances with Egypt, Philistia, and Phoenicia to ward off Assyria's domination. Sweeney argues that the terms used here appear entirely consistent with Isaiah's opposition to Hezekiah's political alliances with foreign nations. Since the reference to horses and chariots reflects the background of preparing for war,[84] Sweeney's position that sets the setting of the passage to ca. 715-701 BCE[85] can be sustained.

6.5.4. Tradition and Theological Comments in the Light of Tripartite Relationship

As stated in the TCC on v.5b, the invitation "come let us walk in the light of Yahweh" (v.5) and the accusation speech (vv.6-8) reiterate the prohibition of the Torah and its tradition. "The light of Yahweh" refers to the teaching of Torah in which the practice of divination[86] and the accumulation of horses, chariots, silver and gold for oneself are strongly prohibited. This is particularly stated in a later development of the divine constitution of monarchy, "When you have come into the land… [and] set over you a king… Even so, he must not acquire many horses for himself, or return the people to Egypt in order to acquire more horses…. also

[77] Kaiser compares this unit with Amos 7:1ff; Isa. 6:11; Jer.14:1-15:4. Kaiser, *Isaiah 1-12*, 33.

[78] Kaiser, *Isaiah 1-12*, 33.

[79] Jeffrey S. Rogers, "An Allusion to Coronation in Isaiah 2:6," *CBQ* 51 (1989) 234-235.

[80] Rogers, "An Allusion to Coronation in Isaiah 2:6," 234.

[81] Rogers, "An Allusion to Coronation in Isaiah 2:6," 235.

[82] Sweeney, *Isaiah 1-39*, 103.

[83] Sweeney, *Isaiah* 1-39, 103-104.

[84] R. Davidson, "The Interpretation of Isaiah II 6ff.," *VT* 16 (1966) 6.

[85] Sweeney, *Isaiah* 1-39, 104.

[86] Cf. Lev. 19:26; Deut. 18:10.

silver and gold he must not acquire in great quantity for himself" (Deut. 18:10). It is striking that the accusative language of Isaiah against his people in vv-6-9 reflects the Torah teaching. As such, we can presuppose that the invitation "to walk in the light" refers to the Torah directed way of life.

The invitation to the Torah way of life is followed by a preposition כי (v.6), which states the reason for the prophetic warning cry: "You [Yahweh] have forsaken your people." The object of נטשתה "you forsake" is עמך "your people". Why Yahweh has forsaken his people is stated by another כי which connects the indictment: "they are filled with diviners from the east" and "soothsayers" (ועננים).[87] Citing 4:5 and Gen 9:14 where the term ענן is rendered as "cloud," Delitzsch contends that עננים probably refers to "cloud gatherers" or "storm raisers."[88] Delitzsch's contention can be sustained in the context of growing agricultural economy in the eighth century. The natural answer to both the fear of drought and the desire to maximize agricultural productions lies with rain. Since bumper crops depend on timely rain, the agricultural population in their passion to maximize the profit may have been tempted to followed pagan rites of invoking rain through some magical means.

Another term of indictment is שפק, which is interpreted differently as "the conclusion of contracts,"[89] "a ritual for warding off demonic powers,"[90] and "clapping of hands associated with coronation."[91] However, as stated in the TCC on v.6e and in view of the presence of pagan practices and description of wealth and military strength (v.7), שפק could be interpreted as clasping of hands in a sense of political alliances and trade agreement with the foreign nations (cf. Hos. 12:1).[92] The procurement of military equipment, such as horses and chariots (v.7) could have been the result of such political and trade alliance.[93] Though the text is not clear about how the wealth was gained, what appears clear is that the wealth was invested for acquiring military equipment (horses and chariots) probably to strengthen the combat forces in order to revolt against the

---

[87] Young, *Isaiah* 1-18, 116; Kaiser, *Isaiah* 1-12, 31; Alexander, *The Prophecies of Isaiah*, 99.

[88] Delitzsch, *Isaiah*, 118.

[89] B. Duhm, *Das Buch Jesaia* (5th ed.; Göttingen: Vandenhœck & Ruprecht, 1968), 40. Cited in Rogers, "An Allusion to Coronation in Isaiah 2:6," 233.

[90] H. Wildberger, *Jesaja* (BKAT) 10/1 cited in Rogers, "An Allusion to Coronation in Isaiah 2:6," 233.

[91] Rogers, "An Allusion to Coronation in Isaiah 2:6," 234.

[92] Walter Brueggemann states that ""clasping of hands with foreigners" means to enter into economic agreements that erode the distinctive self-identity of Israel". Brueggemann, *Isaiah 1-39*, 28.

[93] Kaiser, *Isaiah 1-12*, 35. According to Kaiser, it fits the milieu of Jeroboam II and Uzziah (Azariah) and his successor, Jotham. "The Ammonites paid tribute to Uzziah…." (2 Chro. 26:8); "He (Jotham) fought with the king of the Ammonites… . And the Ammonites gave him that year a hundred talents of silver, and ten thousand cors of wheat and ten thousand of barley. The Ammonites paid him the same amount in the second and the third years (2 Chro. 27:5)".

Assyrians and to protect their land. In this connection ארץ "land" appears twice (v.7) and in both the cases ארץ is connected with an unending national treasure and military equipment, which were acquired to defend the land from possible foreign invasion. In this case, ארץ conveys the understanding of land in a sense of political territory of the land of Judah.

ארץ appears again in the final indictment: "their land is filled with idols" (v.8). Two observations can be noted here. First, the term appears in connection with the national apostasy indicating that ארץ is associated with the entire land of Judah in a sense of a political nation. Second, ארץ appears in connection with theological apostasy of Judah. The reference to idols in the land and bowing down before the idols indicates that Judah remained religious but their religiosity was not according to the teachings of the Torah. Such idolatry is a violation of the second commandment (Ex. 20:4-5; Deut 5:8-9). As already noted above, to maximize the crop production of their cultivable land, pagan practices particularly the magic to cause rain was erroneously followed. To defend their political land from Assyria's tyranny, political alliances were formed and military equipment (horses and chariots) was accumulated apart from Yahweh. Such national piety, prosperity and defense apart from Yahweh cannot protect the people of Judah and their land. Instead, they would be "humbled" and "brought low" (v.9), which probably refer to the defeat from the enemies and consequent exile and loss of their land to a foreign nation (cf.1:7).

The foregoing exegesis shows that Judah has forsaken to walk in the way of the Torah instruction ("in the light of Yahweh" v.5) by following the pagan agricultural rites ("cloud raisers" v.6) to cause the rain so as to make the cultivation of the land fruitful. Also to defend their land from possible Assyrian invasion, Judah made alliance with foreign nations (clasping of hands, v.8) bringing along with it national prosperity and foreign practices against the teaching of the Torah. In this context of national prosperity and apostasy, the term "land" appears indicating that ארץ is used in a sense of political nation. However, religious piety (vv.6, 8), economic prosperity (v.7) and military equipment (v.7) apart from Yahweh and teaching of the Torah is futile and cannot offer security to the nation (v.9). Deviation from the teaching of Yahweh will only bring the loss of land and exile to other nations (v.9).

6.6. Covenant Tradition (Is. 3:12-15)

The expression "my people" (vv.12, 15) and "vineyard" (v.14) are the terms rooted in the covenant tradition. The spoiling and devouring of the economic resources of the poor (vv.12, 14) are contrary to the practice of neighborliness envisaged in the covenant tradition. The tripartite relationship in vv.12-15 is thus rooted in the covenant tradition in which Yahweh is portrayed in terms of his commitment to defend poor victims (who are identified as my people) and the cultivable land that is expressed as "vineyard".

6.6.1. Translation on Is. 3:12-15

12 My people![a] children[b] are their oppressors, and usurers[c] rule over them. O my people, your leaders mislead you, and swallow up the way of your paths.

13 Yahweh rises to argue his case; he stands to judge the peoples.[a]

14 Yahweh enters into judgment with the [a]elders and princes[a] of his people: It is you who have devoured the vineyard[b]; the spoil of the poor is in your houses.

15 What do you mean by crushing my people, by grinding the face of the poor? says the Lord Yahweh of hosts.

6.6.2. Text Critical Comments on Is. 3:12-15

V.12a: The Codex Vaticanus renders a third person singular "his people". The MT's usage of first person עמי "my people" is also rendered in the First Isaiah Manuscript (Qumran). עמי, which appears twice in v.12 and once in v.15, is generally understood as a covenant term and since the term appears in the context of court trial, עמי is understood in terms of covenant violation by the people of Judah.[94]

V.12b: מעולל is a problematic term as it appears in singular number. Alexander explains that in the predicative sentence, if the subject is plural the adjective remains singular. Thus, he interprets it adjectively as "childish."[95] The Vulgate renders it as *spoliaverunt* "have despoiled." The MT's rendering "children" could be retained in view of vv.4 and 5, where a synonymous term נער "boy" is used.

V.12c: LXX, Aquila, Theodotion, and Targum read *nosim*, "creditor, distrainers," instead of נשים, "women" in MT.[96] Motyer, on the other hand, thinks that נשים refers to "royal harem," possibly referring to those "manipulative" and "demanding" wives that king Ahaz acquired. Thus, Motyer interprets the term as women who had "power behind the throne."[97] Sweeney seems to suggest that originally the term is *nosim*, which may have changed to נשים in order to associate it to מלולל "children."[98] Likewise, Stacey also thinks that נשים "women" is unlikely and proposes a slight change in pointing to read it as "usurers."[99] In the context of Isaiah's oracle against corrupt social practices (cf. 1:12; 23; 3:5), we can assume, as most scholars agree,[100] that נשים refers to "usurers" who played an exploitative role in the agrarian society of the eighth century Israel. As Stacey comments, the problem of soil erosion and climatic changes especially in the hill areas makes the

[94] Herbert, *Isaiah 1-39*, 43.

[95] Alexander, *The Prophecies of Isaiah*, 115. Young also interprets in a similar vein, "the oppressors are each one as children." Young, *Isaiah 1-18*, 155.

[96] See, Blenkinsopp, *Isaiah 1-39*, 198.

[97] Motyer, *The Prophecy of Isaiah*, 62.

[98] Blenkinsopp, *Isaiah 1-39*,198.

[99] Stacey, *Isaiah 1-39*, 25.

[100] Stacey, *Isaiah 1-39*, 25; Kaiser, *Isaiah 1-12*, 44; Gray, *Isaiah 1-27*, 62.

crop yielding unpredictable. On such eventuality, the failed farmers borrowed from the usurers, usually with a high rate of interest.[101]

V.13a: BHS reads עמים "peoples," however, the LXX renders τον λαον αυτου "his peoples". As H. D. Hummel suggests, if the final ם is an "enclitic *Mem*", which was originally attached to the following word but that is now lost, then the possible reading would be עמי-ם "my people."[102] Whether it is interpreted as "peoples" or "his peoples," it does not change the key message of the oracle.

V.14a-a: The accused people are mentioned here as "elders" and "princes". זקן refers to the officials of the old tribal order of governance in which the clan and family elders hold responsibility to dispense justice related to socioeconomic and moral disputes. שׂר "princes", on the other hand, refers to the royal officials in a new centralized form of palace government who held administrative and judicial powers.[103] Both the officials are responsible to protect and care for the people. However, instead of dispensing justice, these accused leaders became the perpetrators of injustice and exploiters of economic systems and denied justice to the "poor".

V.14b: הכרם "the vineyard" that is spoiled by the elders and princes can be understood metaphorically as referring to the people of Judah (cf. 5:1-7). However, according to the ancient covenant code, הכרם also has a literal sense in which Yahweh obligates Israel to keep the vineyard fallow in the seventh year along with the fields and olive groves so that the poor of the land and beasts of the field may eat whatever grows from there (Ex. 23:10-11. Cf. Deut. 24:19-22).[104] Since the present oracle is apparently rooted in the covenant tradition, we can assume that the vineyard imagery is employed here both metaphorically to depict the devastation of the poor and literally to state the violation of the land tillage pattern against the covenant norms.

6.6.3. Form Critical Comments on Is. 3:12-15

Some scholars consider v.12 as an independent saying of Isaiah believed to have been placed here by the redactor to connect with the preceding unit vv.1-9 (10-11).[105] Duhm, Skinner, Scott, Watts, Tucker, and others argue that v.13 begins a new subunit and ends with v.15,[106] while Kissane, Oswalt and Kaiser

---

[101] Stacey, *Isaiah 1-39*, 25.

[102] H. D. Hummel "Enclitic Mem," *JBL* 76 (1957) 100.

[103] Leclerc, *Yahweh is Exalted in Justice*, 53.

[104] Leclerc, *Yahweh is Exalted in Justice*, 53.

[105] Vv.11 and 12 is understood as later addition. Cf. Sweeney, *Isaiah 1-4 and the Post-Exilic Understanding of the Isaianic Tradition*, BZAW 171 (Berlin: de Gruyter, 1988), 177-81. Cited in Leclerc, *Yahweh is Exalted in Justice,* 51; Gary, *Isaiah 1-39*, 66).

[106] Scholars who consider vv.13-15 as separate subunit include J. Skinner, *The Book of the Prophet Isaiah* (Cambridge: Cambridge University, 1925; Scott, "Introduction and Exegesis of the

consider vv.12-15 as unit.[107] It appears clear that v.13 introduces a new setting of lawsuit speech that indicts the leaders for exploiting the people. However, v.12 cannot be delinked from vv.13-15, as the context of oppression and misrule in v.12 provides the setting for the following indictment in vv.13-15.[108] Thus, we consider that v.12 serves as a linking verse to the following court speech and indictment in vv.13-15.

The present unit belongs to the genre of judgment speech, which takes the form of lawsuit. This is made clear by the usage of terms, ריב "to contend," דין "judge," and משפט "judgment." V.12 takes up the "accusation" for the widespread economic exploitation and prevailing social chaos in the land.[109] The accusation serves as a basis for Yahweh to initiate the lawsuit against the indicted leaders in vv.13-15. The lawsuit (vv.13-15) takes the form of "an oracular report of Yahweh's court speech, including Yahweh's rhetorical questions: What do you mean by crushing my people or what do you mean by grinding the face of the poor?"[110] The unit of this judgment oracle can be outlined as follows:

General Indictment:	... children are their oppressors, and usurers rule over them... your leaders mislead you, and swallow up the way of your paths (v.12).
Name of the Accuser:	Yahweh rises to argue his case; he stands to judge the peoples... (vv.13-14).
Name of the Accused:	elders and princes of his people (v.14)
Specific Indictment:	... you have devoured the vineyard; the spoil of the poor is in your houses (v.14).
Rhetorical Question:	What do you mean by crushing my people, by grinding the face of the poor? (v.15).

According to Kaiser, the reference to "my people" suggests that the *Sitz im Leben* could be the occasion of cultic festivals where Yahweh is believed to occupy the seat of judgment.[111] He further states that the historical setting of the unit could be during the early period of the prophet's ministry. Since there is no indication of any looming Assyrian threat that comes at the later part of Isaiah's ministry in vv.12-15, we consider that the unit matches up with Isaiah's early part of ministry.

Book of Isaiah, Chapters 1-39," 190; Barry Webb, *The Message of Isaiah: On Eagles' Wings,* BST (England: IVP, 1996), 50.

[107] E.J. Kissane, *The Book of Isaiah* (Dublin: Bowne and Nalon, 1926), cited in Oswalt, *Isaiah 1-39,* 131; Kaiser, *Isaiah 1-12,* 43-44; Sweeney, *Isaiah 1-39,* 107.

[108] Motyer, *The Prophecy of Isaiah*, 61.

[109] Sweeney, *Isaiah 1-39*, 108.

[110] Sweeney, *Isaiah 1-39*, 107.

[111] Kaiser, *Isaiah 1-12*, 45.

6.6.4. Tradition and Theological Comments in the Light of Tripartite Relationship

As stated in the above preliminary remarks, vv.12-15 is rooted in the covenant tradition as indicated by the terms עמי "my people" (vv.12 and 15) and הכרם "vineyard" (v.14). By employing the term עמי, Yahweh not only identifies himself with the poor victims of injustice but also affirms that the people are in covenant relation with him. As Wildberger states, the fact that Yahweh laments for the people proves that he is intimately bound with the people.[112] Also הכרם "vineyard", as stated in the TCC on v.14b, is rooted in the ancient covenant code in which Israel is commanded to let the הכרם "vineyard" remain fallow in the seventh year for the poor of the land and beasts of the field (Ex. 23:10-11). As such, though the term covenant is not mentioned, we assume that the present oracle is rooted in the covenant tradition and that the indictment (v.12) of oppressing "the poor" and "devouring the vineyard" (v.14) can be understood as a violation of the covenant ordinance that specifies that the rulers should care for the poor, widows and orphans[113] and the land usage pattern.

The people with whom Yahweh relates with and on whose behalf he speaks and laments are identified as עמי "my people." It appears twice in v.12 indicating emphatic emphasis.[114] This is followed by an indictment against the perpetrators of exploitation who are identified as מעולל (children), probably referring to the incompetent leaders[115] and נשים referring to "usurers" (v.12) who charge a high rate of interest from poor borrowers.[116] The victims of these incompetent leaders and usurers are identified as "the poor" (v.14) with whom Yahweh shows his solidarity (my people!).

A key term that expresses the indictment is √נגש (to oppress).[117] In Ex. 3:7, the term appears in connection with the Egyptian overseers who exerted oppressive pressure of labor. In 2 Kgs 23:35 and Dan. 11:20, the term appears in the context of forcible and oppressive taxation. We assume that נגשׂיו in v.12 conveys a similar oppressive role especially in the light of the term "usurers" (v.12) who, as argued in the TCC on v.12c, lend to poor peasants with high interest rate. In the event of the peasants' failure to repay due to the surmounting interest rate, the lenders would foreclose the peasants' land in lieu of the borrowed money and thereby added to themselves houses and fields as their properties (cf. Is.5:8). However what appears significant here in terms of the tripartite relationship is that in Ex. 2:23 the oppressed victims cried out to God for intervention, but in

[112] Wildberger, *Isaiah 1-12*, 138.

[113] Pss. 71:12.cf. Is.1:17.

[114] Stacey, *Isaiah 1-39*, 25.

[115] Oswalt, *Isaiah 1-39*, 138.

[116] Stacey, *Isaiah 1-39*, 25.

[117] Qal participle masculine plural + 3rd-person singular suffix, literally "his oppressor."

Isaiah 3:12ff, there is neither a cry for divine intervention nor any complaint of injustice from the victims. If so, what compels Yahweh to take a court case against the oppressors? Following Abraham Heschel's argument that "those who know how to exploit are endowed with the skill to justify their acts, while those who are easily exploited possess no skill in pleading their own cause,"[118] Leclerc contends that the victimized poor are helpless to act for their own cause.[119] Further, citing Prov. 13:41, "The one who oppresses the poor profanes his maker," Leclerc argues that "though the poor have suffered, it is YHWH who is wronged... ."[120] If Leclerc's arguments can be taken into consideration, then it is the incapability of the poor to raise their voice and the prevailing oppression that amounts to an offense against God, which compels Yahweh, the accuser, to take a court case against the oppressors (v.13).

In this court trial, the accused oppressors and usurers are identified as "elders" (זקן) and "princes" (שׂר) of the people (v.14). As mentioned in the TCC on v.14a-a, the elders were the head of the families and tribes who had responsibility in legal decision during the early tribal amphictyony, whereas, princes were the royally appointed officials who had the administrative and judicial power. The reference to "elders" and "princes" (v.14) indicate that both the older and newer mode of leaders existed as two parallel forms of judicial functions during Isaiah's period.[121] In any case, Yahweh indicts both the officials in an emphatic and direct accusation: בערתם הכּרם, "you who have devoured the vineyard". The term בערתם refers to "burning" "gleaning" or "stripping bare by grazing," which was an unusual way of treating the vineyard.[122] As stated in the TCC on v.14b, the covenant law forbids total gleaning of harvest for the sake of the poor and the wild animals.[123] Thus the accusation of devouring the vineyard here includes the misuse of land tillage system and deprivation of the poor for the leftover of the produce of the land, which is against the covenant tradition (Ex. 23:10-11; Lev.19:9-10; Deut. 24:20-21).[124] Such practice of total gleaning and violation of land tillage system is presumably carried out by the landowners in their greed to maximize the agricultural exports for economic gain. In other words, as greediness is pushed into the society, the covenant norms of humanitarian concerns were pushed out of the social practice, which leads to exploitation and corruption in the Judahite society.

The accusation is further stated in v.14b, "the spoil of the poor is in your houses." The word spoil "גזלת" in the present context refers to the plundering or

---

[118] Abraham J. Heschel, *The Prophets* (New York: Harper and Row, 1969), 204.

[119] Leclerc, *Yahweh is Exalted in Justice*, 52.

[120] Leclerc, *Yahweh is Exalted in Justice*, 52.

[121] Leclerc, *Yahweh is Exalted in Justice*, 53.

[122] Motyer, *The Prophecy of Isaiah*, 62.

[123] Leclerc, *Yahweh is Exalted in Justice*, 53.

[124] Motyer, *The Prophecy of Isaiah*, 62.

robbing the poor.[125] Since in Lev. 5:21, 23 (Eng. 6:2, 4), גזלה is used along with √כחשׁ "to deceive" and √עשׁק "to defraud or oppress", Leclerc contends that גזלה in 3:14b can be interpreted as "acts of fraud and deceit accomplished under the guise of legal means."[126] If Leclerc's interpretation can be sustained, then the accusation, גזלה "spoil" of the poor is "in your houses" refers to the appropriation of cultivable land and agricultural products of the poor through the manipulation of the legal system. The victims of "spoil" are described as העני "poor/needy", which according to Dearman refers to "disenfranchisement and the loss of possession."[127] In such context, Dearman contends that העני does not refer to those who lack possession and property but those who lose their land and right of possession.[128] Dearman's contention can be sustained in the context of 3:12-15 as Isaiah has already accused the "usurers" in v. 12 (see the above TCC on v.12c). During the eighth century the practice of money lending with high interest rate became rampant as the problem of soil erosion and erratic rainfall especially in the hill areas frequently caused crop failures, which compelled the farmers to borrow from usurers by mortgaging the land. However, when the harvest fails again and the indebted peasants fail to repay the borrowed amount, the usurers take away the peasants' land in lieu of the borrowed money. Such practices are against the covenant stipulation and Yahweh demands to know by what right the leaders treat the people in this way (v.15).

In sum the above exegesis shows to us that Yahweh enters into the court trial for two reasons: first, because of the widespread oppression that includes surging interest rate, which finally leads to the loss of the poor peasants' land (changing the ownership of land); second, because of violating the land tillage pattern especially the vineyard, which is a violation of the covenant pattern of land use. This indicates that the understanding of land embedded in vv.12-15 is of cultivable/tillable land. Also, in this trial scene the tripartite relationship is brought to the fore by portraying Yahweh as the accuser who takes the case for the victims who are considered as Yahweh's covenanted people ("my people") and who also defends the cultivable land "vineyard" of his people. As Yahweh defends his people he also defends their land. People of Judah and their land are thus seen to belong to each other in which Yahweh is seen as the God who holds the ultimate authority to appeal to and defend both the people and the land.

6.7. Covenant Tradition (Isaiah 5:1-7)

6.7.1. Translation (Isaiah 5:1-7)

1 Let me sing for my beloved[a] my love-song[b] concerning his vineyard: My beloved[c] had a vineyard on a very fertile hill[d].

[125] Motyer, *The Prophecy of Isaiah*, 63.

[126] Leclerc, *Yahweh is Exalted in Justice*, 54.

[127] Dearman, *Property Rights*, 53.

[128] Dearman, *Property Rights*, 53.

2 He dug it and cleared it of stones, and planted it with choice vines; he built a watchtower in the midst of it, and hewed out a wine vat in it; he expected it to yield grapes, but it yielded wild grapes[a].

3 And now[a], inhabitants of Jerusalem and people of Judah, judge between me and my vineyard.

4 What more was there to do for my vineyard that I have not done in it? When I expected it to yield grapes, why did it yield wild grapes?

5 And now I will tell you what I will do to my vineyard. I will remove its hedge, and it shall be devoured; I will break down its wall, and it shall be trampled down.

6 I will make it a waste; it shall not be pruned or hoed, and it shall be overgrown with briers and thorns; I will also command the clouds that they rain no rain upon it.

7 For the vineyard of Yahweh of hosts is the house of Israel[a], and the people of Judah are his pleasant planting; he expected justice, but saw bloodshed; righteousness, but heard a cry!

6.7.2. Text Critical Comments on Isaiah 5:1-7

V.1a: Herbert rejects the interpretation of "my beloved" as referring to Yahweh by arguing that the Hebrew word for "beloved" has a close meaning with fertility myth.[129] Though Stacey agrees that Isaiah perhaps adapted the line from the secular song to suit his purpose, he cautions the danger of interpreting the term along the line of fertility cult of Baal and suggests that it is appropriate to retain the "beloved" as referring to Yahweh.[130] Since v.7 identifies Yahweh as the owner of the vineyard, the term "beloved" in v.1 who is also stated as owner can be interpreted as referring to "Yahweh".

V. 1b. Mostly the verb שיר and its related nominal forms refer to the expressions of praise or joy. G.R. Williams thus argues that שיר which is followed by preposition ל and a noun designates the one to be praised by a song (cf. Ex. 15:1; Judg. 5:3; Pss 13:6; 27:6) with the expression of joy.[131] However as stated in the following FCC, the context here is of a court setting so we consider that שיר assumes a different meaning than the praise of joy. Gale A. Yee compares שיר with the song of Moses (Deut 31:19) in which God, after foretelling Israel's transgression of the covenant, commands Moses to write "the song" (השירה), which would function as a "witness" (לעד) against the people during times of trouble. Yee concludes that both the units thematically contrast the covenantal love of Yahweh and his people's infidelity by designating שיר "song". Since the court setting is

---

[129] Herbert, *The Book of the Prophet Isaiah 1-39*, 48.

[130] Stacy, *Isaiah 1-39*, 32. See also, *Webb, The Message of Isaiah*, 55.

[131] Gray Roye Williams, "Frustrated Expectation in Isaiah v. 1-7: A Literary Interpretation," *VT* 35/4 (1985) 459.

apparent in the following v.3, we assume that the "song" here functions as witness to indict the accused of their wrongdoings.

V.1c. ידיד some scholars think the term here has sexual connotations as in Jer. 11:15.[132] Such view led some scholars to conjecture that the song is a love song. Following the Vulgate, Luther interprets it as "cousin," which Delitzsch rejects and affirms it to be his dearest one.[133] John Oswalt rightly notes that the song is more an accusation than a love ballad.[134]

V.1d. קרן, which is interpreted here as "hill," basically refers to "horn". Blenkinsopp thinks that קרן has Arabic cognate, such as, "names of the mountains like Horns of Hattin, Matterhorn,"[135] which he thinks signifies a prominent hill top that remains like a horn.[136] In view of v.7 where "the house of Israel" is identified as Yahweh's vineyard, the phrase "a vineyard on a fertile hill" suggests Yahweh placing his people in a prosperous land of Canaan in contrast to a dry desert land.

V. 2a. באשים from √באשׁ "to stink," "be odious," as with manna in Ex. 16:24, which is rendered here as "sour grapes" is interpreted differently among the scholars. R.F. Youngblood interpreted the root meaning of באשים as "shameful thing,"[137] while Motyer interpreted it as "stinking fruit."[138] The LXX translates "thorn-plants, thistles" and Vulgate as *labruscas* "wild vines". In any case, באשים serves to explain the unexpected fruits that do not measure up to the standard of invested labor.

V.3a: ועתה "and now" as in v.5 introduces a new and unexpected shift of the speakers. Instead of the singer (vv.1-2) who now fades to the background, the owner of the vineyard himself begins to speak in a first person.

V.7a: Yee asserts that בית ישראל "house of Israel" specifically refers to the Northern Kingdom, Israel. She argues that prior to Isaiah, the prophets Hosea and Amos refer to the north as בית ישראל[139] and that the description בית ישראל in Is. 5:1-7 as the vineyard of the Lord of Host was a customary description that represents the people of the north in the corpus of the eighth century prophets.[140] Yee thus concludes that the usage of vine imagery and the description of Northern

---

[132] Oswalt, *The Book of Isaiah Chapters 1-39*, 152; Gray Roye Williams, "Frustrated Expectations in Isaiah v.1-7," 459.

[133] Delitzsch, *Isaiah*, 160.

[134] Oswalt, *The Book of Isaiah Chapters 1-39*, 152.

[135] Blenkinsopp, *Isaiah 1-39*, 206.

[136] Blenkinsopp, *Isaiah 1-39*, 206.

[137] Ronald F. Youngblood, *The Book of Isaiah: An Introductory Commentary*, 2nd ed. (Grand Rapids, Michigan: Baker, 1993), 38.

[138] Motyer, *The Prophecy of Isaiah*, 68.

[139] Cf. Hos. 1:4, 6; 5:1; 6:10; 12:1; Amos 5:1, 3, 4, 25; 6:1, 14; 7:10; 9:9.

[140] In Hosea, Israel is described as "a luxuriant vine that yields its fruit" (10:1); "Like grapes in the wilderness, I found Israel" (9:10); "They (Israel) shall blossom as the vine" (14:8).

Kingdom as בית ישראל was a vogue characterization to describe the Northern Kingdom, Israel.[141] However, whether the house of Israel is used in a generic sense referring to the whole population or whether it refers to the ruling family is left unanswered in Yee's work. Chaney argues that lexicographically בית refers to the "dynastic house" or "ruling dynast" of the house of Israel.[142] Alec Motyer, David Stacy and other early scholars assert that בית ישראל refers to the whole nation and the "men of Judah" as a part within the whole.[143] In any case, "house of Israel" appears in parallel to "men of Judah" (v.7) so we consider that both Israel and Judah are indicted here.

6.7.3. Form Critical Comments on Isaiah 5:1-7

The passage opens with a definitive introduction in v.1 and moves to a clear conclusion in v.7 indicating that vv.1-7 is a unit. The self contained unit of the passage remains unchallenged, however, scholars have debated whether vv.1-7 is satirical polemic, fable, allegory, *rib* saying or love song. Since the work of John T. Willis on "The Genre of Isaiah 5:1-7," the issue is settled to a great extent, if not entirely. Willis argues that the form of this pericope is "parable" and its contents are "a parabolic song of a discontented husbandman" involving an element of lawsuit or accusations.[144] Willis thus rejects the view of restricting vv.1-7 only within the category of "lawsuit form" arguing that the legal genre can also belong to a "parable."[145] In other words, Willis makes clear that the form of lawsuit in the vineyard song is embodied within the larger literary form of "parable." Despite his excellent analysis of the form of the unit, Willis, however, did not demonstrate how the parable as an "intentional decoy" seeking to entrap the listeners, functions within Isaiah 5:1-7.

In a distinctive line, Gale A. Yee compares vv.1-7 with the song of Moses (Deut. 32) that contains the lawsuit and with Nathan's juridical parable (2 Sam. 12:1-14)[146] that ensnares David into self-judgment and concludes that vv.1-7 is conjoined with two literary forms: a "song" and a "juridical parable."[147] Though Yee's analysis has been commended, one important issue has also been raised since in other instances of juridical parables in the OT,[148] the verdict comes

---

[141] Yee, "A Form-Critical Study of Isaiah 5:1-7," 37-38. See also R. Davidson, "The Interpretation of Isaiah II 6ff", *VT* 16 (1966) 3-4.

[142] Cf. Chaney, "Whose Sour Grapes," 117.

[143] Motyer, *The Prophecy of Isaiah,* 69; Stacy, *Isaiah 1-39*, 33; older scholars include, F. Delitzsch, E. Young, and O. Kaiser. Cited in Yee, "A Form-Critical Study of Isaiah 5:1-7," 37.

[144] Willis, "The Genre of Isaiah 5:1-7", 361.

[145] Willis, "The Genre of Isaiah 5:1-7", 361.

[146] Yee, "A Form-Critical Study of Isaiah 5:1-7", 31-32.

[147] Yee, "A Form-Critical Study of Isaiah 5:1-7,"40; U. Simon, "The Poor Man's Ewe-Lamb: An Example of a Juridical Parable", *Bib* 48 (1967) 220-21.

[148] For example, 2 Sam. 12:1-14; 14:1-20; 1 Kgs 20:35-43; and Jer 3:1-5.

always after the "indictment" and "interpretation" but in the present unit, the verdict (vv. 5-6) comes before the interpretation (v. 7). To settle this form critical issue, Gerald T. Sheppard employs 3:14-15 to reconstruct the juridical parable of 5:1-7, which he thinks is a "fragmentary character" of the original juridical parable preserved in 5:1-7.[149] If viewed synoptically, Sheppard's attempt to combine 3:13-15 with 5:1-7 appears convincing as both the texts deal with the vineyard theme. The question remains, however, whether a thematic closeness between the two passages necessarily indicates a scribal displacement? Sheppard's proposal raises more issues than solving the form critical problem. Following Yee's argument, we consider that 5:1-7 consists of a "song" and "juridical parable" in which the prophet sang a vintage song by employing the rhetoric of entrapment with a purpose to setup the hearers to condemn their own actions of which they are guilty. The issue concerning the precedence of "verdict" (vv.5-6) before the interpretation of "indictment" (v.7) can be seen as a distinctive passage of Isaian juridical parable. This means, unlike other juridical parables in the OT, the present text immediately pronounces a "verdict" before the "indictment" but in enigmatic terms. This is a skillful presentation to heighten the severity of judgment and to lead the listeners to self condemnation.

The unit begins with an introduction of "song" about the vineyard and employs the parable in which Isaiah presents the "case" of the unproductive vineyard (vv.l-2). The original genre appears to be of a complaint in a court setting as indicated by legal overtones of accusation and disputes between the accused and the accuser. The accuser brings in his proof by describing the fulfillment of his responsibilities (v.2) and charged the accused with failing to fulfill the responsibilities (v.4) by appealing the court for judgment (v.3). Based on the accusation, the sentence is pronounced (vv.5-6). V.7 finally gives interpretation of the parable by identifying Yahweh as the owner, Israel and Judah as the vineyard and the wild grapes as injustice and bloodshed in the society. The unit can thus be briefly outlined as follows:

Introduction of parable in a form of "song":	v.1
Benevolent care of the vineyard owner:	v.2
Presentation of the case for judgment:	v.3
Indictment in the form of rhetorical questions:	v.4
Sentence of the trial:	vv.5-6
Interpretation/application of parable:	v.7

The precise date of the composition of this song is difficult to determine, however, most scholars agree that the song reflects the occasion of an autumn

[149] Sheppard, "More on Isaiah 5:1-7," 46.

vintage festival in Jerusalem (Deut. 16:13-15) at the end of grape harvest.[150] If the superscription in 1:1 could be considered as authentic to the period of Isaiah, the prophet began his ministry at the time of economic boom ushered by king Uzzaih in the eighth century. This superscription may provide some light concerning the historical setting of the unit. With the growth of international trade, imported luxury goods like military equipment and architectural materials became lured objects, which were paid through the items produced locally, such as, wheat, olive oil, and wine. As such, there was a greater demand for agricultural production that lead to the spiraling growth of viticultural expansion. Such situation eventually altered the ownership of the land in which poor peasants were dispossessed while the elite class became the owners of large landholdings.[151] The vineyard image in 5:1-7 thus provides a proper setting of Isaiah's polemic in relation to land ownership.

6.7.4. Tradition and Theological Comments in the Light of Tripartite Relationship

Although tradition does not appear clearly in vv.1-7, we can assume that the covenant tradition is embedded in the present unit. We have already argued in our exegeses on Hos. 2:2-13; 16-23 that the metaphor of husband-wife relationship speaks of the covenant relationship. In the Israelite culture, a person cannot make a bride his beloved unless they are married and evidenced in the covenant. The use of the term "beloved" in v.1 could thus be understood in terms of bound covenant relationship. Also we have noted in 3:12-15 that "vineyard" is a key term in the covenant tradition. In addition, the failure of "justice" and "righteousness" (v.7), which appear prominently in the eighth century prophets' literature (cf. 1:10-17, 21-22; Am. 5:21-24; Mic. 6:6-8), appear in relation to the failure to establish equitable relationship in the society and loyalty to Yahweh's expectation as envisaged in the covenant tradition. So, we can assume that the present unit is embedded in the covenant tradition.

As mentioned in the above FCC, the unit introduces a juridical parable in a form of song, "Let me sing for my beloved my love-song concerning his vineyard" (v.1), to present a case of the singer's friend. We have noted in the TCC on v.1a, that "beloved" refers to "Yahweh" and "vineyard" to "Israel and Judah" (cf. vv.3, 7) and that the addressees, as Chaney argues, are the people of Judah and Israel particularly the ruling elite.[152] Chaney's argument appears plausible as the form-critical analysis of all the juridical parables in the monarchical history points to the condemnation or judgment intended against the kings. Nathan's

---

150 Kaiser, *Isaiah 1-12*, 59. Webb, *The Message of Isaiah*, 12; Herbert, *The Books of the Prophet Isaiah 1-39*, 48. Stacy, *Isaiah 1-39*, 31; Motyer, *The Prophecy of Isaiah*, 68.

151 Chaney, "Whose Sour Grapes?" 107.

152 For detail discussion, see Marven Chaney, "Whose Sour Grapes? The Addressees of Isaiah 5:1-7?" 105 and 117.

juridical parable condemns king David (2 Sam. 12:1-14); the parable of a disguised mourning woman is directed against the king David (2 Sam 14:5-17); another juridical parable in 1 Kgs 20:35-43 condemns the king Ahab. In all of these, there is an intentional decoy that instigates the kings to pass judgment on themselves. It seems probable that the recipients of the present juridical parable are particularly directed against the ruling elite, especially the offenders of land ownership who joined house to house and added field to field (cf. 5:8). As noted in the above FCC, the prophet has apparently joined the celebration of autumn grapes festival wherein he used a familiar vintage song to metaphorically convey how Yahweh has given proper care and attention to his people and also to pass an indictment and judgment against the people who have failed to reciprocate Yahweh's benevolent act.[153]

The reference to the vineyard's location on "a fertile hill" is significant. Metaphorically, as noted in the TCC on v.1d, the phrase "a vineyard on a fertile hill" can be understood as referring to Yahweh's act of placing his people in a land of Canaan in contrast to a dry desert land. More significantly, during Isaiah's time, the hilly places became the areas where viticulture was intensively cultivated to meet the increasing demand of wine and oil both for domestic consumption and international export.[154] Chaney has noted some archaeological evidence in this regard that "While rock-cut olive and grape processing installations are probably almost as old as agriculture itself in Palestine, archaeological surveys suggest a proliferation of and innovation in such installations in the eighth century B.C.E." He further states that "seal impressions from Judah witness a system of royal vineyards toward the end of the eighth century."[155] This shift in economic mode of production not only leads to the deterioration of village subsistence agriculture but most importantly, in the process, the previously free landholding villagers lost their land into the hands of rich people who have amassed large land for the expansion of viniculture. Such agrarian descriptions suggest that the issue of injustice recounted in this juridical parable deals mostly with the cultivable land as indicated further by the expressions, such as, vineyard's location on a "hill", digging of it, clearing it of stones, building the watch tower (v.2), breaking down its walls, not pruning and commanding the cloud not to rain upon the vineyard (vv.5-6).

The case is presented in v.3 in which the owner (Yahweh) indicts his people in the form of rhetorical questions (v.4) and announces his judgment to devastate the vineyard for producing bad fruit (v.5-6). The indicted people are identified as the "inhabitants" (יושׁב) of Jerusalem and Judah (v.3). The term יושׁב is mostly understood as referring to the one who "sits on the throne" and the one who "rules

[153] Kaiser, *Isaiah 1-12*, 60.

[154] Chaney, "Whose Sour Grapes," 108.

[155] Chaney, "Whose Sour Grapes," 108-109.

or presides in judgment."[156] However, beyond such conventional understanding, Chaney relates the term with the Ugaratic cognate and suggests that "יושב can also include the sense of 'besitting' a major landed estate." He thus argues that יושב in v.3 refers precisely to "… the wealthy landlords who occupy thrones of power, where they sit in judgment on their social inferiors."[157] Chaney's argument can be sustained in the light of v.8 where Isaiah indicts the landholders who have amassed huge land. In this respect, the inhabitants of Jerusalem and Judah who are called in for judgment (v.3) refer to the owners of large landholdings.

Such an act (amassing the land of others) is described metaphorically as "bad fruits", which is contrary to Yahweh's covenantal act of caring, protecting and watching over them (v.2). In the covenant understanding of land, humanitarian concerns are of utmost importance for the use of land. Just as Yahweh has shown compassion in giving the land, Israel and Judah should also show compassion to the poor, widow and orphan and not grab their land. Instead, those who occupy the seat of power have amassed large land against the covenantal concern of sharing the land and its resources. Yahweh thus announces his sentence to devour the vineyard and remove its hedge, break down its wall and not to give rain upon the vineyard. The descriptions here convey a double meaning on the understanding of land. First, the loss of the vineyard's hedge and fence for the predators to destroy (v.5) points to the Assyrian invasion, which is the basic emphasis of chs. 6-16.[158] This means "vineyard" is understood in terms of land as political nation that will be fallen and destroyed by the conquering enemy. Second, to withhold the cloud not to rain upon the vineyard (v.6) points to the drought that will affect cultivation and hence the vineyard is also understood as cultivable land. Thus, Yahweh's sentence against the vineyard can be primarily understood both in terms of land as political nation and land as cultivable plot that will be laid wasted in the future.

As Joseph Blenkinsopp and Yee argue, if Tiglath-Pilesar has extended his border toward the north by the time Isaiah uttered this parable,[159] then the destructive pronouncement upon the vineyard particularly the house of Israel, has begun to be fulfilled. If this argument can be sustained, then the Judeans could have easily passed the judgment that Yahweh had indeed devoured the hedge, broke down the wall of the north through the Assyrian invasion. However, the plot reverses back to the Judeans revealing that the Judeans themselves will face the same fate for causing injustice and distressing cries in the society. The prophet

---

[156] Frank Moore Cross Jr., and D.N. Freedmann, "The Song of Miriam", *JNES* 13 (1955) 248-49; Gottwald, *The Tribes of Yahweh*, 512-34; Wilfred G.E Watson, "David Ousts the City Ruler of Jebus." *VT* 20 (1970) 501-2.

[157] Chaney, "Whose Sour Grapes," 112.

[158] Blenkinsopp, *Isaiah 1-39*, 208.

[159] Blenkinsopp, *Isaiah 1-39*, 208; Stacy, *Isaiah 1-39*, 33; Yee, "The Form-Critical Study of Isaiah 5:1-7," 38.

had thus tactfully concealed the plot to let the Judeans realize their guilt and to let them pronounce judgment upon themselves.

The "fruits" mentioned in v. 2 is clarified in v. 7. The "sweet grapes" Yahweh expects from Israel and Judah is "justice" and "righteousness" but Yahweh saw "bloodshed" and "cry", which are described as "bad fruit" (v.7). The terms justice and righteousness have a broad meaning, but in the present context, the terms appear to have special significance in relation to land (cf. vv8-10). The Hebrew syntax here shows a play of words: Yahweh expected משפט "justice" but found only משפח "bloodshed"; Yahweh looked for צדקה "righteousness" but found צעקה "cries of distress." BDB suggests that the term משפח "bloodshed" refers to outpouring (of the blood), Motyer interprets it as the "inflicting of wrongs"[160] while Delitzsch considers it to be denoting a "forcible appropriation of another man's property."[161] Delitzsch's interpretation appears plausible since in the parable and in other occurrences of Isaiah, the vineyard theme is closely associated with social injustice; moreover, the woe oracle in v. 8 denounces those who added fields after fields. Thus, within the larger setting of the text, משפח probably refers to the encroachment of properties especially the land. As justice failed, the economically and politically powerful people took the advantage of grabbing the landed properties of the weak especially the agricultural plot to intensify their vineyard cultivation and wine business at the international market. Those who lose out their cultivable lands then cry out in distress but justice was not meted out to them. Isaiah considers such act of injustice and unrighteousness to be the unexpected and disappointing fruit, for which the divine judgment became inevitable.

The foregoing exegesis shows to us that the vineyard imagery in 5:1-7 convey the understanding of land in a sense of political nation that will be destroyed as well as a plot of cultivation that will affected by drought. The reason for announcing such destructive punishment is because of prevailing "bloodshed" and "cries" in the society. Yahweh expects "justice" that demands fairness in the social relationship and "righteousness" that demands loyalty to Yahweh, which in the present context, refers to the instruction on proper use and sharing of the land and its resources as envisaged in the covenant tradition of land use pattern. Since Israel and Judah have failed to produce such fruit of justice and righteousness in their interpersonal relationship and in their relationship with God, Yahweh now announces the judgment that will destroy both their land as political nation and their land as cultivable plot.

6.8. Remnant and Creation Traditions (Isaiah 5:8-10)

The following text mentions leaving few people alone in the midst of the land (v.8), which speaks of the remnant tradition while v.10 mentions Yahweh withholding

[160] Motyer, *The Prophecy of Isaiah*, 69.

[161] Delitzsch, *Commentary on the Old Testament in Ten Volumes,* vol. 7, 166.

the yields of the land showing his power and control over the nature, which speaks of the creation tradition. Because of acts of injustice related to land (v.8), Yahweh will remove people from the land (v.9) and the land will not yield crops for people. The tripartite relationship is thus explained in vv.8-10 by employing the remnant and creation traditions.

6.8.1. Translation on Isaiah 5:8-10

8 Woe[a] you who join house to house, who add field to field, until there is no place but you, and you are left to live alone in the midst of the land!

9 Yahweh of hosts has sworn in my hearing,[a] surely many[b] houses shall be desolate, large and beautiful houses, without inhabitant.

10 For ten acres of vineyard shall yield but one bath, and a homer of seed shall yield a mere ephah.

6.8.2. Text Critical Comments on Isaiah 5:8-10

V.8a. הוֹי[162] is not particularly "woe," which is אוֹי. Thus, BDB renders it as "Ah, Alas, Ha" to raise attention.[163] הוֹי as interjection, usually expresses dissatisfaction, pain and lamentation (for further discussion, see TCC on Micah 2:1a).

V.9a. The MT's ב preposition (in), אֹזֶן feminine dual construct (ear) and 1st C. Sg suffix is rendered in the LXX as ηκουσθη γαρ= כי נשמע meaning "for he was heard." BHS suggests לכן נשמע "therefore he heard", but the MT makes better sense since in the present context Isaiah reports what he heard from Yahweh by using prophetic audition formula. By employing this formula, Isaiah authenticates his judgment speech בזני יהוה צבאות (v.9a), literally "in my ear [is] Yahweh of host," which, according to Delitzsch, means "He is here revealing himself to me."[164] He argues that in Hebrew "to say into ears" is "to speak in a distinct and intelligible manner, which precludes the possibility of any misunderstanding."[165] On the other hand, Tucker states that the phrase suggests the prophet's overhearing of Yahweh's judgment in the heavenly court (cf. 6:8).[166] Whatever may be the appropriate translation, the phrase implies that the prophet has heard Yahweh's judgment to reverse the fortune of the landowners that whatever they get, they will lose.

V.9b: Delitzsch contends that רבים (many) "does not mean less than all," but rather that the judgment will be universal in its effect.[167] If Delitzsch's argument can be sustained, although the indictment of wrongdoings is directed against the offenders, the effect of judgment will be felt by the entire people of Judah.

---

162 הוֹי appears frequently in proto Isaiah: Is 1:4, 24; 5:8, 11, 18, 20, 21, 22; 10:1, 5; 16:4; 17:12; 18:1; 28:1; 29:1, 15; 30:1; 31:1.

163 BDB, 222.

164 Delitzsch, *Isaiah,* 167.

165 Delitzsch, *Isaiah,* 167.

166 Tucker, "The Book of Isaiah 1-39," 93.

167 Delitzsch, *Isaiah,* 167-68.

6.8.3. Form Critical Comments on Isaiah 5:8-10

5:8-10 is a unit of judgment oracle within a larger six-fold woe speech in vv.8-24. Westermann argues that woe oracle begins with הוי (woe), which introduces accusation (v.8b) and is followed by the announcement of judgment (vv.9-10).[168] The הוי (v.8a) is followed by a participle מגיעי "those who add" field to field, which ascertains the addressee upon whom the judgment speech is proclaimed. Vv.8-10 are thus a "woe" oracle against the unjust acquisition of land, which can be outlined briefly as follows:

Introduction of Woe Speech:	Woe (v.8a).
Indictment of Wrongdoings:	you who cause to join house to house, who add field to field, until there is no place… (v.8b)
Announcement of Doom:	… houses shall be desolate… without inhabitant. For ten acres of vineyard shall yield but one bath, and a homer of seed shall yield a mere ephah (vv. 9b-10).

Concerning the historical setting of the unit, there is no clear indication in the text. Though it is not possible to assign the text to any particular historical moment, it is generally agreed that ch.5 belongs to the early period of Isaiah's ministry.[169]

6.8.4. Tradition and Theological Comments in the Light of Tripartite Relationship

As mentioned above, the text clearly speaks of leaving few people alone in the midst of the land (v.8), which speaks of the remnant tradition. V.10 also speaks of the authority of Yahweh to withhold the fecundity of the land indicating his power over the creation. We thus assume that the unit of vv.8-10 is rooted in the Remnant and Creation traditions. By employing the remnant tradition, Isaiah affirms that except for a few people there would be no inhabitants in the land while by employing the creation tradition, Isaiah affirms that Yahweh would withhold the fertility of the land and deprive the people of the land's gift (v.10). Such punishment is announced for accumulating the personal estates (v.8) either by oppressive means (Mi. 2:2) or by purchase (cf. 1 Kgs 21:3), which is against the understanding of inalienable land. Isaiah understood such practice of land acquisition as violation of Yahweh's command for which Yahweh announces his judgment to destroy the people, the land and to take away the fertility of the land (vv.9-10). The tripartite relationship in vv.8-10 is thus explained below by employing the remnant and creation traditions.

---

[168] Westermann, *Basic Forms of Prophetic Speech*, 190.

[169] Childs, *Isaiah*, 46.

According to Zimmerli, behind the prophetic cry "woe to those who join house to house and add field to field" there is a "prior knowledge of property law at work in Israel" as envisaged in the Jubilee legislation in Lev. 25.[170] Zimmerli, therefore, rightly argues that Isaiah's woe speech in 5:8 is a cry against the violation of the legislation of land by the land accumulators. The הוי (woe) in 5:8a introduces an accusation, which is followed by the announcement of judgment.[171] Most commentators agree that the woe oracle in 5:8-10 is directed against the unjust practice of land tenure system.[172] Though the identity of those who sequestrate the land is vaguely identified as מגיעי "those who add field to field" (v.8), scholars consider that the perpetrators are the royal officials and wealthy landowners who manipulated the legal procedure to acquire and confiscate the land.[173] Since Isaiah's contemporary, Micah accuses the elders, princes and chief officials of Jerusalem for gross injustice and appropriation of land (cf. Mic. 2:1-2; 3:9-11; cf. Is. 3:12-14), we can assume that the perpetrators are the royal officials and wealthy people. Key terms in the indictment are בית "house" and שׂדה "field". As discussed already in the TCC on Mic. 2:2c, Moran's study on the Accadian *bitu* in Ugaritic documents that deals with the transfer of immovable property has demonstrated that property in ANE texts is referred to as "house" *(bitu)* and "field" *(eqlu)*.[174] Likewise, Chaney argues that בית in the Decalogue originally refers to the neighbor's plot of arable land held in redistributional domain by an Israelite extended family.[175] Arguing along the line of Moran and Chaney, Premnath contends that "houses and fields" in v.8 refer to the accumulation of land and that בתים רבים refers to the acquisition of "large landholdings."[176] Further,

---

[170] Zimmerli, "'Land' in the Pre-Exilic and the early Post-Exilic prophets'", 248.

[171] Westermann, *Basic Forms of Prophetic Speech*, 190.

[172] Gray, *The Book of Isaiah 1-39*, 90-91; Kaiser, *Isaiah 1-12*, 65-67; Oswalt, *The Book of Isaiah Chapters 1-39*, 158; David L. McKenna, *Isaiah 1-39*, vol. 16a (Dallas, Texas: Word Books, 1993), 95.

[173] Blenkinsopp, *Isaiah 1-39*, 213. See also, Gene M. Tucker, "The Book of Isaiah 1-39: Introduction, Commentary and Reflection", in Leander E. Keck and others, *The Interpreter's Bible,* vol. 6 (Nashville: Abingdon Press, 2001), 93; Childs, *Isaiah*, 47.

[174] W. Moran, "The Conclusion of the Decalogue (Ex. 20:17= Dt 5:21)," *CBQ* 29 (1967) 549-52.

[175] M.L. Chaney, "You Shall Not Covet Your Neighbor's House," *Pacific Theological Review* 15 (1982) 6. Cited in D.N. Premnath, "Latifundialization and Isaiah 5:8-10," *JSOT* 40 (1988), 55.

[176] Premnath, "Latifundialization," 55.

along with W. Johnstone[177] and G. R. Driver,[178] Premnath argues that the term מקום "place" (v.8) is used "in a technical sense to refer to the small landholding of the peasants."[179]

If the above mentioned scholars' argument can be sustained, Isaiah's indictment in vv.8-9 is primarily against the accumulation of arable land of the peasants' landholdings. The manner in which the elite carried out such acquisition is expressed by the hiphil participle מַגִּיעֵי, which expresses the exercising of authority over others by claiming the land as one's own, until there is no place available. This is expressed by the term אֶפֶס, which means "brought to nought or no more", indicating that the elite "...launch an all-out drive for the acquisition of as much property as possible, so that there is no room left for others (Isa. 5:8)."[180] Such prevailing practices against the land acquisition presuppose the violation of ancient covenant law related to land.[181] The covenant tradition understood land as inalienable inheritance that can neither be transferred nor sold permanently (Lev. 25:23).[182] V.8 suggests the violation of the ancestral law by reducing the inalienable land to a purchasable property.[183] Although the text is unclear, it is not unthinkable to assume that the royal court enacted laws to legalize the land transfer. In this case, for the prophet Isaiah, "legality" is not so much a problem than the issue of justice.[184] Law could be enacted, ratified or legislated to legalize the land transfer and thereby legally dispossess the poor of their landholding but

---

[177] Citing references such as, Gen. 23.20; Judg. 9: 55; 19: 28; 1 Sam. 2: 20; 27: 5; 29: 4; 2 Sam. 19: 40, Jonhstone states that מקום refers to estate or property, in addition to its general meaning of locality, place or spot. W. Johnstone, "Old Testament Expressions in Property Holding," *Ugaritica* 6 (1969) 314. Cited in Premnath, "Latifundialization," 55.

[178] G.R. Driver translates מקום as a "share of his estate."G.R Driver, *Canaanite Myths and Legends* (Edinburgh: T & T Clark, 1956), 30. Cited in Premnath, "Latifundiazation," 55.

[179] Premnath, "Latifundiazation," 55.

[180] *TWOT*.

[181] Tucker, "The Book of Isaiah 1-39," 93.

[182] Lev. 25:23 states both theological legitimacy for the divine ownership of land (*the land is mine*) and description of the Israelites' status (*you were sojourners*). As such, Israelites cannot sell the land in perpetuity. Cf. 27:1-11; 36:1-12; Ruth 4:1-4.

[183] Tucker, "The Book of Isaiah 1-39," 93. Leclerc argues that there are two reasons that contributed to the shift of land ownership. First, the *monarchy* empowered kings to acquire land either corruptly (for example, Naboth's vineyard in 1 Kgs 21) or legally (for example, through confiscation of land, or other properties of the traitors or criminals), and these acquired land were redistributed to the loyal officials of the kings. Such process lead to the loss of land of the poor peasants. Second, the process of urbanization led to economic interdependence between the peasant farmers and the rich landowners. This is especially the case when an individual farmer suffered economic loss either because of crop failure, or illness or by other factors. The farmers turned to the rich money lenders borrowing money at the cost of high interest or by mortgaging the land. Such practices gradually lead to the loss of land ownership. Leclerc, *Yahweh is Exalted in Justice*, 59.

[184] Blenkinsopp, *Isaiah 1-39*, 212.

such legality from the covenant perspective is injustice and a violation of covenant relationship with Yahweh as well.

The judgment is thus pronounced by employing the term אם־לא "surely", which emphasizes the affirmative character of judgment.[185] The following sentence specifies that "many houses", which are "large" and "beautiful", will remain "desolate" without any inhabitant (v.9). While we have argued that בית "house" in v.8 can refer to a cultivable plot of land, בית also seem to refer to house or land in a sense of residential plot as indicated by the term יושב "inhabitants" who dwell in the בית. If this argument can be sustained, the invective threat here includes both the desolation of land as arable plot and as living space.

The conjunction כי in v.10 states the nature of damage particularly the crop failure, which would follow the judgment of the dissolution of the land.[186] V.10 states that "ten acres of vineyard shall yield but one bath and a homer of seed shall yield but an ephah". Such expression indicates a judgment upon the arable land that involves a crop failure. In the context of the economic growth of the eighth century the rich landlords, against whom Isaiah indicts, acquired arable land to intensify viniculture as wine and oil were in high demand both for domestic consumption as well as for international export. However, against such greed of the landlord to maximize the profit through cultivation, Yahweh responds to it with a total failure of the harvest. Thus, Premnath rightly concludes that "The judgment speaks of depriving the rich of the very things of which they had deprived the peasants."[187] In other words, the occupation of vastness of land will not bring economic prosperity but desolation and loss of land.[188]

The foregoing exegesis shows to us that the terms "בית", "שׂדה" and "ארץ" refer to land as cultivable plot and residential or living space, which is understood as inalienable property. Acquisition of this arable land or residential space permanently either through a purchase or coercion from the original owner is understood as a violation of the landholding pattern. Yahweh pronounces his sentence against people's crime related to land in which the land suffers desolation while the people were deprived of dwelling in the land. Even the blessing of the land was also withdrawn as the land would fail to yield sufficiently. Here the relationship with the land is affected in terms of unproductive yielding despite hard work. The tripartite relationship is not yet broken at this stage for people are still in the land but Isaiah realizes that the relationship is affected leading toward losing the land in the future as Yahweh's judgment looms near.

[185] Delitzsch, *Isaiah*, 167.

[186] Delitzsch, *Isaiah*, 168.

[187] Premanth, "Latifundialization," 56.

[188] R. W. L. Moberly, "Whose Justice? Which Righteousness? The Interpretation of Isaiah V 16," *VT* 51/1 (2001) 65.

6.9. Remnant Tradition (Isaiah 11:11-12)

The term "remnant" (שׁאר) appears in v.11 in connection with God's act of gathering his people from the four corners of the earth (v.12). God's assurance to "acquire", "assemble" and "gather" his people who were earlier alienated from the land can be understood in terms of the return to their homeland. This indicates that vv.11-12 are rooted in the remnant tradition in which the tripartite relationship is explained by stating that the Lord will act on behalf of his people and that the exiled people are given the hope of returning to their land.

6.9.1. Translation on Isaiah 11:11-12

11 In that day[a] the Lord[b] will extend his hand[c] again a second time to acquire the remnant which is left of his people, [d]from Assyria, from Egypt, from Pathros, from Ethiopia, from Elam, from Shinar, from Hamath, and from the coastlands of the sea[d].

12 He will raise an ensign[a] for the nations, and will assemble[b] the outcasts of Israel[c], and gather the dispersed of Judah from the four corners of the earth.

6.9.2. Text Critical Comments on Isaiah 11:11-12

V.11a: ביום ההוא "in that day", which introduces a future promise of salvation appears frequently in Proto-Isaiah (2:11,17, 20; 3:18; 4:1; 5:30; 10:20; 28:5). The formula appears here in the same way as in the other remnant passages (cf. 4:2; 10:20; 28:5). See also the discussion on the TCC on Hos. 2:16a.

V.11b: The MT's אדני "Lord" is rendered in many MSS as יהוה "Yahweh". As אדני is reserved as a designation for Yahweh, either way of rendering addresses Yahweh's sovereign authority of lordship and thus the basic meaning remains unchanged.

V.11c: The hiphil form יוסיף can mean "he will add to do" meaning "he will do again/more" indicating that God will cause to repeat his action. According to Watts יסף "again" concedes the failure of the earlier effort and announces a further attempt. He argues that God will repeat his action as the first one failed.[189] Umeron rejects such interpretation and argues that in the present context יסף "again" conveys that God's hand is repeating an action which has parallels in the past in a more spectacular way that will bring it to completion."[190] If יסף "again" speaks of God's repeating action, which prior action is here referred to? Brueggemann explains that the first action refers to "Yahweh's scattering enterprise" and the second action here refers to "Yahweh's gathering activity."[191] In other words, יסף

[189] Watts, *Isaiah 1-33*, 178.

[190] Gerald Emem Umoren, *The Salvation of the Remnant in Isaiah 11:11-12: An Exegesis of a Prophecy of Hope and Its Relevance Today* (Boca Raton, Florida: Dissertation.com, 2006), 168-169.

[191] Walter Brueggemann, *Isaiah 1-39* (Louisville, KY: Westminister John Knox Press, 1998), 104.

"again" conveys that God will decisively act to restore those alienated and exiled from land by reversing their fortune and bringing them back to their land.

V.11e-e: "From Assyria… coastland of the sea" summarizes the then world from where God would bring back the remnant of Israel and Judah. "Assyria" attacked and deported Israel in 733 BCE (2 Kgs 15:29) and again in 724-721 BCE (2 Kgs 17:6 [18:11]),[192] as such, Israel's diaspora by the time of Isaiah remains unchallenged. However, the presence of a remnant in Egypt as early as Isaiah's time is doubted while the rest of the locations from Pathros to the coastlands of the sea are considered to have added by a later redactor.[193] Against such proposal, Umeron cites 1 Kgs 14:25 and argues that Egypt (and "Pathros" also refers to Egypt, the Nile region) invaded Judah and took captives during the time of Rehoboam.[194] He also argues that there was pro-Egyptian faction during Isaiah's time (cf. 30:1-7; 31:1-3) that did not support Assyrian vassalage; this group may have fled to Egypt for political refuge. Citing Jer. 43, Umeron argues further that some people of Judah migrated to Egypt (ca. 627-560 BCE) and even the Ephraimites, he argues, fled their conquered land and escaped to Egypt.[195] Umeron argues persuasively that all the nations mentioned here show possible diasporas of Israel and Judah before the pre-exilic time.[196] If Umeron's historical analysis can be sustained, then the setting of the present text concerning Israel and Judah's dispersions reflects the pre-exilic dating.

V.12a: נס "ensign" appears earlier in a judgment oracle (5:26, cf. 13:2) in which Yahweh ensigns "נס" to the nations to announce the coming destruction of the land of Judah and deportation of the people from their land. In contrast, God's נס appears here to the nations not to bring the judgment of destruction but to announce the salvation of his people by gathering them back from different scattered nations.

V.12b: ואסף "and he will gather" comes from the root "אסף" conveying the ides of "gathering what is scattered and bringing together". It is used here in a sense of gathering in back to the group or bringing in back to the land of promise after Yahweh has scattered them to Assyria, Egypt, Pathros, Elam, Shinar, Hamath and coastlands of the sea.

V.12c: The niphal participle נדחי "outcast" of Israel (ישׂראל) comes from the root נדח meaning "to drive away or banish". Umeron states that the niphal form evokes the idea of being sent or taken away from the land, denoting "the exiles" and "those who have been scattered."[197] He thus concludes that the phrase ישׂראל

---

[192] Watts, *Isaiah 1-33*, 179.

[193] Cf. Blenkinsopp, *Isaiah 1-39*, 267.

[194] Umeren, *The Salvation of the Remnant in Isaiah 11:11-12*, 153-154.

[195] Umoren, *The Salvation of the Remnant in Isaiah 11:11-12*, 154.

[196] For detail discussion on his arguments see, Umeren, *The Salvation of the Remnant in Isaiah 11:11-12*, 151-160.

[197] Umeren, *The Salvation of the Remnant in Isaiah 11:11-12*, 189.

נדחי "outcast of Israel" basically refers to the people of the Northern Kingdom who "as the result of God's judgment, were displaced from their land and were consequently cut off from the fellowship with their people."[198]

6.9.3. Form Critical Comments on Isaiah 11:11-12

Most scholars consider vv.11-12 as secondary addition and argue for exilic or post-exilic authorship.[199] Such argument is based on the assumption that Isaiah could not have conceived of a time when Jews would be scattered over the known world,[200] since there was no such large scale diaspora during Isaiah's time.[201] Against such viewpoint, Oswalt argues that Isaiah's knowledge of the international political situation could have helped him make the projection of Judah and Israel's diaspora to different parts of nations mentioned in v.11. Further he argues that "the omission of any reference to Babylon is unaccountable if the passage was written after 586 BCE."[202] The authenticity of vv.11-12 is also raised since only Assyria and Egypt are mentioned at the end of the immediate following unit (v.16) from where the remnants would return.[203] However, as argued in the TCC on v.11e-e, Umeron's historical analysis has convincingly demonstrated that all the locations "from Assyria… [to] the coastlands of the sea" (v.11) show the pre-exilic presence of Israel and Judah. As such we affirm that vv.11-12 do not suggest any exilic or post-exilic dating.

Based on the above discussion we consider that vv.11-12 is an authentic passage of Isaiah. The unit consists of a central theme of restoration of the remnant of Judah and Israel upon which vv.13-16 are expanded by emphasizing the result of God's restorative act. Thus, we consider vv.11-12 as a salvation oracle that deals with the promise of future restoration. This is indicated by the formula of the prophetic announcement of salvation ביום ההוא "in that day" (v.11). In this oracle, the Lord promises to extend his hand again for his people (v.11a). The purpose of the extension of God's help is to redeem (acquire) his remnant from the nations (v.11b). The Lord's restoration is carried out by assembling and gathering the alienated and exiled people back to their land (v.12).

[198] Umeren, *The Salvation of the Remnant in Isaiah 11:11-12*, 190.

[199] Since the promise concerning Judah's return (v.12) and the reconciliation between Judah and Israel (vv.13-14) are presumed to be referring to the end of the Babylonian exile and moreover, the terms, such as, "highway" for the returnees in v.15 appears in 40:3; 49:11; "coastlands" in v.11 appears in 41:1,5; 42:2,10,12; 49:1; 51:5. As such, scholars consider that the language and theme of vv.11-16 belong to the exilic period of Deutero Isaiah. Tucker, "The Book of Isaiah 1-39", 145.

[200] Oswalt, *Isaiah 1-39*, 286.

[201] F. Delitzsch, *Isaiah*, vol. 7, trans. by James Martin (Grand Rapids, Michigan: William B. Eerdmans Publishing Company, 1982), 289.

[202] Oswalt, *Isaiah 1-39*, 286.

[203] Blenkinsopp seems to suggest that the remaining locations are added to the list at a later period. Blenkinsopp, *Isaiah 1-39*, 267.

6.9.4. Tradition and Theological Comments in the Light of Tripartite Relationship

As noted in the above preliminary remark, vv.11-12 are rooted in the remnant tradition. "Remnant" (שאר) in v.11 may not be understood in a sense of "pruning, purification ... and new covenant"[204] to preserve Yahweh's people through a few faithful ones as developed later in the post-exilic era. However, the term explicitly affirms God's act of acquiring, assembling and gathering the people of Judah and Israel from the four corners of the earth (vv.11-12), which is a major theme in the remnant tradition. This indicates that the present unit is rooted in the remnant tradition in which "the Lord" promises to act for "his people" in a sense of restoring them back to the land. Thus, the tripartite relationship in the present unit is explicated by employing the remnant tradition.

The divine restoration is announced by employing the prophetic formula ביום ההוא "in that day" (v.11). Whether "in that day" refers to a distant or immediate future is difficult to determine. What appears clear is that the phrase points to a future intervention in which God would decisively act and reverse their present distress and usher a hope for their future. The divine intervention is described in terms of God extending his hand "again" for "his people" (v.11). As argued in the above TCC on v.11c, √יסף "again" implies that God will repeat his spectacular intervention as in past history. וסף also reiterates that just as in the past God intervenes in judgment by bringing destruction upon the land and scattering his people (cf. 1:7; 3:14, 26; 5:5-6, 9) he will now intervene to redeem and gather them (v.12). יסף "again" can thus be understood here as referring to God's decisive act to restore those alienated and exiled from the land by bringing them back to their homeland. In this case, "a second time" does not necessarily refer to the second ingathering of the exiles after the first return had taken place during the Zerubbabel and Ezra's time as Duhm, Kaiser, Fohrer and other argue. Instead, as Hasel argues, "the context makes clear the fact that the first time in which Yahweh recovered his people was the exodus deliverance to which v.16 refers. The "second time" then refers to a new action of God which corresponds to the exodus deliverance."[205]

The people on whose behalf God extends his hand "again" is stated as שאר "remnant" and עמו "his people". The image of "remnant" appears frequently in chs.1-39 (cf. 7:1-9; 10:19-22; 14:22, 30; 15:9; 37:4, 31-32). In the eighth century prophetic literature, "remnant" appears in the context of a judgment oracle that announce a destruction of land and deportation of people (cf. Am. 3:12; 4:11; 5:3; 5:15; 9:1-4). Amidst the impending judgment, Isaiah envisages a

---

[204] Markus Bockmuehl, "1QS and Salvation at Qumran", in D.A. Carson and others (eds), *Justification and Variegated Nomism: The Complexities of Second Temple Judaism*, vol.1 (Grand Rapids, Michigan/Tubingen, Germany: Baker/Mohr Siebeck, 2001), 391.

[205] Gerhard F. Hasel, *The Remnant: The History and Theology of the Remnant Idea from Genesis to Isaiah* (Michigan: Andrews University, 1974), 342.

future hope for the people to return back to the land. This is expressed figuratively through the name of Isaiah's son's "Shear-jasub", meaning "the remnant shall return" (7:1-9). שאר in the present usage presupposes the existing diaspora as a result of God's judgment. This diaspora (remnant) is identified as "his people" (עמו). Since עמו is in construct form, it expresses the relationship between God and Israel/Judah, which is based on the traditional covenant formula/relationship "יהוה עם" (1 Sam. 2:24; 2 Sam. 1:12; 6:21; 2 Kgs 9:6).[206] This means, Isaiah sees God's intention to intervene based on the covenant relationship he shares with the people of Israel/Judah.

The purpose of divine intervention is stated as "to acquire" his remnant from the nations (v.11b). √קנה "to acquire" with preposition ל "to" expresses God's purpose of acting "again". Watts cites Gen 14:19, 22 where קנה appears in creation context and Ex. 15:16 and Ps 74:2 where קנה appears in connection with God's redemption and concludes that קנה in v.11 has the overtone of redemption and creation in which God promises "to bring back the exiles in a way parallel to the Exodus, a way that is like his creation of a people for himself."[207] In a similar vein, Umoren states that לקנות "to acquire" in the present context points to a special relationship in that God by offering his salvation to the remnant would "re-create a new people unto himself."[208] "To acquire" thus refers to God's act of restoring his people (Israel and Judah, cf. v.12) back to their land who are now scattered to different nations and establish a renewed relationship with his people.

The Lord's restoration is carried out by assembling and gathering the exiled Israel and Judah from the four corners of הארץ "the earth" (v.12). הארץ "the earth" from where Israel and Judah will be gathered appears in the context of the then known world "Assyria, Egypt, Pathros, Ethopia, Elam, Shinar, Mahath and coastlands of the sea" (v.11). As such, הארץ can be understood here as referring to the earth in a sense of global world. Such global sense of the term from where "his people" will be rescued is further explained by the expression "the four corners" (v.12).

Based on the foregoing exegesis, the following observations can be made.

הארץ "the earth" refers to the entire earth in a sense of global arena where Israel and Judah are scattered and from where the Lord will carry out his redemptive work.

The Lord's assurance to gather his people refers to the return of Israel and Judah back to their homeland in the future despite the looming exile that threatens their present occupation in the land.

Yahweh's relationship with Israel/Judah is based on the traditional covenant relationship "עמו" (his people) and based on such relationship the hope of Israel/Judah to return and reclaim the land is anchored. In the judgment oracle

---

[206] Lipinski, "עם" in *TDOT*: 11, 172.

[207] Watts, *Isaiah 1-33*, 178.

[208] Umeren, *The Salvation of the Remnant in Isaiah 11:11-12*, 176. no. 219.

Yahweh did not totally eliminate his people but leaves some remnant because of his covenant faithfulness. Likewise, in the salvation oracle Yahweh announces to bring the remnant back to the land because of his commitment to covenant faithfulness. This indicates that the remnant tradition is rooted in the covenant tradition and that the two traditions are interlinked with one another.

6.10. Zion Tradition (Isaiah 33:7-12)

Both the people and land are portrayed to be in desolation because of the enemy's attack (vv.7-9). Amidst such chaotic situation, Yahweh's intervention is envisaged to defeat the enemy and to defend the oppressed (vv.10-12). The motifs of enemy's threat against Jerusalem and Yahweh's intervention on behalf of his people are the major themes in Zion theology (see the tradition and theological comments below). This indicates that vv.7-12 is rooted in Zion tradition through which Isaiah explicates the condition of both the people and land and Yahweh's relationship with them.

6.10.1. Translation on Isaiah 33:7-12

7 Behold, their warriors[a] cry out, "outside"; the envoys of peace weep bitterly.

8 The highways are desolate, the travelers has ceased. Covenant is broken, cities[a] are despised, there is no regard for man.

9 The land mourns[a] and languishes; [b] Lebanon is confounded and withers away; Sharon is like a desert; and Bashan and Carmel[b] shake off their leaves.

10 Now[a] I will arise says Yahweh, now I will lift myself up[b]; now I will be exalted.

11 You conceive chaff, you bring forth stubble; your breath is a fire that will consume you.

12 And the peoples will be as if burned to lime, like thorns cut down, that are burned in the fire.

6.10.2. Text Critical Comments on Isaiah 33:7-12

V.7a: The LXX assumes the root of אראלם as ירא "to fear," and renders the first colon of v.7 as *εν τω φοβω υμων* "in your fear". Such rendering appears to be untenable since vv.8-9 do not speak of the enemies' fear of Judah. Scholars have attempted to emend MT's אראלם to אראלים as rendered in some MSS and argue for the connection with אריאל "Ariel" identified as Jerusalem in 29:1. Though such rendering is possible, Oswalt argues that its contrast with "envoys" in the next phrase appears less striking. Moreover, he questions that such interpretation fails to explain "whether a simple plural *îm* is intended instead of MT *-ām* "their.""[209] A different line is taken by Delitzsch who divides אראלם into ארי אל "lion of God" and derives the meaning as their heroes or valiant one, which he identifies

[209] Oswalt, *Isaiah 1-39*, 596, no. 8.

as Jerusalem's envoy of peace sent to Sennacherib (2 Kgs 18:14).[210] Delitzsch's proposal can be sustained, however, identifying it as envoys of Jerusalem remain difficult as it fails to interpret חצה "outside" appropriately. Assuming that the context reflects Sennacherib's invasion in 701 BCE (see the FCC below), we render אראלם as "warriors" who belong to the Assyrian army. However, since the verb √צעק "to cry out" is followed by חצה, which comes from the noun חוץ with directional ה, together the expression אראלם צעקו חצה can be rendered as "their warriors cry out' 'outside"' indicating that Sennacherib's army were ordering the Judahites out from their home or cities. This line of interpretation is succinctly rendered by Sweeney as "their warriors cry, 'Out!.'"[211] Since 2 Kgs 18:13 mentions that Sennacherib's army stormed into the fortified walls of Jerusalem and took all the cities of Judah, 'their warriors cry out, "outside"' apparently reflects such historical situation.

V.8a: Duhm proposes to emend MT's ערים "cities" to עטים "witnesses" as rendered in the 1QIsa.[212] In a similar vein, recently Katherine H. Hayes demonstrates that the MT's ערים can be emended to עטים by arguing that עטים has its cognate in the Old Aramaic and Akkadian meaning "treaty or treaty stipulation."[213] Though the rendering of 1QIsa "עטים" (witnesses) may be possible as the idea of rejecting the witnesses of covenant is indicated by the term "ברית" (covenant), Motyer contends that there is a possibility of error, which occurred on the part of 1QIsa. Inconclusive debate continues as to whether error occurred in the MT or in 1QIsa. In any case, retaining MT's "cities" is not impossible if one sees that ערים "cities" are despised in the form of invasion by nullifying or not honoring the covenant (ברית).

V.9a: The third masculine singular verb אבל "to mourn" with the feminine subject ארץ "earth" in not uncommon but Hayes rightly points out that the coupling of the masculine verb אבל with the feminine verb אמללה where both refers to the same subject is unusual. By comparing with אבל, which occurs with a masculine subject תירוש "wine" followed by a feminine subject גפן "vine" in 24:7, Hayes thinks that the present order of words in v.7 may have influenced by 24:7.[214] In any case, אבל appears frequently in connection with the feminine noun "earth" (ארץ) as in 24:4; Hos. 4:3 and also in Am. 1:2 where אבל appears in connection with the withering of Carmel.[215] Primarily אבל means "to mourn" and

---

[210] F. Delitzsch, *The Prophecies of Isaiah*, vol. 2 (Grand Rapids, Michigan: William B. Eerdmans Publishing Company, 1982), 59-60.

[211] Sweeney, *Isaiah 1-39*, 423.

[212] 1QIsa refers to the Dead Sea Scroll of Isaiah.

[213] Katherine M. Hayes, *The Earth Mourns: Prophetic Metaphor and Oral Aesthetic* (Atlanta: SBL, 2002), 162.

[214] Hayes, *The Earth Mourns*, 162.

[215] אבל appears in connection with the earth in other prophetic literature see, Jer. 4:28; 12:4, 11; cf. Joel 1:9; 10.

secondarily "to dry up" but, as Hayes argues, the use of אבל "with one meaning could easily bring to mind the other meaning or nuance in particular contexts, creating a prime opportunity for poetic wordplay."[216]

V.9b: The four places mentioned here are all proverbial for luxuriant vegetation. Lebanon, which lies in the north appears frequently in Isaiah to describe the richness of timber particularly cedar.[217] Sharon is situated in the west coast south of Carmel, which is known for its fertility. Bashan lies in the east of Jordan and it appears mostly in the OT to describe lush green fertile land.[218] Carmel, which lies in at the western end of a mountain range, refers to a rich wooded and fertile area.[219] The references to these geographical regions, which are known for their fecundity, have all lost their lushness.

V.10a: עתה "now" announces Yahweh's intervention to bring judgment. It appears three times and follows immediately the helpless situation depicted in vv.7-9 indicating that Yahweh's intervention is present for the helpless sufferers. This is succinctly expressed by Oswalt who states that humans' failure mentioned in vv.7-9 becomes the divine opportunity to intervene in v.10ff.[220]

V.10b: ארומם from √רום "to lift" is rendered in 1QIsa with *taw* performative. The MT has as a shortened from of hithpael, which Motyer explains as poetic assonance.[221]

6.10.3. Form Critical Comments on Isaiah 33:7-12

Vv. 7-9 is a lament in which the present vexation at the enemies' hand is understood to be the result of Yahweh's disengagement.[222] Unlike the speech of future blessing and salvation (vv.1-6), הן "behold" in v.7 introduces a new section, which laments over the warriors' oppression. V.8 describes the disruption of economic activities and betrayal of socio-political relations that affects the lives of people in the cities. V.9 describes the state of the land by depicting it as mourning and withering away. עתה "now" in v.10 announces Yahweh's intervention to judge the enemies, which is based on the wrongdoings inflicted upon the victims described in vv.7-9. Vv.11-12 gives description of judgment by employing the metaphor of fire, which will bring complete destruction. Such thematic linkages indicate that vv.7-12 is a unit. Vv.7-9 employs the form of lament speech, which describes the enemies' oppression that causes the lamentable situation for the people and the land while vv.10-13 employs the form of salvation of salvation oracle by portraying the image of Yahweh's judgment against the oppressors and thereby freedom for the people

[216] Hayes, *The Earth Mourns*, 14.

[217] Isa. 2:13; 10:34; 14:8; 60:13.

[218] Isa. 2:13; Am. 4:1; Pss 22:13; Deut. 32:14; Ezek. 27:6; Jer. 50:9.

[219] Jer. 4:26.

[220] Oswalt, *Isaiah 1-39*, 597.

[221] Cf. Motyer, *The Prophecy of Isaiah*, 265; Oswalt, *Isaiah 1-39*, 594.

[222] Brueggemann, *Isaiah 1-39*, 262.

and land is envisaged. Since v.13 employs a call to attention formula "hear" (שמעו), which normally introduces a new unit, we consider it to be separate and not a part of vv.7-12.

Scholars are not unanimous concerning the historical setting of vv.7-12. Clements assumes that the text reflects the destruction of Jerusalem and suggested the period of Babylonian exile,[223] while Wildberger argues that השרון (v.9) is the name for the northern coastal plain that appears primarily in post-exilic texts and also by considering that there are some similarities in the language, form and style with the post exilic passages of Isa. 24-27, he assigns the unit to the Persian period.[224] Distinctively, Duhm sets the setting in the struggle between Judas Maccabeus and Antiochus Eupatoria in 162 BCE and dates the passage to the Hellenistic period.[225] As the unit assumes foreign invasion, all the above proposals remain possible. However, as Roberts argues there appears no reason not to attribute this unit to Isaiah.[226] A careful perusal of the unit suggests a historical situation of Assyria's invasion of Jerusalem (705-701 BCE) as the situation depicted in vv.7-9 portrays the image of Sennacherib's siege of Jerusalem.[227] As argued in the above TCC on v.7a, 2 Kgs 18:13 mentions that Sennacherib invaded the fortified cities of Jerusalem and took control of all the cities despite the emissaries of Hezekiah attempt to make a peace deal with him at Lachish. The reference to "the envoys of peace weep bitterly" (v.7), "the highways are desolate, the travelers has ceased" and "covenant is broken" (v.8) reflect the situation of Sennacherib's invasion of Jerusalem in 701 BCE.

6.10.4. Tradition and Theological Comments in the Light of Tripartite Relationship

Though "Zion" or "Jerusalem" does not appear in the present unit, within the larger setting of ch.33, which is addressed to Zion (cf. vv.5-6, 13, 20), vv.7-12 seem to be rooted in the Zion tradition. In the Zion tradition, the major emphasis is that Yahweh chooses Zion as his dwelling place and that he defends the city from the threats of natural and supernatural forces.[228] Elements of Zion tradition appear here as indicated by the expressions of enemy's attacks against the land

---

[223] Cf. Clements, *Isaiah 1-39*, 265.

[224] Wildberger, *Jesaja*, 1288. Cited in Hayes, *The Earth Mourns*, 163-164. Cf. Sweeney, *Isaiah 1-39*, 428.

[225] Duhm (*Das Buch Jesaia*, 208–9, 210–11. Cited in Hayes, *The Earth Mourns*, 164. Also see, Kaiser, *Isaiah 13-39*, 342.

[226] J.J.M. Roberts, "The Divine King and the Human Community in Isaiah's Vision of the Future", in H.B.Hoffman and others (eds), *The Quest for the Kingdom of God: Studies in honor of George E. Mendenhall* (Winona Lake: Eisenbrauns, 1983), 127-136.

[227] Delitzsch, *Jesaja*, 348, 350–51; Seitz, *Isaiah 1–39*, 233–35; Lack, *La Symbolique du Livre d'Isaïe*, 69. Cited in Hayes, *The Earth Mourns*, 163-164.

[228] Ollenburger, *Zion the City of the Great King*, 16.

(vv.7-8); that Yahweh rises up "קוּם" on behalf of the people and city (v.10) and consumes the enemy with fire "באשׁ" (vv.11-12).[229] Such emphasis on Yahweh's protective action and his judgment against the enemy are the major themes of Zion tradition.[230] Nevertheless, it needs to be noted that unlike the royal emphasis of Zion theology, which asserts Zion's inviolability, Isaiah presents here that both the people and the land have suffered desolation (vv.7-8) indicating that Jerusalem is vulnerable to defeat. However, by emphasizing Yahweh's intervention (v.10) Isaiah asserts that Jerusalem's enemy will be defeated and the vulnerable Zion will be redeemed so that the people can live securely again in the land. The tripartite relationship in vv.7-12 can thus be seen in terms of Yahweh's intervention on behalf of his people, which conveys a hope for the people to reestablish themselves in the land.

The introductory particle הן "behold" (v.7) calls for the attention of the addressee about the state of the people and the land. The lamentable condition of the people is described in v.7, "their warriors cry out 'outside!'" As argued in the above TCC on v.7a, "their warriors" refer to the Assyria's army that attacked Jerusalem in 701 BCE (cf. 2 Kgs 18:13, 32) while the term "outside!" (חצה) used in connection with "their warriors" refers most likely to Sennacherib's warriors who ordered the Judahites to get "outside" from their home or cities. Such forceful eviction could be the reason for "bitter" (מר) lamentation among the people, which is described by the verb "weep" (√בכה). Both the terms "bitter" and "weep" appear in the contexts of distress and need,[231] indicating that the Judahites were left in a most distressful situation amidst Assyria's attempt to evict them from their place of habitation. As people remained in distressful state of mourning, even the normal activities of the land come to an end. This is depicted in v.8 that the highways are "desolate (נשׁמו)" and travelers have "ceased (שׁבת)" indicating that even the socioeconomic activities have come to a complete standstill.

Such chaotic situation of the people and the land of Judah is stated to be the result of breaking the "covenant" (ברית). As the text does not provide any particular historical context for the breaking of a covenant, consensus on the issue of which covenant is referred to here and who actually broke it is difficult to determine. Blenkinsopp argues that since in 29:1ff Ariel is referred to Jerusalem that is besieged by the Assyrians and since against this background (30:2, 4) Hezekiah attempted to ally with Egypt to overthrow Assyria's domination, he concludes that the breaking of covenant refers to Hezekiah who broke his oath as vassal to the Assyrian overlord.[232] Following Parpola and Watanabe, Blenkinsopp

---

[229] Cf. Brevard S. Childs, *Isaiah and the Assyrian Crisis*, SBT 3 (London: SCM, 1967), 115-116.

[230] Daniel Jones Muthunayagom, *The Relationship Between Election and Israel's Attitude Towards the Nations in the Book of Isaiah* (Delhi: ISPCK, 2000), 7.

[231] For "מר"cf. Ruth 1:20-22; "יבכיון" cf. Job 31:38; Isa. 65:14; Jer. 49:3.

[232] Blenkinsopp, *Isaiah 1-39*, 440.

comments that the lamentable situation described in vv.8-9 is "the outcome of the curses attached to the vassal treaty, including famine and drought."[233] Other scholars, on the other hand, argue that after Assyrian's victory on the coastal areas, Hezekiah realized the futility of resistance and struck a peace deal with Sennacherib by paying him a huge tribute (2 Kgs 18:17ff). However, it is argued that later Sennacherib changed his mind and demanded a total surrender of the city to which Hezekiah refused and this leads to threats of Assyria's invasion against Judah.[234] The breaking of the covenant from this viewpoint is understood to be referring to Sennacherib's reversed military invasion against Jerusalem and not honoring the peace deal with Hezekiah.

Despite the present impasse, there seems to be a common understanding that the "covenant" here refers to a peace agreement reached between Sennacherib and Hezekiah during the Assyrian crisis.[235] In any case, whoever (Hezekiah or Sennacherib) broke the covenant, what appears significant to our investigation is that the breaking of this covenant affects both the people and the land: "cities are despised" and there was "no regard for man" (v.8). ערים "cities" here refers to a place of habitation for the people of Judah, which can also be understood in terms of the political territory of Judah. As argued in the above TCC on v.8a, the Assyrians invaded Judah without honoring the agreement (ברית) of peace reached between Sennacherib and Hezekiah. During such invasion the Assyrians probably ordered the Judahites to get "outside" of their cities (cf.v7) and such eviction carried out against the inhabitants of Judah is understood as an act of despising the "cities" and disregarding the people ("man, cf. v.8). In this case, ערים "cities" refers to the place of habitation as well as territory of political land for the people of Judah.

The term ארץ "land" appears in v.9 in connection with Lebanon, Sharon, Bashan and Carmel. As mentioned in the TCC on v.9b, these regions are known for the richest growth of trees, grass and plants,[236] which indicates that "ארץ" is used here to refer to the arable/cultivable portions of land. Isaiah's emphasis, however, is that these fecund portions of land have turned barren and are now devoid of all life ("withers away", "like a desert" and "shake off their leaves" v.9). Whether the loss of lushness in these arable regions is due to drought or not is difficult to determine. In any case, Isaiah's emphasis is that such transformation of the quality of land has brought severe pain upon the land itself as the text describes it vividly

[233] S. Parpola and K. Watanabe, *Neo Assyrian Treaties and Loyalty Oaths* (Helsinki: Helsinki University Press, 1988), 5, 11, 46-47. Cited in Blenkinsopp, *Isaiah 1-39*, 440.

[234] Scholars who follows this view include, R de Vaux, *Supplement au Dictionnaire de la Bible*, iv (1949), 755ff; J. Scharbert, *Die Propheten Israels bis 700 v. Chr.* (Koln, 1965), 288ff; B. Mazar, "Sennacherib's Judean Campaign", in J. Liver (ed.), *The Military History of the Land of Israel in Biblical Times* (Tel Aviv, 1965), 291ff. cited in Childs, *Isaiah and the Assyrian Crisis*, 12-13.

[235] Cf. Tucker, "The Book of Isaiah 1-39", 271.

[236] Hayes, *The Earth Mourns*, 172.

that the "land mourns and languishes" (אבל אמללה ארץ). What appears significant here is the emphasis on the connection between the people and the land. The description of the mournful state of land (v.9) is immediately preceded by the portrayal of utter distress of the inhabitants of the cities (cf. vv.7-8) indicating a close relationship and solidarity between the people and land.[237] As mentioned in the above FCC, Assyria's invasion of Jerusalem is understood to be the result of breaking the covenant, which creates a precarious situation for the people and the land, as such, humans' conduct in socio-political relations is seen to have direct consequences not only to humanity but also to the land.

As the people and the land of Judah were in a precarious state, Yahweh intervenes by announcing his judgment against the oppressive enemy (v.10). Yahweh's intervention is introduced by עתה "now", which appears three times in v.10 to convey a strong emphasis of his intention. "עתה" is used before three synonymous verbs: "arise" "lift up" and "exalted" to convey the idea of Yahweh's exaltation. Such divine exaltation is carried out through his intervention in judgment to vanquish the enemies and to deliver his people, the idea that is rooted in the Zion tradition. Though עמים "peoples" (v.12) upon whom the judgment is announced remain uncertain, the context makes clear that עמים refers to the destroyer[238] whom we have identified as the Assyrians in the above FCC. Assyria's anger against Jerusalem rages like a "fire", but such rage will in fact consume them just as the thorns are cut down and burned up in the fire (v.12). Such image of judgment by fire conveys the idea of total destruction.

The foregoing exegesis of Isa. 33:7-12 points to us that Isaiah understood land in a sense of a place for habitation and a territory of political nation in which he uses the term ערים "cities". He also uses the term ארץ to convey the land as arable portions, which remains vulnerable to barrenness. Such understanding of land is inextricably linked with people since after the land is invaded, the land as place of habitation becomes a land of mourning (v.7); the land as place of prosperity becomes a deserted place with no economic activity (v.8) and the land as place of fecundity becomes a barren land that is devoid of life (v.9). Such state of land, which affects the lives of people, is seen to be the result of treacherous humans' conduct (breaking the covenant or treaties, cf. vv.7-8). Yahweh demonstrates his relationship with the desolated land and people through his intervention in which the perpetrators of invasion were defeated (vv.10-12) and thereby the possibility for the people to live securely again in the land is envisaged.

6.11. Isaiah's Theology of Land

Based on the foregoing exegesis, we now summarize Isaiah's understanding of land as follows:

---

[237] Oswalt, *Isaiah* 1-39, 597.

[238] Oswalt, *Isaiah* 1-39, 598.

1. *Meaning of the Term Land*

First, Isaiah employs ארץ to refer mostly to the land of Judah and Israel as *territory for political nation.* In Isaiah, land as political nation is envisaged as a place where God intends to make life grow and prosper without intimidation. Such understanding is metaphorically expressed by employing the vineyard imagery (5:1-7). However, land as political nation that was intended to be a secure place of existence became a mourning and languishing land with constant threat of devastation (1:7; 33:8-9). ארץ is portrayed to be in constant tension between the policy of territorial expansion and the desire to defend the nation for secure existence (33:7-12). It is in this context that the issue of annexation and devastation of land is presented in Isaiah's understanding of land as political nation. Nations see ארץ "land" as an arena for territorial expansion (33:7-9) and pursuing such agenda is seen as one of the reasons of destruction upon the land (1:7; 33:8-9) and alienating the people from their nation (33:7). Such precarious state of ארץ "land" is also understood to be the reason of proliferation of military equipment for national defense (2:7). In Isaiah's understanding, ארץ as political nation is thus seen as impermanent in history that can be overthrown and destroyed (1:7). Such vulnerability of land is seen to be the outworking of divine judgment (5:9) in response to the wrong acts of the inhabitants of the land (1:4-7; 2:7-9; 3:12-15; 5:5-7; 8-10; 33:7-12). However, despite its vulnerability, ארץ is presented as an arena upon which Yahweh carried out his redemptive action to bring his people back to their homeland (11:11-12). In short, in Isaiah's understanding of land as political nation Yahweh is presented as a God who controls the destiny and history of the nations.

Second, Isaiah understood land as a *place of habitation and living space.* Key terms that describe such understanding of land include בית "house", שדה "field" and ארץ "land" (5:8), which Isaiah employs to refer to the portion of land where people dwell as residential or living space. Another term that expresses land as living space is עריכם "your cities" (1:7), which refers to the land that people inhabit within a particular political nation as their living space. As a place of habitation, land is understood to be an important aspect of property for secured existence and as property, land became an object to covet and possess. Thus, practices of unjust acquisition of residential plot and forceful eviction of people from their land became rampant (5:8). Denial of land as residential space is seen as deprival of existence, as such, encroachment, acquisition and alienation of and from the land is condemned with a threat of divine judgment in woe oracle (5:8).

Third, Isaiah understands land in the sense of an *arable and cultivable land.* Key terms that describe the arable land are ארץ, אדמה "land" (1:7; 33:9) and שדה "field" (5:8) where vineyard, cucumber and other produces of the land are cultivated (1:8; 5:2, 8, 10). Alongside these commonly occurred terms, בית "house" is also used to refer to an arable land held in redistributional manner (5:8). Arable land is understood as fecund portion of land with rich and luxurious yielding, which is seen as Yahweh's blessing to Israel and Judah (5:1-2). However, being a land where economic activities are engaged, the arable land became a tempting object to covet, which leads to widespread practices of encroachment and dispossession (5:8). Most socioeconomic crimes committed in Israel and Judah during Isaiah's time are associated with the arable land (3:14; 5:7, 8) and such offences are understood as contrary to Yahweh's law on land usage pattern (3:14). Because of the inhabitants' crimes associated with the arable land, Yahweh announces his judgment that affects the cultivable land severely. Yahweh withheld rain (5:6), withdrew the productivity of the land (5:10) and even the lush green and fertile land like Carmel, Lebanon and Bashan withers away (33:9). In Isaiah's understanding, the arable land remains vulnerable to losing its fecundity depending on the behaviors of the inhabitants (5:1-7). Judah's behavior is thus inseparably linked with the outcome of the arable land in which Yahweh is seen as the God who controls the nature of the cultivable land.

2. *Tripartite Relationship*

The above mentioned meaning on land shows a close relationship between Yahweh, Israel/Judah and land. In Isaiah's understanding Israel/Judah as political nations and their relationship with the land stands or falls based on their relationship with Yahweh. The relationship with Yahweh is mostly seen in terms of apostasy, such as, forsaking Yahweh (1:4), following idolatry (2:8), and practicing injustice (3:12-15; 5:7, 8), which brings the consequences of the failure of cultivable land (5:10; 33:9) and the destruction of and alienation from their political land (1:7; 2:9; 5:5-6). The reason for breaking the tripartite relationship is thus understood in terms of Israel/Judah's alienation form Yahweh in which estrangement from Yahweh is seen as alienation from the land itself (1:4-9). Israel and Judah's occupation of and alienation from the land are understood in terms of their relationship with Yahweh.

Yahweh and Israel's relationship is also described by employing with the metaphors of sonship "בנים" (1:4) and vineyard "כרם" (5:1-7) in which land comes to a central focus by emphasizing Yahweh's personal care bestowed upon the land and people (5:1-2). However, instead of remaining in close relationship with Yahweh as "sons", Judah despised and forsook God (1:4) and instead of bearing the fruit of justice and righteousness as Yahweh's vineyard, Judah and Israel bore bloodshed and violence (5:7). As a result, the land was overthrown (1:7), devoured and Yahweh's protection was withdrawn from the land (5:5). In other words, the blessing of the land is denied to Israel/Judah because of their deviant relationship with Yahweh. Land as political nation, as place of habitation and as cultivable portion appear in constant tension in Isaiah's understanding due to Judah/Israel's deviant relationship with Yahweh. The destruction of the land and its consequent bearing upon Israel/Judah is thus seen as the outworking of Yahweh's punishment against his people. However, despite severing the tripartite relationship because of Israel/Judah's apostasy, Isaiah envisaged a hope of restoring the relationship between Yahweh, Israel/Judah and land in the eschatological day of salvation. Israel/Judah's distress of alienation from their homeland would be reversed in the future as Yahweh would act decisively to restore the alienated and exiled people of Israel and Judah back to their land from different parts of the world (11:11-12).

In other words, in Isaiah's understanding of tripartite relationship, the land remains vulnerable to destruction and desolation based on Israel/Judah's relationship with Yahweh. When Israel/Judah remained faithful to Yahweh, the land enjoyed protection and prosperity but when Israel/Judah became estranged from Yahweh, the land fails its agricultural yields and Israel/Judah were also alienated from the land and thereby the tripartite relationship was severed. However, severing the tripartite relationship is not the end of Yahweh's relationship with his people and the land. Isaiah offers a hope of restoring Israel/Judah's relationship with Yahweh in the eschatological day in which the land is also restored back to Israel and Judah. In Isaiah's understanding of tripartite relationship, the land remains affected when Yahweh judges Israel/Judah and likewise the land is restored when Yahweh restores Israel/Judah.

3. *Traditions*

The above summary on the meaning of land and tripartite relationship in Isaiah's understanding is shaped by various traditions. They are summarized as follows:

By employing the *covenant tradition* Isaiah shows how Judah has contravened her privileged position. Instead of being a holy nation (גוי קדוש) as envisioned in the covenant tradition (Ex. 19:6), Judah became a "sinful nation" (גוי חטא), full of "iniquity" (עון) and alienated (זור) herself from Yahweh (1:4). Contrary to the covenant norms of land tillage pattern (Lev. 25:1-7, 23) and the obligation to care for the unprivileged (Ps. 71:12), exploitation and injustice became rampant by dispossessing the poor of their land and economic resources (3:12-15; 5:7, 8-10). Isaiah sees such offences as contrary to the covenant tradition and announces Yahweh's judgment in the form of agricultural failure (5:6, 10; 33:9), the destruction of their living space (5:9) and political territory (1:7; 33:8-9) and alienation of people from the land (33:7). Such destruction of land announced by Isaiah is envisaged in the covenant curse tradition in the event of violating the covenant obligation (Lev. 26, cf. Deut. 28-29). By employing the covenant tradition Isaiah reiterates that covenantal loyalty to Yahweh is the condition for Israel/Judah to live in the land and any form of disloyalty to the covenant would bring destruction to the land and alienation of people from the land (2:7). By affirming the covenant tradition, Isaiah shows that the perpetuity of the tripartite relationship remains conditional to covenantal loyalty and that loyalty to the covenant is binding for Israel/Judah to live in the land.

Despite the above judgment of destruction, Isaiah asserts that some survivors continued to dwell in the land. This is expressed by employing the *remnant tradition* in which Yahweh's kind act is understood to be the only reason for sparing some survivors in the land. Though by employing the covenant tradition Isaiah announces the destruction of land as a consequence of Judah's disloyalty, by affirming the remnant tradition Isaiah also asserts that the tripartite relationship was not entirely severed as Yahweh still placed some survivors (1:9) who lived alone in the midst of the land (5:8). Isaiah understood that the total annihilation of the people and complete destruction of the land is prevented because of Yahweh's kindness upon the remnants (1:9). Though Israel/Judah were alienated from their land and scattered to different nations, by employing the remnant tradition Isaiah affirms that Yahweh will acquire and gather his people from the four corners of the earth and envisages a hope for the exiles to return back to their homeland (11:11-12). The reestablished tripartite relationship is thus envisaged by employing the remnant tradition in Isaiah.

Isaiah employs *Torah tradition* to emphasize how Judah has deviated from the teachings of Yahweh (2:6, 8) and its consequent exile and alienation from the land, which is expressed as humiliation for the people (2:9). Practicing divination (2:6), worshipping idols (2:8) and acquiring chariots and horses (2:7) are understood as contrary to the tradition of Torah for which reason Isaiah states that Yahweh has rejected Judah (2:6). Judah followed idolatrous practices to enhance the productivity of the cultivable land (2:6) and to defend their nation from external invasion (2:7). However, by employing Torah tradition, Isaiah asserts that apart from the light (instruction) of Yahweh, any attempt to defend the land and to enhance economic prosperity is futile.

By employing the *Zion Tradition*, Isaiah emphasizes how the tripartite relationship is reestablished. Unlike the popular understanding that affirms Yahweh's presence and protection and thereby the inviolability of Zion, Isaiah understood that the land is vulnerable to destruction (33:8-9). However, by emphasizing the Zion tradition, Isaiah affirms that Yahweh will intervene to defend both the people of Judah and their land. In Isaiah's understanding of Zion tradition, the defeated people and the devastated land will again be restored by Yahweh and thereby Yahweh will be lifted up and exalted through his intervention of vanquishing the Judah's enemies (33:10-12).

Chapter 7

Conclusion
Theology of Land in the Eighth Century Prophets

7.1. Meaning of Land

The foregoing exegeses have shown us that various land terminologies employed by prophets Amos, Hosea, Micah and Isaiah basically convey four levels of meaning. First, ארץ "land" is used to refer to *the entire known earth* in which the existence of various different nations is acknowledged. Second, ארץ "land" is understood in a sense of *particular political nation* but mostly the term refers to the land of Israel and/or Judah. Other terms like מקום and ערים also appear to refer to the places and cities of particular political nation. Third, land is understood as *cultivable or arable portion* where economic activities are engaged. Such understanding is expressed by employing the terms like, בית, שדה, נחלה, חלק, האדמה and ארץ. Sometimes, however, land is also understood as an open and uncultivable area. Fourth, land is also understood in the sense of *residential space* which people inhabit as expressed by the terms like בית and ערים. Each term conveys one meaning in a particular text but maybe another in another occurrence. The contexts of a particular text best determine meaning for each term.

7.2. Traditions and Tripartite Relationship

In what follows, we have briefly highlighted the way each prophet used the traditions showing some commonalities and differences. This is done by way of comparing the way each tradition is used by the prophets in the light of tripartite relationship. Based on the comparative insights on traditions, some theological and ethical significance are drawn in the following section.

7.2.1. Brotherhood Tradition

Brotherhood tradition appears only in Amos in the context of the relationship between Tyre and Israel (Am. 1:9-10). It refers to the political relationship between the nations that was supposed to be characterized by the nature of cooperation and solidarity. In the brotherhood tradition, Yahweh is understood as the sovereign ruler, ultimate judge and observer of the affairs of nations. Yahweh expects brotherhood relationship to be perpetuated among the nations so as to preclude any form of war for territorial expansions. Amos employed the brotherhood tradition to envisage peaceful existence among the nations. Violation of brotherhood relationship between the nations brings alienation from and destruction of the land Amos considers the breaking of brotherhood tradition as an act of transgression (פשע), which is stated as the reason of Yahweh's intervention for the destruction of land.

7.2.2. Kinship Tradition

The kinship and brotherhood traditions appear to be similar but they are used in different contexts. On the one hand, the brotherhood tradition appears in the context of political pact between the nations though not related to each other as kinfolk, while the kinship tradition, on the other hand, is used between the nations related to each other as uterine brothers. It appears only in Amos in the context of bilateral relations between Edom and Israel (Am. 1:11-12). Violation of kinship tradition affects the tripartite relationship as follows: First, by breaking the kinship tradition, nations started to infringe into each others' territories and began to alienate the inhabitants from their homeland. Second, disregarding kinship tradition and its consequent territorial infringement is seen as an affront to Yahweh's land gift tradition. Yahweh demands the exercise of kinship responsibility between the nations so as to forbid war for territorial expansions. Such understanding of kinship tradition has ethical implication to promote peace, harmony and territorial respect among the nations. It envisages co-operation rather than infightings and alienation of people from the land as uprooted refugees.

7.2.3. Torah Tradition

The Torah tradition affirms that its stipulations are meant to govern the lifestyle of the people in the land. Failure to live by its instructions will result in destruction and expulsion from the land. Amos and Hosea employed the Torah tradition in the context of religious apostasy (Am. 2:4-5) and in the context of growing military strength and political threat from the surrounding nations (Hos. 8:9-13; 10:13-15 and Is. 2:5-9). Hosea also employs the Torah tradition to contrast Israel's "ways" of trusting in her military strength (Hos. 10:14) instead of trusting Yahweh. Such idea of contrasting Israel and Judah's "way" with Yahweh's way is metaphorically expressed in Isaiah as "walking" in "the light of Yahweh" (Is. 2:5-9). Torah is thus compared to or understood as Yahweh's way indicating that to walk in the light and to walk in the way of Yahweh is to follow the teaching of Torah. Unlike other eighth century prophets, Micah employs the Torah tradition to affirm the universal legitimacy of its teachings for peace and justice. Amidst the growing context of conflicts for territorial expansions, Micah sees the Torah tradition and its teachings as viable option for ensuring international peace and disarmament.

In the Torah tradition of tripartite relationship, Yahweh is affirmed as Israel and Judah's God while Israel and Judah are understood as Yahweh's "people". Israel and Judah's loyalty to Yahweh as instructed in the Torah became the condition for secured survival in the land. Obedience to Yahweh's instruction sustains the tripartite relationship in that Yahweh not only ensures peace and justice among the nations but also guarantees the survival in and cultivation of the land (Mic. 4:1-5, cf. Is. 2:2-4). On the other hand, rejection of Torah brings Yahweh's punishment upon Israel and Judah and the consequence of Yahweh's judgment affects the land in the form of agricultural failures, devastation of land (Am. 2:4-6) and alienating the people from their homeland (Hos. 8:12-13; 10:15; Is. 2:9). In the Torah tradition of tripartite relationship the eighth century prophets affirms that to remain loyal to the teaching of Torah is to remain rooted in the land while to deviate from Yahweh's Torah is to alienate oneself from the land.

7.2.4. Exodus Tradition

The Exodus tradition perpetuates the memory of Yahweh's redemptive act and his giving of the land to Israel in fulfillment of his land promise. Israel's existence in the land is remembered as a result of Yahweh's salvific act. In Am. 2:6-16 the Exodus tradition is employed in the context of injustice and oppression related to land. Amos' usage of the Exodus tradition delegitimizes any form of injustice that uproots and alienates the vulnerable people from the land. In Am. 9: 5-8, the Exodus tradition is recounted to challenge Israel that Yahweh's past intervention do not confer them a favorite position. Two distinctive features can be observed in Amos' usage of the Exodus tradition. First, he reinterprets Yahweh's past intervention on Israel's behalf as model to emulate and to show kindness to the landless poor. Second, Amos gives a new meaning to Exodus by affirming that Yahweh is not just Israel's God but he is a universal Lord who has also been active in the history of other nations. In a little different line, Hosea reinterprets the Exodus tradition to explain Israel's historical identity in relation to Yahweh's kind act (Hos. 2:15; 11:1; 13:4). Mostly, the Exodus tradition appears in Hosea to justify the coming judgment for Israel's failure to reciprocate Yahweh's kind intervention (Hos. 7:16; 8:13; 12:9; 12:13-14; 13:4). The distinctiveness feature in Hosea's usage of the Exodus tradition is that it does not guarantee Yahweh's kind intervention as in the past but to sentence Israel to her former status of bondage (Hos. 8:13). Unlike Amos and Hosea who reiterated the Exodus tradition mostly in the judgment oracle, Micah distinctively employed the Exodus tradition to assure Yahweh's kind intervention (Mic. 7:8-20). As Yahweh defeated Israel's enemy during the Exodus, Yahweh will yet again intervene with mighty act and defeat the encroaching nation (Assyria) so as to ensure his protection for the people and the land. Yahweh's mighty intervention is the result of Judah's repentance (Mic. 7:9) and Yahweh's forgiving nature (Mic. 7:18).[1]

In the Exodus tradition of tripartite relationship, Yahweh is affirmed as Israel's "deliverer", "shepherd" and "God" (Hos. 2:23; Mic. 2:14) and Israel as Yahweh's "people", "sheep" and "inheritance" (Mic. 2:14) while the land is seen as Yahweh's object of promise to Israel and Israel's object of possession (Mic. 7:11, 14). Yahweh's kind act initiates the establishment of tripartite relationship, which enables landless Israel to possess the land in the Exodus period (Am. 2:10). Israel was expected to follow Yahweh's model and show kindness to the fellow landless people. However, Israel failed Yahweh by alienating and uprooting the defenseless from their land. This results in disturbing tripartite relationship in which Yahweh intervenes and sentences Israel to destruction of and exile from their land (Am. 2:10-16; Hos. 8:13). As the ethical aspect of the Exodus tradition was not perpetuated, Israel's relationship both with Yahweh and her land failed, which is expressed in terms of alienation from the land.

In the Exodus tradition, Yahweh is portrayed as a God of liberation, who delivers nations and destines a separate territory to each nation. Yahweh is presented as the hope for the conflicted infested world. Yahweh's kind act on behalf of the marginalized de-warrants any form of mistreatment of fellow members in the land and encourages kindness as model to emulate in societal relations. God wants people to have their own land and live in freedom and dignity as such; nobody should be under slavery without the rights to their land to govern themselves.

7.2.5. Covenant Tradition

The covenant tradition reiterates that just as Israel and Judah exist in the land because of Yahweh's loyalty to his covenantal promise, Yahweh also demands their loyalty to covenant relationship in order to sustain their continual existence in the land. In the covenant tradition, disloyalty to the covenant relationship with Yahweh is seen as a rejection to the right and privileges for Israel and Judah to dwell in a God-given land (Am. 2:4-5; Hos. 8:12-13). Whereas, Hosea mostly employs the covenant tradition in the context of Israel's following of other gods (Hos. 1:2; 2:2-8; 17), in Amos, Micah and Isaiah the covenant tradition appears mostly in the context of judgment against injustice related to socioeconomic offences (Am. 5:6-11; 5:21-27; Mic. 2:1-5; Is. 1:4-9; 3:12-15; 5:1-7). Hosea's emphasis on covenant tradition appears different from Amos, Micah and Isaiah in at least another two ways. First, unlike other prophets, Hosea sees Israel's

[1] It is worthy to note in this context that the Deutro-Isaiah used Exodus tradition in his salvation oracle as second exodus from exile to their land. Cf. Isa.41:9-10; 43:6; 44:24-28; 45:13-14; 46:9, 13; 48:20-21.

reliance on her military strength and her political alliances with other nations as manifestation of unfaithfulness to her covenant partner, Yahweh (Hos. 8:9-13; 10:13b-15). Probably because Hosea sees Israel's reliance on military power as an expression of distrusting Yahweh and also alliances with nations could invite temptation for Israel to follow the gods of other nations. Second, Hosea also uses covenant as the basis of Yahweh's future restoration of both Israel and her land (Hos. 2:16-23; 14:4-7). Though the term covenant does not always appear in all the texts, in Hosea it is conveyed metaphorically through husband-wife relation while in Amos, Micah and Isaiah, the idea is expressed through the invoking of the covenant curse judgment. Despite the above differences, at least two broad observations on the common emphasis on covenant violations can be noted. First, covenant violation is understood in terms of theological apostasy: they rejected Yahweh's Torah (Am. 2:4; Hos. 8:12), followed idols (Am. 2:4; 5:26; Hos. 2:7-8), practiced divination (Isa. 2:6) and did not trust Yahweh (Hos. 5:13; 10:13b). Second, covenant violation is emphasized in relation to socioeconomic injustice related to land: they encroach upon the territory of each other (Hos. 5:10), covet the field and houses (Mic. 2:2; Isa. 5:8), seized and evicted the poor from their inheritance (Am. 2:6; Mic. 2:2; Isa. 5:8), robbed the poor peasants of their crops (Isa. 3:12, 14), and failed justice system due to bribery (Am. 2:7; Mic. 3:9, 11). In violating the covenant, Israel and Judah not only alienated themselves from Yahweh but they themselves were alienated from the land and its produce as Yahweh's judgment causes drought and agricultural failures upon the land.

Just as covenant tradition is employed to explain the breaking of tripartite relationship, the prophets also employed it as the basis to envisage a future restoration of the relationship. Israel's repentance, "you are my God" (Hos. 2:23) and Yahweh's "forgiveness" and "love" (Hos. 14:4) that accepts Israel again as "you are my people" (Hos. 2:23) re-establishes the covenant relationship between Yahweh and Israel. The restored relationship between Yahweh and Israel further restores the blessing and gifts of land to Israel (Hos. 2:22-23; 14:5-7). This is stated in terms of Yahweh's answer to the land with fertility and the land's response to Israel with prosperity making Israel's existence in the land possible. For Israel, prosperity and secured survival in the land depends on her covenant faithfulness with Yahweh. In the covenant tradition, relationship with the land either stands or falls based on her commitment to the covenant relationship with Yahweh.

Israel possessed the land as her inheritance and Yahweh possesses Israel as his inheritance, which indicates that belongingness governs the tripartite relationship. Yahweh is not a detached God but he is a God who longs for relationship with humanity. Human beings are God's people[2] and God assures humanity's survival in the land if they remain loyal to him. Loyalty to Yahweh is the way to the fullness of life while alienation from God is an estrangement from the life of blessing in

[2] Cf. Isa.19:24-25.

the land.[3] The covenant tradition of tripartite relationship teaches us that our right relationship with God determines our relationship with fellow humans and with the land.

7.2.6. Theophany Tradition

Theophany tradition affirms the earth as an arena where Yahweh appears in majesty and demonstrates his sovereign authority on the earth that evokes the attention of both the people and nature. Though Isa. 6 narrates Yahweh's manifestation, its account is different in that it does not mention the convulsion of the earth and the disturbance of nature following Yahweh's appearances on earth as in Amos and Micah. Both Amos and Micah employed the theophany tradition in the context of judgment against the land of Israel and Judah (Am. 9:8; Mic. 1:4-5), however, unlike Micah, Amos links the theophany tradition with the creation and Exodus traditions. By intertwining these traditions, Amos shows that Yahweh as creator (creation tradition) intervenes upon the earth (theophany tradition) and delivers other nations like he did to Israel (Exodus tradition) and destined each nation a separate political territory (Am. 9:5-8). Apart from this difference, both the prophets emphasized that Yahweh's manifestation was occasioned by sin, which caused disturbances upon the entire nature (Am. 9:5; Mic. 1:3-4).

Both Amos and Micah reinterpreted the theophany tradition to suit their message of judgment. Whereas, in the tradition of Sinai theophany Yahweh's arrival was occasioned by Israel's affirmed allegiance to Yahweh (Ex. 19:5-6, 8), in Amos and Micah the theophany was occasioned by "sin" of Israel and Judah (Am. 9:8; Mic. 1:4-5). Second, whereas, in Deborah's narrative the theophany was occasioned by Yahweh's promise to rescue Israel and her land from enemies (Judg. 5:1-5ff), in Amos and Micah it was occasioned by Yahweh's judgment to announce the destruction upon Israel and Judah and their land (Am. 9:5-8; Mic. 1:4-6). In theophany tradition, "land" is seen as an arena of Yahweh's manifestation and a sphere of human existence, while the nations are seen as inhabitants of land as Yahweh designated to them. Yahweh is portrayed as the God of history who rules, intervenes and controls the affairs of humanity. Yahweh and Israel/Judah relationship are understood to be in precarious state and such strained relationship between Yahweh and Israel/Judah put the land in precarious state of devastation (Am. 9:5-8; Mic. 1:2-7). Theophany tradition in Amos and Micah, therefore, announces the strained tripartite relationship in which Yahweh's manifestation to deal with Israel and Judah's sin causes unrest upon Israel and disturbs the life forces on the land.

Yahweh's appearance on the earth and the responses of nature to Yahweh's arrival delegitimizes humans' attempt to deify nature as god. Nature is an arena for humanity to survive as God's gift and not an object of worship. Humans' ethical behaviors are linked with the state of nature. Humanity's behavior ("sins" and

[3] Cf. Lev. 28:25-28. Karl A. Deurloo, "Erets: Erd-Land Fur Menschen", *CV* 46/1 (2004) 9.

"rebellions") affects the land and the life forces to vulnerable state of "mourning". Humans' rebellion against God is contrary to the law of nature that Yahweh has ordained. This calls for proper ethical values of humanity to live in harmony with God as well as with nature. Such understanding can contribute to Christian's perspective on ecological crisis.

7.2.7. Creation Tradition

Creation tradition affirms Yahweh as the creator of all the earth and the controller of nature (Am. 9:5-6; Hos. 2:8-9). Both the humanity and land are linked together as Yahweh's creation and Yahweh is presented as the God who is active in the affairs of his creation. Whereas, technical creation term like ברא does not appear in Hos. 2:16-12 and Isa. 5:8-10 but by emphasizing Yahweh's power over the entire creation, he is presented as the creator God and the sovereign controller over the entire nature (cf. Gen. 1-2). Unlike Hosea and Isaiah, the prophet Amos uses creation terms, such as, "builder" and "founder" (Am. 9:6) to assert Yahweh as the creator and thereby his ultimate ownership of the earth is affirmed. Also unlike Hosea and Isaiah, Amos links the creation tradition with the Exodus tradition to establish Yahweh's sovereignty as creator and owner and thereby his authority to designate a territory for each political nation is affirmed (Am. 9:5-8). Two significant emphases of the eighth century prophets' usages of creation tradition can be noted. First, as creator Yahweh is understood as a God who controls nature: he sends rain to moisturize the land (Hos. 2:21-23; 14:4-5); he withholds rain that affects the cultivation of the land (Am. 4:6-8; Isa. 5:6); he bestows fertility upon the land (Am. 9:13) and withdraws the yielding of the land (Hos. 2:9, 13; 14:4-5; Isa. 5:10). Yahweh's favorable or unfavorable responses to natural forces are understood in terms of Israel and Judah's relation with Yahweh. Second, as creator Yahweh is the ultimate owner of the earth who holds absolute authority over the destiny of the nations. As such, Yahweh determines which nation settles in which particular territory of land (Am. 9:7).

In the creation tradition Yahweh is portrayed as the creator and both the humanity and land are linked together as Yahweh's creation (Am. 9:5-8; Hos. 2:2-12).[4] The land remains under Yahweh's control and its produces are seen as Yahweh's gift upon the land for the survival of humanity (Hos. 2:16-23). Because both the humanity and land are Yahweh's creation, both remain answerable to each other and to Yahweh. As such, when humanity sins against God, Yahweh intervenes in judgment against humanity by causing destruction upon the land (Am. 9:5-8; Hos. 2:2-12; Isa. 5:10). Also, in response to humans' failed relationship with Yahweh the land fails to respond to humans' need by turning into a parched land and failing to produce its yielding (Hos. 2:3, 9). Likewise, in response to humans' answer to Yahweh's directed way of life, the

[4] The understanding of God as the creator and Lord of all the earth and everything in it is affirmed in the NT (cf. Acts 17:24).

land answers to humans' needs by yielding its crops abundantly. Yahweh's answer to the land and the land's answer to humans' need are seen to be dependent upon humanity's answer to Yahweh as the ultimate controller of nature and the only God (cf. Hos. 2:20-23). In the tripartite relationship of creation tradition, land appears to be an arena of struggle between Yahweh and Israel and that the precarious state of land is the result of disturbing relationship between Yahweh and Israel/Judah (Am. 9:5-8; Hos. 2:2-12; Isa. 5:10). Yahweh's pronouncement of judgment against Israel affects the land severely, which in return affects the lives of the Israelites in the land.

Yahweh is the God of creation. As such he controls the law of nature either to provide or withhold the blessing of the land. Land and all its vitalities are Yahweh's creation and such understanding delegitimizes any attempt to deify nature as an object of worship. All the gifts of land belong to Yahweh as creator. As such, Yahweh is the only provider and the only way back for humanity to the life of blessing upon the land is to affirm the allegiance to Yahweh.

7.2.8. Zion Tradition

Zion tradition affirms the sanctity and inviolability of Jerusalem based on the belief that Yahweh's dwells in Zion. Zion is believed to be divinely protected and that no evil and destruction can befall upon Zion (Mic. 3:11). Micah and Isaiah (Mic. 3:11-13; 7:8-10; Isa. 33:7-12) employ the Zion tradition in the context of Assyrian threat in which both the people and land were in precarious state. Amidst such situation, Micah and Isaiah envisaged Yahweh's intervention to defeat the enemy and to protect his people and land. Unlike Isaiah, Micah emphasizes further on Zion tradition in the light of the sins of Jerusalem. In Micah, Judah understood that the looming destruction of her land is the result of her sin (Mic. 7:9), while the nations understood it as Yahweh's inability to defend his people and land (Mic. 7:10). Yahweh's relationship with his people and the land is thus put at stake. Amidst such context, Yahweh defeats the nations to empower his people and protect their land from certain defeat (Mic. 4:13).

Some distinctive emphases on Micah's usage of Zion tradition can be noted. Micah did not emphasize on Yahweh's intervention exclusively to deal with Jerusalem's enemy but also to deal with Jerusalem's sin. Like the Psalmists (65:4[5]; 68:29[30]; 122:1; 122: 9), Micah affirms divine presence in Jerusalem ("the house of Yahweh", Mic. 4:1). However, unlike the Psalmists, Micah understood that because Yahweh is in their midst, he will punish Jerusalem and "plough" her land like a field (Mic. 3:11-12). Such destruction is seen to be the way of divine justice taking its course of action for failing to deliver justice (Mic. 3:9). Unlike other prophets, Micah employed Zion tradition to affirm Yahweh's presence that envisages international peace. Yahweh dwells in Jerusalem to teach justice to the nations, which she had failed to deliver, as the way of life. This would ensure peace among the nations and safe dwelling in the land (Mic. 4:1-5). This indicates that Yahweh's protection on both the people and the land is ensured only when justice is practiced as the way of life. Micah also links Zion tradition with the Exodus tradition amidst the context of Assyria's threat to assures that Yahweh will bring liberation by subjugating the powerful nation that threatens Jerusalem as Yahweh did amidst the Egyptian in the past (Mic. 7:8-14).

In the Zion tradition of tripartite relationship, justice is seen as a way of life, which Yahweh demands from his people for secured existence in the land. Affirmation on Yahweh's presence among the people and the protection of the land (Zion tradition) is seen as an elusive hope if Judah's ethical life is unaccompanied by justice. Because of her injustice, Yahweh himself comes against Zion and "ruined" her land (Mic. 3:9-11). As justice system failed, the vulnerable and helpless were denied protection (Mic. 3:9-12). Likewise, Yahweh denies his protection upon the vulnerable Zion. As a consequence, the land was ploughed and ruined to destruction (3:12) and the people were deprived of their dwelling in the land. Injustice is thus seen to be the reason of debarring Yahweh's protection and denial of land to Zion.

However, the tripartite relationship is yet again reestablished after Zion suffers Yahweh's indignation in relation to her sin (Mic. 7:9-10). Yahweh assures to protect his people and the land from the enemies (Mic. 4:11-13; 7:8ff). As Yahweh intervenes on behalf of Jerusalem, Judah was given a hope to reoccupy the land, rebuild the cities, and extent the boundary of their land (Mic. 7:10). Such affirmation on Yahweh's intervention once again reaffirms the tripartite relationship between Yahweh, Judah and the land. This picture of a harmonious relationship between Yahweh, Judah as well as nations and land (the tripartite relationship) is envisaged in the setting of accepting Yahweh's justice as the way of life (Mic. 4:1-5).

Yahweh is not a detached God but he dwells amidst the people. God's presence in our lives does not immune us from suffering his punishment. Because Yahweh dwells amongst the people he observes injustice and deals with judgment to correct the wrongs.

7.2.9. Remnant Tradition

It affirms that despite Yahweh's punishment, both the people and the land would not be totally destroyed as Yahweh would leave a few survivors in the land. It also assures the alienated people that God would "assemble" and "gather" them back to their homeland. Isaiah affirms that Yahweh exiled the people of Judah from their homeland for their act of injustice related to land (Isa. 5:8; Mic. 2:2 cf. Am. 5:3). In the context of massive destruction from the enemies, the hope of rebuilding and reoccupying the land become impossible. However, Isaiah affirms that Yahweh left a few people in the midst of the land (Is. 5:8-10) indicating that the tripartite relationship was not totally severed. Also, despite the judgment of destruction, Yahweh in his kind act promises to acquire and gather his people from the four corners of the earth and bring the exiles back to their homeland (11:11-12). The reestablished tripartite relationship is thus envisaged by employing the remnant tradition in Isaiah.

Isaiah explains the tripartite relationship by employing the remnant tradition. In such understanding the disturbed tripartite relationship, which was occasioned by Judah's sin, was not seen to be entirely severed. The judgment to exile the people and desolate the land that was announced earlier was not carried out in totality as Yahweh placed some survivors (Isa. 1:9) in the midst of the land (Isa. 5:8). Total annihilation of the people and complete destruction of the land is prevented because of Yahweh kindness in his relationship with the land and people (Isa. 1:9). Despite Yahweh's judgment of exile, his people would also not be forever alienated from their land as Yahweh assures to gather his people from all the corners of the earth and give them back their land (Isa. 11:11-12). Though the basis of such tripartite relationship is not stated clearly, what appears clear is that the act of gathering back the exiles is stated as Yahweh's act. The reestablished tripartite relationship is thus envisaged by employing the remnant tradition in Isaiah.

Yahweh never destroys his people completely nor alienates them forever from the land for he is the God who keeps his covenant promise. Yahweh is the God of restoration who does not want to alienate his people forever from the land. He is the God who forgives and longs to restore his people back to him and to the land. The theological implication of remnant tradition affirms that in confession there is forgiveness and in repentance there is always restoration. God's forgiveness and humans' repentance result in restoration of fortunes of the people and the land. Such understanding of remnant tradition has ethical relevance in that it teaches humanity that the way back to genuine life is through repentance to God.

7.3. Conclusion

In sum, whether referring to the entire earth, or a particular political nation, or a cultivable land or a place of habitation, "land" almost always appears in connection with Yahweh and Israel/Judah conveying to us that the land theology of the eighth century prophets is the tripartite relationship. If Israel remains loyal to Yahweh, she finds herself located in the land and enjoyed its bountiful blessing. However, if Israel alienates herself from Yahweh she finds herself alienated from the land (exile). Such understanding of land as tripartite relationship is rooted in various historical and religious traditions, namely, Brotherhood, Kinship, Torah, Exodus, Covenant, Theophany, Creation, Zion and Remnant traditions as explained above.

By employing various traditions, the eighth century prophets understood land as Yahweh's creation in its entirety and therefore Yahweh is seen as the ultimate ruler, owner and controller of the earth who apportions land to every nation as separate political territory, judges the affairs of every political nation and controls the cycle of nature of the land. Land is understood as a gift of Yahweh and such understanding of land as gift is seen as a blessing of Yahweh's covenantal promise. Land is also understood to be an arena in which its inhabitants do the will of Yahweh and enjoy Yahweh's blessing. Israel's occupation of the land and her disobedience to Yahweh's command are understood to be mutually exclusive. For Israel and Judah to go astray from Yahweh is to depart from the land but to remain loyal to Yahweh is to remain located in the land. The destruction of and exile from the land is not understood as total breakdown of the tripartite relationship as Yahweh leaves some people in the land and also assures to gather the exiles back to their land. Israel/Judah can always look towards the future with hope of restoring their relationship with Yahweh as well as the land as Yahweh is understood as the God who restores the fortune of his people and the land. Land is also seen to be a place of habitation in which safe dwelling of people as individual and as nation is envisaged. As such, harmonious existence between the members of the society and between the nations is encouraged by stressing the ethos of tolerance and respect for territorial integrity among the inhabitants of the land.

7.4. Role of Churches today

Taking together the message of the eighth century prophets and teachings for a wider tripartite relationship can enhance the ministry of churches today. A blueprint plan of action cannot be discussed here since the Indian context is vast, complex and pluralistic. But the necessity to promote the relationship between people and land can be emphasized by the churches and involve in the following roles:

i. Re-reading the history and tradition of the OT for the teaching of the tripartite relationship. Such kind of teaching would delegitimize humans' autonomy and shows that people belong to land and land belong to God and both the people and land belong to God as his creation. The emphasis on tripartite relationship would promote relation with the nature and fellow human beings and offer a hope for peace and harmony and justice.

ii. Systematic preaching on the text of tripartite relationship particularly from the prophetical books can help the congregation understand how humans' conduct affects the relationship with other people and also with the land and God. One of the important problems related to tripartite relationship is that many poor people have been alienated from their land in villages because of loans, burden of debts, exploitation of money lenders and booming real-estate business. In ancient Israel, Jubilee year was introduced to re-establish their relationship with the land (Lev. 25:20-25). Churches need to dialogue with the Government to restore the alienated people to their land, offer micro-credit to promote their agriculture.

iii. Reflecting on our own historical experience under the British rule and estranged relationship with our mother land India without political freedom and being a colony for their market. By perpetuating the memory of our own Independence struggles and theologizing it as our tradition, we can challenge the public for more patriotism and taking care of the land and people. One way of doing it is to create awareness programme among Communities about the problems of globalization, multi-national finance capitalism and neo-colonial trend that foreign companies can buy land and water resources for their industries.

iv. Some action plans can be sorted out to relate our people to our land. Such action plans can include: projects on environment protection, enacting laws to stop the alienation and uprooting of people from the land especially the farmers for real estate purpose, offer a micro-credit to promote agriculture and non-formal education to strengthen the ties between people and land. Environmental degradation is one of the reasons for villages to break their ties with their land and move to cities as refugees. Churches can support some of the national movements such as Narmada Bachau, Chipko Movement, Wild Life Association to stop environmental degradations and alienation of land from people.

Bibliography

Books and Commentaries

Alexander, Joseph A. *The Prophet Isaiah: A Commentary*. Grand Rapids, Michigan: Zondervan, 1978.

Alexander, T. Desmond. *From Paradise to the Promised Land: An Introduction to the Main Themes of the Pentateuch*. Grand Rapids, Michigan: Baker, 1995.

Alfaro, Juan I. *Justice and Loyalty*. Grand Rapids, Michigan: William B. Eerdmans Publishing Comapany, 1989.

Allen, Leslie C. *The Book of Joel, Obadaiah, Jonah and Micah*. NICOT. Grand Rapids, Michigan: William B. Eerdmans Publishing Comapany, 1976.

Andersen, Francis I. and David Noel Freedman. *Hosea: A New Translation with Introduction and Commentary*. AB 24. New York: Doubleday, 1980.

_______ *Amos: A New Translation with Introduction and Commentary*, AB 24A. New York: Doubleday, 1989.

_______ *Micah: A New Translation with Introduction and Commentary*. AB 24E. New York: Doubleday, 2000.

Baker, Kenneth L. and Waylon Bailey. *Micah, Nahum, Habakkuk, Zephaniah*. NAC 20. Nashville, Tennessee: Broadman, 1999.

Barnes, William Hamilton. *Studies in the Chronology of the Davidic Monarchy of Israel*. Altants: Scholars, 1991.

Barrick, W. Boyd. *BMH as Body Language: A Lexical and Iconographical Study of the Word BHM When Not a Reference to Cultic Phenomena in Biblical and Post-Biblical Hebrew*. New York/London: T & T Clark, 2008.

Barry, Webb. *The Message of Isaiah: On Eagles' Wing*. BST. England: IVP, 1996.

Barstad, Hans M. *The Religious Polemics of Amos: Studies in the Preaching of Am: 7b-8; 4:1-13; 5:1-27; 6:4-7; 8:14*. Leiden: Brill, 1984.

Barton, John. *Amos's Oracles Against the Nations*. The Society for Old Testament Studies Monograph Series, 6. Cambridge: Cambridge University, 1980.

Bimson, John J. *Redating the Exodus and Conquest*. Sheffield: Almond, 1981.

Blenkinsopp, Joseph. *A History of Prophecy in Israel: From Settlement in the Land to the Hellenistic Period.* Philadelphia: Westminster John Knox Press, 1983.

_______ *Isaiah 1-39* AB19. New York, Doubleday: Anchor, 2000.

_______ *Treasures Old and New: Essays in the Theology of Pentateuch.* Grand Rapids, Michigan:/Cambridge, UK: Michigan: William B. Eerdmans Publishing Comapany, 2004.

Brich, Bruce C. and others (eds). *A Theological Introduction to the Old Testament.* Nashville: Abingdon Press, 1999.

Brich, Bruce. *Hosea, Joel and Amos.* Westminster Bible Companion. Louisville, Kentucky: Westminister John Knox Press, 1997.

Bright, John. *A History of Israel.* 4th edn. Louisville, Kentucky: Westminister John Knox Press, 2000.

Broyles, Craug C. and Craig A. Evans (eds). *Writing and Reading the Scroll of Isaiah Studies of an Interpretive Studies.* Vol.1. Leiden: Brill, 1997.

Brueggemann, Walter. *Tradition in Crisis: A Study in Hosea.* Richmond, Virginia: Westminister John Knox Press, 1968.

_______ *The Land: Places as Gift, Promise, and Challenge in Biblical Faith.* London: SPCK, 1978.

_______ *Isaiah 1-39.* Louisville, KY: Westminister John Knox Press, 1998.

_______ Walter. *Isaiah 1-39.* Louisville, Kentucky: Westminster John Knox Press, 1998.

_______ *The Covenanted Self: Explorations in Law and Covenant.* Minneapolis: Fortress Press, 1999.

_______ *The Prophetic Imagination.* 2nd edn. Minneapolis: Fortress Press, 2001.

Bullock, C. Hassell. *An Introduction to the Old Testament Prophetic Books.* Chicago: Moody, 1986.

Cathcart, Kevin J. and others (eds). *The Targum of the Minor Prophets: Translated, with a Critical Introduction, Apparatus and Notes.* Vol. 14. Edinburgh: T & T Clark, 1989.

Chacko, Modayil Mani. *Liberation and Service of God: A Theological Evaluation of Exodus 1:1-15:21.* Delhi: ISPCK, 2002.

Childs, Brevard S. *Isaiah and the Assyrian Crisis.* SBT 3. London: SCM, 1967.

_______ *Isaiah*, OTL. Louisville, Kentucky: Westminister John Knox Press, 2001.

Clements, R.E. *Old Testament Theology: A Fresh Approach.* London: Marshall, Morgan & Scott, 1978.

_______ *Isaiah 1-39.* NCB. London/ Grand Rapids, Michigan: Marshall, Morgan & Scott/Eerdmans, 1980.

Clines, David J. A. *The Theme of the Pentateuch.* JSOTSS 10. England; Sheffield, 1978.

Cogan, M. *Imperialism and Religion: Assyria, Judah and Israel in the Eight and Seventh Centuries BCE*. Missoula, Mont.: Scholars, 1973.

Coote, Robert B. *Amos Among the Prophets: Composition and Theology*. Philadelphia Fortress Press, 1981.

Cotterell, Peter and Max Turner. *Linguistics and Biblical Interpretation*. Downers Grove, Illinois: IVP, 1989.

Craigie, Peter C. *The Twelve Prophets*. Vol. 2. Louisville, Kentucky: Westminister John Knox Press, 1985.

Cripps, Richard. S. *A Critical and Exegetical Commentary on the Book of Amos*. Great Britain: SPCK, 1960.

Crusemann, Frank. *The Torah: Theology and Social History of the Old Testament Law*. Trans. by Allan W. Mahnke. Edinburgh: T & T Clark, 1996.

Davies, Graham I. *Hosea*. Sheffield: JSOT, 1993.

Davies, W.D. *The Gospel and the Land: Early Christianity and Jewish Territorial Doctrine*. Los Angeles: University of California, 1974.

Dearman, John Andrew. *Property Rights in the Eight Century Israel*. SBL Dissertation Series 106. Atlanta: Scholars, 1988.

Delitzsch, F. *Isaiah*. Vol. 7. Trans. by James Martin. Grand Rapids, Michigan: William B. Eerdmans Publishing Company, 1982.

Dempsey, Carol J. *The Prophets: A Liberation-Critical Reading*. Minneapolis: Fortress Press, 2000.

Dobba-Allsopp, F.W. *Weep, O Daughter: A Study of the City-Lament Genre in the Hebrew Bible*, Biblica et Orientalia 44. Rome: Pontificio Instituto Biblico, 1993.

Dozeman, Thomas B. *God on the Mountain: A Study on Redaction, Theology and Canon in Exodus 19-24*. SBL 37. Atlanta, Georgia: Scholars, 1989.

Driver, G.R. *Canaanite Myths and Legends*. Edinburgh: T & T Clark, 1956.

Driver, S. R. *The Books of Joel and Amos*. Cambridge: Cambridge Bible, 1897.

_______ *An Introduction to the Literature of the Old Testament*. Edinburgh: T & T Clark, 1913.

Engnell, I. *A Rigid Scrutiny*. Nashville: Vanderbilt University, 1969.

Fager, Jeffrey A. *Land Tenure and Biblical Jubilee: Uncovering Hebrew Ethics through the Sociology of Knowledge*. JSOTSup. 155. Sheffield: JSOT, 1993.

Finley, Thomas J. *Joel, Amos and Obadiah*. The Wycliffe Exegetical Commentary. Chicago: Moody, 1990.

Fohrer, Georg. *Introduction to the Old Testament*. Trans. by David E. Green. Nashville, New York: Abingdon Press, 1968.

Garret, Duane A. *Hosea, Joel*, NAC. Broadman & Holman, 1997.

Gemeren, Van. *Interpreting the Prophetic Word*. Grand Rapids, Michigan: Zondervan, 1990.

Goldingay, John. *Old Testament Theology: Israel's Gospel.* Vol. 1. Downers Grove, Illinois: IVP, 2003.

Goshen-Gottstein, M. H. *The Book of Isaiah.* Jerusalem: Magnes, 1975.

Gottwald, Norman. K. *The Hebrew Bible: A Socio-Literary Introduction.* Philadelphia: Fortress Press, 1985.

Gowan, Donald E. *The Book of Amos: Introduction, Commentary and Reflection.* NIB 7 Nashville: Abingdon Press, 1996.

Gray, George Buchanan. *The Book of Isaiah 1-27.* Vol.1. ICC. Edinburgh: T & T Clark, 1980.

Guenther, Allen R. *Hosea, Amos.* Scottdale, Pennsylvania/Waterloo, Ontario: Herald, 1998.

_______ *Hosea, Amos,* Believers Church Bible Commentary. Ontario: Herad, 1997.

Habel, Norman C. *The Land is Mine: Six Biblical Land Ideologies.* Minneapolis: Fortress Press, 1995.

Hailey, Homer. *A Commentary on the Minor Prophets.* Grand Rapids, Michigan: Baker, 1972.

Harper, William Rainey. *Amos and Hosea.* ICC. Edinburgh: T & T Clark, 1979. Blackwell, 1970.

Harrison, R.K. *The Archaeology of the Old Testament.* New York: Harper and Row, 1963.

Hasel, G. *The Remnant.* Berrien Springs: Andrews University, 1972.

_______ *Understanding the Book of Amos: Basic Issues in Current Interpretations.* Grand Rapids, Michigan: Baker, 1991.

Hayes, John H. *Amos, Eight Century Prophet: His Times and His Preaching.* Nashsville: Abingdon Press, 1988.

Hayes, John H. and J. Maxwell Miller (eds). *Israelite and Judean History.* London, Philadelphia: SCM, Trinity International Press, 1997.

Hayes, Katherine M. *The Earth Mourns: Prophetic Metaphor and Oral Aesthetic.* Atlanta: SBL, 2002.

Heibert, Theodore. *The Yahwehist's Landscape: Nature and Religion in Early Israel.* New York/Oxford: Oxford, 1996.

Herbert, A.S. *The Book of the Prophet Isaiah Chapters 1-39.* CBC. Cambridge: Cambridge University, 1973.

Heschel, Abraham J. *The Prophets.* New York: Harper and Row, 1969.

Hillers, Dilbert R. *Micah.* Hermenia. Philadelphia: Fortress Press, 1994.

Holladay,W. L. *The Root SUBH in the Old Testament.* Leiden: E. J. Brill, 1958.

Horeth, Alfred J and others. Eds. *Peoples of the Old Testament World.* Grand Rapids, Michigan/Cambridge: Baker/Lutterworth, 1994.

Hubbard, David Allen. *Hosea.* TOTC. Leicester, England: IVP, 1989.

Jeremias, Jorg. *The Book of Amos: A Commentary*. OTL. Louisville, Kentucky: Westminster John Knox Press, 1995.

Kaiser, Otto. *Isaiah 1-12: A Commentary*. OTL; Philadelphia: Westminster John Knox Press, 1983.

Kaiser, Walter C. *A History of Israel: From Bronze Age through the Jewish Wars*. Nashville, Tennessee: Broadman & Holman, 1998.

Keil, C.F. *Minor Prophets*. Vol. 10. Grand Rapids, Michigan: William B. Eerdmans Publishing Company, 1982.

Kidner, Derek. *The Message of Hosea*. BST. Leicester, England/Downers Grove, Illinois: IVP, 1981.

Knight, George A.F. *Theology as Narration: A Commentary on the Book of Exodus*. Grand Rapids, Michigal: 1976.

Koehler-Baumgartner, *Hebraisches und aramaisches Lexicon Zum AT*. Leiden, 1953.

Leclerc, Thomas. *Yahweh is Exalted in Justice: Solidarity and Conflict in Isaiah*. Minneapolis: Fortress Press, 2001.

Limburg, James. *Hosea-Micah*. Interpretation. Atlanta, Georgia: Westminister John Knox Press, 1988.

Macintosh, A.A. *Hosea*. ICC. Edinburgh: T & T Clark, 1977.

Martens, Elmer A. *God's Design: A Focus on Old Testament Theology*. 2nd edn. Grand Rapids, Michigan: Baker Books, 1994.

Mason, R. *Micah, Nahum, Obadiah*. Sheffield: JSOT, 1991.

Mays, James Luther. *Amos: A Commentary*. OTL. Philadelphia: Westminster John Knox Press, 1969.

_______ *Hosea: A Commentary*, OTL. Philadelphia: Westminster John Knox Press, 1969.

_______ *Micah*, OTL. Philadelphia: Westminster John Knox Press, 1976.

McCarthy, Dennis J. *Treaty and Covenant: A Study in Form in the Ancient Oriental Documents and in the Old Testament*. Analecta Biblica 21a. Rome: Biblical Institute, 1978.

McKay, J. *Religion in Judah Under the Assyrian*. London: SCM, 1973.

McKenna, David L. *Isaiah 1-39*, The Communicator's Commentary. Vol. 16A. Dallas, Texas: Word Books, 1993.

Melanchton, Monica J. *Rejection by God: The History and Significance of the Rejection Motif in the Hebrew Bible*. SBL 22. New York: Peter Lang, 2001.

Milgrom, Jacob. *Leviticus 23-27*. AB 3B. New York: Doubleday, 2000.

Miller, J. Maxwell and John Hayes. *A History of Ancient Israel and Judah*. Philadelphia: Westminster John Knox Press, 1980.

Miller, John W. *Meet the Prophet: A Beginner's Guide to the Book of the Biblical Prophets*. New York: Paulist, 1987.

Motyer, Alec. *Isaiah.* TOTC. Leicester, England: IVP, 1999.

Mowvley, Harry. *The Book of Amos and Hosea.* London: Epworth, 1991.

Muthunayagom, Daniel Jones. *The Relationship Between Election and Israel's Attitude Towards the Nations in the Book of Isaiah.* Delhi: ISPCK, 2000.

Nogalski, James. *Literary Precursors to the Book of Twelve.* New York: de Gruyter, 1993.

Noth, Martin. *The History of* Israel. Trans. by Peter Ackroyd. New York: Harper & Row, 1958.

Ogilvie, Lloyd J. *Hosea, Joel, Amos, Jonah,* The Communicator's Commentary 20. Dallas, Texas: Waco, 1990.

Oswalt, John. *The Book of Isaiah Chapters 1-39.* NICOT. Grand Rapids, Michigan: William B. Eerdmans Publishing Company, 1986.

Pagolu, Augustine. *The Religion of the Patriarch.* JSOTSS 277. England: Sheffield, 1988.

Parpola, S. and K. Watanabe. *Neo Assyrian Treaties and Loyalty Oaths.* Helsinki: Helsinki University Press, 1988.

Patrick, Dale. *The Rhetoric of Revelation in the Hebrew Bible.* Minneapolis, Fortress Press, 1999.

Paul, Shalom M. *Amos.* Minneapolis: Fortress Press, 1991.

Pitchard, J.B. (ed.). *Ancient Near East Texts.* Princeton: Princeton University Press, 1954.

Rendtorff, Rolf. *The Old Testament: An Introduction.* Philadelphia: Fortress Press, 1986.

_______ *The Covenant Formula: An Exegetical and Theological Investigation.* Trans. by Margaret Kohl. Edinburgh: T & T Clark, 1998.

Robinson, H.W. *Amos: Hebrew Text.* London: SPCK, 1923.

Robinson, Th. and F. Horst, *Die Zwolf Kleinen Propheten, HAT* 1/14. Tubingen, 1964.

Rudolph, W. *Jeremiah HAT* 1/12. Tubingen: Mohr, 1958.

Schmidt, Werner H. *Old Testament Introduction.* Bombay: St. Paul, 1992.

Seitz, Christopher R. *Zion's Final Destiny: The Development of the Book of Isaiah a Reassessment of Isaiah 36-39.* Minneapolis: Fortress Press, 1991.

Sellin, E. *Das Zwolfprophetenbach, KAT* 12/1. Leipzig, 1929.

Shaw, Charles S. *The Speeches of Micah: A Rhetorical-Historical Analysis.* JSOTSS 145 Sheffield: JSOT, 1993.

Sherwood, Yvonne. *The Prostitute and the Prophet: Hosea's Marriage in Literary-Theoritical Perspective.* JSOTSS 212. Sheffield: Sheffield Academic, 1996.

Skinner, J. *The Book of the Prophet Isaiah.* Cambridge Bible. Cambridge: Cambridge University, 1925.

Smith, Billy K. and Frank S. Page. *Amos, Obadiah, Jonah*, NAC, 19b. Nashville, Tennessee: Broadman & Holman, 1995.

Smith, Gray V. *An Introduction to the Hebrew Prophets: The Prophets as Preachers.* Nashville, Tennessee: Broadman and Holman, 1994.

_______ *Isaiah 1-39: An Exegetical and Theological Exposition of the Holy Scripture.* NAC. Nashville, Tennessee: Broadman and Holman, 2007.

Smith, J.M.P. *A Critical and Exegetical Commentary on Micah, Zephaniah, Nahum, Obadiah, Joel.* ICC. Edinburgh: T & T Clark, 1911.

Smith, Mark S. *The Early History of God: Yahweh and the Other Deities in the Ancient Israel.* 2nd edn. Grand Rapids, Michigan: William B. Eerdmans Publishing Company, 2002.

Smith, Ralph L. *Micah-Malachi*, WBC. Vol. 32. Dallas, Texas: Word Books, 1998.

Soggin, J. Alberto *The Prophet Amos: A Translation and Commentary.* England: SCM, 1987.

Stacey, David. *Isaiah 1-39.* London: Epworth, 1993.

Steck, Odil Hannes. *Old Testament Exegesis: A Guide to the Methodology.* Trans. by James D. Nogalski. Atlants, Georgia: Scholars, 1998.

Stuart, Douglas. *Hosea-Jonah.* WBC 31. Dallas, Texas: Word Books, 1998.

Sweeney, Marvin A. *Isaiah 1-39.* FOTL 16. Grand Rapids, Michigan/Cambridge, UK: William B. Eerdmans Publishing Company, 1996.

_______ *The Twelve Prophets.* Berit Olam. Vol. 1, Collegeville, Minnesota: Liturgical, 2000.

_______ *The Twelve Prophets.* Berit Olam. Vol. 2. Collegeville, Minnesota: Liturgical, 2000.

Thiele, Edwin R. *The Mysterious Numbers of the Hebrew Kings: A Reconstruction of the Chronology of the Kingdoms of Israel and Judah.* Grand Rapids, Michigan: 1965.

Thomas, P.P. *Jeroboam II the King and Amos the Prophet: A Social-Scientific Study on the Israelite Society During the 8th Century BCE.* Delhi: ISPCK, 2003.

Umoren, Gerald Emem. *The Salvation of the Remnant in Isaiah 11:11-12: An Exegesis of a Prophecy Hope and Its Relevance Today.* Boca Raton, Florida: Dissertation, 2006.

Van Gelderen, C. and H.W. Gispen, *Het Bock Hosea*, COT. Kampen, 1953.

von Rad, Gerhard. *The Message of the Prophets.* Trans. by D.M.G. Stalker. New York: Harper & Row, 1962.

_______. *Old Testament Theology.* Vol. 2. Edinburgh: Oliver & Boyd, 1965.

Wagenaar, Jan A. *Judgment and Salvation: The Composition and Redaction.* Leiden: Brill, 2001.

Waltke, Bruce. *Obadiah, Jonah, Micah.* TOTC. England: IVP, 1988.

Watts, John D. *Vision and Prophecy in Amos*. Leiden: Brill, 1958.

Weiser, *Das Bauch der Zwolf Kleinen Propheten* ATD 24. Gottingen, 1949.

Wenell, Karen. Jesus and Land: Sacred and Social Space in Second Temple Judaism. London: T & T Clark, 2007.

Westermann, Claus. *Prophetic Oracles of Salvation in the Old Testament*. Trans. by Keith Crim. Edinburgh: T & T Clark, 1987.

_______ *Forms of Prophetic Speech*. Trans. by Hugh Clayton White. Cambridge/ Louisville, KY: Lutterworth/Westminister John Knox Press, 1991.

Wildberger, Hans. *Isaiah 1-12*. Trans. by Thomas H. Trapp. Minneapolis, Fortress Press, 1991.

Wildberger, Hans. *Isaiah 13-27*. Trans. by Thomas H. Trapp. Minneapolis, Fortress Press, 1997.

Williamson, H.G.M. *The Book Called Isaiah: Deutro Isaiah's Role in Composition and Reduction*. Oxford: Clarendon, 1994.

Winward, Stephen. *A Guide to the Prophets*. London: Hodder & Stoughton, 1968.

Wolff, Hans Walter. *Hosea*. Trans. by Gray Stenser. Philadelphia: Fortress Press, 1974.

_______ *Joel and Amos*. Trans. by Waldemar Janzen. Philadelphia: Fortress Press, 1977.

_______ *Micah: A Commentary*. Continental Commentary. Minneapolis: Augsburg, 1990.

Wood, Leon J. *The Prophets of Israel*. Schaumberg, Illinois: Regular Baptist, 1979.

Word, Stephan Win. *A Guide to Prophet*. London: Hodder and Stoughton, 1968.

Wright, Christopher J.H. *God's People in God's Land: Family, Land and Property in the Old Testament*. England/Grand Rapids, Michigan: Paternoster/William B. Eerdmans Publishing Company, 1990.

_______ *The Mission of God: Unlocking the Bible's Grand Narrative*. Downers Groove, Illinois: IVP, 2006.

Youngblood, Ronald F. *The Book of Isaiah: An Introductory Commentary*. 2nd ed. Grand Rapids, Michigan: Baker, 1993.

Zimmerli, Walter. *The Old Testament and the World*. Trans. by. John J. Scullion. Atlanta: Westminister John Knox Press, 1971.

Zvi, Ben Ehud. *Micah*. FOTL 21B. Grand Rapids, Michigan/Cambridge, UK: William B. Eedrmans Publishing Company, 2000.

Articles from Books

Allen Ronald B. "זכר", in R. Lrid Harris, Gleason L. Archer Jr., and Bruce K. Waltke (eds). *TWOT:* 1. Chicago: Moody, 1980. 241-243.

Bockmuhel, Markus. "1QS and Salvation at Qumran", in D.A. Carson and others (eds). *Justification and Variegated Nomism: The Complexities of Second Temple Judaism.* Vol. 1. Grand Rapids, Michigan/Tubingen, Germany: Baker/Mohr Siebeck, 2001. 381-414.

Claus Westerman. "The Way of the Promise through the Old Testament", in Bernherd W. Andersen (ed). *The Old Testament and the Christian Faith.* New York: Harper and Row, 1963. 200-224.

Driver, G.R. "Difficult Words in the Hebrew Prophets", in H.H. Rowley (ed.). *Studies in Old Testament Prophecy.* Edinburgh: T & T Clark, 1950. 52-72.

Freedman, David Noel. "Prolegomenon", in George Buchanan Gray. *The Forms of Hebrew Poetry.* New York, KTAV. 1972.

Grogan, "Isaiah," in Frank E. Gaebelein (ed). *Isaiah, Jeremiah, Lamentations, Ezekiel.* The Expositor's Bible Commentary. Vol. 6. Grand Rapids, Michigan: Zondervan, 1986. 3-354.

Gunkel, Hermann. "The Close of Micah: A Prophetic Liturgy. A Study in Literary History", *in What Remains in the Old Testament and Other Essays.* Trans. by A.K. Dallas. London: George Allan and Unwin, 1928.

Harrelson, Walter. "Faith, Life, and the Emergence of Tradition", in Douglas A. Knight (ed). *Tradition and Theology in the Old Testament.* Philadelphia: Fortress Press, 1977. 11-30.

Knight, Douglas A. "Tradition and Theology", in Douglas A. Knight (ed). *Tradition and Theology in the Old Testament.* Philadelphia: Fortress Press, 1977. 358-360.

Koopmans, William T. "אחזה", in Willem A. VanGemeren (ed), *NIDOTTE.* Vol. 1. Carlisle, Cumbria: Paternoster, 1997. 258-360.

Lipinski. "עם", in G. Johannes Botterweck and Helmer Ringgren (eds). *TDOT:* 11. Trans. by David E. Green. Grand Rapids, Michigan: William B. Eerdmans Publishing Company, 1974. 163-177.

Marrs, Rick. R. "Back to the Future": Zion in the Book of Micah", in Bernard F. Batto and Kathryn L. Roberts (eds). *David and Zion: Biblical Studies in Honor of J.J.M. Roberts.* USA: Eisenbraums, 2004. 77-96.

Martin, John A. "Micah", in John F. Walvoord and Roy B. Zuck (eds). *The Bible Knowledge Commentary.* Colorado: David C. Cook, 1983. 1475-1492.

McComisky, Thomas Edward. "Amos", in Frank E. Gæbelein and others (eds), *Daniel and the Minor Prophets.* The Expositor's Bible Commentary. Vol. 7. Grand Rapids, Michigan: Zondervan, 1985. 269-331.

Mendenhall, George E. "Amorites", in David Noel Freedman and others. *ABD.* Vol.1. New York: Doubleday, 1992. 199-202.

Niehaus, Jeffery. "Amos", in Thomas Edward McComisky. Ed. *The Minor Prophets*. Vol. 1 Grand Rapids, Michigan: Baker, 1992. 315-494.

Ottosson. "ארץ", in G. Johannes Botterweck and Helmer Ringgren (eds). *TDOT:* 1. Trans. by John T. Wallis. Grand Rapids, Michigan: William B. Eerdmans Publishing Company, 1974. 400. 388-405.

Peter, Stanley E. "The Book of Amos", in David Noel Freedman and others. *ABD*. Vol. 1. New York: Doubleday, 1992. 203-212.

Ploger, J. G. "אדמה", in G. Johannes Botterweck and Helmer Ringgren (eds). *TDOT:* 1. Trans. by John T. Wallis. Grand Rapids, Michigan: William B. Eerdmans Publishing Company, 1974. 88-98.

Roberts, J.J.M. "The Divine King and the Human Community in Isaiah's Vision of the Future", in H.B. Hoffman and others (eds). *The Quest for the Kingdom of God: Studies in honor of George E. Mendenhall.* Winona Lake: Eisenbrauns, 1983. 127-136.

Schmid, H.H. "ארץ", in Ernst Jenni and Claus Westermann (eds). *TLOT.* Vol. 1. Trans. by Mark E. Biddle. Massachusetts: Hendrickson, 1997. 172-179.

Scott, R.B.Y. "Introduction and Exegesis of the Book of Isaiah, Chapters 1-39", in G. Buttrick and others (eds). *NIB*. Vol. 5. Nashville: Abingdon Press, 1956. 156-381

Seow, C.L. "The Book of Hosea", in David Noel Freedman and others (eds). *ABD*. Vol. 3. New York: Doubleday, 1992. 291-297.

Simundson, Daniel J. "The Book of Micah: Introduction, Commentary and Reflection", in Lender E. Keck and others (eds). *Introduction to Apocalyptic Literature, Daniel and Twelve Prophets*. NIB 7. Nashville: Abingdon Press, 1996. 533-597.

Smart, J. D. "Amos" in *IDB*. Vol. 1. Nashville: Abingdon Press, 1962. 116-120.

Tucker, Gene M. "The Book of Isaiah 1-39: Introduction, Commentary and Reflection", in Leander E. Keck and others (eds). *NIB*. Vol. 6. Nashville: Abingdon Press, 2001.

van Meeteren. "חבל", in G. Johannes Botterweck and Helmer Ringgren (eds). *TDOT:* 15. Trans. by David E. Green. Grand Rapids, Michigan: William B. Eerdmans Publishing Company, 1996. 557-564.

von Rad, Gerhard. "The Promised Land and Yahweh's Land", in *The Problem in the Hexateuch and Other Essays*. Trans. by Trueman Dicken. Philadelphia/ London: Fortress Press/SCM, 1984. 79-93.

Wanke, G. "נחלה" in Ernst Jenni and Claus Westermann (eds). *TLOT.* Vol. 2. Trans. by Mark. E Biddle. Peabody, Massachusetts: Hendrickson, 1997. 731-734.

Wright. "חבל", in Willem A. VanGemeren (ed). *NIDOTE:* Carlislie, Cumbria: Paternoster, 1996. 518-523.

Wright, Christopher J. H. "ארץ" in Willem A. VanGemeren (ed). *NIDOTTE:* 1. Carlislie, Cumbria: Paternoster, 1996. 518-523.

______ "נחלה" in Willem A. VanGemeren (ed). *NIDOTTE:* 4. Carlislie, Cumbria: Paternoster, 1996. 272-273.

Wright, G.E. "The Lawsuit of God: A Form Critical Study of Deuteronomy 32", in Anderson, Bernhard W. and Walter Harrelson (eds). *Israel's Prophetic Heritage: Essays in Honor of James Mulinburg.* New York: Harper, 1962. 26-67

Yee, Gale A. "The Book of Hosea: Introduction, Commentary and Reflections", in Leander E. Keck and others (eds). *Introduction to Prophetic Literature, Daniel, the Twelve Prophets.* NIB. Vol. 7. Nashville: Abingdon Press, 1996. 197-297.

Zimmerli, Walter. "The 'Land' in the Pre-exilic and the Early Post-Exilic Prophets", in James T. Butler, Edgar W. Conard and Ben C. Ollenburger (eds). *Understanding the Word: Essays in Honour of Bernhard W. Anderson.* JSOTSS 37. Sheffield: JSOT, 1985. 247-267.

Journals

Abraham, A. T. "Three Bible Studies on Struggle for Social Justice", *Religion and Society* 22 (1975) 3-10.

Albright, W.F "The Israelite Conquest in the Light of Archaeology", *BASOR* 74 (1939) 8-63.

Assis, Elie. "How Long Are you Slack to go to Posses the Land" (Jos. 28:3): Ideal and Reality in the Distribution Discriptions in Joshua 13-24", *VT* 53/1 (2003) 1-25.

Barré, Michael L. "*'rṣ (h)hyym-* 'The Land of the Living'?", *JSOT* 41 (1988) 37-59.

Barre, Michael L. "Amos 1:11 Reconsidered", *CBQ* 47 (1985) 420-427.

Bartlett, J.R. "The Use of the Word ראש as a Title in the Old Testament", *VT* 19/1 (1963) 1-10.

Berkowitz, Abraham. "The Law and the Land: Why Biblical Israel has Artificial Territorial Boundaries?", *Tradition* 28/2 (1994) 34-43.

Bimson, John. "Merenpath's Israel and Recent Theories", *JSOT* 49 (1991) 3-29.

Blenkinsopp, J. "Fragments of Ancient Exegesis in an Isaian Poem (Jes 26:22)," *ZAW* 93/1 (1981) 51-62.

Bosma, Carl J. "Creation in Jeopardy: A Warning to Priests (Hosea 4:1-3), *CTJ* 34 (1999) 64.

Boyle, Marjorie O'rourke. "The Covenant Lawsuit of the Prophet Amos: 3:1-4:13", *VT* 21/3 (1971) 338-363.

Bramer, Stephen J. "The Structure of Amos 9:7-15", *Bibliotheca Sacra* 156 (1999) 272-281.

Brueggemann, Walter. "Amos 4:4-16 and Israel's Covenant Worship", *VT* 15 (1965) 1-15.

_______ "Vine and Fig Tree": A Case Study in Imagination and Criticism", *CBQ* 43/2 (1981) 188-204.

_______ "To Whom Does the Land Belong? 2 Sam. 3:13", *Journal for Preachers* 30/3 (2007) 28-35.

Burrows, Eric. "Cuneiform and Old Testament: Three Notes," *JThS,* 28 (1927), 184.

Cannawurf, E. "the Authenticity of Micah 4:1-4", *VT* 13/1 (1963) 26-33.

Chaney, M. L. "You Shall Not Covet Your Neighbor's House", *Pacific Theological Review* 15 (1982) 3-15.

Chaney, Marvin L. "Whose Sour Grapes? The Addressees of Isaiah 5:1-7 in the Light of Political Economy," *Semeia* 87 (1999) 105-122.

Charles H. Silva, "Literary Features in the Book of Hosea", *Bibliotheca Sacra* 164 (2007) 34-48.

Christensen, Daune L. "The Prosodic Structure of Amos 1-2", *HTR* 67 (1974) 427-436.

Clifford, R.J. "The Use of HOY in the Prophets" *CBQ* 28/4 (1966) 458-466.

Cornelius, F. "Genesis 14", *ZAW* 72/1 (1960) 1-7.

Crawford, Timothy G. "Taking the Promised Land, Leaving the Promised Land: Luke's Use of Joshua for a Christian Foundation Story", *Review and Expositor* 95/2 (1998) 251-261.

Cross, Frank Moore and D.N. Freedmann. "The Song of Miriam", *JNES* 13 (1955) 237-250.

Davidson, R. "The Interpretation of Isaiah II 6ff.," *VT* 16 (1966) 1-7.

Deurloo, Karel A. "Erets: Erd-Land Fur Menschen", *Communio Viatorum* 46/1 (2004) 6-14.

Driver, G.R. "Studies in the Vocabulary of the Old Testament III", *JTS* 32 (1931) 361-363.

Dus, Jan. "Der Beitrag des benjaminitischen Heidentums zur Religion Israels" *Communio Viatorum* 6/1 (1963) 61-80.

Eckardt, A. Roy. "Land of Promise and City of God", *Theology Today* 10/4 (1954) 482-491.

Fishbane, "Critical Note: Additional Remarks on RHMYW (Amos 1:11)", *JBL* 91 (1972) 391-392.

Gerstenberger, E. "Covenant and Commandment", *JBL* 84/1 (1965) 38-51.

Gerstenberger, E. "The Woe Oracles of the Prophets" *JBL* 81 (1962) 249-263.

Gevirtz, S. "A New Look at an Old Crux: Amos 5:26", JBL 87/3 (1968) 267-276.

Glass, Zipporah G. "Land, Slave Labor and Law: Engaging Ancient Israel's Economy", *JSOT 91* (2000) 27-39.

Gordis, R. "The Asseverative *Kaph* in Ugaratic and Hebrew", *JAOS* 63 (1943) 176-178.

Graham, W. "Notes on the Interpretation of Isaiah 5:1-14," *AJSL* 45 (1928-1929) 167-178.

Haupt, P. "Isaiah's Parable of the Vineyard," *AJSL* 19 (1902/1903) 193-202.

Hauser, Alan J. "Israel's Conquest of Palestine: A Peasant's Rebellion?", *JSOT* 7 (1978) 2-19.

Hayes, John H. "Amos's Oracles Against the Nations (1:2-2:16)", *Review and Expositor* 92 (1995) 153-167.

_______ "The Tradition of Zion's Inviolability", *JBL* 82/4 (1963) 419-426.

Hess, Richard K. "Early Israel in Canaan: A Survey of Recent Evidence and Interpretation", *PEQ* 12 (19930) 125-132.

Hoffmeyer, Jeffrey H. "Covenant and Creation: Hosea 4:1-3 Exposition", *Review and Expositor* 102/1 (2005) 143-151.

Huffmon, Herbert B. "The Covenant Lawsuit in the Prophets" *JBL* 78/4 (1959) 285-295.

Hummel, H. D. "Enclitic Mem in Northwest Semetic Especially Hebrew", *JBL* 76 (1957) 85-104.

Irvine, Stuart A. "The Southern Boarder of Syria Reconstructed", *CBQ* 56/1 (1994) 21-41.

Jeyaraj, Jesudasan B. "Ownership, Tenancy and Care of Land in Leviticus 25-27", *AJTR* 4/2 (1991) 18-31.

Johnstone, W. "Old Testament Expressions in Property Holding," *Ugaritica* 6 (1969) 308-317.

Jones, Dorothy. "Surveying the Promised Land: Elizabeth Jolley's Milk and Honey", *Semeia* 88 (2001) 97-111.

Kaiser, Walter C. "The Promised Land: A Biblical-Historical View", *Bibliotheca Sacra* (1981) 302-312.

Kurht, A. "The Cyrus Cylinder and Archaemenid Policy", *JSOT* 25 (1983), 69-72.

Lang, Bernhard. "The Social Organization of Peasant Poverty in Biblical Israel", *JSOT* 24 (1982) 47-63;

_______ "Sklaven und Unfreie im Buch Amos (2:6, 8:6)", *VT* 31/4 (1981) 482-488.

Levine, Etan. "The Land of Milk and Honey", *JSOT* 87 (2000) 43-57;

Light, Gray W. "The New Covenant in the Book of Hosea", *Review & Expositor* 90 (1993) 221.

Limburg, James. "Sevenfold Structures in the Book of Amos", *JBL* 106/2 (1987) 217-222.

Lundbom, J. "Poetic Structure and Prophetic Rhetoric in Hosea", *VT* 29/3 (1979) 300-308.

Machinist, Peter. "Assyria and Its Images in the First Isaiah", *Journal of the American Oriental Society* 103 (1983) 719-737.

Mann, Thomas W. "Israel and the Land: A Note From a Christian Perspective", *Theology Today* 35/4 (1979) 421-426;

Mariottini, Claude F. "Joel 3:10 [H 4:10]: "Beat Your Plowshares into Swords", *Perspectives in Religious Studies* (1987) 125-130.

Mariottini, Claude F. "Warfare in the Eighth Century: Swords into Plowshare", *Biblical Illustrator* 12 (1986) 11.

Mariottini, Claude F. "Joel 3:10 [H 4:10]: "Beat Your Plowshares into Swords", *Perspectives in Religious Studies* 14 (1987) 125-130.

Marshal, Bruce S. "Israel's Stake in the Land", *Theology Today* 35/4 (1979) 413-420.

Martens, Elmer. "The Promise of the Land to Israel", *Direction* 5/2 (1976) 8-13.

McKane, William. "Micah 2:1-5: Text and Commentary", *JSS* 42/1 (1997) 7-22.

Mendenhall, G.E. "The Hebrew Conquest of the Palestine", *BA* 25/3 (1962).

Milgrom, Jacob. "Did Isaiah Prophecy During the Reign of Uzzaiah?", *VT* 14 (1964) 164-167.

Miller, P.D. "Fire in the Mythology of Canaan and Israel", *CBQ* 27/3 (1965) 256-261.

Miller, Patrick D. "The Gift of God: The Deuteronomic Theology of the Land", *Interpretation* 23/4 (1969) 451-465.

Moberly, R. W. L. "Whose Justice? Which Righteousness? The Interpretation of Isaiah V 16", *VT* 51/1 (2001) 55-68.

Moran, W. "The Conclusion of the Decalogue (Ex. 20:17= Dt 5:21)," *CBQ* 29 (1967) 549-52.

Mordecai A. Friedman, "Israel's Response in Hosea 2:17b: "You are My Husband", *JBL* 99/2 (1980) 199-204.

Newman, Murray Lee. *The People of the Covenant: A Study of Israel from Moses to Monarchy.* London: Carey Kingsgate, 1962.

Nogalski, James D. "The Problematic Suffixes of Amos ix 11" *VT* 43/3 (1993) 411-418.

Obed, B. "The Historical Background of Syro-Epharmite War Reconsidered", *CBQ* 34 (1972) 153-165.

Ollenburger, Ben C. *Zion The City of the Great King: A Theological Symbol of the Jerusalem Cult*, JSOTSS 41. Sheffield: JSOT, 1987.

Owens, John Joseph. "Exegetical Studies in the Book of Amos", *Review & Expositor* 63/4 (1966) 429-440.

Kruger, P.A. "Israel, the Harlot (Hos. 2:4-9)", *JNLS* 11 (1983) 107-116.

Partlow, Jonathan A. "Amos's Use of Rhetorical Entrapment as a Means for Climactic Preaching in Amos 1:3-2:16", *Restoration Quarterly* 49/1 (2007) 23-32.

Paul, S. "Amos 1:3-2:3: A Concatenous Literary Pattern", *JBL* 90/4 (1971) 397-403.

Premnath, D.N. "Amos and Hosea: Sociohistorical Background and Prophetic Critique", *Word & World* 28/2 (2008) 125-132.

Premnath, D.N. "Latifundialization and Isaiah 5:8-10", *JSOT* 40 (1988) 49-60.

Rector, Larry J. "Israel's Rejected Worship: An Exegesis of Amos 5", *Restoration Quarterly* 21/3 (1978) 161-175.

Rector, Larry J. "Israel's Rejected Worship: An Exegesis of Amos 5" *Restoration Quarterly* 21/3 (1978) 161-175.

Reicke, Bo. "Liturgical Traditions in Micah 7", *HTR* 60 (1967) 349-357.

Richard, D. Patterson, "Portraits from a Prophet's Portfolio: Hosea 4", *Bibliotheca Sacra* 165 (2008) 294-308.

Richardson, H. Neil. "*SKT* (Amos 9:11): "Booth" or "Succoth"?", *JBL* 92/3 (1973) 375-381.

Robert, D. Bergen, "Calling Forth Yahweh's curses: Hosea's Judgment of Israel in 8:1-10:15", *Criswell Theological Review* 7/1 (1993) 39-50.

Rogers, Jeffrey S. "An Allusion to Coronation in Isaiah 2:6," *CBQ* 51 (1989) 234-235.

Ruprecht, Eberhard. "Vorgegebene Tradition Und Theologische Gestaltung in Genesis 12:1-3", *VT* 29/2 (1979) 171-188.

Schmidt, Ludwig. "Genesis 15", *VT* 56/2 (2006) 251-267.

Seebass, Horst. "Holy" Land in the Old Testament: Numbers and Joshua", *VT* 56/1 (2006) 92-104.

Seeligmann, I.L. "On the History and Nature of Prophecy in Israel," *Erets-Israel* 3 (1954) 129.

Sheppard, Gerald T. "More on Isaiah 5:1-7 as a Juridical Parable," *CBQ* 44 (1982) 45-47.

Simon, U. "The Poor Man's Ewe-Lamb: An Example of a Juridical Parable", *Bib* 48 (1967) 220-21.

Smith, Gray V. "Continuity and Discontinuity in Amos' Use of Tradition", *JETS* 34/1 (1991) 33-42.

Speiser, E.A. "Of Shoes and Shekels", *BASOR* 77 (1990) 1-35.

Speiser, E. A. "Note on Amos 5:26," *BASOR* 108 (1947) 5.

Steve Mckenzie, "Exodus Typology in Hosea", *Restoration Quarterly* 22/1-2 (1979) 100-108.

Sweeney, Marvin A. "Micah's Debate with Isaiah", *JSOT* 93 (2001) 111-124.

Thomas, D. Winton "The Text of Jesaia II6 and the Word *spq" ZAW* 75 (1963) 88-90.

Torrey, C. "On the Text of Amos v. 26; vi. 1, 2 ; vii. 2," *JBL,* 13 (1894) 1-15.

Townsend, Jeffrey L. "Fulfillment of the Land Promise in the Old Testament", *Bibliotheca Sacra* (1985) 320-337.

Vahrenhorst, Martin. "Land und Landverheuβung im Neuen Testament", *JBTh* 23 (2008) 123-148.

Wainwright, G.A. "Capthor-Cappodicia", *VT* 6 (1956) 199-210.

Wainwright, G.A. "Some Early Philistine History", *VT* 9 (1959) 73-84.

Wainwright, G.A. "The Septuagint's *Καππαδοκια* for Capthor", *JJS* 7 (1956) 91-92.

Warshal, Bruce S. "Israel's Stake in the Land" *Tradition Today* 35/4 (1979) 414.

Watson, Wilfred G.E. "David Ousts the City Ruler of Jebus", *VT* 20 (1970) 501-2.

Weingreen, J. "The Title Moreh Sedek", *JSS* 6 (1961) 162-174.

Weiss, Meir. "The Pattern of Numerical Sequence in Amos 1-2: A Re-examination", *JBL* 86 (1967) 416-423.

Wessels, W.J. "Micah 7:8-20: An Apt Conclusion to the Book of Micah", *Verbutm Ecclesia* 24/1 (2003) 254.

Wharton, James A. "Hosea 4:1-3", *Interpretation* 32/1 (1978) 78-83.

Whitelam, Keith W. "Israel's Traditions of Origin: Reclaiming the Land", *JSOT* 44 (1989) 19-42.

Wijngaards, J. "הוציא and העלה: A Twofold Approaches to the Exodus", *VT* 15 (1965) 91-102.

Wildberger, Hans. "Die Völkerwallfahrt zum Zion: Jes 2:1-5", *VT* 7/1 (1957) 62-81.

Williams, Gray Roye. "Frustrated Expectation in Isaiah v 1-7: A Literary Interpretation," *VT* 35/4 (1985) 459-465.

Willis, John T. "Some Suggestions on the Interpretation of Micah 1:2", *VT* 18 (1968) 372-379.

Willis, John T. "A Reapplied Prophetic Hope Oracle" *VTS* 26 (1974) 64-76.

Wolff, Hans Walter. "Guilt and Salvation: A Study of the Prophecy of Hosea", *Interpretation* 15/3 (1961) 274-285.

Wood, Joyce Rilett. "Speech and Action in Micah's Prophecy", *CBQ* 62 (2000) 658.

Yee, Gale A. "She is not my Wife and I am Not her Husband": A Materialist Analysis of Hosea 1-2", *BibInt* 9 (2001) 369-371.